CONSTITUTIONAL POLITICS IN THE PROGRESSIVE ERA

Constitutional Politics in the Progressive Era

Child Labor and the Law

STEPHEN B. WOOD

THE UNIVERSITY OF CHICAGO PRESS
CHICAGO & LONDON

Library of Congress Catalog Card Number: 67–25525

THE UNIVERSITY OF CHICAGO PRESS, CHICAGO & LONDON
The University of Toronto Press, Toronto 5, Canada

© *1968 by The University of Chicago*
All rights reserved
Published 1968
Printed in the United States of America

To Judith

To Judith

Acknowledgments

Every author has many debts, some of which can never be satisfactorily acknowledged. Two former colleagues at the University of Chicago, Marvin Meyers and Calvin Stillman, have shown confidence and given counsel in ways so numerous that I can neither describe nor properly credit their contribution to this book; only they know what I owe them. Among others who have read the manuscript, my thanks are due especially to C. Herman Pritchett, an adviser of rare humanity, and Herbert Storing, a discerning critic. Throughout the manuscript another kind of obligation is apparent: to many commentators who have sought to enhance our knowledge of the judicial process. Appreciation also is due several persons and numerous publishers who have kindly granted permission to reprint copyrighted materials.

Introduction

"The central problem involved in the constitutional adjudication of the last half century," Benjamin F. Wright, Jr., observed in 1942, "was the accelerated movement toward an ever-increasing intervention of government in social and economic life. . . . Toward the end of the [nineteenth] century the vast increase in regulatory statutes coming before the [Supreme] Court raised a question quite as fundamental as that produced by the slavery crisis, whether the Constitution of 1787 could be interpreted to serve as an instrument of government for an industrialized population."[1]

An important phase of this regulatory movement involved efforts to employ congressional powers to accomplish, by indirection, social welfare purposes. This study concerns the major thrust of that development: the campaign during the progressive era to establish national child labor standards. The reform legislation that was enacted carried the two most potent congressional powers to acknowledged constitutional frontiers and beyond judicially acceptable limits — for several decades in the case of the commerce power and until the present day in the case of the taxing power. By comprehensively portraying the events that comprise the child labor history, this study seeks to enhance our knowledge of the deeply political processes by which constitutional law is formed.

These processes, in our highly legalistic system, center upon constitutional adjudication. As Edward S. Corwin pointed out, "all the more important questions of governmental *purpose* or *power* come to be translated sooner or later — *and sooner rather than later* — into questions of constitutional power."[2] The government-

[1] *The Growth of American Constitutional Law* (Boston: Houghton Mifflin Co., 1942), p. 110.
[2] *Constitutional Revolution, Ltd.* (Claremont, Calif.: Claremont Colleges, 1941), p. 7. See also Felix Frankfurter and James M. Landis, *The Business of the Supreme Court* (New York: Macmillan Co., 1928), p. 14.

by-lawsuit that results is "perhaps the most significant feature of our system of judicial review of the constitutionality of legislation," Paul A. Freund has written.[3] But an understanding of constitutional development involves more than insight, however penetrating, into the operation of federal judicial power. It necessitates exploration of every phase of democratic policy formation — from the coalescence of politically relevant opinion and the enactment of public policies by the popular branches of government through judicial construction of the limits of the powers and the legitimacy of the purposes embodied in legislation and the political consequences called forth by the results of Supreme Court decision-making. Viewed separately, each phase exerts a powerful claim upon our attention. However, the struggle for constitutional acceptance of new policies, which have few, if any, analogues in the past, is essentially a seamless process of adapting law to changed social and economic conditions.

At bottom, the effort to understand constitutional development forces us to examine the nature of popular government and the rightful place within it of the distinctively American institution of judicial review. The indispensable starting point is the formative period of constitutional interpretation. Justice Story proclaimed, in *Martin* v. *Hunter's Lessee*,[4] the primacy of the democratic will in what is perhaps its classic formulation in our legal tradition.

> The Constitution, unavoidably, deals in general language. It did not suit the purposes of the people, in framing this great charter of our liberties, to provide for minute specifications of its powers, or to declare the means by which those powers should be carried into execution. It was foreseen that this would be a perilous and difficult, if not impracticable task. The instrument was not intended to provide merely for the exigencies of a few years, but was to endure through a long lapse of ages, the events of which were locked up in the inscrutable purposes of Providence. It could not be foreseen what new changes and modifications of power might be indispensable to effectuate the general objects of the charter; and restrictions and specifications, which at the present might seem salutary, might, in the end, prove the overthrow of the system itself. Hence, its powers are expressed in general terms, leaving to the legislature, from time to time, to adopt its own means to effectuate legitimate objects, and to mould and model

[3] *On Understanding the Supreme Court* (Boston: Little, Brown and Co., 1949), p. 82.
[4] 1 Wheaton 304 (1816).

the exercise of its powers, as its own wisdom and the public interest should require.[5]

John Marshall reiterated this principle in *McCulloch* v. *Maryland*.[6] Though limited in its powers, the national government was supreme within its sphere of action. "But the question respecting the extent of the powers actually granted, is perpetually arising, and will probably continue to arise, as long as our system shall exist."[7] Constitutional ambiguity unavoidably attached to the purposes and powers of American democracy and contention about them would continue unabated. To the popular branches fell responsibility to adapt the great powers on which the welfare of the nation essentially depended to the various crises of human affairs, exigencies that could best be provided for as they occurred. Again, in *Gibbons* v. *Ogden*,[8] Marshall affirmed the primacy of popular sovereignty, despite its ever present risks.

> The wisdom and discretion of Congress, their identity with the people, and the influence which their constituents possess at elections, are, in this, as in many other instances . . . the sole restraints on which they have relied, to secure them from its abuse. They are the restraints on which the people must often rely solely, in all representative governments.[9]

Here was the fundamental check upon Congress when it exercised explicitly granted powers. The principle acquired peculiar force from the fact that Marshall enunciated it immediately after his famous exposition of the scope of the commerce power.[10]

On the other hand, in *McCulloch*, Marshall also gave classic expression to the inherent rightness of the principle of judicial review. The Constitution devolved upon the Supreme Court the important duty of construing the limits of the general powers granted to the national government. As the ultimate arbiter of the Constitution's meaning, the bench had to determine, when its judgment was properly sought, whether or not the new constructions the popular branches had applied in acts of governance were legitimate. If an illegitimate enlargement of powers, as distin-

---

5 *Ibid.*, pp. 326–27.
6 4 Wheaton 316 (1819).
7 *Ibid.*, p. 405.
8 9 Wheaton 1 (1824).
9 *Ibid.*, p. 9.
10 "It is the power to regulate; that is, to prescribe the rule by which commerce is to be governed. This power, like all others vested in Congress, is complete in itself, may be exercised to its utmost extent, and acknowledges no limitations other than are prescribed in the Constitution." *Ibid.*

guished from a permissible extension, had occurred, a declaration
of invalidity became mandatory.

> Should Congress, in the exertion of its powers, adopt measures
> which are prohibited by the Constitution; or should Congress,
> under the pretext of executing its powers, pass laws for the accom-
> plishment of objects not entrusted to the government; it would
> become the painful duty of this tribunal, should a case requiring
> such a decision come before it, to say that such an act was not the
> law of the land.[11]

The Court, Marshall stated, disclaimed all pretensions to whittle
down the legislature's prerogative. All the same, the Court's discretionary power to construe the Constitution authoritatively
would soon be firmly entrenched.

The course of American democracy since that time has been
determined, in substantial measure, by the results of collisions
between popular sovereignty and judicial control. "There must
be power in the States and the Nation to remold, through experience, our economic practices and institutions to meet changing
social and economic needs," Justice Brandeis argued in dissenting,
in 1932, from a ruling that invalidated state regulatory legislation.[12] His opinion, which self-consciously recurred to Marshall's
formulation about the extent of constitutional powers and purposes, represented the popular claim to adapt governmental authority to altered circumstances. The claim to judicial supervisory
power, on the other hand, is represented in numerous decisions
that cut down by interpretation or explicitly invalidated regulatory measures. Many of these holdings — for example, *Bailey* v.
Drexel,[13] which figures prominently in this history — just as self-
consciously rephrased Marshall's expressed reluctance to intrude
upon popular processes unless this was absolutely necesary to limit
unfounded exertions of government powers.

The truly important aspect of these collisions concerns the guidelines available to the legislator and to the jurist when interpreting
the general constitutional grants that afford wide latitude to
choice. No one has ever enumerated these guidelines definitively
but we tend to agree about the main elements: the fundamental
values of the American creed; the traditions of American constitutionalism, whether incorporated in formal institutions and procedures or embodied in long-standing, customary rules; and the
practical imperatives of policy-making that are generated by

11 *McCulloch* v. *Maryland*, 4 Wheaton 316, 423 (1819).
12 *New State Ice Co.* v. *Liebmann*, 285 U.S. 262, 311 (1932).
13 259 U.S. 20 (1922).

deeply felt public needs. Not that these elements remain ever the same, although some rights have been held to be so vital to the existence of democratic society that they may never be subjected to popular vote.[14] Our political tradition, just as our collective life, changes — if only in part and ordinarily with exceeding slowness.

The problem comes in applying these guidelines, in our efforts to retain certainty in the law while accommodating the Constitution to contemporary conditions. The task usually involves a choice among conflicting values and among evolving conceptions of how life should be lived in situations in which convictions often assume great intensity. Which guidelines should be determinative, and to what extent should these legitimated interpretations control the future? What, for example, is the nature of the federal system? How, in the language of the Sugar Trust case,[15] can we simultaneously maintain the bond of union and preserve the autonomy of the states?

The answer, American experience clearly teaches, is that this conflict is no more amenable to permanent settlement than are questions about the extent of national powers and purposes. From the outset, when Federalists and Republicans clashed over what the nation should become, our search for boundary lines in the use of power has centered upon concrete issues, not abstract ideals about government. These controversies, as Thomas Reed Powell observed during a later period of pronounced constitutional discord, turn "on what people do or do not want to have government do or to have government capable of doing."[16] American experience also teaches that technological innovation and social change may drastically alter areas of conflict within short periods of time.

Our tendency, therefore, is to reach constitutional conclusions that resolve significant problems tentatively; that is, to fashion practical answers for the time being. This does not mean that the work of translating guidelines into legislation and judicial decisions necessarily produces results that accord with dominant opinion and the political tradition. No one, for example, could plausibly argue that the holding in *Hammer* v. *Dagenhart*,[17] the second significant case treated in this study, conformed to public expectations and to precedent. It means, rather, that our constitutional answers, and thereby progress in the law, usually depend

14 See especially *West Virginia State Board of Education* v. *Barnette*, 319 U.S. 624 (1943).

15 *United States* v. *E. C. Knight Co.*, 156 U.S. 1 (1895).

16 "Constitutional Reform," *American Law School Review* (May, 1936), pp. 474–75.

17 247 U.S. 251 (1918).

more upon attaining agreement about the facts at issue and the consequences of pursuing alternative courses of action than upon legal considerations. It matters little whether the facts in conflict concern "a private eleemosynary institution" in early-nineteenth-century New England,[18] newly developed grain "elevating facilities" in the principal midwestern transshipping terminal in the 1870's,[19] or the stoppage of "productive activities" by industrial strife within "a great basic industry" in the 1930's.[20] It matters greatly, in every instance, however, what agreement is reached by public officials who confront new conditions and formulate policies to meet new problems.

The conflict between popular sovereignty and judicial supervision provides the context for understanding the child labor history. Indeed, Marshall's broad constructions of national powers in *McCulloch* and in *Gibbons* and his justification for judicial nullification in *McCulloch*, when these powers were overstepped or exercised to accomplish improper purposes, comprise the informing themes of this study of constitutional politics. Although the history spans several decades, from 1907, when Senator Albert Beveridge originally proposed federal legislation, until 1941, when the Supreme Court unanimously sustained the Fair Labor Standards Act, the vital events occurred during the progressive era. At that time, the child labor reform movement powerfully affected politics and law; subsequently, its role was subsidiary, an appendage to larger events.

For this reason the study concerns the earlier, formative period, when child labor reform constituted an integral part of the process of adjusting American life to industrial conditions. It traces the rise of the reform movement, the enactment by Congress of the Keating-Owen law in 1916, the law's destruction at the hands of the Supreme Court, the public response to unconstitutionality that culminated in the passage of the Pomerene amendment to the Revenue Act of 1918, and this measure's involved and ultimately fatal career in the courts. The interplay of reform politics and legal processes, when related to the rise and wane of the progressive movement and to the parallel trend of judicial construction — growing toleration and then reaction — provides the necessary perspective for understanding how change in the law is brought about.

18 *The Trustees of Dartmouth College* v. *Woodward*, 4 Wheaton 518 (1819).
19 *Munn* v. *Illinois*, 94 U.S. 113 (1877).
20 *National Labor Relations Board* v. *Jones and Laughlin Steel Corporation*, 301 U.S. 1 (1937).

Contents

Contents

1

The Rise of Child Labor Reform

Industrialization and Progressivism

Modern America emerged from the Civil War. By the turn of the century, the industrial revolution had remolded American life. The powerful industrial nation, which spanned the continent in 1900, differed profoundly from the predominantly rural society of the ante bellum years. Railroad mileage, steel tonnage, prodigious immigration, technological innovation and business consolidation, and the relentless westward surge that swept away the frontier were vivid evidence of a new social order. As the nature of American society changed during these momentous years the character and scope of many of its significant problems also changed. Grave economic and political abuses began to accumulate behind the traditional forms of freedom as industrialism and urbanization developed with a minimum of social control. Vast business organizations, geared to national and international markets, curtailed the scope of competition and restrained economic opportunities in many fields. Hardships, dislocations, and injustices attended the rapid massing of country-bred Americans and Europeans in expanding cities and their employment as wage earners in immense, impersonal factory systems. Traditional political institutions, adapted to a smaller, simpler society, were severely strained by the pressures of the new industrial society.

These conditions bred widespread discontent. Basic shifts in public attitudes and in political alignments began to occur. Across the history of the period stormed angry farm-belt Granger and urban-patrician reformers, single-taxers and Socialists, trade unionists and Populists. They aroused fear and produced excitement, laid siege to state legislatures, and forced their demands on the attention of the nation. As the conditions that they criticized adversely affected more and more persons, the volume of protest swelled louder. Despite unparalleled economic progress, a spirit of disquiet hung over Main Street.

As the twentieth century began, a far-reaching revolution in public opinion swept the country, and America set about the task of social reconstruction. Ten years before, when bitter Populist protests rose from the distressed plainsmen, the national majority had remained staunchly conservative; but now Bryan and Populism had captured the Democratic convention. The short, happy reign of William McKinley, the symbol of post-Civil War Republican conservatism, was ended abruptly by an assassin's bullet and by the accession of Theodore Roosevelt. As the decade advanced, Roosevelt emerged as the first President to represent the rising progressive movement, bent on far-reaching social reconstruction.[1]

In their attempts to ensure the promise of the young Republic, progressive thinkers evolved new concepts of social responsibility for the general welfare, new forms of public regulation, and new institutions of popular control. The progressives hoped to make government more responsive to the reform temper of the nation. In addition, they sought to expand governmental powers and to direct the nation's energies toward new purposes. Intervention by powerful instrumentalities of government into previously immune areas of life was deemed necessary for curbing unrestrained economic individualism and rectifying serious social and economic injustices. The experiences of the more advanced industrial nations of western Europe afforded precedents for action and undoubtedly made the path easier.[2]

The progressive assault gathered momentum and went forward on many fronts. Great cities turned out corrupt bosses, elected reform mayors, and expanded municipal ownership of public facilities. States enacted humanitarian legislation, expanded their regulation of economic forces, and introduced democratic experiments. In the nation's capitol, dynamic leaders advanced pioneer measures of social control, sought to dissolve the most flagrantly abusive large industrial combinations, and championed the public welfare. Sanction for state action was found in the doctrine of the police powers, the sovereign power to govern men and

[1] Eric F. Goldman, *Rendezvous with Destiny* (New York: Alfred A. Knopf, 1953), p. 162.
[2] Harold U. Faulkner, *The Quest for Social Justice* (*A History of American Life*, eds. Arthur M. Schlesinger and Dixon Ryan Fox, Vol. XI [12 vols.; New York: Macmillan Co., 1937]), p. 129.

things. At the federal level, the commerce and taxing powers of Congress, scarcely exercised during much of the laissez faire nineteenth century, were considered the most appropriate bases for action. The Roosevelt administration was a period of beginnings. The powerful momentum of the reform movement approached flood tide in 1908. It would soon sweep over America.

Child Labor: Emergence of the Problem

Of all the grave social abuses that began to excite the concern of reformers at the turn of the century, none more clearly challenged humanitarian values than that of child labor. Although the problem had existed in America in various forms from the time of the earliest settlements, the modern form had been created by the swift and largely uncontrolled industrialization of the nation.[3] In virtually every region, the spread of the factory system, with its simplified repetitive processes, swept children into industrial occupations as wage earners.[4] This was especially true in the last decades of the nineteenth century, when the problem of exploitation rapidly assumed serious proportions.

Between 1870, when the Census Bureau first collected occupational information about persons ten through fourteen years of age, and 1910, the census figures reveal a startling rise in both the number and the proportion of children entering the labor force.[5] By 1900, one child in six between the ages of ten and fif-

[3] The federal Children's Bureau has defined child labor in the following manner: "The employment of young persons is a social problem whenever and wherever it deprives them of the opportunity for normal development. If children go to work too soon or work under unfavorable conditions, the result is harmful not only to the individual but also to society. . . . The problem should be visualized as a changing one, which lessens as higher standards are adopted, regulations improved, and employment restricted, but which increases as new light is shed upon the effects of industrial work on growing boys and girls." U.S. Children's Bureau, *Child Labor: Facts and Figures* (Washington, D.C.: Government Printing Office, 1933), p. 1.

These propositions point up a serious problem encountered by the social justice movement: changing conceptions of socially desirable practices made it difficult, at any particular moment, to characterize abuses precisely and to formulate effective remedial programs.

[4] For the most authoritative accounts of child labor conditions during the nineteenth century, see *The Beginnings of Child Labor Legislation in Certain States* and *Cotton Textile Industry* (*Report on Women and Child Wage Earners in the United States*), U.S. Department of Labor, Vols. VI and I (19 vols.; Washington, D.C.: Government Printing Office, 1910–13), and Edith Abbott, "Early History of Child Labor in America," *American Journal of Sociology* (July, 1908), pp. 15–37.

[5] *Child Labor: Facts and Figures*, p. 70.

teen was gainfully employed, and there were more than 1,750,000 child laborers in America.[6] Further, the conditions under which hundreds of thousands of these children toiled were sharply distinguished from those that prevailed in the past. Traditionally, parental supervision or apprenticeship afforded safeguards against excessive labor, but industrial wage earners now were harnessed to a system of production in which long hours and arduous and dangerous labor were commonplace. These changes in the size and scope of productive units, and changes in legal conceptions about personal freedom and private property, which revolutionized the adult workman's relationship with his employer — from fellow hand in the workshop to dependent wage laborer in an immense, impersonal corporation — also denied children their former protection against exploitation.

Public consciousness about child labor developed slowly, however. At the beginning of the nineteenth century, traditional American social values, notably the Puritan precept against childhood idleness, reinforced by commercial incentives, generally condoned the employment of children in manufacturing establishments.[7] The practice was regarded as morally correct and socially beneficial.[8] As the impact of the industrial revolution became more apparent during the 1830's and 1840's, most of the northeastern states, following England's precedent, slowly began to regulate the most flagrantly abusive and dangerous conditions of employment, primarily through legislation that was based on the police powers.[9] The principal objective of this rudimentary social control was to restrict the hours of labor for all classes of employees.[10] In addition, children were sometimes accorded special consideration through the establishment of minimum-age legislation, but this came later.[11] By 1860, six states had curtailed the workday to ten hours for children who were engaged in industry, and four states ex-

---

[6] Approximately 60 per cent of these children were agricultural workers, farm labor traditionally forming the most important single source of child employment. However, the worst conditions of employment existed in manufacturing, where 16 per cent of the children (280,000) were at work. Domestic and personal services, street trades, and similar pursuits engaged the remaining 24 per cent. *Ibid., passim.* (Throughout this study census figures have been rounded to the nearest thousand.)

[7] *Ibid.*, p. 68.

[8] *The Beginnings of Child Labor Legislation*, p. 27.

[9] *Ibid.*, pp. 37–42.

[10] *Ibid.*, pp. 32–36.

[11] *Ibid.*

cluded children below designated ages.[12] However, these pioneering statutes "were largely ineffective because [they were] inade-
quately framed and enforced, and because the standards, low as
they seem by modern comparison, did not command general support, either from parents or from employers."[13] Child labor, in
short, was practically unregulated in America before the Civil
War.[14]

The spectacular expansion of the factory system and mechaniza-
tion of industry after the Civil War rapidly increased the number
of industrial child laborers.[15] Faced with greatly increased competition in a swiftly changing economy, the entrepreneurial class frequently sought — where the work made it feasible — to reap the
apparent economic advantages afforded by child operatives. Ra-
tionalizing productive processes by cutting costs to the bone, they
adopted the customary social practice, despite the drastic transformation that had occurred in the conditions of employment.
Productive processes were widely adapted to accommodate child
labor. As in other phases of industrial administration, the profit
motive took precedence over humane labor practices.

Neither the dominant laissez faire economic ethic nor prevailing
social attitudes provided much basis for objection to these practices. The former, especially after it was reinforced by the pseudo-
scientific spirit of Social Darwinism, condemned as irrational and
unjust any interference with the "natural harmony" of the economic order. And traditional American individualism, with its
pervasive images of personal initiative and self-reliance, usually
resulted in an unquestioning acceptance of poverty and misery for
members of the community who were deficient in the "economic
virtues." Work was natural and inevitable for many children, it
was commonly agreed; early remunerative employment inculcated
beneficial habits of discipline and developed technical skills that
improved the likelihood of success in the competitive struggles
that would be waged in adulthood. That the children of immi-

12 *Ibid.*, p. 209. See also Elizabeth Sands Johnson, "Child Labor Legislation,"
in John R. Commons *et al., History of Labor in the United States* (4 vols.; New
York: Macmillan Co., 1935), III, 403.

13 *Child Labor: Facts and Figures*, p. 69.

14 Edith Abbott, "Child Labor in America before 1870," in Grace Abbott,
The Child and the State (Chicago: University of Chicago Press, 1938), p. 275.

15 See Vincent A. McQuade, *The American Catholic Attitude on Child
Labor since 1891* (Washington, D.C.: The Catholic University of America Press,
1938), pp. 10–20, and Elizabeth H. Davidson, *Child Labor Legislation in the
Southern Textile States* (Chapel Hill: University of North Carolina Press,
1939), p. 1.

grants, of southern hill folk, of the growing urban working classes, and of other groups on the bottom rung of the social ladder entered industrial occupations as a consequence of poverty or personal choice usually was looked upon as an unavoidable, if perhaps somewhat unfortunate, aspect of the nature of things.

These conditions gave rise to a second phase of state legislation, but the results were hardly more satisfactory than before. Most statutes were impaired by faulty construction or debilitating amendments or were rendered ineffective as the result of lax or nonexistent administration.[16] As substantial industrial systems were developed in various sections of the country during the 1870's and 1880's, the experiences of the northeastern states tended to be repeated. Many children were drawn into industrial employment and criticism — usually very limited in extent and voiced chiefly by trade unionists, religious leaders, and urban-patrician reformers — slowly developed, as did the defensive response of industrial interests. Rudimentary regulatory statutes were wrung from reluctant state legislatures. Despite these occasional, scattered enactments, the great mass of Americans was largely uninformed and, essentially, unconcerned about the plight of child laborers.

By 1900, most industrial states had enacted some form of child labor regulation; however, most of this legislation was inferior to the standards that had been established in the more progressive northeastern states — although the latter usually afforded minimal protection for children, compared with the standards commonly agreed upon only a decade later. During this period, however, the social conceptions that would make significant legislative advancement possible in the future were beginning to work their way into popular attitudes.[17] Child labor, once viewed as a beneficial social institution, was slowly — in part, unconsciously — taking on the stigma of an unrighteous and harmful consequence of industrial capitalism, destructive to child and community. The child labor reform movement of the twentieth century did not initiate public regulation; rather, it sought to enact meaningful standards, progressively to improve these standards, and to ensure their enforcement.

The Peculiar Role of the South

As the twentieth century began, child labor attracted widespread national attention for the first time and the progressive reform

---

[16] Faulkner, *The Quest for Social Justice*, p. 186, and Katharine Lumpkin and Dorothy Douglas, *Child Workers in America* (New York: Robert M. McBride and Co., 1937), p. 258.

[17] *Child Labor: Facts and Figures*, pp. 70–71.

movement developed effective political strength.[18] The south played an especially important role in forming this public awareness. Its post-Civil War industrial system developed under circumstances that sanctioned community sacrifice and tended to present formidable barriers to social legislation. The Civil War, which had accelerated northern industrial expansion, left the south virtually in ruins, and the region sought to restore its prosperity — its very life — by establishing a viable system of agriculture that "integrated" white labor and colored freedman, and by turning — where its capital resources were sufficient or northern financing was available — to manufacturing. The new factories took on extraordinary importance.[19] The new oligarchy, composed of factory masters and financiers but bearing a marked resemblance to the ante bellum plantation aristocracy, became influential community leaders in a society that cherished strong conservative traditions.[20] Southern opinion, by and large, vigorously opposed efforts to regulate the new industries, which promised the rehabilitation of the region and the restoration of white supremacy.[21] More than in most other regions, the laissez faire attitude toward industry persisted well into the twentieth century in the south, as did the heritage of industrial child labor.

By 1900, significant industrial growth had occurred, chiefly in cotton manufacture, and child labor had become a pervasive social problem. A new empire of cotton mills "sprang into existence in the piedmont area of the Carolinas and Georgia . . . wherever water power was available," Simkins observes. As the new century began, the federal census stated that the growth of the cotton industry had been "the one great fact in [the south's] history during the past ten years."[22] Child labor was intimately connected to that growth. The problem, Woodward points out, "was not an occa-

[18] Lumpkin and Douglas, *Child Workers in America*, p. 254.

[19] For the development of southern industrialism, see especially C. Vann Woodward, *Origins of the New South, 1877–1913 (A History of the South*, eds. Wendell Holmes Stephenson and E. Merton Coulter, Vol. IX [10 vols.; Baton Rouge: Louisiana State University Press, 1951]), and Francis Butler Simkins, *The South Old and New* (New York: Alfred A. Knopf, 1947). Also see Davidson, *Child Labor Legislation in the Southern Textile States*, pp. 3–9, 55, 235, and W. J. Cash, *The Mind of the South* (Anchor Books ed.; Garden City, N.Y.: Doubleday, 1954), pp. 195–242.

[20] See Woodward, *Origins of the New South, 1877–1913, passim*; Simkins, *The South Old and New, passim*; V. O. Key, *Southern Politics* (New York: Alfred A. Knopf, 1949), *passim*; and Davidson, *Child Labor Legislation in the Southern Textile States*, pp. 52–68.

[21] See Cash, *The Mind of the South*, pp. 195–242.

[22] Simkins, *The South Old and New*, p. 239.

sional abuse or passing phenomenon. It was an entrenched interest, a growing evil that had become a normal feature of the textile industry and the foundation of fortunes." [23]

The mills, which symbolized the "new south," drew an ample labor supply of poor whites from the mountains and surrounding farms. "These folk," the lower sill of white society, "eagerly sought industrial employment as a means of improving their low economic status." [24] As mill hands, they "remained docile, ignorant, and proud, deaf to appeals that they forget their inherited prejudices and join labor unions advocating social legislation." [25] They clustered in the proprietary villages that surrounded the mills and looked upon whatever subsidized uplift activities were provided as improvements upon their previous circumstances. As a consequence:

> Two new classes had been added to Southern society, the mill operative and the mill owner. The latter often outdid the town merchant and banker in wealth and prestige. His mansions overshadowed the small cottages of the mill village in much the same manner that the big house of the planter once had dominated the slave quarters. This new regime was almost as feudalistic as the earlier economy. If the mill workers, in the exercise of their prerogatives as white men, were not as docile as Negroes, they certainly did not question the economic and social pre-eminence of the mill master, or his right to control the moral, political and industrial life of the usually unincorporated mill villages. It was a mild form of bondage in an age supposedly dominated by individual self-expression.[26]

Those who suffered most were the children of the mill operatives, who heeded the monetary and prescriptive inducements — to augment family income and to maintain employment and housing — to put their offspring to work in the mills. Historically, before preventive legislation was enacted — first in England and later in New England — various machine operations in the cotton

---

[23] Woodward, *Origins of the New South*, p. 416. "In 1900 three out of ten workers in the mills of the south were children under sixteen years of age, and 57.5 per cent of these children were between ten and thirteen. Those under ten, of whom there were many, were not enumerated. A former president of the American Cotton Manufacturers' Association declared that the adoption of an age limit of fourteen would close every mill in North Carolina, because 75 per cent of the spinners in that state were fourteen or younger." *Ibid.*

[24] Simkins, *The South Old and New*, p. 240.

[25] *Ibid.*, pp. 240–41.

[26] *Ibid.*, p. 241.

textile industry had been assigned to children. These same, supposedly safe and non-exacting tasks, tending spindles and the like,
were the lot of tens of thousands of children in the south Atlantic
states (some of them less than ten years of age), and usually precluded continuation of their education. By 1900, the southern
mills employed more child laborers than any other sector of American industry.

Two factors chiefly drew national attention to the south's child
labor conditions at the time: community crusades to enact remedial
state legislation and the competitive threat that some branches of
southern industry had begun to pose to manufacturers in other
regions. Local reform groups, incensed by particularly objectionable manifestations of exploitation, launched sustained campaigns
whose disclosures shocked the entire nation.[27] It was this publicity,
widely disseminated by the militant organs of the muckrackers
and sensational, mass publications, more than any other cause,
that brought the national child labor reform movement into being.
In addition, northern manufacturers, including but by no means
restricted to the New England textile industry, pointed to the
contrast in labor conditions between the two regions and charged
that the south's competitive advantage resulted principally from
the exploitation of children and the consequent depressed scale
of adult wages. This explanation was close to the truth. The industrial progress of the south rested upon a surplus of unorgan-
ized, adult workmen.[28] This "enthusiastic labor," as it was eu-
phemistically described in advertisements, tended to perpetuate
child labor and to dampen interest in trade unionism.

The humanitarian and the economic criticisms centered upon
the conspicuous failure of the principal southern textile states to
enact child labor legislation that in any way kept pace with the
other regions of the country. Because the disparity in standards
persisted, the south, during the ensuing two decades, was inex-
orably bound up with the national movement for child labor
reform. Initially, with few, and gradually more, exceptions, southern manufacturers — especially the cotton mill men — resisted
adopting the labor conditions that prevailed in the national
economy. The southern populace, though less intransigent, generally remained suspicious of governmental intervention in the
economic order.

27 See Edgar Gardner Murphy, *Problems of the Present South* (New York:
Macmillan Co., 1904), pp. 95–150.

28 See Woodward, *Origins of the New South*, p. 307; Simkins, *The South
Old and New*, p. 244; and Cash, *The Mind of the South*, pp. 203–6.

As a consequence, although the industrial exploitation of children was by no means confined to the south,[29] the south remained the main focus of national publicity. As a further consequence, it became the chief target for the reform movement's activities. The south, in turn, furnished the most persistent opposition to these activities. This opposition, formed to control state legislation, later fought in Congress and before the Supreme Court to preserve its interests against what it considered outside and improper interference.

Organizing for Reform: Establishment of the National Child Labor Committee

As reliable information was acquired, the leaders of the nascent reform movement perceived that industrial child labor had become a national problem. Edgar Gardner Murphy, the chief figure in awakening the south to child labor conditions, took the lead in informing the country about the facts. In communications with interested persons and within existing social action agencies, this Alabama minister argued that child labor involved the welfare of all the states; therefore, a united demand for remedial legislation was required to alleviate and, eventually, solve the problem.[30] In advocating national cooperation as the sole means of correcting child labor abuses, Murphy, like those he influenced, envisioned legislative action within the states, not federal control. Indeed, Murphy specifically disavowed using the word "national" in a political sense:

> The conditions of industry vary so greatly and so decisively from State to State and locality to locality that the enactment of a federal child labor law, applicable to all conditions and under all circumstances, would be inadequate if not unfortunate.[31]

Murphy also rejected the simplistic explanation that exploitation resulted primarily from the unprincipled action of avaricious individuals. He believed, instead, that a complex system of industrial life had engulfed the nation before the public understood what had occurred and could devise adequate modes of social control.

In common with other reform movements, the growth of public

---

[29] Only one-tenth of the 280,000 children reported as engaged in industrial pursuits by the federal census in 1900 were employed in the south.

[30] Davidson, *Child Labor Legislation in the Southern Textile States*, pp. 122–23.

[31] Murphy, *Problems of the Present South*, p. 129.

concern led to an organizational effort to channel public opinion into purposeful action. The most important effect was the formation, on April 15, 1904, of the National Child Labor Committee. Local committees had previously been established in several states and in a number of urban communities. As Murphy's ideas gained prominence, it was natural that a national organization should have been created to foster public awareness and coordinate legislative campaigns. It was natural, also, that Murphy was the moving spirit in founding the new reform agency.[32] From the beginning, the National Committee's policies reflected his conception of the national character of child labor and the necessity for coordinated remedial action throughout the country.

The founders of the N.C.L.C. included many prominent members of existing reform organizations, and some whose names were soon to become synonymous with the new progressive movement. Typically, they represented the major geographic areas, political parties, and religious faiths. From the beginning, therefore, the committee rightfully claimed to be a national rather than a sectional organization. The dominant influence in policy-making, however, was exercised by social workers, educators, and philanthropists, most of them from the major cities of the eastern seaboard. Although the committee's membership remained small, seldom numbering more than 10,000 persons, the committee rapidly acquired a reputation for getting things done. Its highly effective leaders and recruits, its success in raising funds (chiefly from membership fees and private gifts), its skillful planning and execution of programs, and the public support it enlisted soon made the committee the main force behind modern efforts to abolish child labor in America.

The dominant ideals of the committee were humanitarian: to fill the urgent need for "a national body which would be a great moral force for the protection of children."[33] Like other reform groups, it sought to counter one set of ideas with another. Specifically, it tried to overcome traditional, individualistic attitudes, the inflexible dictates of Social Darwinism, and social indifference, by emphasizing common ideals, by relating the claims of social justice to traditional American aspirations, and by formulating action-compelling interpretations of the facts of contemporary

[32] *The Long Road*, Fortieth Anniversary Report of the National Child Labor Committee (New York, 1944), p. 11.
[33] Quoted in *Child Labor at the Mid-Century*, Annual Report, N.C.L.C., September 30, 1950 (New York, 1950), p. 5.

society. "American civilization," stated Felix Adler, the founder of the Society for Ethical Culture and the committee's first chairman, "is characterized by compassionateness toward human suffering," but its most distinctive and dominant principle was "the moral equality of all human beings." [34] In Adler's view, child labor perverted those principles, and menaced the progress of civilization itself. Its terrible social costs could no longer be tolerated; its atrociously inhumane practices had to cease, as soon as possible.[35]

The National Committee's program called for investigations to establish the facts concerning child labor, publication of these findings and other publicity to arouse public opinion and heighten parental responsibility, and enactment of legislation to provide protection against premature and other injurious employment and to ensure educational opportunities.[36] Its main efforts attempted to bar children below fourteen years of age from employment in industry and commerce and to ensure that children between fourteen and sixteen years of age would be protected against excessive hours of labor and night work. This legislation was sought at the state rather than the national level, however. Indeed, the original program prospectus specifically disavowed federal legislation as a means of controlling or abolishing the evils of child labor.[37]

During the National Committee's first decade of existence, its programs helped achieve significant child labor reform. The first of two periods of marked progress spanned the years 1905 to 1907, roughly coinciding with Theodore Roosevelt's second presidential term. The progressive ground swell was gathering strength in the states, where the quest for social justice centered. Throughout the country, state legislatures enacted measures to improve working conditions and secure humane objectives, to curb economic malefactors and extend democratic processes. The activities of the National Committee and other reform organizations converted public concern into public pressure for change. The increasingly clear contrast between widely professed social aspirations and the intolerable conditions that surrounded the employment of children in industry spurred two-thirds of the states either to

---

34 "The Basis for the Anti-Child Labor Movement in the Idea of American Civilization," *Child Labor and Social Progress*, Proceedings of the Fourth Annual Meeting, N.C.L.C. (New York, 1908), pp. 1–2.

35 *Ibid.*

36 *Objectives of the Committee*, N.C.L.C. leaflet (New York, 1904).

37 Samuel M. Lindsey, "National Child Labor Standards," *Child Labor Bulletin* (May, 1914), pp. 25–26.

initiate protective legislation or greatly to strengthen existing laws.[38]

There was little change in the southern textile states during this period, despite strenuous efforts by the National Committee and other reform organizations. The committee's investigations and the resulting publicity, as well as criticism of other aspects of southern life, especially from northern sources, strengthened the feeling throughout much of the region that the reform movement was an "alien" force.[39] This resentment against "northern" interference seriously impaired the efforts that were being made within the region to improve regulatory standards. The captains of industry and commerce skillfully exploited the ingrained reluctance of the southern community to tolerate examination of its peculiar institutions as a means of rallying southern public opinion to the defense of so-called southern interests. It was, of course, merely another version of the familiar southern plea for local control, which had earlier been applied to abolitionists, reconstructionists, desegregaters, and other intruders. "Let us alone and we'll remedy acknowledged problems — our way!"

Beveridge and Federal Child Labor Regulation

Near the end of this initial period of accomplishment, in January, 1907, the first important appeal for federal regulation of child labor was made. The appeal may well be the most significant address on the subject ever delivered in America, the now famous exposé that Albert Beveridge presented on the floor of the United States Senate. Beveridge had become a popular, national figure, in the years just after the Spanish-American War, as a flamboyant advocate of overseas expansion. Later, he championed progressive causes and became an acknowledged leader in the emerging anti-child labor movement. His intention in speaking, which was thoroughly publicized in the preceding weeks (Beveridge was a skilled politician), was to shock the sensibilities of the nation and to demand national legislative action to abolish "child slavery."[40]

Hour after hour, during three days of debate, Beveridge read

[38] Faulkner, *The Quest for Social Justice*, p. 186.

[39] Davidson, *Child Labor Legislation in the Southern Textile States*, pp. 1–2, 126–29, 137–48. Discussing the south's reaction to this criticism, Davidson observed: "This was a natural feeling on the part of a people still sore from the wounds of the Civil War and reconstruction . . ." *Ibid.*, p. 2.

[40] Claude G. Bowers, *Beveridge and the Progressive Era* (Boston: Houghton Mifflin Co., 1932), pp. 250–52.

an indictment, documented by months of careful research, depicting an evil "as brutal and horrible in its inhumanity as anything the pen of Dickens ever painted."[41] In his judgment, a national abuse of appalling scope existed: hundreds of thousands of children throughout the country were being systematically exploited. Beveridge adduced voluminous evidence to confirm the number of child laborers and to describe conditions in such conspicuously offending industries as Pennsylvania coal breakers, Ohio glass factories, New Jersey sweatshops, and southern textile mills.[42] He told of human suffering and destroyed youth, of ruthless impairment of adulthood and national impoverishment, for what he regarded as a few men's profit. The tone was angry and insistent, the images vivid and arresting. The speech is a striking illustration of dramatic criticism in an age of outspoken social protest.[43]

His facts, Beveridge hoped, would make the necessity for federal legislation abundantly clear. Child labor was national in scope, so widely prevalent that the states were unable to deal with it. Their laws, with rare exceptions, failed to meet desirable standards, and enforcement was lax, sometimes virtually nonexistent.[44] On the other hand, states that enacted effective statutes found themselves at a pronounced disadvantage in competing with "backward" areas.[45] Uniform law was the only practical remedy, and Congress alone could apply this curative. Beveridge proposed that the commerce power be used to bar the products of manufacturing establishments that employed child laborers from interstate shipment.[46]

The Supreme Court's decision in *Champion* v. *Ames*,[47] less than four years before, sustaining the first significant exercise of federal authority for police power purposes, greatly encouraged Beveridge and largely shaped his constitutional argument. Justice Harlan had held:

[41] *Ibid.*, p. 253.

[42] *Congressional Record*, 59th Cong., 2nd Sess. (Washington, D.C.: Government Printing Office 1907), pp. 1552–57, 1792–826, 1867–83. The speeches were delivered January 23, 28, and 29, 1907.

[43] Beveridge spoke of "the presentation of the evidence in this case — because that is what it amounts to, evidence in a case," as if he were a prosecuting attorney for the nation, presenting a suit against the perpetrators of an enormous crime.

[44] *Congressional Record*, 59th Cong., 2d Sess., p. 1817.

[45] *Ibid.*, p. 1807.

[46] The bill (59th Congress, 2d Sess., S. 6562) provided penalties against interstate carriers who transported goods produced by factories that employed children under fourteen years of age.

[47] 188 U.S. 321 (1903).

As a State may, for the purpose of guarding the morals of its own people, forbid all sales of lottery tickets within its limits, so Congress, for the purpose of guarding the people of the United States against the "widespread pestilence of lotteries" and to protect the commerce which concerns all the States, may prohibit the carrying of lottery tickets from one State to another. . . . We should hesitate long before adjudging that an evil of such appalling character, carried on through interstate commerce, cannot be met and crushed by the only power competent to that end. We say competent to that end, because Congress alone has power to occupy by legislation, the whole field of interstate commerce.[48]

But what was the scope of this power? How far might federal social legislation go? The opinion provided scant guidance: "The present case does not require the court to declare the full extent of the power that Congress may exercise in the regulation of commerce among the states."[49]

This conclusion stopped short of the broad declaration of congressional authority that counsel for the government had urged during argument in the case. The unlimited power over external commerce that the individual states had exercised under the Articles of Confederation had, with the Constitution, passed to Congress; "no residuum was left to the states."[50] The only limitations on this transferred plenary power were the minor qualifications expressly stated in the Constitution. "*That the power to prohibit is absolute*, and the legislature is the final authority of the wisdom of its exercise, seems to be clearly established upon both principle and authority," counsel concluded.[51]

Harlan's opinion, however, greatly distressed the four dissenters. The arbitrary classification of lottery tickets, Chief Justice Fuller charged:

breaks down all the differences between that which is, and that which is not, an article of commerce, and the necessary consequence is to take from the States all jurisdiction over the subject so far as interstate communication is concerned. It is a long step in the direction of wiping out all traces of state lines, and the creation of a centralized Government.[52]

The power to promote the public health, good order, and prosperity inhered exclusively in the states and had never been surrendered to the national government. Fuller maintained:

48 *Ibid.*, pp. 357–58.
49 *Ibid.*, pp. 362–63.
50 *Ibid.*, p. 335.

51 *Ibid.*, p. 340.
52 *Ibid.*, p. 371.

It will not do to say — a suggestion which has heretofore been
made in this case — that state laws have been found to be ineffective for the suppression of lotteries, and therefore Congress should
interfere. *The scope of the commerce clause of the Constitution
can not be enlarged because of the present views of public interest.*[53]

Fuller's opinion closely followed the contention of the counsel
for the lottery interests, who sought to undermine any basis for
federal police powers and to prevent federal interference with
so-called internal affairs of the states. In addition, Fuller prepared
a second line of defense: the doctrine that the power to prohibit
commerce was confined strictly to articles that were inherently
deleterious. In some measure, Harlan's statement that lottery
tickets "polluted commerce" appeared to represent a victory for
this doctrine, for it could be construed to mean that Congress
might prohibit only articles that caused harm during transit or
when utilized. Nevertheless, Fuller's bitter protest disclosed the
fundamental facts: the Court's holding permitted a congressional
majority to interfere indirectly with substantive property rights;
the threat of prohibition was a powerful instrument for securing
compliance with legislative conceptions of socially desirable practices; and, once such power was sustained, it might be impossible
to restrict it.

Beveridge's constitutional position essentially recapitulated the
sweeping interpretation of the commerce power that governmental
counsel had developed. To demonstrate the "entire legality" of
federal child labor legislation, he traced the history of the commerce clause, citing recent congressional enactments that, he
asserted, sought similar social welfare objectives. He applied the
broadest possible construction to Harlan's purposefully vague
holding: as an incident to its power to regulate commerce among
the states, Congress possessed absolute discretion to exclude any
and all articles from interstate transportation. The exact determination depended, at any moment, upon Congress's conception
of the current requirements of proper public policy.[54]

This interpretation became linked to the most important
achievement in Beveridge's life, his now famous biography of
Chief Justice Marshall, the Constitution's great expounder. In
the child labor debate, Beveridge drew the link between Marshallian construction and the nationalistic interpretation of federal

53 *Ibid.*, p. 372. Emphasis added.
54 *Congressional Record*, 59th Cong., 2d Sess., pp. 1822–26, 1869–83.

powers that underlay progressivism: the belief that Congress should mold its exercise of national powers to fit exigencies undreamed of by the founders.

Most of Beveridge's colleagues agreed with him about the need for child labor reform, although the concurrence was variously expressed. Some senators joined Beveridge in condemning child labor abuses; others, although critical of exploitation, contended that the problem had been magnified, or that exceptional instances, admittedly cruel and offensive, had been invalidly generalized to condemn entire industries or regions.

The Beveridge bill, nevertheless, provoked strong and persistent opposition. Hostile senators, whether uncompromising defenders of the fundamental principles of laissez faire or progressive legislators who were unable to discern how Congress could regulate the conditions of production, repeatedly interrupted Beveridge's presentation, challenging his interpretation of the commerce power. Federal legislation, according to the opponents' argument, would go beyond constitutional limitations and invade the legitimate powers that were reserved to the states. More important, especially for conservative members, such an enactment would furnish a ready precedent for further federal regulatory enactments under the guise of the commerce power, whose nature, extent, and destructiveness no one could predict.[55] Most of the opponents were convinced that state legislation afforded an adequate regulatory, and the only constitutionally allowable, remedy.[56]

From the Beveridge Bill to the Report on Women and Child Wage Earners: Interlude and Resurgence in Reform

Beveridge's remarkable address accomplished his immediate aim: the impassioned performance on the Senate floor compelled the attention of a nation quickening to the quest for social justice. Despite the convincing demonstration that there was nothing

[55] In an analysis of congressional reaction to legislation at "constitutional frontiers," Thomas G. Karis states that the crucial and suggestive question, more often asked than any other by opponents and some supporters of federal regulations in the course of the Beveridge debate, was "Where would regulation under the commerce clause end?" This analysis traces congressional debate on attempts to establish federal child labor legislation ("Congressional Behavior at Constitutional Frontiers: from 1906, the Beveridge Child Labor Bill, to 1938, the Fair Labor Standards Act [unpublished Ph.D. dissertation, Department of Political Science, Columbia University, 1951], p. 31).

[56] *Congressional Record*, 59th Cong., 2d Sess., pp. 1822–26, 1869–83, *passim*.

illusory about child labor, however, neither the populace nor the progressive President, whom Beveridge greatly admired, was prepared to use the doctrines of the Lottery case as a precedent for the proposed social reform. Congress showed little interest in the Beveridge bill, and, of greater moment, the decisive public opinion that would have been necessary to enact federal legislation did not materialize. Many persons, nevertheless, were indignant about child labor abuses. In two consecutive presidential messages to Congress, Theodore Roosevelt had recommended a comprehensive investigation of the condition of women and child wage earners throughout the country. In correspondence that was made public at the time, he indicated his expectation that the investigation would lead to appropriate legislation, either by Congress or by the states, if the necessity was demonstrated.[57] Within a month after the Beveridge debate, Congress appropriated $150,000 to carry out such an investigation; but Americans were not ready to go further. Less than a generation had passed since Congress, with the enactment of the Sherman Antitrust Act, had begun to explore the possibility of using the commerce power to regulate the economic order.

The failure of the Beveridge bill to arouse significant public support proved greatly disappointing to many, but not all, of the National Committee's trustees. In preparation for his Senate appearance, Beveridge had twice consulted the board, on November 22 and December 6, 1906. After prolonged and discordant discussion, the committee endorsed the Beveridge bill,[58] but this decision divided the leadership and alienated some of the members. Edgar Gardner Murphy spoke for a group of trustees who believed that the bill was unconstitutional, that endorsement of federal legislation violated the organizing principles of the committee, and that such action would do irreparable harm to the reform movement, especially to state campaigns in the south.[59]

[57] Letter to the Secretary of Commerce and Labor, in *Congressional Record*, 59th Cong., 1st Sess., p. 3579.

[58] Davidson, *Child Labor Legislation in the Southern Textile States*, pp. 130–37. In 1954, on the National Committee's fiftieth anniversary, the early records of the organization, together with an extensive though incomplete collection of its publications, letters, and working papers (chiefly reports drafted for policy purposes), were deposited in the Library of Congress. In the process, some pieces were lost or misplaced, notably the minutes of the board of trustees for most of the committee's first ten years. It has been necessary, as a result, to rely upon Davidson's reports for this period because they are the most nearly complete record in print.

[59] *Ibid.*, pp. 132–37.

Internal differences within the committee had not sharply emerged before, but Beveridge's proposal precipitated an open conflict over the means for attaining reforms. The motion endorsing federal legislation formalized the belief that state laws generally lacked adequate inspection provisions and often were not enforced: that a national standard was necessary "to correct the evils of child labor in their important national aspects, especially in the deterioration of our racial stock, and will tend to establish equality of economic competition, without minimizing state responsibility." [60] The division within the committee was sectional in that the southern trustees, without exception, opposed federal action; however, they received support from various northern members, seemingly without regard to political affiliation, who objected on principle.

When it became clear that there was no chance of enacting federal legislation, the trustees sought to reunite the leadership and to assuage the discontented. On October 25, 1907, they adopted a resolution that acknowledged the wide disagreement within the National Committee and withdrew their endorsement of the Beveridge bill.[61] The resolution left the members free to take any position they chose, and committed the board to wait until the results of the investigation into the condition of women and child wage earners were reported before deciding on an official stand for the National Committee.[62]

The executive secretary, Samuel M. Lindsay, a vigorous advocate of federal legislation, resigned, ostensibly because of the pressure of his responsibilities as a faculty member at Columbia University. His replacement, Owen Lovejoy, previously the committee's northern secretary, wrote Murphy, in January, 1908, that the Beveridge bill was dead as far as the committee was concerned. "My own feeling is that the less said about this matter of our relation to Federal Legislation the better, and I regret some of the things the newspapers are publishing on the subject." [63] Thereafter, the committee revitalized its program to secure legislation within the states and energetically backed its new campaign for a federal children's bureau.[64]

During the next few years, child labor bills were regularly intro-

[60] Quoted in *ibid.,* p. 132.
[61] *Lindsay,* p. 27.
[62] *Ibid.*
[63] Quoted in Davidson, *Child Labor Legislation in the Southern Textile States,* p. 137.
[64] *Ibid.,* pp. 136–37.

duced in Congress. However, without the leadership of a progressive President or strong and persistent public pressure, the lawmakers were not inclined to disturb the status quo. Like the National Committee, persons interested in reform tended to adopt a wait-and-see attitude on federal regulation.[65] Within the states, legislation was passed very slowly. An important factor was the Supreme Court's five-to-four decision in the *Lochner* case [66] in which New York's maximum-hour law for bakers had been invalidated. The Court majority had admonished state legislatures, saying that states' interference with the ordinary trades and occupations of the people seemed to be on the increase. These justices made it absolutely clear that they did not believe in the soundness of the philosophy that upheld such regulatory laws as that of New York. The economic liberties of men could not be entrusted to the paternal wisdom of legislatures.

The *Lochner* decision had a marked effect in arresting social reform in the states, for legislatures were reluctant to risk the destruction of statutes that seemed to run counter to the Court's trend of decision. This retarding influence extended to child labor enactments, even though state courts had consistently affirmed the right of legislatures to outlaw child labor abuses.[67] This situation persisted, until the Oregon Ten-Hour Law for women came before the Court, in the *Muller* case.[68]

The leaders of the social justice movement perceived that a crisis of major importance had arrived and they sought an outstanding attorney to defend the statute. At the suggestion of Florence Kelley, the general secretary of the National Consumer's League and a National Committee trustee, the services of Louis D. Brandeis were secured. By his unconventional argument, based on "the living facts of industrial America," and because of the growing political force of progressivism, Brandeis won a tremen-

[65] When the 60th Congress convened, in December, 1907, Beveridge reintroduced the regulatory measure he had drafted the session before. Again, it failed to receive significant support and Beveridge did not thereafter actively pursue federal legislation in Congress. His defeat for reelection in 1910, although not attributable to his child labor stand, removed the reform movement's most vigorous advocate within the national legislature.

[66] *Lochner* v. *New York*, 198 U.S. 45 (1905).

[67] State decisions upholding child labor legislation as a valid exercise of the police powers were so numerous, positively stated, and widely accepted that the first case was carried to the Supreme Court only in 1913. The result was an affirmative opinion, in *Sturges Manufacturing Co.* v. *Beauchamp*, 231 U.S. 320 (1913).

[68] *Muller* v. *Oregon*, 208 U.S. 412 (1908).

dous victory for sociological jurisprudence and twentieth-century reform. With this decision, and later decisions after the Court's conversion to the principle of judicial toleration, the floodgates that had retarded social legislation swung open. State legislatures, in the immediately succeeding years, received great impetus for the enactment of measures that regulated industrial conditions.[69]

The child labor reform movement benefited from this stimulus and from the publication, beginning in June, 1910, of the nineteen volumes of the federal report on women and child wage earners.[70] The living facts, never before comprehensively documented, supported the data from the National Committee's investigations. The offensive conditions disclosed by this study and by other social research stimulated public interest, and, added to the liberal sentiment of the times, sharpened the demand for remedial legislation. In the states, the second period of distinct progress in regulatory legislation was underway,[71] to last until the nation went to war.

[69] Arthur S. Link, *American Epoch* (New York: Alfred A. Knopf, 1955), pp. 70–71.

[70] United States Department of Labor, *Report on the Condition of Women and Child Wage Earners* (19 vols.; Washington, D.C.: Government Printing Office, 1910–13).

[71] The National Committee reported that its seventh year, 1910–11, had been notable for the number and importance of legislative changes. A summary showed that improvements had been made in the law of thirty states during this time. "Seventh Annual Report, N.C.L.C.," September 30, 1911, in *Child Labor Bulletin* (November, 1911), p. 187.

The following year was similarly successful; progress was reported in twelve of the fourteen states that held legislative sessions. "Eighth Annual Report, N.C.L.C." September 30, 1912, *ibid.* (November 1912), p. 1.

2

Progress and Paradox:
Recourse to the Nation

Child Labor after a Decade of National Reform

By 1912 the progressive movement had become a permanent force in American life. During the summer, Roosevelt's candidacy drove a wedge between the conservative and insurgent wings of the Republican party, and shortly thereafter the standard of the New Nationalism was raised in a feverish convention in Chicago. The Democrats countered with the Princeton-scholar-turned-reformer, and a campaign of epic proportions moved to its inevitable conclusion. William Howard Taft, weakened by the defection of important conservatives as well as liberals in his party, ran a poor third. Theodore Roosevelt also suffered defeat; but the nation was overwhelmingly progressive, and the new President, Woodrow Wilson, symbolized its vitality as well as its reform sentiment.[1]

America was prepared for drastic action — the platforms of both the Democratic and the Progressive parties called for liberal legislation of national scope to recreate the promise of the young Republic — and it would not be disappointed.[2] Wilson drove Congress forward. In his own dramatic words: "The old order changeth — changeth under our very eyes, not quietly and equably, but swiftly and with the noise and heat and tumult of reconstruc-

---

[1] "Individuals might disagree over a definition of progressivism," Link writes, "but a large majority of them were discontented with Old Guard policies and in a rebellious mood. . . . Even Taft . . . would have denied he was a conservative." Arthur S. Link, *Woodrow Wilson and the Progressive Era* ("The New American Nation Series," eds. Henry Steel Commager and Richard B. Morris, Vol. I [New York: Harper & Row, 1954]), p. 22.

[2] Herbert Croly summed up the matter in an epochal volume. The national promise, he said, could no longer be considered destined to automatic fulfillment but had "been transformed into a closer equivalent of a national purpose, the fulfillment of which was a matter of conscious work." *The Promise of American Life* (New York: Macmillan Co., 1909), pp. 20–21.

tion."[3] The legislation of the New Freedom poured forth at an unheard-of pace. The Roosevelt era, in Eric F. Goldman's characterization, "had been a period of beginnings, of a scattering of pioneer legislation and a mounting favorable opinion. The Wilson era, building on this foundation, was a period of sweeping achievement."[4]

As the era began, the National Committee could look back upon significant progress in child labor reform that had been accomplished largely through its efforts. During the previous decade, as its tenth Annual Report (issued in September, 1914) pointed out, forty-six of the forty-eight states had improved their protective legislation or had provided enhanced educational opportunities for children.[5] On the other hand, despite these satisfying legislative strides and the pervasive character of progressive sentiment, the extent of child labor appeared to be unchanged and progress in the advancement and enforcement of protective standards was becoming more difficult to sustain. An impasse to further gains seemed to be developing.

In understanding this paradoxical situation, two facts are important: progress toward achieving the committee's objectives had been differential, and success had caused the committee to shift its emphasis. As for exclusion, through which the committee had sought to end the inhumane conditions associated with the industrial employment of grade-school-age children by imposing a minimum-age standard for fourteen-year-olds, success had in large measure been attained. Indeed, a memorial to Edgar Gardner Murphy in 1913 declared that the first stage in reform had come to an end. Except for conspicuously backward areas, the worst horrors were almost gone.[6] As for protection, however, through which the committee had sought to afford adequate safeguards by establishing an eight-hour day and exclusion from night work for children fourteen and fifteen years of age, progress, although significant, was less marked.

These results had caused the National Committee to concentrate its efforts on the enactment of protective legislation, an objective that aroused less emotionally charged popular response than ending "the holocaust of the children." In addition, the committee consciously revised this program of safeguards to take

---

[3] *The New Freedom* (Garden City, N. Y.: Doubleday, 1913), p. 29.

[4] *Rendezvous with Destiny* (New York: Alfred A. Knopf, 1952), pp. 225–26.

[5] "Tenth Annual Report, N.C.L.C.," September 30, 1914, in *Child Labor Bulletin* (November, 1914), p. 8.

[6] "Passing of a Pioneer," *Child Labor Bulletin* (November, 1913), p. 9.

account of experience and to embody new objectives, particularly
for adequate administrative structures and enforcement provisions.[7] These employment standards were incorporated into a
Uniform Child Labor Law, which was recommended to the states.
By 1914, however, only a few states met these standards in all
respects.[8]

The situation took on added significance after the 1910 census
data revealed that the number of children at work had increased
since 1900. To be sure, those engaged in industrial pursuits had
declined slightly during the decade, from 284,000 to 261,000, but
the number of child workers had increased, from 1,750,000 in
1900 to 1,990,000 in 1910, thereby keeping pace with the rise in
the nation's population. It was still true that one child in every
six between the ages of ten and fifteen was gainfully employed.[9]
Neither the demand for youthful workers nor the supply of children seeking remunerative employment showed a tendency to
decline. State enactments had changed the nature of child labor
as an industrial phenomenon by eliminating the worst physical
abuses, but they were far from ending exploitation. Indeed, the
significant reduction in the number of child laborers under fourteen meant only one thing: industrial employment for children
over that age was becoming institutionalized. Of equal importance, conditions in other areas of child employment had been
little affected. In agriculture, the number of child workers had
increased, and it was discovered that almost one-fifth worked in
for-hire positions, unsupervised by their parents. The census
termed them "farm laborers working out."

Against this background of partial success in legislative campaigns but persistent use of child labor, a summary statement in

---

[7] At the same time, the committee was slowly redefining child labor, calling
attention to the plight of children engaged in commercial activities and street
trades, exploring the possibilities of ameliorating the conditions of agricultural child laborers, and considering whether higher minimum standards in
industry might not be desirable. See especially *ibid.*, pp. 5–10, 45–47, and
Elizabeth H. Davidson, *Child Labor Legislation in the Southern Textile States*
(Chapel Hill: University of North Carolina Press, 1939), pp. 249–52.

[8] In 1904, thirteen states had a minimum-age requirement of fourteen years
for industrial employment; thirty-six states established this standard by 1914.
At the earlier date, only one state restricted the hours of labor for children
under sixteen to eight hours a day, but eighteen states had done this ten years
later. Similarly, five states prohibited night work for children in 1904, and
thirteen states made provisions for factory inspection; by 1914, thirty-four
states prohibited night work and thirty-six states had some form of factory-
inspection legislation. "Tenth Annual Report, N.C.L.C.," p. 8.

[9] *Child Labor: Facts and Figures*, U.S. Children's Bureau (Washington,
D.C.: Government Printing Office, 1933), *passim*.

the National Committee's tenth Annual Report takes on full meaning: "It was hoped in 1904," wrote the general secretary, Owen Lovejoy, "that child labor could be abolished in ten years of hard work. We have been disillusioned. More has been done than seemed possible within the period, but the field is immensely larger than was supposed." [10]

Overshadowing all else was the growing resistance to legislative progress in the states. This phenomenon was attributable, in substantial measure, to the lack of uniformity in protective standards from state to state and to the possibly greater disparity between provisions for factory inspection and the enforcement of such legislation.[11] The course of reform had been far from even throughout the country, and, within the states, legislation usually had accumulated piecemeal, and often without much reference to suggested standards, local interests almost invariably affecting the outcome. Not only was there great variation in legislation, but some states — especially those of the southern piedmont area — lagged far behind the general level of regulation. The economic and competitive advantages supposedly (and often actually) enjoyed by backward states tended to retard reform efforts in almost every state in which manufacturing was of any importance.[12]

State legislatures were increasingly reluctant to make further reform advances at what seemed the expense of the industrial interests of the locality. With each succeeding legislative term it became more evident that uniformity of standards was impossible to achieve through state-by-state campaigns, and that — unless another avenue of control was found — the time required to attain reform goals might lengthen interminably.

The National Committee Decides to Seek Congressional Legislation

Although local prospects for child labor reform seemed discouraging in 1913, one all-important circumstance gave hope to the movement: the nation had turned progressive in its politics.

[10] "Tenth Annual Report, N.C.L.C." pp. 8–9.

[11] Inspection provisions varied in stringency and enforcement processes often were inadequate, and sometimes rendered useless by failure to vote appropriations or to provide necessary personnel. When it came to penalizing, violators were tried in local courts and convictions were difficult to secure. In many communities, particularly semi-rural ones and those with seasonal industries or one dominant industry, prosecutors often were reluctant to institute proceedings, juries to convict, and judges to impose penalties.

[12] Raymond G. Fuller, "Child Labor," *Encyclopaedia of the Social Sciences*, eds. Erwin R. A. Seligman and Alvin Johnson (15 vols.; New York: Macmillan Co., 1937), III, 419.

This change mitigated the fear of Leviathan, which throughout American experience has been a constant of politics. In 1906, as popular discontent had mounted, Elihu Root cautioned:

> It may be that [public] control would be better exercised in particular instances by the governments of the states, but the people will have the control they need, either from the states or from the national government; and if the states fail to furnish it in due measure, sooner or later constructions of the constitution will be found to vest the power where it will be exercised — in the national government.[13]

The traditional commitment to dispersed power did not disappear, but, as Woodrow Wilson's first administration began, progressives enthusiastically heralded the efficacy of national legislation for fulfilling the reform program. "The great impulses of the several movements for social and economic justice were now pulsating more strongly than before." [14]

Federal regulation of child labor no longer appeared to be foreclosed, as it had seemed to be six years before. At that time, public opinion had rejected child labor as a subject for national control because of uncertainty about the constitutionality of the Beveridge bill and because exploitation was not generally regarded as a national economic problem. In the intervening years, many statutes, utilizing the commerce and taxing powers to accomplish police power purposes, accustomed the masses of persons to this form of social control. In addition, the implications of child labor for industrial competition had become widely recognized. As a result, states that were not willing to advance alone appeared ready to advance in company, thereby ending the advantages enjoyed by communities that pursued short-sighted social policies. Moreover, progressivism's equalitarian tendencies and urban orientation had produced lively concern for the interests of children, especially the offspring of the poor. The nation's future adults were owed every educational opportunity and every chance for social betterment that society could provide.[15] As the old order of political align-

---

[13] Address to the Pennsylvania Society, September, 1906, quoted in Commission on Intergovernmental Relations, *A Report to the President* (Washington, D.C.: Government Printing Office, 1956), p. 56.

[14] Link, *Woodrow Wilson and the Progressive Era*, pp. 54–55.

[15] In the judgment of Schlesinger and Fox, and a judgment shared by other students of the social justice movement, the generation that ended with American entry into World War I "made perhaps its greatest humanitarian contribution in an energetic concern for the long-neglected rights of childhood." Editor's introduction to Harold U. Faulkner, *The Quest for Social Justice (A*

ments changed, humanitarian, economic, and civic arguments for remedial action began to merge; child labor reform was coming to mean the equalization of labor conditions as well as social justice.

Any doubts that might have remained about the constitutionality of federal social legislation were largely dispelled early in 1913, when the Supreme Court unanimously sustained the Mann Act. Indeed, the decision marked a decisive turning point in national reform, for the Court's sweeping language caused the leaders of various branches of the social justice movement to shift their efforts to obtaining national legislation that could effect social improvements. The Mann Act, the most important statute to that time for extending federal control over matters of health, morals, and welfare where state legislation had proved ineffectual, struck at the systematic inducement of women to become prostitutes. Like child labor, this issue had aroused the nation. Convinced that the whiteslave trade had become a national problem that demanded a national remedy, congressional majorities proceeded to purify the streams of commerce. In upholding the act, in *Hoke* v. *United States*, Justice McKenna affirmed that Congress had power "to occupy, by legislation, the whole field of interstate commerce." [16]

> The principle established by the cases is the simple one, when rid of confusing and distracting considerations, that Congress has power over transportation "among the several states"; that the power is complete in itself, and that Congress, as an incident to it, may adopt not only means necessary but convenient to its exercise, and the means may have the quality of police regulations. [17]

In these circumstances, the National Committee changed its policy; it now seemed possible to accelerate the entire reform program. In one decisive campaign, the principal barriers of the past might be swept aside. Late in 1913 the trustees decided to initiate a campaign to establish uniform child labor standards throughout the country by the enactment of federal legislation. In 1907, Florence Kelley recalled, "lingering doubts as to the power of Congress to deal with child labor in the states beset the minds of members of the National Child Labor Committee, and deprived Senator Beveridge of whole-hearted, unanimous backing for his bill." [18] But all this had changed. Edgar Gardner Murphy

History of American Life, eds., Arthur M. Schlesinger and Dixon Ryan Fox, Vol. XI [12 vols.; New York: Macmillan Co., 1937]), p. xvi.

[16] 227 U.S. 308, 320 (1913).

[17] *Ibid.*, p. 323.

[18] "The Federal Child Labor Law," *Survey* (August 26, 1916), p. 523.

was dead, and federal legislation had almost the unanimous support of the officers and trustees, Samuel M. Lindsay, the vice-
chairman, reported.[19]

In part, the new policy had resulted from discouragement about
the progress of reform during the previous decade.[20] For the most
part, however, it resulted from agreement among the committee's
leaders on the kind of social control that was needed to end industrial child labor and from their judgment that this remedy was
now attainable.[21] "To combat child labor successfully we need to
unite all the forces of the national authority to those of the state
and local authorities, each acting within their respective and
proper jurisdiction but so united, cooperative, and comprehensive
that there is no 'twilight zone' in which no authority acts or in
which conflicting authorities may nullify each other's activities,"
Lindsay said.[22]

Selection of the Commerce Power

The Sixty-third Congress had convened in April, 1913, called
into special session by President Wilson. At that time, Senator
Kenyon, an insurgent Republican from Iowa and a leading congressional progressive, re-introduced the Beveridge bill, unsuccessfully presented in every Congress since 1908. Four other measures,
also based on the commerce power, were introduced; one of them,
the Coply-Poindexter bill, was a Progressive party proposal.[23] But
Congress had been summoned to enact the priority measures of
the New Freedom — the Federal Reserve Act and tariff reduction —
and lesser matters were postponed.

When, months later, the National Committee decided to support federal legislation, the trustees reviewed the child labor bills
that had been introduced. All were found defective in that they
failed to meet desirable standards or were directed toward interstate carriers rather than toward industrial establishments in

[19] "National Child Labor Standards," *Child Labor Bulletin* (May, 1914),
p. 28.

[20] For the testimony of a long-time trustee, see Homer Folks, *Changes and
Trends in Child Labor and Its Control* (New York: National Child Labor Committee, 1938), p. 18.

[21] "Tenth Annual Report, N.C.L.C.," p. 8.

[22] "National Child Labor Standards," pp. 29–30.

[23] It differed from previous bills by defining "antisocial child labor" with
greater specificity and inclusiveness than any other had done. Every form of
manufacturing activity — factory, cannery, workshop, and mechanical establishment — was to be subject to regulation.

which child laborers were employed.[24] They decided that a measure that incorporated the provisions deemed essential by the committee should be formulated and introduced in Congress.[25]

The draft of this bill was worked out by a number of eminent constitutional lawyers who were associated with the committee, after extensive correspondence with other prominent attorneys, numerous state officials, and spokesmen for reform groups, and after consultations with federal administrative officers (particularly, officials of the Children's Bureau) and liberal congressmen. Two of the men who were chiefly responsible for its form and substance were William Draper Lewis, Dean of the University of Pennsylvania Law School, and Charles P. Neill, former Commissioner of the Bureau of Labor. Neill had supervised the unprecedented federal investigation into the condition of women and child wage earners, and, earlier in 1913, had become a trustee of the National Committee (as would Lewis five years later). The previous summer, Lewis had chaired the platform committee at the Progressive convention and had reported a plank that advocated the use of federal power to cope with grave national problems that had "expanded beyond the reach of the individual states."[26] The measure he now helped draft applied this same principle, in the belief that state legislation was not and could not be made adequate to control the national problem of child labor.

The decision about the congressional power that should be invoked involved a judgment on which power would best withstand attack on constitutional grounds and best ensure effective administration and enforcement of the stipulated restrictions.[27] Although selection of the commerce power was almost certain, the merits of the commerce and the taxing powers were carefully considered.[28] In each instance, the constitutional experts scrutinized a body of recent federal legislation that had the character-

[24] Owen R. Lovejoy, "Federal Government and Child Labor," *Child Labor Bulletin* (February, 1914), pp. 19–25, and "Minutes of the Board of Trustees, N.C.L.C.," cited in Davidson, *Child Labor Legislation in the Southern Textile States*, pp. 250–52.

[25] *Ibid.*

[26] Kirk Porter, *National Party Platforms* (New York: Macmillan Co., 1924), p. 336.

[27] Lovejoy, "Federal Government and Child Labor," p. 20.

[28] Hearings before the Committee on Labor, U.S. House of Representatives, 63d Cong., 2d Sess., on H.R. 12292, The Child Labor Bill, February 27, March 9, and May 22, 1914 (Washington, D.C.: Government Printing Office, 1914), pp. 19–20.

istics of police regulations and Supreme Court decisions that had
legitimated these measures. For the commerce power, there was
the well-developed regulatory movement that included legislation
barring lottery tickets, impure foods and drugs, obscene literature,
and the transportation of women for immoral purposes from
interstate commerce. The most significant of the approving judicial holdings were *Champion* v. *Ames* [29] and *Hoke* v. *United
States*.[30]

The taxing power presented a less definite pattern of regulatory
legislation; nevertheless, the drafting committee closely examined
the prohibitive excise that had been levied upon colored oleomargarine and the levy that had destroyed the manufacture of
poisonous white phosphorus matches. The former had been sustained in *McCray* v. *United States*,[31] despite the fact the tax had
been so oppressive it had halted the sale of the commodity, thereby
seeming to open the way to further regulatory experiments. The
latter case had not been tested in the courts; because of the loud
public outcry, the manufacturers had capitulated to the congressional purpose without a contest.

All things considered, the commerce power appeared the
sounder of the two congressional powers, and the trustees accord-
ingly selected it.[32] Thus the National Committee chose the principal means by which national regulatory authority had been
extended in the United States.

The employment standards and administrative procedures incorporated in the proposed statute were considered a great improvement over the child labor bills previously introduced in
Congress. The main provisions prohibited the shipment in interstate commerce of products in whose manufacture children under
fourteen years of age had been employed or children from fourteen
to sixteen had worked more than eight hours in any day or more
than forty-eight hours in any week.[33] For the especially hazardous
occupations of mining and quarrying, products were excluded if
children under sixteen had been employed. The measure thus
differed significantly from the Beveridge bill, which provided

29 188 U.S. 321 (1903).

30 227 U.S. 308 (1913).

31 195 U.S. 27 (1904).

32 See Lovejoy, "Federal Government and Child Labor," pp. 19–24, and
Hearings on the Child Labor Bill, pp. 19–20.

33 The other major provisions made it illegal to employ children from fourteen to sixteen years of age for more than six days in any week or at night
(between seven in the evening and seven in the morning).

only for excluding children under fourteen years of age from industrial employment. As Lovejoy wrote: "It does not seek to penalize the interstate carrier, but attempts to place responsibility upon the real offender, i.e., 'the person, partnership, association or corporation or any agent thereof' producing the goods." [34] In addition, the proposed statute contained effective enforcement provisions, avoiding the conspicuous failure of the Beveridge bill to provide for administration in unambiguous terms. Finally the penalty provisions were adjusted to meet varying situations, by making every delivery for illegal shipment constitute a separate offense.[35]

Congressional Hearings on the Palmer-Owen Bill

In 1908 the National Committee established a Washington office that served as a clearinghouse for the legislative and educational efforts of organizations that were cooperating to achieve child labor reform. In the years that followed, the director of this office, Dr. Alexander J. McKelway (like Edgar Gardner Murphy, a southerner in origin and allegiance), was in continuous contact with governmental officials and gained valuable experience in legislative matters. His capable hands guided the congressional campaign, steadily and surely.

Shortly after it was drafted, the committee's reform bill was introduced in Congress, first in the House, on January 16, 1914, and four weeks later in the Senate.[36] Its sponsors were two men sympathetic to federal regulation, Representative A. Mitchell Palmer, a young, reform-minded Democrat from Pennsylvania, who later became Wilson's Attorney General, and Senator Robert L. Owen, also a democrat, and a leading Wilsonian progressive from the new state of Oklahoma, who had been one of the principal architects of the Federal Reserve Act. The House Committee on Labor, which previously had ignored child labor bills, promptly announced that hearings on child labor legislation would be held.

The hearings, in three sessions, were devoted exclusively to consideration of the Palmer-Owen bill and were dominated by its advocates. Representative Palmer testified briefly at the first session, on February 27, 1914.[37] At the crucial second session, March 9, 1914, nine witnesses, representing organizations that endorsed the

---

[34] "Federal Government and Child Labor," p. 21.

[35] *Ibid.*, p. 22.

[36] 63d Cong., 2d Sess., H.R. 12292 (January 26, 1914) and S. 4571 (February 21, 1914).

[37] Hearings on the Child Labor Bill, pp. 3–9.

bill, were heard and the bulk of the testimony making up the hearings was taken.[38] Four of the witnesses spoke for groups other than the National Committee — for the American Federation of Labor, the Children's Bureau, the National Consumers' League, and the New Jersey Federation of Women's Clubs — but their short statements were expressions of sentiment rather than contributions to the substantive discussion. Spokesmen for the National Committee argued the necessity for creating national standards for child labor regulation, developed the constitutional justification for congressional action, and coordinated the testimony of the other speakers.

The most striking aspect of the testimony was the virtual absence of any attempt to convince the congressmen that child labor was a serious social problem and that it was national in scope. The dangers to children were so universally recognized, it was felt, that a dramatic exposé of evils was unnecessary, and common acceptance of the need for effective legal restriction also was taken for granted. As a consequence, the hearings involved little of the emotional intensity of the Beveridge debate; rather, they were characterized by dispassionate analyses of the merits and constitutionality of the Palmer-Owen bill.

The policy argument was constructed from the "facts" about the contemporary economic order and the National Committee's experiences with state campaigns. America had developed a truly national economy, in which most industrial production had acquired an interstate function, Palmer stated.[39] The practical difficulties encountered in state reform efforts reflected this development and showed that interstate commerce was "the root of this great evil." Time after time, Lovejoy recalled, state legislatures, concerned with protecting local industrial interests, had been unwilling to improve their legislative standards unilaterally.[40] McKelway stressed the main argument that had been raised against reform: states, if they adopted desirable protective standards and rigorously enforced them, were placed at a disadvantage, especially in competition with neighboring states with similar industries.[41] For these reasons, it was difficult to achieve effective state regulation and impossible to establish uniform legislative standards throughout the country.

In the latter connection, the National Committee's representa-

38 *Ibid.*, pp. 11–83.
39 *Ibid.*, pp. 4–6.
40 *Ibid.*, p. 12.
41 *Ibid.*, p. 74.

tives placed special emphasis on the problem in the south. On the basis of personal investigations that had lasted two years, Wiley Swift built a case specifically against the southern textile industry as one of the most flagrant violators of state child labor laws.[42] In his judgment, state action could not be expected to remedy the situation for many years, for the influential cotton manufacturers controlled their states and were likely to do so for many more years.[43]

Lovejoy challenged the oligarchy of mill men:

> The point of view of those opposed to [the Palmer-Owen bill] is most frankly expressed in a recent article in the Charlotte North Carolina *Observer*. In its issue of January 31, 1914, the *Observer* says: "Not a cotton mill in the South could ship its goods out of the State in which they are made if this bill were a law."
>
> The same . . . opposition is shown by the organ of the glass manufacturers in Pennsylvania and by champions of other special interests elsewhere. We are pleased to have the issue so clearly drawn.
>
> If this statement is not true, the mills that are manufacturing cotton under humane conditions in Southern states should publicly repudiate this gratuitous defense of a condition of child employment which has become intolerable to the national conscience. If, however, the plea is true, it is time all Americans should know about it. It is desirable that the cottonmill interests, which have for 10 years professed to be leaders in child labor reform, but which have through this period, opposed every specific attempt to improve the laws, should have their position set forth. If the statement is true, we are no longer left in doubt as to the motive which has killed every creditable child labor bill in the past 10 years in any prominent Southern cotton manufacturing state, and has as consistently opposed every such measure in Northern cotton manufacturing states.[44]

McKelway, however, pointed out that substandard regulatory legislation in the south Atlantic states differed only in degree from that in the north and east, where by far the largest number of toiling children was employed.[45]

To round out their treatment of its merits, Lovejoy and McKelway discussed the reasonableness and expediency of the Palmer-Owen bill. Many of its provisions, Lovejoy showed, had been in-

42 *Ibid.*, p. 36.
43 *Ibid.*, pp. 37–38.
44 *Ibid.*, p. 23.
45 *Ibid.*, p. 74.

corporated in state legislation;[46] moreover, the crucial provision, the eight-hour day, had been applied to adult labor, presumably as a protective measure, in both state and federal enactments affecting convict labor and persons employed under government contracts.[47] If these standards were widely approved in their present form, he argued, the Palmer-Owen bill could not be condemned as drastic legislation.[48] The efficacy of the measure was equally apparent; the retarding influence of backward states would be overcome; conditions of industrial competition would be equalized, and effective enforcement made possible; progressive states would be protected from child-made goods that otherwise would cross their borders in interstate commerce.[49] McKelway's view was that the Palmer-Owen bill could be enforced; state laws often were not.[50]

"The Power of Congress . . . Is the Ultimate Determining Question" [51]

The National Committee's constitutional justification for federal control was set forth in a brief submitted to the Labor Committee and amplified in testimony. The brief urged a broad interpretation of the commerce power but stopped short of Beveridge's conception of virtually unlimited congressional authority. However, it adopted his contention that the power to regulate extended to outright prohibition of objectionable commerce, whatever its nature. The precedents Beveridge had relied upon were quoted approvingly, and the *Hoke* case repeatedly cited. Taken together, these decisions were understood to have constitutionally legitimated the doctrine of federal police powers. This interpretation rested upon a view of interstate commerce that comprehended more than mere transportation across state lines. It included activities that were intrastate in character, when considered separately, but directly affected national welfare or morality. However, the brief contained no suggestion of a stream of commerce – a definite and well-understood business traffic across state lines, such as had been developed in the Stockyards case.[52]

All of the important constitutional objections that would be

46 *Ibid.*, pp. 12–13.
47 *Ibid.*, p. 13.
48 *Ibid.*, p. 14.
49 *Ibid.*, pp. 15–24, 30–33.
50 *Ibid.*, pp. 76–77.
51 *Hoke* v. *United States*, 227 U.S. 308, 320.
52 *Swift and Co.* v. *United States*, 196 U.S. 375 (1905).

raised against the principle of federal regulation in succeeding years — that it exceeded congressional authority, constituted a camouflaged regulation of hours, interfered with the exclusive rights of the states, violated the Fifth Amendment, infringed upon liberty of contract, and established a dangerous precedent — were anticipated and answered. The brief sought especially to forestall criticism on the basis of interference with state autonomy. Justice McKenna's opinion in *Hoke* was said to be decisive:

> There is a domain which the States cannot reach and over which Congress alone has power; and if such power be exerted to control what the States cannot, it is an argument for — not against — its legality. Its exertion does not encroach upon the jurisdiction of the States. We have examples; others may be adduced. The Pure Food and Drug Act is a conspicuous instance. In all of the instances a clash of national legislation with the power of the States was urged, and in all rejected.[53]

This holding, the National Committee's leaders felt, cancelled out any hitherto existing "twilight zone" between national and state power, and gave special relevance to a conception of cooperative federalism that had been set forth in the decision. "Our dual form of government has its perplexities, State and Nation having different spheres of jurisdiction . . . but it must be kept in mind that we are one people; and the powers reserved to the states and those conferred on the nation are adapted to be exercised, whether independently or concurrently, to promote the general welfare, material and moral."[54]

Throughout, the brief recurred to one central idea: that the Palmer-Owen bill proposed a regulation of interstate commerce in order to eliminate conditions that were patently injurious to the public welfare. This proposition derived immediately from McKenna's most important declaration in *Hoke*.

> The power of Congress under the commerce clause of the Constitution is the ultimate determining question. If the statute be a valid exercise of that power, how it may affect persons or States is not material to be considered. It is the supreme law of the land and persons and States are subject to it.[55]

[53] *Hoke* v. *United States*, 227 U.S. 308, 321–22, quoted in Hearings on the Child Labor Bill, p. 30.

[54] *Ibid.*, p. 322, quoted in "Memorandum in Reply to Questions on the Constitutionality of the Palmer Federal Child Labor Bill," *Child Labor Bulletin* (February, 1914), pp. 25–34.

[55] *Ibid.*, p. 320.

Like Wilson, whose New Freedom speeches espoused the position that the Constitution should be interpreted "according to the darwinian principle . . . that a nation is a living thing and not a machine," the National Committee envisioned a Constitution of powers that authorized the government to meet the problems of a rapidly expanding industrial society, not an instrument of limited purposes.[56]

Two legal spokesmen for the National Committee, Dean Lewis and Jasper I. Brinton, former Attorney General of Pennsylvania and chairman of that state's Child Labor Association, discussed the constitutional issues at length. American constitutional development, Lewis told the congressmen, had produced two interpretations of congressional authority over commercial activities. One view, identified with Chief Justice Marshall, maintained that national power over interstate commerce was just as extensive as state power over intrastate commerce. The crucial question was whether regulatory legislation violated express constitutional limitations, of either the Fifth or the Ninth Amendment. (The Tenth Amendment was not regarded as a limitation, for the power over interstate commerce was delegated, and the Tenth Amendment reserved only powers that were not delegated.[57]) In effect, Lewis argued that specious distinctions based upon the Tenth Amendment could not qualify or limit the extent of the enumerated powers vested in Congress. The conflicting view, identified with former President Taft, maintained that congressional authority was limited not only by express provisions but also by the principle that it must not be exercised indirectly to accomplish results that could not be accomplished directly — in effect, making the Tenth Amendment nugatory.[58] According to this constitutional doctrine, congressional authority over interstate commerce was less extensive than its power over foreign commerce.

It was hardly necessary for Congress to spend time deciding between these two views, Lewis declared, "because the decisions of the Supreme Court . . . have made it entirely clear that that tribunal adhered always, and especially lately — and if I may emphasize the words 'especially lately' — to the Marshall view."[59] Lewis concluded: "At least as far as the Supreme Court . . . is concerned, this question is a closed question, and therefore those

---

[56] Hearings on the Child Labor Bill, p. 33.
[57] *Ibid.*, pp. 59–60.
[58] *Ibid.*, pp. 60–61.
[59] *Ibid.*, p. 61.

of you who feel that that is controlling would regard any further argument as a work of supererogation." [60]

Earlier, Brinton had acknowledged, in responding to a question, that the Court had not yet decided a case in which the conditions of production of an article shipped in interstate commerce had been considered. He denied, however, that a distinction could be drawn between detrimental effects following upon shipment and those that preceded shipment. He supported this conclusion by citations from recognized authorities, some of whom had only recently changed their minds. Particularly telling was a statement of W. W. Willoughby, probably the most respected constitutional scholar then occupying a chair in political science:

> The distinction between conditions of production and purposes, or modes of use, of commodities, though a real one, will probably not be held controlling. In neither case has Congress a direct regulative power — over neither the conditions of production nor the modes or use of consumption. If, therefore, in either case, the prohibition can be construed to be, in fact, a regulation of interstate or foreign commerce, neither the ultimate effect nor the legislative intent embodied in the law may be inquired into by the courts.[61]

In effect, Lewis and Brinton treated the constitutional issue as settled, but they were careful not to thrust their views upon the lawmakers as the only appropriate position for wise and humane men. Should congressmen feel reasonable doubts about extending the commerce power or anticipate adverse judicial action, the two lawyers, by implication, counseled the representatives to vote against the measure. This position was not an argument for legislative supremacy in the controversy between popularly determined policies and judicial supervision; rather, the National Committee stressed deference to the judiciary, assuming that recent precedents provided ample justification for federal social legislation and that the Supreme Court would not inquire into congressional purposes or the incidental effects of valid legislation. The position assumed that progressivism had permeated the constitutional philosophy of the bench.

The House Passes the Palmer-Owen Bill

Near the end of the session, Arthur E. Holder, representing the American Federation of Labor, commented happily upon the

---

[60] Hearings on the Child Labor Bill, pp. 61–62.
[61] Quoted in *ibid.*, p. 50.

unanimity of those present.[62] Seven years before, Senator Beveridge had been ridiculed for advocating federal child labor legislation, but not a single voice was raised against any feature of the
Palmer-Owen bill. The National Committee reported the congressmen's receptiveness to its membership with obvious pleasure; the
representatives listened closely, kept their questions free of ob-
structiveness, and displayed wholehearted bipartisan support.[63]
Julia Lathrop, chief of the federal Children's Bureau,[64] testified
to strong, nation-wide interest in decisive action that would end
child labor abuses by federal legislation, such as the Palmer-Owen
bill.[65] In the following weeks the chairman of the Labor Committee endeavored to notify all presumably interested parties
throughout the country that the bill was pending. Again, the
National Committee and congressmen were surprised, for the expected sizable opposition failed to materialize.[66]

Two and a half months later, on May 22, 1914, the Labor Committee assembled to listen to three prominent cotton manufacturers from South Carolina.[67] Their spokesman, Lewis K. Parker, an
important figure in the southern textile industry, disavowed any
interest in perpetuating child labor and asserted that conditions
in the south were gradually improving. In the transition from
agriculture to industrialism, however, state legislatures, intimately
familiar with local circumstances, should be free to support local

[62] *Ibid.*, p. 81. Throughout the campaign to establish federal child labor
legislation the A. F. of L. was an intensely interested ally; however, other
objectives of public policy took precedence in its political priorities.

[63] *Child Labor Bulletin* (May, 1914), p. 3.

[64] The agency Miss Lathrop headed had been created by Congress in 1912,
after eight years of agitation by interested groups. Although limited in funds
and authority, the bureau was given the broad function of investigating and
reporting upon all matters pertaining to child life and welfare. In addition
to initiating a series of studies, the bureau established close ties with groups that
were concerned with child welfare and cooperated with them — cautiously at
first, so as not to prejudice future congressional support — in the advancement
of substantive policies. Relationships were especially cordial with the National
Committee, whose main ally it became in the long struggle to establish national child labor standards. In 1914, the bureau's role was more circumspect
than later, seemingly because of its initial insecurity. The crucial factor in
the campaign to establish the bureau was the publication of the *Report on
the Condition of Women and Child Wage Earners*. The National Committee,
which had started the campaign, saw its choice for the head of the agency
appointed. Prior to coming to the bureau, Miss Lathrop had been one of the
notable group of lieutenants surrounding Jane Addams at Hull House.

[65] Hearings on the Child Labor Bill, pp. 40–41.

[66] *Ibid.*, pp. 83–84.

[67] *Ibid.*, pp. 85–117.

instruments of material well-being and to provide children the forms of protection that were locally approved. With the development of a skilled adult labor force, he contended, the problem of child labor would inevitably decline, for the public would exclude children from industrial employment and require their attendance in school.[68]

The South Carolinians condemned the minimum-age standard but their attack centered on the eight-hour-day provision. Under existing conditions of competition, especially those imposed by foreign producers, the Labor Committee was told, the southern mills could not survive if they were forced to curtail their workday; their single shift of eleven or twelve hours had to be maintained. Because the operations in which children were engaged could not be adjusted separately, the manufacturers would be compelled, should Congress enact the Palmer-Owen law, to discharge all mill hands under sixteen years of age. In no other way could the struggling southern industry, with its small profit margins, meet its competition. "It will be absolutely impossible . . . to conform to that law," Parker declared. "The whole salvation of the cotton manufacturer is dependent upon full production."[69] Because the mills represented virtually the entire industry of South Carolina, employing directly, or in subsidiary activities, nearly one-fifth of the population, the repercussions would be far-reaching. McKelway, however, sought to refute these arguments. He introduced evidence that showed the textile mills of Massachusetts had successfully adjusted their operations after the passage of an eight-hour law by the state legislature.[70]

This ended the hearings. Their most important aspect was revealed not in the testimony but in the almost complete silence of the opposition. The belated appearance of the mill owners was an anticlimax, seemingly unimportant in view of the remarkable unanimity and enthusiasm otherwise evident – a fact that would not be lost on Congress. The hearings brought into direct confrontation the organization most determined to enact federal legislation and the industrial interest most vehemently opposed, and the National Committee had easily discredited the manufacturers' apologies for exploitation. Future congressional hearings, should there be need for any, it seemed clear, would center on constitutionality. The National Committee had correctly assumed that public sentiment supported federal control of child labor; the southern textile manufacturers' only plausible defense against popular action lay in convincing Congress of the measure's invalidity.

It was mid-August, nearly three months after the last session of the hearings, before the Committee on Labor reported the Palmer-Owen bill, and not until February 13, 1915, six months later, was its unanimous report submitted to the House.[71] The unanimity of the committee and the substance of its report made it seem improbable that the delay of nearly a year resulted from doubts about the merits or constitutionality of the measure.[72] The report, which closely followed the National Committee's presentations, found that child labor was a national evil of appalling scope and so obvious that argument was unnecessary, and it declared that the federal government alone possessed the power to overcome the evil.[73] Ten years before, a serious question might have been raised about the legal issues, but now it seemed clear that

> this doubt has probably been effectively dispelled by a steady current of judicial thought, running in the same direction as that current of public opinion which has demanded, as a public right, that the Federal Government should assume the burdens of many new responsibilities, as the only practical means of remedying grave national evils inherent in the conflicting commercial interests of the States.[74]

On February 15, 1915, two days after the report was submitted, Representative Palmer moved to suspend the rules and brought the bill before the full House. There was little discussion, but several representatives from southern textile states tried unsuccessfully to employ parliamentary delaying tactics. Although the session was drawing to a close, the margin of victory the bill subsequently received strongly suggests that these tactics were undertaken more to make a "record" than to oppose the measure.

---

[71] U.S. Congress, House, Committee on Labor, House Rep. 1400, to accompany H.R. 12292, the Palmer-Owen Bill, 63d Cong., 3d Sess. (Washington, D.C.: Government Printing Office, 1915).

[72] Thomas G. Karis, "Congressional Behavior at Constitutional Frontiers: From 1906, the Beveridge Child Labor Bill, to 1938, the Fair Labor Standards Act" (unpublished Ph.D. dissertation, Columbia University, 1951), p. 50.

[73] House Report 1400, pp. 6–12. "The entire problem has become an interstate problem rather than a problem of isolated States, and is a problem which must be faced and solved only by a power stronger than any state," the report stated (p. 7).

[74] *Ibid.*, p. 14.

The final vote was an overwhelming 233 to 43.[75] During the debate, in anticipation of a victory of this magnitude, Palmer had asserted that the country decisively favored the bill. "The Republican Party, and the Progressive Party, and the Democratic Party, and the Nation have declared for this kind of legislation. The country is for it, as it is for very few things in either branch of Congress today." [76]

The outcome plainly depicted the sectional character of the developing political struggle. Thirty-five of the forty-three votes against the bill were cast by representatives from six southern states. But the contest was not to pit the "solid south" against the remainder of the nation; rather, a portion of the region, the south Atlantic states in which textile manufacturing was centered, would issue the challenge. A majority of representatives from only four states — North Carolina, South Carolina, Georgia, and Mississippi — opposed the bill.

It is more difficult to evaluate the impact upon the vote (if any) of the congressional elections held three months earlier. The Democratic majority in the Senate was not affected, but the party's strength in the House was significantly reduced — to a mere twenty-five-vote margin. The Republicans had regained ground in the populous northern industrial states, but only one Republican representative voted against the Democratic party measure. Party lines, clearly, were submerged; neither side could claim exclusive credit for the result.

Two weeks after the affirmative action in the House, on March 1, 1915, the Senate Committee on Interstate Commerce reported the bill favorably.[77] The committee dispensed with hearings and required only one sentence to affirm its members' conviction that the evils of child labor were generally recognized and that Congress could exclude from interstate commerce articles produced by child labor. However, the report acknowledged that some persons controverted the constitutionality of legislation of this nature.[78] Because the session was virtually over, the bill's managers made an attempt to bring it directly to the floor, but Senator Lee Overman of North Carolina dissented on a unanimous consent motion to

[75] *Congressional Record*, 63d Cong., 3d Sess. (Washington, D.C.: Government Printing Office, 1915), p. 3836.

[76] *Ibid.*, p. 3834.

[77] U.S. Congress, Senate, Committee on Interstate Commerce, Senate Rep. 1050, to accompany S. 4571, the Palmer-Owen Bill, 63d Cong., 3d Sess. (Washington, D.C.: Government Printing Office, 1915).

[78] *Ibid.*, p. 2.

advance the bill on the calendar. As often happens in the Senate, a special interest was served — this time the southern textile manufacturers — and the measure was dead for the session. Three days later, March 4, 1915, the Sixty-third Congress adjourned.

David Clark's "Engine for Fighting"

The editor of a small textile journal published in Charlotte, North Carolina, who had taken exception to Parker's representations before the Labor Committee and who welcomed the challenge of the reform groups, set about organizing a group of southern cotton manufacturers with the intention of countering the movement to establish federal child labor legislation. This man, David Clark, was a member of a family that had been prominent for many generations in the history of his home state and the south. His father, Walter Clark, had served with distinction as a youthful Confederate colonel and for twenty-six years had been a member of the North Carolina supreme court, including sixteen years as its presiding officer. Recognized throughout America as one of the south's outstanding liberals, Chief Justice Clark claimed the friendship of such men as Theodore Roosevelt, William Jennings Bryan, Samuel Gompers, and Robert La Follette. Before the turn of the century he became known as "the jurist of the Populist movement"; and in 1906, in a notable speech at the University of Pennsylvania, he systematically developed the thesis that the Constitution had been written to frustrate the democratic will. His subsequent attacks upon "government by judges" helped inform the progressives' attack upon conservative ideology and jurisprudence.[79] David Clark's mother was a Graham, descendant of another illustrious family long accustomed to influencing affairs in the south. Her lineage traced back to Marmaduke Norfleet, a notable seventeenth-century settler, and included blood ties to George Washington. Her father, William A. Graham, had had an especially distinguished political career, having served as governor of North Carolina, United States senator, Secretary of the Navy, Whig candidate for Vice-President, and a senator in the Confederacy.

Unlike his father, David Clark was a crusty, uncompromising conservative. After limited success as an engineer, he founded the *Southern Textile Bulletin*, in 1911, with the firm conviction (as

[79] See Aubrey Lee Brooks, *Walter Clark, Fighting Judge* (Chapel Hill: University of North Carolina Press, 1944), and *The Papers of Walter Clark*, eds. Aubrey Lee Brooks and Hugh Talmage Lefler (2 vols.; Chapel Hill: University of North Carolina Press, 1950).

he stated forty years later) "that no trade journal can justify its existence unless it renders service to the industry with which it is affiliated."[80] True to this conviction, Clark published the *Bulletin* with almost single-minded devotion to the interests of the cotton textile industry of the south. Every advance in the size and productivity of southern mills was chronicled in its pages, and the *Bulletin* trumpeted such events as the decline of the venerable northern textile giant, the Amoskeag Mills (of Manchester, New Hampshire).[81] Clark used its columns to lead the industry in opposition to governmental intervention, unionism, and other similar "evils," and was inclined to criticize the mill owners only when he thought they had acted against their best material interests.

There was little restraint in Clark's personality; he possessed absolute faith in the correctness of his beliefs and acted with great certainty of purpose. These traits were reflected to a marked degree in his management of the *Bulletin*. It was a "personal" journal, written in pithy, fervent language that Clark employed undeviatingly, sometimes savagely, to serve his purposes.[82] Besides serving the southern textile industry, it seems inescapable that Clark meant to attain public prominence in the southern community; otherwise, through the years, there would have been more constructive criticism of the textile industry in the pages of the *Bulletin*, less irresponsible polemics and distortion, and surely less glorification of his services so that the mill owners would understand his claim to their gratitude.[83]

---

[80] *Southern Textile Bulletin* (March, 1951), p. 84.

[81] *Ibid.*, February 7, 1918, p. 10.

[82] Although Walter Clark's collected papers indicate very little correspondence with his son, in a letter of May 6, 1923, the jurist acknowledged the "splendid success" of the *Bulletin*, his son's editorial skill, and the fact that he had "faithfully and ably represented the mill interests." However, he set down a long admonition against making personal attacks upon others that might be considered insulting or contemptuous. The reason for this reproof seems to have been the bitter attacks upon union leaders in *Bulletin* editorials during the early twenties. In the background was the first large-scale attempt at organizing industrial workers in the south, which, coming when the over-expanded mills had been hard hit by the postwar depression, led to violence at Gastonia, North Carolina, and elsewhere. See *The Papers of Walter Clark*, II, 459.

[83] Perhaps the best reflection of Clark's personality and his need for public recognition is the comprehensive way in which he documented, within the editorial columns of the *Bulletin*, the fight against the creation of national child labor standards. Had he been less interested in the textile manufacturers' acclaim, it would have been far more difficult, perhaps even impossible, to

Clark, when he began to publish the *Bulletin,* wholeheartedly endorsed the manufacturers' stand on child labor. Children were employed extensively in southern mills; progress in legislation represented only what the manufacturers were driven to grant by the pressure of public opinion; every new law was a compromise and no gain was ever complete, for reformers could not "convert the majority of mill men to an acceptance of the theories that child labor was morally wrong or practically avoidable."[84] The *Bulletin* frequently criticized reform efforts — particularly those undertaken by the National Committee, which Clark derisively referred to as "the New England organization" — and justified the child labor statutes of the principal textile manufacturing states. Clark's editorials charged that rival northern interests were trying to destroy the southern industry, that the work children engaged in within the mills was neither arduous nor dangerous, and that the south was being maligned by sensationalist publicity that was based upon exceptional instances or upon practices that long ago had been outlawed in the region.

Clark's direct assault upon the reform movement began in the early spring of 1915. At the invitation of Captain Ellison Smyth, an influential South Carolina textile manufacturer,[85] seven prominent mill owners, "selected for their fighting qualities," met at Greenville, South Carolina, and formed the Executive Committee of Southern Cotton Manufacturers.[86] The meeting had been called

reconstruct in a relatively full way much that follows, and the events themselves might have been quite different.

[84] Davidson, *Child Labor Legislation in the Southern Textile States,* p. 148.

[85] Captain Ellison Smyth should be carefully distinguished from another South Carolinian with virtually the same name, Ellison Durant "Cotton Ed" Smith, the junior senator from the state and special protector of cotton interests in Congress.

Captain Smyth was the president of four cotton mills in South Carolina (his son and son-in-law managed four other mills). Among his holdings was the famous Pelzer Mills, a modern, highly integrated factory, one of the show places of the southern textile industry. In addition, Smyth helped found the Cotton Manufacturers' Association of South Carolina and had served continuously for eleven years as its president. "Cotton Ed" Smith went to the Senate in 1908, elected by the votes of South Carolina's dirt farmers. "For over 30 years his platform remained unchanged: states' rights, white supremacy, and a tariff for revenue only." An inveterate foe of centralized government, he fought unstintingly to preserve the Constitution as he thought the founders had constructed it, and energetically looked after the interests of the cotton farmers. See Ernst M. Lander, Jr., *A History of South Carolina* (Chapel Hill: University of North Carolina Press, 1960), pp. 77–78.

[86] *Southern Textile Bulletin* (May 18, 1922), p. 18. In addition to Clark and Smyth, the original members of the committee were: S. F. Patterson, Roanoke

on Clark's initiative, and he chose the men who were to attend, who "insisted" that Clark be the secretary and treasurer and "handle the affairs" of the organization.[87] This he emphatically did, assisted by the chairman, S. F. Patterson, another North Carolinian.

According to its public statements, the Executive Committee was an independent association, founded to promote the interests of the southern textile industry, but experience soon demonstrated that its efforts were devoted exclusively to preventing the establishment of federal child labor standards.[88] Nor was the committee an entirely independent agency. To be sure, its leaders exercised virtually unrestrained initiative, policies being chosen without recourse — and sometimes even in opposition — to what might be termed constituent opinion. But from the outset its relations with the textile manufacturers' associations of the southern states were very close. The annual Proceedings of these organizations, particularly North Carolina's, attest to this cooperation, as well as instances of parallel leadership. For the next ten years, Sam Patterson, the chairman of the Executive Committee, served simultaneously as chairman of the legislative committee of the North Carolina association. Moreover, during this period Patterson and W. C. Ruffin held the presidency of that association. In addition, Captain Ellison Smyth continued as president of the South Carolina association, and a few years later the president of the Georgia association also became a member.

In sum, a militant group of mill owners, led by an able and determined publicist, set about defending their interests as employers of child labor against what they believed was an immediate threat of federal intervention. For more than a decade the Executive Committee played an enormously important role in the struggle over national child labor standards. Its members sought unremittingly to defeat these attempts and their efforts, alone or in company with other conservative interests, uniformly succeeded.

Rapids, North Carolina; W. C. Ruffin, Mayodan, North Carolina; A. F. McKessick, Greenwood, South Carolina; W. J. Vereen, Moultrie, Georgia; Garnett Andrews, Rossville, Georgia; Scott Roberts, Anniston, Alabama; and T. L. Wainwright, Stonewall, Mississippi.

[87] *Ibid.*

[88] In 1925, Patterson said the committee had been formed solely for the purpose of defeating the Keating-Owen law. See "Legislative Committee Report," *Proceedings of the Nineteenth Annual Convention of the Cotton Manufacturers' Association of North Carolina* (Charlotte: Observer Printing House, 1925), p. 89.

Throughout this period the group perfectly illustrated Madison's definition (in the *Federalist Papers*) of "faction"; actuated by particular and local economic interests, the Executive Committee sought a partisan objective that was clearly detrimental to the permanent and aggregate interests of the nation. David Clark, moreover, personified the ambitious man energetically contending for preeminence.

3

Progressivism Climaxed:
The First Federal Child Labor Law

The Textile Manufacturers' Attack on the
Child Labor Bill

The Sixty-fourth Congress, elected a generation before the Twentieth Amendment became part of the Constitution, did not
convene until December, 1915. In the long first session, acute
problems of neutrality and preparedness, forced upon the consciousness of the nation by the war in Europe, vied with important
domestic legislation for the attention of its members.

At the very start of the session Senator Owen re-introduced the
child labor bill, originated by the National Committee, and one
month later Representative Edward Keating, a Democrat from
Colorado, with strong labor-organization ties (who took Palmer's
place as sponsor), introduced the measure in the House.[1] Henceforth it would be known as the Keating-Owen bill. Three days
later, on January 10, 1916, hearings were begun before the House
Committee on Labor, and, one month later, on February 15, 1916,
before the Senate Committee on Interstate Commerce.[2]

At first glance these hearings appear strikingly similar to those
that were held two years before. Although five other bills that
were based on the commerce power were introduced, only the bill
drafted by the National Committee received serious attention; and
the same interest groups that had clashed in 1914 again confronted

---

[1] 64th Cong., 1st Sess., S. 1083 (December 7, 1915), and H.R. 8234 (January 7, 1916).

[2] U.S. Congress, Hearings before the Committee on Labor, U.S. House of
Representatives, 64th Cong., 1st Sess., on H.R. 8234, The Child Labor Bill,
January 10–13, 1916 (Washington, D.C.: Government Printing Office, 1916),
and U.S. Congress, Hearings before the Committee on Interstate Commerce
U.S. Senate, 64th Cong., 1st Sess., on H.R. 8234, Interstate Commerce in Products of Child Labor, February 15–21, March 17, 1916 (Washington, D.C.: Government Printing Office, 1916).

each other. Despite these similarities there were important differences. The 1914 hearings had been called at the request of the National Committee and had largely been given over to presentations by its spokesmen in support of federal regulation; the southern textile manufacturers' protest had been voiced by individual mill owners ineffectually. Now, however, David Clark's Executive Committee, tightly organized and skillfully led, represented the industry and grasped the initiative. Clark requested the hearings and used them to mount an attack on the merits and the constitutionality of federal child labor legislation. The National Committee, in answering this attack, thought the unanimity of the Labor Committee's report and the decisiveness of the House vote the year before had settled the first issue, and therefore shifted the burden of argument on the second issue to those who opposed national action.

Because the campaigns to develop public support had met with notable success and reform of industrial child labor by congressional action had become a national purpose, Clark knew that his Executive Committee had to undermine the congressional vote and the public sentiment that stood behind it. Immediately after the Executive Committee's organizational meeting, Clark made plans "for fighting or at least delaying" the Keating-Owen bill.[3] In one of his first steps, he employed former Governor W. W. Kitchin of North Carolina to represent the committee in Washington.[4]

Still a prestigious figure in the south, Kitchin also was a familiar presence in Washington (after twelve years of congressional service) and intimately acquainted with legislative procedures and congressional attitudes. Moreover, as a former congressman, and also because his brother, Claude, was floor leader for the New Freedom in the House, Kitchin had access to party councils and to leading men within the legislative chambers of the Capitol.

The strategy that Clark and Kitchin worked out had two main approaches: (1) demonstrating that federal regulation of child labor was unnecessary because industrial conditions in the south were satisfactory, and impolitic because it was certain to prove injurious to the textile mills, their operatives, and the southern community; and (2) demonstrating that the Keating-Owen bill was constitutionally infirm because it exceeded congressional authority and invaded the exclusive jurisdiction of the states. Running through both attacks was a plea, sometimes explicit but

---

[3] *Southern Textile Bulletin* (March 4, 1926), p. 21.
[4] *Ibid.*

more often implicit, that the south be permitted to solve its own problems of industrial development because the good faith of its people, especially the cotton manufacturers, was apparent to all reasonable men.

Kitchin took the lead in discussing the facts before the Labor Committee, assisted by a delegation of mill owners and managers, including several members of the Executive Committee. Here were some of the south's "best people"; they represented the new industrial oligarchy that had transformed the life of the region and they were accustomed to exercising wide political influence. The unavoidable starting point, Kitchin declared, was that many destitute and poverty-stricken children in the south had to work in order to live, for public welfare agencies were few in number and had very limited resources. The mills provided beneficial employment and their villages afforded educational and moral opportunities that were not available in other work situations. In addition, Kitchin insisted, the mill owners were deeply interested in improving the conditions of labor, as their record of radical changes over the past decade showed. Although child labor standards admittedly were not what they should be, southerners could be trusted to make further improvements as fast as circumstances permitted.[5] The thirteen mill representatives similarly testified that conditions in the mills and their surrounding villages had been grossly misrepresented,[6] and Clark urged the congressmen to tour the mill districts, implying the manufacturers had nothing to hide.

From the beginning, however, the mill men placed their greatest emphasis on the disastrous consequences that could be anticipated from the enactment of the eight-hour provision for children fourteen to sixteen years of age.[7] The congressmen were told that this restriction would force the mills to discharge children under sixteen or to curtail the workday for all employees. In the former instance, many discharged children and their families would again experience the grinding poverty they had previously known. In

[5] Hearings on the Child Labor Bill (1916), pp. 12–16.
[6] *Ibid.*, pp. 3–133.
[7] The minimum-age limit had ceased to be a major issue, except in North Carolina; it had been incorporated in legislation in all of the other southern textile states (save South Carolina, where passage was expected momentarily). After successfully resisting the age limit for many years, the South Carolina manufacturers decided to lend their support to the provision, ensuring its enactment, evidently with the idea of improving the chances to forestall federal legislation.

the latter instance, the mills would suffer a grave and perhaps ruinous decrease in the efficiency of their operations.

Witness after witness unhesitatingly affirmed that, faced with this distasteful choice, virtually every cotton mill in the south would necessarily dismiss its youthful employees. Hence they repeatedly categorized the Keating-Owen bill as a discriminatory attack upon their struggling industry. Clark put the proposition bluntly: the measure meant, unmistakably, that no person under sixteen years of age would be employed in southern textile mills.[8] When pressed by Keating and other congressmen, the manufacturers vigorously denied the feasibility of a third alternative: reducing the hours for children while retaining the longer work shifts for adults. Prohibitive capital expenditures would be called for and labor conditions seriously disrupted, it was argued.

The most significant aspect of the manufacturers' testimony was just this narrow concentration on the consequences of the Keating-Owen bill for the southern textile industry. None of the mill representatives applied their arguments to other regions or industries: they viewed the problem of child labor entirely within the framework of a local and special economic interest. McKelway seized upon this singularity when he commented upon the manufacturers' testimony,[9] challenging their right to represent southern opinion and their interpretation of child labor conditions. Throughout the region, public sentiment favored reform and eminent men endorsed the Keating-Owen bill. These leaders and the organizations they represented, not the mill owners, he claimed, best reflected the sentiment of their states. Further, the manufacturers had misrepresented the nature of state legislation, and especially their own efforts to improve conditions. Time after time, he charged, they had defeated reform legislation, thereby frustrating popular opinion. "Why, out of the thousands of industries in this country, do the cotton mills alone protest against this measure?" The answer was self-evident: the owners knew they could resist meaningful state legislation for many years to come.[10]

Although McKelway failed to draw the conclusion directly, the manufacturers' plea that the south be permitted to solve the prob-

8 *Ibid.*, pp. 3–12, 16–31.

9 To expedite the hearings, McKelway agreed with Kitchin not to introduce new testimony on the merits, merely to ask that the relevant portions of the 1914 hearings be included, along with a compendium of state child labor laws. *Ibid.*, p. 238.

10 *Ibid.*, pp. 235–55.

lem of child labor by itself was actually a request that the mill men be allowed to handle it very much as they pleased. Moreover, McKelway did not point out the full implications of the Keating-Owen bill for the manufacturers: it threatened the contractual relationships that forced children into permanent cotton mill employment and the closed character of most of the mill villages. Child laborers tended to become poorly compensated adult workmen, handicapped by lack of education and technical training and tied to cotton manufacture. They were docile employees, and unlikely to support labor organizations or exert much pressure for higher wages. At the same time, the manufacturers' stewardship over their operatives' welfare, a dependence the more progressive mill owners ordinarily did not institutionalize, served in large measure, if often unconsciously, to mask economic self-interest.[11] Federal regulation, however, would inevitably foster pressure for modern industrial conditions and strike a sharp blow at the outmoded paternalism. The villages would not be transformed overnight, but they would never be the same again.

Laissez Faire Constitutionalism versus Federal Police Powers

The Executive Committee's challenge to the constitutionality of the Keating-Owen bill sought to hedge the extent (for it could not deny the existence) of judicially approved exercises of congressional authority for police power purposes. Kitchin, who set forth this attack, argued that Congress did not possess "the power to exclude from interstate commerce any article that is in itself sound, healthy, not immoral and that can do no possible injury in the State into which it goes." [12] In reaching this conclusion, Kitchin relied upon the distinction between manufacturing and commerce that had been drawn in the Sugar Trust case.[13] Commerce, the Court had held, succeeded to manufacture and was no part of it. Therefore, Congress could exercise its authority only after articles became part of interstate commerce; it could not reach back to the conditions of production.[14]

11 For a discussion of the mill villages as paternal philanthropy, see Elizabeth H. Davidson, *Child Labor Legislation in the Southern Textile States* (Chapel Hill: University of North Carolina Press, 1939), pp. 152–53, 235–55. A generally accurate though sometimes romantic study of a typical village is presented in Marjorie A. Potwin, *Cotton Mill People of the Piedmont* (New York: Columbia University Press, 1927).

12 Hearings on the Child Labor Bill (1916), pp. 137–57.

13 *United States* v. *E. C. Knight Co.*, 156 U.S. 1 (1895).

14 Hearings on the Child Labor Bill (1916), p. 141.

Kitchin's general view of the Constitution, however, was more important to his position than any precedent. The authority of Congress over interstate commerce may have been unlimited when the Constitution was ratified, he acknowledged, but the adoption of the first ten amendments changed that situation.[15] The due process clause of the Fifth Amendment and the reservations incorporated in the Tenth imposed clear limitations. Of the two, the due process clause was more fundamental because it incorporated the freedom to engage in lawful commerce, guaranteed by the higher law.[16] The rights to buy, sell, and transport honest and wholesome merchandise were sacred under the Constitution. The Tenth Amendment guaranteed the states control over their internal affairs, especially labor conditions within their borders. Hence any federal enactment that attempted to equalize conditions of production was fatally defective.

The Executive Committee at last found an ally in James Emery, the general counsel of the National Association of Manufacturers, who joined the attack on the principle of federal regulation. The prestige of the business community had declined sharply since the halcyon days of McKinley (when the nation "vibrated ecstatically to the magic word 'prosperity' "[17]). As progressive enthusiasm waxed stronger and business fell in public esteem, Emery had pioneered the techniques of national pressure politics to restore his clients' influence. He knew that the old-style lobby, a creature of closed politics, had been thoroughly discredited and that, in the new democratic circumstances, control over the formation of public policy depended upon exerting organizational power and affecting public attitudes.[18]

Emery declared that he welcomed the abolition of child labor and approved the standards incorporated in the Keating-Owen bill, but the method of control it invoked was revolutionary and posed a far-reaching threat to industrial freedom.[19] Like Kitchin,

[15] *Ibid.*, p. 142.

[16] *Ibid.*, p. 140.

[17] Walter Lippmann, *A Preface to Politics* (New York: Mitchell Kennerley, 1913), p. 89.

[18] See E. Pendleton Herring, *Group Representation before Congress* (Baltimore: The Johns Hopkins Press, 1929).

[19] Hearings on the Child Labor Bill (1916), pp. 157–58. Emery claimed to speak for the American business community; however, questioning by Keating disclosed that Emery had generated opposition to the Keating-Owen bill within the N.A.M.'s board of directors and that his appearance did not result from a resolution adopted at the association's annual convention (*ibid.*, pp. 157–58, 174–76).

Emery tried to circumscribe the extent of the commerce power. Although plenary in nature, the congressional grant did not extend to the conditions of production; nothing was more clear in all the judicial history of the country.[20] Nor did it extend to unrestricted prohibition. The absolute power the individual states possessed prior to the Constitution to exclude from their territory articles manufactured in other states had been partially destroyed. The founders intended, Emery asserted, to ensure that legitimate enterprise could be freely pursued. Congress could regulate only such things as retarded the free flow of commerce, whether "'physical or economic, a mob, a monopoly, or a sand bank.'"[21] Congressional authority, in short, was protective only and not prohibitive, except with regard to elements injurious to commerce.

For Emery, the significance of the Keating-Owen bill lay chiefly in the precedent it would establish. His analysis of the facts differed only in its conclusion from the analysis developed two years before by the bill's proponents. The N.A.M. counsel asserted that, because 90 per cent of all commodities were disposed of outside the state in which they were produced, whoever controlled the conduct of interstate commerce became the regulator of American business. If the child labor bill was enacted, the national government would become this regulator.[22] Where would this enormous power lead? Assuming that Congress would readily heed the clamor for federal regulation, Emery unfolded a grisly parade of horrors. The police powers of the states would rapidly become an empty thing and the federal government would exercise virtually unrestricted control over American business.[23] Like many another defender of business interests since the Granger era, Emery sought to invoke what Lerner has termed the "Grand Peur" — apprehension about the destruction of constitutional rights that would irresistibly follow from the enactment of progressive regulatory legislation.

Although Emery's and Kitchin's constitutional theories did not coincide at every point, they were greatly similar. Both men applied a highly restrictive interpretation to the Constitution, in numerous clauses that limited the scope of congressional authority. Both hewed to the well-worn laissez faire doctrine that national powers could not be exercised to accomplish indirectly what Congress could not accomplish directly. And both rested

20 *Ibid.*, pp. 163–65.
21 *Ibid.*, p. 170.
22 *Ibid.*
23 *Ibid.*, p. 173.

their interpretations on decisions that antedated the era of judicial toleration, and were noticeably wary of contemporary precedents. On the other hand, where Emery tended to cite authorities to prove that the Constitution was more an instrument of prohibitions than affirmations,[24] Kitchin held that the principles of the higher law transcended its positive grants. Moreover, when Emery steadfastly contended that the Constitution absolutely precluded the Keating-Owen bill, Kitchin grudgingly protested: "I do not think the evil is sufficient to justify the remedy that you are going to apply, even if you have the power."[25]

The National Committee's rejoinder was presented by Thomas I. Parkinson, the director of the Legislative Drafting Bureau at Columbia University. After the 1914 hearings, the bureau, which specialized in research in law and its administration, had been retained to prepare reports to meet criticism of the Palmer-Owen bill.[26] Parkinson's testimony is chiefly noteworthy because of his handling of the subject of congressional responsibility for constitutionality when considering prospective legislation.

There were two distinct questions before the committee, the desirability and the constitutionality of the child labor bill, Parkinson stated. Congress possessed ultimate authority with respect to desirability; but only the Supreme Court could determine the constitutional issue. For this reason it was unnecessary to demonstrate the constitutionality of the measure beyond all doubt before Congress acted. This did not mean that legislators should disregard the issue; rather, they should enact reasonable statutes, according to their conscientious interpretation of constitutional powers, when the altered conditions of society necessitated action. It had to be kept in mind, Parkinson said, that the Court constantly extended federal authority in the field of interstate commerce beyond the preconceived notions of its limitations.[27] The argument assumed that, in the ordinary course of events, controversial legislation that chartered new constitutional paths would be passed up to the Court through the process of test litigation. It assumed further that, in a period of pronounced judicial tolera-

---

[24] Emery gave the committee an exact count of the prohibitions placed upon national government, compared to the affirmations, and seriously argued that the former, being more numerous, gave the Constitution its essential character. There was no hint of qualitative differences between the various clauses in this surprisingly artless analysis.

[25] Hearings on the Child Labor Bill (1916), p. 154.

[26] *Child Labor Bulletin* (November, 1915), p. 15.

[27] Hearings on the Child Labor Bill (1916), pp. 177–79.

tion of legislative experimentation, the Court was unlikely to invalidate federal social legislation.

Turning to the bill itself, Parkinson cautioned that any skillful lawyer, by using selective citations, could construct an argument that would leave the impression that it was clearly unconstitutional. Unrelated and vague propositions, however, were not
an adequate basis for determining the question; only full examination of the pertinent provisions of the Constitution would
suffice.

The remainder of Parkinson's testimony involved a systematic
examination of what the Constitution said about the commerce
power.[28] The restrictions urged by Kitchin and Emery were dismissed as constitutional fallacies. In particular, Parkinson criticized the contention that the Tenth Amendment diminished the
original grant of authority to Congress. It was logic-chopping of
the worst kind to infer that the amendment limited the extent of
enumerated powers. Like Lewis and Brinton before him, Parkinson narrowed the question to whether a distinction could be
drawn between legislation that tried to protect the consumer and
that which tried to protect the producer. The precedents, notably
Champion and *Hoke*, belied it, he stated. "In neither case was
there any purpose of protecting commerce itself, or the instrumentalities of commerce." The contested statutes were sustained
as federal police power measures. Men might quarrel with this
interpretation, Parkinson said, but to do so was to quarrel with the
justices.[29]

House Passage and Clark's Plans

On January 17, 1916, four days after the conclusion of its hearings and only ten days after the introduction of the Keating-Owen
bill in the House, the Labor Committee reported it favorably in
a statement that practically duplicated the language of the unanimous report of the previous February.[30] Most of the earlier report,
in fact, was copied directly, the only important additions being
several sections, largely derived from the National Committee's
presentations, that countered the Executive Committee's policy
arguments or bolstered the conclusion that the proposed statute

[28] *Ibid.*, p. 179–87.

[29] *Ibid.*, pp. 186–87.

[30] U.S. Congress, House, Committee on Labor, To Prevent Interstate Com-
merce in the Products of Child Labor, House Rep. 46, to accompany
H. R. 8234, The Keating-Owen Bill, 64th Cong., 1st Sess. (Washington, D.C.:
Government Printing Office, 1916).

was constitutional. The parochial approach taken by the Executive Committee's delegation magnified the mill owners' self-interest rather than induced sympathy for their position. Emery, too, faced an unresponsive audience, despite the fact that the interest he represented was somewhat broader and his argument less vulnerable to special pleading.

The opposition, however, had a limited effect; in contrast with the previous year, a minority report was presented by three representatives from southern states.[31] The three lawmakers set down against the Keating-Owen bill the legal arguments that Kitchin had made, thereby reporting the Executive Committee's position formally to the House. Their summation chiefly invoked apprehension about future legislation, following James Emery's example. Even if national regulation was admitted to be constitutional, they urged that the bill be rejected because the evil was too limited in scope (and remedial by local law) to justify the exercise of immense legislative power by Congress.[32]

Ten days later, Keating skillfully managed to bring the bill before the Committee of the Whole, and on February 2, 1916, the bill passed overwhelmingly, for the second time, 337 to 46.[33] Although the size of the opposition was virtually unchanged, the number of representatives who supported the bill had increased by nearly 50 per cent over the previous year. Again, the debate was brief, especially in view of the acknowledged importance of the bill; and, again, futile delaying tactics were employed by a small but active opposition that consisted almost exclusively of representatives from the southern textile district.[34]

Analysis of the vote plainly shows a definite alignment of south Atlantic states against the bill, as in the previous year. The entire delegations from North Carolina and South Carolina voted to defeat it, as did the majority of representatives from two other southern states, Georgia and Mississippi, where the textile industry was a major force in political affairs. As Davidson points out: "From the other southern states where manufacturing was not so firmly entrenched but where the state rights appeal was presum-

31 *Ibid.*, Part II.

32 *Ibid.*, p. 11.

33 *Congressional Record*, 64th Cong., 1st Sess. (Washington, D.C.: Government Printing Office, 1916), p. 2035. For a discussion of the congressional maneuvers associated with the enactment of the child labor bill, see Edward Keating, *The Gentleman from Colorado* (Denver: Sage Books, 1964), pp. 347–53. (The reader should be cautious about Keating's propensity to exaggerate his role and his failure to remember events correctly.)

34 *Congressional Record, ibid.*, pp. 2007–35.

ably strong, there was no such united opposition." [35] In six of those states, solid delegations supported the bill, and in the other five the majority voted for it. In thirty-eight states, every representative who was recorded voted affirmatively. Only one congressman from outside the south cast a negative vote, and only two Republicans, Parker of New Jersey and Britt of North Carolina, opposed the bill's passage.

The day after the House's action, the National Committee's annual conference convened in Asheville, North Carolina, as if confronting the opposition on its own ground. McKelway analyzed the congressional vote and jubilantly told the delegates that the majority of southerns, as well as the overwhelming number of legislators from other regions, had favored the Keating-Owen bill. (He also pointed out that more states than would be needed favored and ensured the passage of a constitutional amendment if this should become necessary.) Caustically, McKelway recited the most telling criticism of the southern textile states:

> The plain question for plain folks is, Are all the constitutional lawyers from North Carolina and South Carolina, or does it just happen that these are the two biggest cotton manufacturing states in the union, as well as the two states in the South which have not yet reached the 14-year age limit for the employment of children? The question will not down — Why are the only two solid delegations against this bill from the two states with the worst conditions of child labor? [36]

Representative Keating, who also addressed the conference, forecast the future with remarkable accuracy:

> The cotton mill interests know that if we are beaten in this Congress, we will bob up serenely in the next. They know this fight is going on until the law is on the statute books, and no power but the Supreme Court can defeat this child labor legislation.

The congressional backers of the bill had only one request, Keating said, "the privilege of voting in the Senate of the United States on this bill in order that it may be passed up to the Supreme Court." [37] In this he acknowledged the fear of the bill's strategists that southern senators might try to "filibuster it to death." Unless prevented by adverse public opinion, the Carolina senators, thor-

[35] Davidson, *Child Labor Legislation in the Southern Textile States*, p. 257.

[36] Alexander J. McKelway, "The South for Child Labor Reform," *Child Labor Bulletin* (May, 1916), p. 57.

[37] Edward Keating, "Federal Child Labor Legislation," *Child Labor Bulletin* (May, 1916), p. 70.

oughly versed in delaying unwanted legislation in caucus and committee, or strangling it in procedural entanglements, were expected to take the lead in obstructionist tactics.

It was plain, however, after the decisive action in the House, that the Executive Committee's fight against the Keating-Owen bill had been lost. What had only recently been an empowering public consensus was now determinative. The only matter in doubt was how long defeat could be staved off. Although Clark may have cherished illusions about successful resistance, the evidence suggests that he and Kitchin knew that such efforts were destined to fail. Nevertheless, they continued their resistance, mounting another full-scale attack upon the measure in hearings, which they requested, before the Senate Committee on Interstate Commerce. Perhaps Clark could not admit defeat; perhaps he and Kitchin hoped for an unexpected turn of events. Most likely, however, they had enlarged their conception of the nature of the political struggle and were looking beyond Congress to the Supreme Court and mass opinion. If the southern textile industry was to be saved from sycophantic reformers and swarming federal agents (Clark's derisive characterization), it was not enough to defeat a single piece of legislation; rather, the pervasive support for federal child labor regulation had to be reversed, once and for all. More than a last stand in Congress, the hearings became a forum for the future.

Senate Hearings on the Child Labor Bill

From the beginning, the Senate hearings — starting on February 15, 1916, and running through five consecutive sessions — closely corresponded to the House committee hearings. Again, misrepresentation was the rationale for the textile manufacturers' attack, set forth, in the main, by members of the Executive Committee. If the south's peculiar history and circumstances were correctly understood, it would be seen that satisfactory child labor standards had been established and that further progress was assured. Again, however, the ruinous consequences of federal legislation preoccupied the southern delegation.[38] Captain Ellison D. Smyth summarized the mill owner's complaint: the Keating-Owen bill "practically fixes the age at 16, because it says they cannot work under 16 except eight hours," and the bill provided for "federal inspection and control of our internal affairs by the General Government." Sam Patterson unequivocally asserted that, be-

[38] Hearings, Interstate Commerce in Products of Child Labor, pp. 7–94, 236–40.

cause of the excessive costs, "we are not going on the eight hour system until we are compelled to do so." [39] And Scott Roberts uncompromisingly defended child labor. He had sufficient audacity, he said, to attack the bill solely on its demerits, as an infringement upon the inherent human rights of impoverished children to find remunerative work.[40] Not the plight of children but rather the most profitable work schedule remained the heart of the matter.

When Senator Clapp of Minnesota, a leading insurgent Republican, asked why so much testimony was being presented about the southern textile mills, Patterson restated the allegation that the southern mills were the sole reason for agitating the Keating-Owen bill. Logically, then, if the Senate found southern conditions were satisfactory (an invitation to visit the textile districts was again extended), there would be no necessity for the bill. Shortly afterward, the committee chairman, Newlands of Nevada, a progressive, administration Democrat, told Patterson that he regarded passage of the bill, perhaps in somewhat modified form, as practically assured.

> "I think the feeling is — I may be mistaken — that this subject will not be left exclusively to the States in the fear that even though the States may pass wise laws upon the subject the laws themselves may not be properly enforced." [41]

Despite every assurance of success, McKelway and Wiley Swift responded to the Executive Committee's charges at considerable length, no doubt to ensure that every conceivable advantage was exploited.[42] In particular, McKelway reviewed the National Committee's history as a means "to lift away the sectional prejudice that its work was directed against the South or one of its industries."

Constitutionality, the only line of defense for the Executive Committe, had worn thin, but Kitchin again raised the barriers of states' rights and the "eternal verities" of the higher law. He advanced a static conception of the law, contending that congressional powers did not vary in extent from period to period, having been firmly molded when the nation was formed. In the 1850's, the view that Congress could bar products from market would not have been accepted. "If that clause did not contain that power 60 years ago, is it right to insist that it has it now?" Kitchin in-

39 *Ibid.*, pp. 10, 46.
40 *Ibid.*, p. 33–49.
41 *Ibid.*, p. 68.
42 *Ibid.*, pp. 189–236.

quired. The lawmaker, fully as much as the jurist, was required to transmit, unimpaired, the immutable laws of equity and justice to future generations.

Kitchin, however, seemed to acknowledge that his efforts to raise constitutional objections had little chance of success, as his closing statement reveals.

> The sovereignty of this Government is in the people. They have power to give Congress more power. Congress has only the power granted in the Constitution. . . . When a citizen is deprived of a guaranteed right by Congress on the ground that it is reasonable to so deprive him, . . . it is the spirit of an unrestrained acting majority. Constitutions are made to protect minorities. Majorities usually are able to take care of themselves.[43]

In contrast, James Emery gave not an inch.[44] If anything, the indictment he had earlier laid against the Keating-Owen bill was urged with even greater vigor. He importuned the senators to protect industrial freedom and not to open the way to a vast remolding of the economic order by the federal government. Two features of Parkinson's position especially alarmed him. He brusquely dismissed Parkinson's contention that the Supreme Court had recurrently extended congressional authority in the field of interstate commerce beyond the previously understood limits. The powers of Congress were neither increased in their extent nor changed in their nature by the words of men nor by passing expressions of public opinion.[45] And against Parkinson's contention that congressmen might, in good conscience, enact legislation about whose constitutionality they were not entirely certain, because the Supreme Court would settle the issue upon review, he countered with one of Judge Cooley's celebrated commentaries

> Legislators have their authority measured by the Constitution. They are chosen to do what it permits and nothing more, and they take solemn oaths to obey and support it. When they disregard its provisions they usurp authority, abuse their trust, and violate the promise they have confirmed by an oath. To pass an act when they are in doubt whether it is not violating the Constitution is to treat as of no force the most imperative obligation any person can assume.[46]

43 *Ibid.*, pp. 83–94, 100, 111.
44 *Ibid.*, pp. 241–82.
45 *Ibid.*, p. 279.
46 Thomas M. Cooley, *The General Principles of Constitutional Law in the United States*, ed. Andrew C. McLaughlin (3d. ed.; Boston: Little, Brown and Co., 1898), p. 150; quoted in Hearings, p. 246.

In Emery's view, the lawmakers' conscientious reading of an immutable Constitution was no less obligatory than that of the Court. In a period during which the supreme bench increasingly deferred to legislative judgment, the Cooley doctrine had become an especially important element in the conservative defense against federal social and economic legislation. If the Court displayed reluctance to supervise congressional intent, the congressional chambers became a more important battleground than ever before in the political struggle to decide how and for what purposes national powers would be exercised.

Parkinson's testimony covered much the same ground as before, but he submitted a lengthy accompanying brief, making a much fuller aggregate statement than he had presented to the House Labor Committee. The only difficult constitutional point, he argued, involved the effect of the Fifth Amendment upon the power of Congress to regulate interstate commerce. What, in fact, constituted unreasonable confiscatory interference with liberty or property? The problem arose because the test of reasonableness was vague, the Court having said that no hard and fast rule "separates the constitutional from the unconstitutional in this field of the police power and the due process clause." [47] This appraisal, as before, assumed that the Court would determine the constitutionality of federal social legislation on a case-by-case basis, relating exercises of power to existing conditions. Hence Congress should not fear to undertake reasonable regulatory experiments.

In addition, Parkinson treated directly what was probably the most important objection to the Keating-Owen bill — Emery's warning that it would encourage a flood of demands for far-reaching regulatory legislation. His rejoinder, brief but penetrating, assessed the pressure of American democracy more realistically than Kitchin's peroration or Emery's grim parade of horrors.

> It does not matter in the slightest what this committee or what this Congress may do with this bill so far as future requests and future demands for the extension of the Federal powers are concerned. You can not hold up that demand by any action which you may take on this bill. . . . You will be flooded with those demands whatever you do with this bill, and you will be flooded with them until the limitations of the congressional power are more definitely prescribed by the Supreme Court. [48]

[47] *Ibid.*, pp. 113–52; quotation on p. 122.
[48] *Ibid.*, p. 128.

There is little evidence in the history of subsequent regulatory measures (the Adamson Act, for example) to dispute Parkinson's prediction that the demands for expanded federal powers would continue, and largely without reference to congressional action on the child labor bill.

Although the hearings concluded, for all practical purposes, on February 21, after the testimony of the interested groups, the Interstate Commerce Committee met once more in public session, one month later, to hear from two self-styled representatives of a women's organization — extreme conservatives who could be counted upon to oppose any form of progressive social action. The committee chairman, Senator Newlands, said that the communications he had received indicated a strong public demand that the Keating-Owen bill be passed. Senator Lippitt of Rhode Island, the committee member most likely to reflect the views of the northern business community, reported that his experiences confirmed Newlands', although he thought there was another side to the question. Stacks of petitions, all urging passage of the bill, had come to him, and to other senators, but not a single statement in opposition.[49]

The Residuum of the Commerce Power Rests with Congress

When the Committee on Interstate Commerce submitted its report,[50] a month later, a number of substantial amendments were offered. Instead of closing the channels of interstate commerce merely to products in whose manufacture child laborers had taken part, the Senate version of the bill excluded the entire output of industrial establishments in which children were employed.[51] Not only would enforcement be made easier, the committee stated, by obviating the need to prove that children had worked on a specified product, the entire evil of industrial child labor would be reached by extending protection to children who were not directly engaged in manufacturing processes. On the merits, the committee concluded that child labor regulation was not a field in which diversity between the states was desirable. The exploitation of children was prejudicial to the welfare of the nation and

49 *Ibid.*, pp. 291–302.

50 To Prevent Interstate Commerce in the Products of Child Labor, Senate Rep. 358.

51 Another amendment made the bill's provisions applicable against shipments in foreign commerce, correcting an oversight in the National Committee's original draft.

shocking to the moral sense of the community. After reviewing the Executive Committee's testimony and noting the textile manufacturers' resistance to state reform, the committee pointedly observed:

> It seems hardly reasonable, therefore, that the representations . . . by the employers of the children, and their counsel, should have great weight in defeating the enactment of a bill which applies to all mining, mechanical and manufacturing occupations throughout the United States.[52]

Overall, the report conveyed the impression of complete assurance that Congress could enact federal child labor legislation under the commerce power. Specifically, the committee set down fundamental principles, which, in its opinion, were so well established that they were no longer open to controversy: (1) the commerce power was complete, except as constitutionally limited; (2) the power included the authority absolutely to prohibit specified persons and things from interstate transit; (3) the only limitation upon this authority, as far as the Keating-Owen bill was concerned, was the Fifth Amendment, which protected against arbitrary interference with private rights; and (4) this authority might be exercised in the interest of the public welfare as well as in the direct interest of commerce. The entire history of legislation and adjudication under the Constitution was cited as conclusive proof of the validity of the construction.[53]

Not only was the Keating-Owen bill clearly constitutional when tested against these standards, the committee declared, the practical inability of the states to eliminate child labor made its enactment essential. As long as a single state still chose to exploit its children, making it impossible for other states to protect their industries and consumers, this urgent need would continue.[54] But the report did not end with this emphatic conclusion; the committee tried to silence any constitutional doubts that might remain as a consequence of the arguments that had been said to invalidate the bill. Most significantly, it sought to discredit the idea that there could be a twilight zone of economic activity that was immune from governmental regulation.

> That somewhere between the States and Congress there exists full and complete power effectively to regulate the evil of child labor

52 To Prevent Interstate Commerce in the Products of Child Labor, Senate Rep. 358, p. 16.
53 *Ibid.*, pp. 16–17.
54 *Ibid.*, pp. 20–21.

is incontrovertible; that part of that power is no longer possessed by the States because they have delegated it to Congress is established by the cases beyond doubt; it must necessarily follow that the residuum of this power is vested in Congress.[55]

Next, the committee dismissed Emery's and Kitchin's basic criticism of the Keating-Owen bill.

The fact, often adverted to by opponents of the bill that most of the previous legislation under the commerce clause has not been directed primarily to the protection of the producer, is merely incidental, and in the opinion of the committee does not rise to the dignity of an argument against the constitutionality of the bill.[56]

The supposed distinction, the report stated, was based on the erroneous view that congressional authority extended only to persons who were directly affected by commercial intercourse. However, legislation was never sustained on such a narrow basis, but rather on the bases of "benefits ultimately accruing to the public health and welfare."[57] Justice McKenna's opinion in the *Hoke* case made it unmistakably clear the Court understood that the principles sustained in the various police power cases impliedly sanctioned such legislation as the Keating-Owen bill. For McKenna had declared:

It may be that Congress could not prohibit the manufacture of the article in a State. It may be that Congress could not prohibit in all its conditions its sale within a State. But Congress may prohibit its transportation between the states, and by this means defeat the motive and evil of its manufacture.[58]

The report concluded, in short, that Congress could legislate — virtually without limitation — to stem, by indirect means, dangers arising from or augmented by interstate commerce.

The National Conventions: Politics Principles, and Progressivism

Although Ellison D. Smith was the ranking Democratic member of the Committee on Interstate Commerce, there was no minority report. No doubt the southern senators realized that drafting a dissent would be wasted effort. Instead, the opponents made plans to prevent the Keating-Owen bill from reaching the

55 *Ibid.*, p. 21.
56 *Ibid.*
57 *Ibid.*, p. 22.
58 *Ibid.*

floor. The intricacies of the Senate calendar, the nature of Senate conventions and procedures (especially the difficulty in imposing the cloture rule), and the sheer power of personal privilege seemed to offer ample opportunities for protecting the interests of the textile oligarchy. When the substitute bill came before the Committee of the Whole, on June 3, Senator Overman's objections, in a situation that required unanimous consent, set it aside for a second time, seemingly indefinitely. Once again the south's remarkable capacity to protect its peculiar interests had been given practical effect within the Senate. Later that day, Congress recessed for the national conventions.

In 1912 the delegates to the Progressive party convention had pledged to work unceasingly, in state and nation, for the prohibition of child labor (among other reforms) and had declared that "up to the limits of the Constitution, and later by amendment of the Constitution, if found necessary, we advocate bringing under effective national jurisdiction those problems which have expanded beyond the reach of the individual states." [59] For Albert Beveridge, who keynoted the insurgent gatherings (as well as for many other Progressives), child labor was just such a problem. Their adversaries in the major parties had treated the subject ambiguously, but the situation changed dramatically in 1916.

Just as the Populist platform in 1892 had provided a foundation for the first phase of American progressivism, many of the measures embodied in the Progressive platform had been taken over by the New Freedom and the reunited Republicans. [60] The Democrats renominated Woodrow Wilson, on a platform that stressed progressive achievements, and the Republicans selected an equally distinguished public official, Charles Evan Hughes, and adopted a platform that was designed to prove the party's dedication to social justice. Both platforms contained unequivocal planks that called for the immediate enactment and effective enforcement of comprehensive federal child labor legislation. [61]

When the Senate reconvened, it seemed certain to most observers that the convention pledges, already fulfilled in the House, would be promptly redeemed, but this assessment failed to take into account the strategic position the intransigent southerners

[59] Kirk Porter, *National Party Platforms* (New York: Macmillan Co., 1924), p. 336.
[60] Arthur S. Link, *Woodrow Wilson and the Progressive Era* ("The New American Nation Series," eds. Henry Steel Commager and Richard B. Morris, Vol. I [New York: Harper & Row, 1954]), p. 16.
[61] See Porter, *National Party Platforms*, pp. 383, 402.

occupied in the Democratic caucus — and their potential bargaining power if they threatened a filibuster. Redemption seemed to be forthcoming when the Republican Conference Committee and the Democratic Steering Committee met to seek agreement on a program of imperative legislation for the remainder of the session, especially because — after initial reluctance — the Republican minority had announced its willingness to facilitate the passage of the Keating-Owen bill.[62] When the Democratic caucus next met, however, the cotton mill spokesmen, Lee Overman and Ellison D. Smith, threatened prolonged discussion on the floor if the child labor bill was not struck from the list of priority legislation, and the caucus yielded. The Democratic leadership, apparently, felt that a full-scale filibuster would impede, perhaps preclude, the passage of other important legislative proposals.[63] After learning what had happened, McKelway and various liberal congressmen and administrative officials urged President Wilson to intervene at once. They warned that reformers looked upon the Keating-Owen bill as a test of the administration's progressivism.[64] Wilson, however, was already acutely aware of the implications of what had occurred. The next day, July 18, he went to the President's Room at the capitol. The assembled Democratic leaders were forcefully reminded of the child labor pledge in the party's platform and they were enjoined to fulfill that pledge.[65]

Whether politics or humanity was the dominant motive behind Wilson's dramatic eleventh-hour demand for the passage of the child labor law could not be determined, according to the *Literary Digest*. Although it was only eight years since he had written that the Beveridge bill represented "an obviously absurd" extension of congressional power,[66] Wilson was fully prepared — though his constitutional reservations may not have been entirely allayed — to support federal child labor legislation. The years immediately preceding his presidential candidacy saw changes in his attitudes toward the use of federal power to achieve social justice, and these changes were accelerated as he presided over the bloodless revolution. During the 1912 campaign, discussing what had to be

62 *Child Labor Bulletin* (August, 1916), pp. 91–92.

63 *Ibid.*, p. 92; *Independent* (July 31, 1916), p. 150.

64 Davidson, *Child Labor Legislation in the Southern Textile States*, p. 258; Link, *Woodrow Wilson*, p. 227.

65 *New York Times*, July 19, 1916, p. 6; *Literary Digest* (August 5, 1916), p. 290; *Independent* (July 31, 1916), p. 150.

66 Woodrow Wilson, *Constitutional Government in the United States* (New York: Columbia University Press, 1908), pp. 170–71.

done to conserve the nation's human resources, he had cited the regulation of child labor and had accepted this and other aspects of the social justice program as partially federal as well as state questions.[67] Although he had not at that time decided how much the national government should do, his decision had been made in 1916, and it dramatized the ideological distance America had traveled.[68]

Obviously, Wilson's charge to the Democratic Steering Committee also was motivated by political considerations. He faced a hard campaign (the closest presidential election of the century). Theodore Roosevelt's third party no longer threatened Republican unity, and Charles Evans Hughes, a man of great popular appeal, had achieved a notable record as a reform governor of New York and on the Supreme Court bench. Wilson appreciated the unifying effects that would follow from enactment of a genuinely popular measure, such as the Keating-Owen bill — especially after the divisive consequences of the Brandeis appointment and in the midst of the controversy caused by the proposed eight-hour workday law for railway labor. He clearly recognized, in the words of the *Independent*, that the matter would "probably have an important effect upon the presidential campaign, because the Progressives and the labor unions are unanimously in favor of federal restriction of child labor, and any failure on the part of the Democratic administration to deal with the question would be remembered against it in November." [69] Indeed, it seemed that the victory would go to the major party that won most of the former Progressives.[70]

[67] John Wells Davidson, "Wilson in the Campaign of 1912," in *The Philosophy and Politics of Woodrow Wilson*, ed. Earl Latham (Chicago: University of Chicago Press, 1958), pp. 95–97.

[68] Grace Abbott, who succeeded Julia Lathrop as chief of the Children's Bureau, told a House committee in 1924 that Wilson "had been very active in support of both the first and second child labor laws" and that, after the first law was declared unconstitutional, "he indicated that he had every intention of keeping up the fight for the protection of children to the very end." U.S. Congress, Proposed Child Labor Amendments to the Constitution of the United States, Hearings before the Committee on the Judiciary, U.S. House of Representatives, 68th Cong., 2d Sess. (Washington, D.C.: Government Printing Office, 1924), pp. 275, 276.

[69] July 31, 1916, p. 150.

[70] The influence of political calculations should not be exaggerated. Link, for example (*Woodrow Wilson*, pp. 54–80, 223–51, and *Wilson, The New Freedom* [Princeton: Princeton University Press, 1956], pp. 241–76, 445–71), argues that Wilson's conversion to progressivism occurred only in early 1916 and almost entirely as a campaign expedient to lure the "advanced progressives" (his term for the leaders of the social justice movement) into the Democratic

After Wilson's intervention, the Senate Republicans, who had planned to make political capital of the caucus action, pressed for immediate passage of the Keating-Owen bill. The crucial battle, however, took place later in a second meeting of the Democratic caucus. Still unwilling to concede defeat, the southerners sought to add crippling amendments and to attach a previously vetoed immigration bill as a rider,[71] but they were hopelessly outnumbered and could not persuade their colleagues to resist the powerful presidential injunction.[72] Firmly managed by the majority leader, Senator Kern of Indiana, the caucus agreed, on July 25, to pass the bill, unamended, before adjournment.[73]

ranks. Wilson, he implies, forced the Senate to enact legislation about whose constitutionality he had serious reservations. But Link does not explain satisfactorily why Wilson should have acted in such a Machiavellian way. He largely ignores the rapid shift in public attitudes about the constitutional issues between 1907 and 1916 (illustrated by the *Hoke* case and the Interstate Commerce Committee's report [the latter certainly was not produced by "advanced progressives"]), the widespread public and congressional support for effective national child labor regulation, and the fact that both radical agrarian and conservative states' rights Democrats enthusiastically supported the Keating-Owen bill. If other constitutional authorities had changed their minds, why not Wilson?

In February, 1914, it is true, when representatives from the National Committee sought support for the Palmer-Owen bill, Wilson declined, for constitutional reasons, to give his endorsement (see Link, *Wilson, the New Freedom*, pp. 256–57). However, Link's more recent treatments of Wilson's relationship to social justice legislation in 1916 *(Wilson: Confusions and Crises, 1915–1916* [Princeton: Princeton University Press, 1964], pp. 319–23, and *Wilson: Campaigns for Progressivism and Peace* [Princeton: Princeton University Press, 1965], pp. 56–60) seem to mark a change of mind about Wilson's thought and motivations, but they do not deal directly with the Keating-Owen bill.

Link, moreover, stereotypes the National Child Labor Committee and the motivations of its leaders. He seems to feel that Florence Kelley's flirtations with socialism characterized child labor reformers generally, and that they hoped to extend federal control into many sectors of industrial life. But those who were most representative of the committee (Felix Adler, Homer Folks, Owen Lovejoy, and Rabbi Stephen A. Wise, to name a few) were not "advanced progressives," in Link's description. They were single-minded pragmatists, impelled by humanitarian motives, who wanted to use federal authority to abolish a great evil. They did not consciously intend to reshape the economic order.

[71] *Child Labor Bulletin* (August, 1916), p. 92.

[72] On July 31 the *Independent* commented: "President Wilson is reported to have postponed the date of the notification of his renomination by the Democratic party until he receives assurances that the child labor bill and the federal workingmen's compensation bill are to be pushed thru to enactment."

[73] *Child Labor Bulletin* (August, 1916), p. 92.

The Obligations of Congress

On August 3, Senator Robinson of Arkansas, who had taken over leadership of the child labor bill after Senator Owen became absorbed in other matters, moved to take it up on the Senate floor. The Keating-Owen bill was made the unfinished order of business, to be superseded by other legislation only on unanimous consent.[74] Supporters and opponents alike agreed that its passage, by an overwhelming majority of votes, was assured. Robinson, a young, progressive Democrat, claimed that this result was universally conceded, and Hardwick of Georgia, one of the leaders of the southern opposition, spoke of the enormous political power behind the bill, frankly admitting that he was utterly without hope that anything could be done to stop it.[75] Despite this certainty about the outcome, the Senate exchanged all of the constitutional arguments for and against the bill.

That Congress was at a constitutional frontier was acknowledged by almost every senator who took the floor; however, there were sharp differences of opinion about how Congress should proceed. These differences stemmed principally from contrasting views about the purposes for which the commerce power could be exercised and the extent of congressional responsibility for determining the constitutionality, as well as the desirability, of proposed legislation. Opening the debate, Robinson contended that congressional authority was subject to constant re-definition as the conditions of society changed.

> While the power to regulate commerce remains the same, in an abstract sense, as it was at the time of the adoption of the Constitution, nevertheless its application has been a subject of constant development, and the process is still going on. . . . [Congress] has not in any one act, nor in all the laws heretofore passed concerning commerce, exhausted its power, and it will not do so if this measure becomes a law.[76]

The same progressive proposition was repeated by others who supported the bill, Democrats and Republicans alike, chiefly from midwestern states. Although the proponents were not in perfect accord over how far Congress could go in developing and extending its powers to take account of new social and industrial conditions, they agreed that the words of the Constitution did not

---

[74] *Congressional Record*, 64th Cong., 1st Sess. (Washington, D.C.: Government Printing Office, 1916), p. 12034.

[75] *Ibid.*, pp. 12062–64.

[76] *Ibid.*, pp. 12055–56.

remain fixed in meaning. Kenyon of Iowa, a long-time advocate of federal child labor legislation and Robinson's partner on the Repubican side in managing the Keating-Owen bill, stated that "the fathers who formed this instrument had no idea of what was coming, of the new conditions and the changes which would ensue, and the Constitution has been construed in a way to meet most of them." [77] It was not intended to block the progressive legislation that was required by the interest of all the people.

Robinson and others admitted that path-breaking legislation often raised questions of constitutional limitation, but these problems, they said, were not insurmountable, for Congress's responsibility was limited. If, after careful examination, legislators thought a measure clearly violated the Constitution, or they had very grave doubts about its constitutionality, they were duty-bound to defeat it. If, however, lesser doubts existed, they should be resolved in favor of an otherwise desirable measure. In this way the lawmakers met their obligation to the country, and the constitutional question was passed on to the Supreme Court, which had final responsibility for settling it. The determining factor for Congress, said Kenyon, was simply the gravity of a legislator's doubts on any piece of legislation; he had to interpret the Constitution, as if he were a member of the Supreme bench, but he need not anticipate how the Court would actually construe the Constitution. Senator Colt of Rhode Island summed up the position in this way.

> Mr. President, there may be a doubt about the constitutionality of this bill, but if it is not manifestly unconstitutional, and if it is just, if it meets the great humanitarian sentiment of the nation, if it accords with our higher aspirations toward social reform, let us pass it; and then, if subsequently it should be shown, upon very careful investigation, to be clearly in violation of the Constitution of the United States, we have, thank God, under our form of Government, a tribunal which will so declare it to be.[78]

This position showed remarkable deference to a Court that had displayed considerable hostility to progressive legislation only a few years before; indeed, the progressive attack upon judicial conservatism had reached its climax in 1913. For virtually every progressive who discussed the issue, Republican as well as Democratic, to have acknowledged the Supreme Court as the final seat of authority is not easily explained. A partial answer no doubt lies in the new atmosphere of judicial toleration that followed the *Muller*

[77] *Ibid.*, p. 12218.
[78] *Ibid.*, p. 12285.

case and the expectation that the chastened bench would continue to defer to legislative discretion. The senatorial statements strongly suggest, however, that the Court's peculiar place and function in American government had not been as seriously undermined by liberal criticism in the progressive era as later generations have come to believe.

Among the bill's supporters, some, like Robinson, said they had few or no doubts about its constitutionality: others admitted to fairly substantial doubts; but none professed sufficient uncertainty to condemn the bill. No one, Kenyon argued, could be absolutely sure that it was constitutional, though he thought the courts would so hold it. This confidence in the outcome of judicial review was expressed again and again. Every progressive measure that had been enacted in the previous twenty years had encountered doctrinaire criticism from able lawyers and had been bitterly assailed in Congress, Robinson said, but none had been invalidated by the Supreme Court.

Gallinger of New Hampshire, the Republican minority leader, perhaps best summed up the congressional censensus. At the time of the Beveridge debate, the New England legislator said, he had been told by eminent lawyers in the Senate, men from both parties, in whose legal knowledge he had great confidence, that the proposed statute was "in all human probability unconstitutional." However, he continued.

> I have since had occasion to consult some of those same Senators and they have told me that they have changed their views, as the President of the United States has changed his views, and that they now believe the legislation to be constitutional. For that reason, having a strong inclination to support this kind of legislation, I have no hesitancy today in voting for the bill, assuming that it will go to the Supreme Court of the United States for interpretation and decision.[79]

The bill's opponents, chiefly senators from the southern textile states, dissented fiercely. Hardwick said that the bill clearly distorted congressional authority beyond all reasonable interpretation. With this certainty went the conviction, repeatedly expressed, that Congress was at a parting of the ways, and the whole structure of government was in jeopardy. Hardwick characterized the bill as a "Pandora's box," which, once opened, would sooner or later destroy the American people.[80] Similar warnings about the trend

---

[79] *Ibid.*, p. 12301.
[80] For a particularly memorable expression of Hardwick's apprehensions

of federal legislation were the major arguments against the bill.
The Constitution, if viewed "properly" as a scheme of prohibitions, contravened the progressives' position that legislators could
enact statutes even if they were not certain about their constitutionality. If there was serious doubt about the propriety of a proposed measure, congressmen were unconditionally bound to resolve
this uncertainty against the measure. To do otherwise, in Cooley's
characterization, was "to treat as of no force the most important
obligation any person can assume." [81]

This responsibility of Congress ought particularly to be observed, Hardwick argued, because the courts deferred to legislative
judgment, construing every doubt in favor of the constitutionality
of legislation. Legislators, in turn, were solemnly bound to support
the courts, rather than to shift their responsibilities to the justices.
Brandegee of Connecticut, one of the few senators from a northern
state who opposed the bill, stressed the implications at length.

> . . . The Supreme Court of this country ought to have some
> support; but if we are constantly going to throw upon the Supreme
> Court all the responsibility of setting aside acts we thought were
> unwise but that we passed in response to public clamor, we are, to
> a certain extent, depriving the Supreme Court of its right to have
> the support of a coordinate branch of the Government in trying
> to maintain the Constitution of the United States.
>
> We all know what effect it has when a high court sets aside an
> act of Congress or an act of a State legislature the passage of which
> benevolent people had been able to procure. All the journals of
> the country, the magazine writers, and the "uplifters," a great
> many of whom deal in language and not brains, who know noth-
> ing about the law, but are very versatile with epithets, denounce
> the Supreme Court and say it is time to haul off the bench and to
> have referendums and recalls and all that sort of thing.[82]

Brandegee later took part in an illuminating colloquy with another Republican, Kenyon's colleague from Iowa, Senator Cummins, the ranking minority member of the Committee on Interstate
Commerce and one of the most prominent insurgents in Congress,

about federal social legislation, see Charles Warren, *The Supreme Court in
United States History* (Boston: Little, Brown and Co., 1923), p. 460.

[81] *Congressional Record*, 64th Cong., 1st Sess., p. 12075; quotation from
Cooley on p. 150.

[82] *Congressional Record, ibid.*, pp. 12092–93. Brandegee said he was not
inclined to oppose the bill, that he would not hesitate for a moment to support it if agreement could be reached to pass it and stop there, but he feared
the dangerous consequences that would follow if it should be sustained by the
Court. When the time came to vote, he was paired.

about the conflicting positions on how Congress should approach legislation whose constitutionality was in doubt. Cummins stated that he personally knew, absolutely and certainly, how he would decide upon the Keating-Owen law if he were a justice (that it was clearly constitutional) "but when I am asked, 'What will the Supreme Court decide . . . ,' the doubt arises. I do not know." Brandegee (who felt the bill was unconstitutional) replied: "I did not use the word 'doubt' in that way at all. I am talking about the doubts in the Senators' minds as to the constitutionality of the legislation. . . ." In the end, both men agreed that every congressman had to decide the question for himself but that, once the Supreme Court applied an authoritative construction, "it is his duty" — as Brandegee said — "to construe the Constitution as the court has done, although he may think they really erred." [83]

Hardwick, however, vigorously rejected their conclusion. The decisions of the Court were binding on litigants, he said, and, if a ruling was plain and clear, Congress also was bound. But, because the Court had sometimes reversed itself, every legislator had to form his own honest judgments on the meaning of the Constitution. He ought "to do what he thinks is right, provided his conviction is so profound, so fixed, that it does not yield to the persuasive influence of the logic and reasoning of the court's decision." [84] To clarify his position, the Georgian said he had never viewed the holding in the Lottery case [85] as sound law. The usurpations of power, which had culminated in the legislative outrage now before the Senate, had their source in that holding's erroneous doctrines.

Despite this reservation, Hardwick thought that the child labor bill would encounter insuperable difficulties when it was reviewed by the justices. The bench, he implied, would set the statute alongside the Constitution and quickly discern its inherent defects — rather than distort constitutional provisions to accommodate the measure. Overman was more cautious about the judicial result, and Brandegee stated that, although the Court would have found the bill unconstitutional only a year or two before, he did not know how it would now decide. Thomas of Colorado, a Bryan Democrat, quoted the famous Mr. Dooley remark that the Supreme Court followed the election returns, and openly confessed, although he feared the precedent, that the justices probably would

[83] *Ibid.*, pp. 12228–29.
[84] *Ibid.*, p. 12076.
[85] *Champion* v. *Ames*, 188 U.S. 321 (1903).

sustain the measure. "The court, like others, is human and largely controlled by public opinion whenever its manifestation seems to be undoubted." [86]

Perhaps the most striking aspect of the senatorial debate was the deferential approach to judicial authority taken by liberal and conservative senators alike. Both sides regarded the Supreme Court as the guardian of the fundamental law, and neither side challenged the Court's interpretative prerogative. Indeed, the apparent reversal of positions hardly could be more surprising. Conservatives quoted Mr. Dooley and regarded the Court's decisions skeptically, contending that they were not necessarily binding upon Congress, while insurgents appealed to the sacred authority of the bench. Obviously, the changing character of the Supreme Court's interpretations of the Constitution influenced the legislators' thoughts and statements. For progressives, recent judicial decisions foretold the validity of the Keating-Owen law; for opponents of the bill, the opposite was true, although they were less sure about the outcome. Neither side, however, was certain that the justices would follow the construction they contended should be apparent to all.

Two distinctly minority views about the proper congressional approach to pioneering legislation should be noted. Senator Works of California, even though he thought the measure would be declared unconstitutional, said that he would vote for it.

> I think it will furnish the best opportunity the Supreme Court of the United States has ever had to determine this question definitely and for all time; and the question is not going to be settled until it is finally settled in that way. So we may just as well give the Supreme Court the opportunity to determine it now as at any later time.[87]

Senator Lane of Oregon was not awed by constitutional provisions, believing the courts had been overly zealous about the rights behind which special interests hide.

> So far as the Constitution goes it is just as good as it is and not one whit better than it works out to be. I have no veneration for any ordinance that prevents a great government from doing what is right by its people, or respect for any man's theories as to how unfortunate it would be if we should go ahead despite it and do that thing which we were chosen to do for the people. If it is right,

86 *Congressional Record*, 64th Cong., 1st Sess., pp. 12133–34.
87 *Ibid.*, p. 12212.

I would do it regardless of constitutions or constitutional cavilings of anybody. The general health and well-being of the community at large are of greater importance than any constitution or any author of any constitution, for that matter. . . .

There is a larger and broader aspect to this question than constitutional rights and interference with the dicta of some court and fine whittlings of law points here and the interpretation of someone long ago who knew not what the country was coming to or what this day would bring forth.[88]

Lane's attitude reflected the impatience of some radical reformers who felt that the need for new forms of social control was more important than the ordinary considerations of constitutionality. Theirs, to be sure, was a new "higher law," but it did not have great appeal in a society that was preoccupied with legalism.

Outside Congress, Samuel Gompers, writing in the *American Federationist*, said that what was right should be legislated, despite what lawyers and judges might say about constitutional limitations.

Whether the child labor law may be held legally constitutional is not the potential consideration. Child labor is morally wrong, economically improvident and nationally unwise. And a law enacted by the United States Congress and signed by the President solemnly so declaring can not be disregarded.

The nation demands limitation or abolition of child labor. If the courts shall hold that the Constitution interferes with this purpose then the Constitution must and will be changed.[89]

The Senate Passes the Keating-Owen Bill

It was a southerner, "Pitchfork Ben" Tillman of South Carolina, the leader of radical agrarian forces during the Populist days and onetime member of the National Child Labor Committee, who indicted the southern textile manufacturers most severely.[90] Tillman, although he condemned the Keating-Owen bill, also condemned his mill-owning constituents. Congress lacked authority to enact the proposed legislation, he charged; the majority was simply pandering to public opinion and cowardly surrendering to the insidious forces of centralization. But his deadliest fire was aimed at the textile manufacturers, in his own and in neighboring states.

[88] *Ibid.*, p. 12291.
[89] Samuel Gompers, "Lift the Burdens from Child Life," *American Federationist* (September 1916), p. 844.
[90] For background on Tillman, see Francis Butler Simkins, *The Tillman Movement in South Carolina* (Durham: Duke University Press, 1926).

The quibbling and selfishness of the cotton-mill owners makes me almost willing to vote for the Keating bill despite my honest conviction of its unconstitutionality — and I have told them so in my replies to their letters. The reasons they advance against the measure lead me to think that they oppose it, not because it sets a bad and dangerous precedent but because it reduces their dividends.[91]

Faced with certain defeat, the senators from the southern textile district no longer attempted to obstruct the bill's passage. Overman, however, sought to wrest a major concession and moved to amend the bill to provide a two-year period (rather than the stipulated single year) before the provisions took effect. Ellison D. Smith and Hardwick, who repeated the familiar argument that the southern mills would need the longer period to adjust their operations, were decisively answered by Senator Lippett. Lippett entered the debate reluctantly, he said, because, as the representative of a northern textile state (Lippett also had large holdings in cotton mills), his remarks might be misinterpreted. New England's experience, he said, proved that the southerners' contention was groundless — the necessary changes could be effected in no more than two months' time, without great difficulty and at small expense. Hardwick then revived the discredited charge that the force behind the bill arose in large measure from commercial rivalry. Lippett admitted that the New England mills had suffered from the "differences in customs" between the two sections, and that some types of cotton manufacture had been lost to southern producers, but the northern manufacturers did not compain about this nor seek to attack the south.[92] The real force behind the bill was humanitarianism, Lippett declared. The organization that had skillfully advocated its enactment had no financial assistance from New England mills. Nor had he ever before received as

---

91 *Congressional Record*, 64th Cong., 1st Sess., p. 12294. Tillman also said he would heartily favor federal child labor legislation if Congress were empowered to enact such legislation, and there is no reason to doubt his sincerity.

92 Hardwick was wrong, Lippett argued, when he described New England's attitude toward the south as selfishness: "He should describe it as generosity of the highest order. I want to say to the Senator from Georgia that the only reason why the cotton manufacturing industry was ever established in the South was on account of the humanitarian labor laws that were enacted in Massachusetts and in Rhode Island and Connecticut. . . . As for the matter of selfishness, I fail to see what selfishness there is in running our industry without protest under these more humanitarian conditions when we allow a competitor in our own country to go on under other conditions without protest on our part." *Ibid.*, p. 12308.

many communications in support of a prospective statute. Senator Weeks of Massachusetts, a leading conservative in the Senate, who described himself as the spokesman for the largest textile interests in the north, said that his experience had paralleled Lippett's. In short, Overman's amendment was defeated.

Late in the evening of August 8, the Senate voted 52 to 12 to pass the Keating-Owen bill.[93] It seems unlikely that the long hours of debate in oppressive weather changed the minds of more than a handful of senators, if any, but the drama was played to its conclusion. In part, this was simply the regular process of congressional conflict, but the expectations of constituents and the anticipated closeness of the approaching presidential election also accounted for the legislative struggle. However, the support for the bill was nonpartisan and the opposition was still sectional. Of the twelve negative votes, six came from the three principal southern textile states — North Carolina, South Carolina, and Georgia — and four were cast by senators from Alabama, Mississippi, and Florida. As had twice been true in the House, several southern states voted unanimously for the bill, and the majority of southern senators also supported it. The only non-Southern votes against the bill were cast by the two Republican senators from Pennsylvania.

Within a week after the Senate vote, a conference committee agreed upon the Senate's version of the bill and House acceptance followed. On September 1, before a large gathering of interested persons, President Wilson signed the bill

> with real emotion . . . because I know how long the struggle has been to secure legislation of this sort and what it is going to mean to the health and the vigor of the country, and also the happiness of those whom it affects. It is with genuine pride that I play my part in completing this legislation.[94]

In the language of his first inaugural address, it was a duty met — part of the task of purifying and humanizing the vital processes of American life.

The President's statement, however, was crowded off the front pages by news of the war in Europe and by upper case headlines

---

[93] *Ibid.*, p. 12313. That the hour was late, the session near an end, and the outcome absolutely certain probably explains, in large part, why a third of the Senate did not vote. Of those who were absent and asked to have their preferences recorded, or paired, nearly all (15 to 3) indicated that they supported the bill.

[94] *New York Times*, September 2, 1916, p. 4.

announcing that the House had passed the Adamson bill. The next day Wilson formally accepted the presidential nomination of the Democratic Party for the second time. In doing so, he announced that he stood squarely on his record of achievement, one part of which consisted of "the emancipation of the children of the nation by releasing them from hurtful labor." Summarizing the accomplishments of his administration, Wilson said: "We have in four years come very near to carrying out the platform of the Progressive Party, as well as our own: for we also are Progressives."[95] Once again the headlines were preempted. The front page of the *New York Times* thundered that a crippling, nation-wide railway strike had been averted by the signing of the "Eight Hour Bill."

The Crowning Achievement of Progressivism

The Keating-Owen law evoked immense popular approval in the autumn of 1916. The two parties had declared for federal legislation in their platforms, their spokesmen now vied with each other in claiming credit for enacting the statute, and the two presidential candidates endorsed it wholeheartedly. Congressional leaders said that the mass of the people emphatically favored it — as they favored few other contemporary measures — and that this sentiment extended throughout much of the south.[96] The evidence left little room for controversy; even the congressional opponents of the law admitted the solidity of its public support.

Newspapers of widely varying political persuasions hailed the emancipation of the children. Unanimity was not as common in the south as elsewhere, but many southern newspapers, including leading journals of opinion, expressed their approval. In the industrial east, the *New York Times* found that the measure was "rather startling to conservatives, and especially to reactionary minds, but . . . it is not unprecedented or revolutionary."[97] The leading Republican editorial voice in the midwest, the *Chicago*

95 *Ibid.*, September 3, 1916, p. 4.

96 Robinson had pointed out during the Senate debate that, with few exceptionos, the southern states had already passed child labor laws analogous in one or more ways to the Keating-Owen bill, and that these measures had been "enacted in most instances in spite of and over the opposition of the industries and organizations employing child labor." *Congressional Record*, 64th Cong., 1st Sess., p. 12054.

97 August 5, 1916, p. 8. The editorial suggested that the wisdom of the statute was still open to discussion and that opinions might differ, but the *Times* supported Wilson's re-election on the basis of his proven progressivism.

Tribune, without repudiating either its conservatism or its hostility to the expansion of federal power, singled out the two Republican senators who had voted against the bill (Boies Penrose and George T. Oliver of Pennsylvania) for "individual criticism and censure"; they had "defied community welfare" and "committed an offense in defiance of public opinion for special interest."[98] The *New Orleans Picayune,* the most influential newspaper in the south's largest city, said:

> Time has convinced the country that the only way in which relief could be obtained was through a national law; that the present system of working children in mines and factories is abominable, is against every instinct of humanity today, and further that there is no truth in the claim that the southern mills, situated in the midst of cotton fields and with everything in their favor, can not compete with establishments a thousand miles away.[99]

Many manufacturers throughout the nation, those whose economic interests seemed most immediately involved, either supported the bill or remained silent. As the *New York Times* observed, they had for some time "been content — or discontent — to accept such restrictions as are inevitable and to do little more than call attention as they could to the unfairness of compelling them to compete with manufacturers still permitted to use child labor."[100] James Emery's warning about a vast increase of federal intervention in the economic order implicit in the Keating-Owen bill had failed to produce the hoped for response within the business community.

The Republican *New York Tribune,* representative of the New Nationalism brand of liberalism, summed up the basis for the national consensus when it described the measures as "in the non-partisan field — the field of social and economic progress."[101] It was another response to the felt needs of the times, another impulse in that current of reform striving, as William Allen White put it, "to lift men to higher things, to fuller enjoyment of the

---

[98] August 10, 1916, p. 6. The *Tribune* did not censure the southern senators because the states they represented had "no conception of what industrialism is or what it demands for the protection of the wage earner and the average human being." It endorsed Hughes for the presidency because Wilson's re-election would mean turning national affairs over to backward southerners.

[99] Quoted in extension of Representative Keating's remarks in the *Congressional Record,* 64th Cong., 1st Sess., Appendix, p. 1809.

[100] August 5, 1916, p. 8.

[101] August 10, 1916, p. 6.

fruits of civilization, to wider participation in the blessings of modern society." [102]

This impressive public and congressional consensus had evolved slowly, after many years of effort by a small group of local and national organizations that were dedicated to creating public interest in reforming child labor abuses. It had emerged, however, from an immensely larger and more significant national reform movement, which sought far-reaching social and economic readjustments in American life. This movement had captured the imagination and enlisted the enthusiasm of the vast majority of citizens.

Progressivism reached a climax during Wilson's first term, the Keating-Owen law being perhaps its greatest advance. Two circumstances, in particular, help to explain its passage. First, a distinct pattern of federal police power exercises had been developed. Social theories, favorable to national control, had evolved — as Elihu Root warned would happen — because the states had neglected community responsibilities and popular opinion unmistakably supported their implementation. Second, there had been a long period of experience and progress in state child labor legislation. By 1916 most of the states had established regulatory standards that approximated those of the Keating-Owen law. There were more fundamental progressive advances, for example, the Federal Reserve and Clayton Antitrust acts, but probably none evoked more pervasive public approval or greater depth of emotional commitment. [103]

---

[102] William Allen White, *The Old Order Changeth* (New York: Macmillan Co., 1909), p. 30.

[103] The National Committee's leaders took no exception to, and even encouraged, the popular notion that the Keating-Owen law was another emancipation proclamation, but they labored under no illusion that it would end child labor in America. To be sure, they thought it would go a long way toward eliminating industrial abuses (at least 150,000 children subject to the worst forms of exploitation would be immediately affected), but most of the child laborers were at work in other sectors of the economy. It was felt, however, that there would be a marked indirect effect upon these forms of exploitation and that the states would be influenced to raise the standards of their legislation, improve enforcement, and enact better school-attendance and other child welfare legislation. See "Twelfth Annual Report, N.C.L.C.," *Child Labor Bulletin* (November, 1916), p. 141.

4

Judge and Company: Raising the Test Case

The Decision to Initiate Test Litigation

After the passage of the Adamson Act, it was announced that the nation's railroads, which in company with other large business interests had bitterly opposed the enactment, would immediately institute proceedings in the federal courts, challenging its validity. Under the commerce power, Congress had established a mandatory eight-hour day for a major segment of American industry and had, crucially, temporarily adjusted wages. This was federal intervention into an area of labor relations that hitherto had been immune to national regulation; moreover, it took the form of emergency legislation, enacted in the face of a threatened, calamitous nation-wide strike after only cursory consideration in the two houses. The passage of the Keating-Owen bill, on the other hand, attracted less attention and there was no public notice that its constitutionality would be contested. Immediately after the Senate vote, however, the readers of the *Southern Textile Bulletin* were informed that the Executive Committee would undertake a court test.[1] Six weeks later, in mid-September of 1916, David Clark insisted — in the face of publicly expressed skepticism — that the statute would be carried to the Supreme Court.[2]

The Executive Committee's decision seemingly was inevitable. Having been defeated in Congress, the group could hardly fail to transfer the contest to the courts. Nevertheless, Clark later admitted that there had been substantial disagreement about the advisability of instituting legal proceedings. Three members, he stated, thought "there was no possibility of winning and only two

[1] *Southern Textile Bulletin* (August 10, 1916), p. 10.
[2] *Ibid.*, September 21, 1916, p. 10.

of them really thought we had any chance of winning."[3] The determining factors in the concurrence to proceed despite the internal division cannot be known with certainty, but Clark's tenacity and resolve to exhaust every means for defeating the operation of the law (characteristics shared by the two other members from North Carolina, Patterson and Ruffin) must surely have been significant and may well have been decisive.[4]

In addition, the long public debate about the constitutionality of federal child labor regulation and the fact that the Supreme Court had never reviewed a case that involved an exercise of the commerce power directly analogous to the Keating-Owen law gave grounds for hope. If the Court so chose, the statute could be distinguished from the legislation that had been upheld in previous police power decisions. With this possibility in mind, Clark assessed the probable alignment of the justices and interpreted the result as not definitely settling the matter against the Executive Committee.[5] Nevertheless, the legal challenge was undertaken with considerably less confidence than the attack the railway managers had launched, without the slightest hesitation, against the Adamson Act.

The Executive Committee's militant spirit had little counterpart in the southern textile industry, however. A large section of the mill-owning community did not condone test litigation. Some manufacturers were openly critical of Clark's plan, and many urged him to withdraw the case after proceedings were begun.[6] The overwhelming majority of manufacturers opposed the Keating-Owen law as inconvenient and possibly injurious, as an arbitrary interference in private economic rights, and as a portent of future interference that would be more difficult to resist as a result of the erosion of the protecting shield of states' rights.

---

3 *Ibid.*, June 6, 1918, p. 14; see also *ibid.*, May 18, 1922, p. 18, and March 4, 1926, p. 21.

4 In a memorial to Patterson in 1926, Clark stated: "There were many men who advised against any contest against the enactment of a Federal Child Labor Law, and I honestly believe that if it had not been for the determination of Patterson and Ruffin the cotton mills of the South would today be under the domination of agents of the U.S. Department of Labor. . . . " *Proceedings of the Twentieth Annual Conference of the Cotton Manufacturers' Association of North Carolina* (Charlotte: Observer Printing House, 1926), p. 77.

5 *Southern Textile Bulletin* (June 6, 1918), p. 14.

6 Clark later stated, in a summary issue of the *Bulletin*: "It was the opinion of 75 per cent of the cotton manufacturers and fully that per cent of the lawyers that it was useless to contest the constitutionality of the laws." *Ibid.*, May 18, 1922, p. 18, and March 4, 1926, p. 21.

Nevertheless, many mill owners considered court action to be ill advised and almost certainly destined to prove fruitless.[7] In their view, it could do no more than arouse additional antagonism against the industry. They were prepared, however grudgingly, to adjust their operations to the statute's requirements.[8]

The weight of their numbers notwithstanding, these man had no influence upon the Executive Committee's decision; Clark persisted in his efforts to institute test proceedings despite continued criticism from various mill spokesmen and from other southern interests. Although he did not represent the prevailing opinion within the cotton textile industry, he was free to serve it as he thought best. Throughout the litigation, Patterson and Ruffin vigorously supported Clark within the Executive Committee, and, together with other prominent manufacturers from North Carolina and South Carolina, they steadfastly supported him in public.[9] That the aggressively active opposition was largely confined to these two states speaks for itself: the Keating-Owen law threatened their child labor practices more than those of other states.

Seeking to justify the constitutional challenge, Clark charged that the Keating-Owen law was "in reality a bill to force the cotton mills of the South to conform to the ideas of agitators and competitors in other states."[10] Thereby, he flatly disclosed the fundamental reason for the Executive Committee's opposition: the belief that the statute was a discriminatory attack, originated outside the south, which directly endangered the southern textile manufacturers' control of their labor and their profits. A less parochial reason for continuing the struggle — the threat of increased

[7] Addressing the National Child Labor Committee's annual conference in 1916, Dr. George T. Winston, former president of the University of North Carolina, appraised the manufacturers' motives: "Many mill men — I believe a majority of them, probably three-fourths of them — are in favor of reform. But the minority raises a cry, a class cry, which arouses feelings and 'pride of profession' and rallies the mill men who then rally a lobby and fight legislation against the better sentiments of some of them, probably most of them. They promise to make the reformation themselves, and then they don't do it." "Child Labor in North Carolina," *Child Labor Bulletin* (May, 1916), pp. 71–72.

[8] Among the manufacturers who welcomed the legislation were the owners of some of the largest and most efficient cotton mills in the south. These men employed few, if any, child laborers (as defined by the statute), or did so only because they were compelled by competition. They felt that national child labor standards, like other progressive advances in labor relations, would prove advantageous to southern industry.

[9] *Southern Textile Bulletin* (May 18, 1922), p. 18.

[10] *Ibid.*, August 17, 1916, p. 10.

governmental control of the economy — was emphasized in Clark's broadsides for general public consumption. He dramatically portrayed an extreme form of this purported danger:

> If it is constitutional for the government to thus control the operation of industries in the sovereign states, it can take away from the States almost every power and every vestige of States Rights and Congress will control all our internal affairs. Already a bill has been prepared for introduction in Congress to prevent the interstate shipment of goods manufactured by persons who are paid less than a certain wage.[11]

By seeking to associate the Keating-Owen law with other supposedly projected and far-reaching encroachments upon economic liberties, Clark sought to divert attention from the nature of the cotton maufacturers' interests and to enlarge the number of persons who might come to believe that their own economic concerns were placed in jeopardy by such legislation.[12] Although charges of this nature did not recruit many adherents, they touched upon a sensitive area in American thinking, even during a period dominated by progressive ideas.

Securing Counsel and Financial Support

The first step in Clark's plan was to secure counsel of outstanding reputation and ability. As the son of a distinguished state jurist he had acquired intimate knowledge of judicial procedures, personnel, and tactics. In late September, 1916, the readers of the *Southern Textile Bulletin* were informed that negotiations were under way with a Philadelphia lawyer of national reputation, and, at the end of November, they were told that this man had been retained.[13] To describe the Philadelphian simply as a lawyer of national standing was a marked understatement. John G. Johnson, a brilliant corporation counsel, had been acknowledged for thirty years as the leader of the American bar, one of the first among the elite who — in Edward S. Corwin's scathing terms — had originated and shaped the American Bar Association into a "sort of juristic sewing circle for mutual education in the gospel of Laissez Faire." At the height of his powers he had argued and

11 *Ibid.*, August 16, 1917, p. 10.

12 At the time there was broad agreement that wage regulation constituted a more severe breach of economic freedom than the regulation of hours and other working conditions. Clark endeavored to nourish fears of such departures from liberty of contract by portraying extreme examples.

13 *Ibid.*, September 21 and November 30, 1916, p. 10.

won the Sugar Trust case,[14] contributing immeasurably to the creation of the twilight zone between federal and state regulation of commerce, and "from then on there was really no great case defended in which he did not lead." [15]

Clark could have made no better choice of counsel than the advocate whom the supreme bench had styled the "Knight of the American Bar." Clark, nevertheless, met opposition within the Executive Committee to retaining a "business lawyer," for some of his associates preferred a "political lawyer," former Senator Bailey of Texas. Bailey was regarded, even by progressive leaders in Congress, as an outstanding authority on constitutional law. Apparently, a compromise was effected, for Clark announced that if sufficient funds were available after the retention of the Philadelphian, an effort would be made to secure the services of the former senator.[16] Johnson, however, died in April, 1917, and, for reasons that were not disclosed, the Executive Committee did not retain Bailey.

After Johnson's death, Clark traveled to New York City, where he engaged the law firm of O'Brien, Boardman, Parker, and Fox. His reasons for choosing this firm, though Clark never disclosed them, are readily apparent. Junius Parker, a native North Carolinian, had practiced law in his home state before going to New York, where he became the assistant counsel and then general counsel for the American Tobacco Company. He had participated in the landmark antitrust suit in which the Supreme Court had declared that company a monopoly and ordered its dissolution,[17] and had there been associated as counsel with John G. Johnson. It is not surprising that Clark had high regard for the general counsel for one of the largest corporate enterprises in the south or that he recognized the advantage to be gained by employing such a notable Carolinian in the court of first instance.

Parker's firm, moreover, was one of the best-known corporate law organizations in the country. Its senior partner, Morgan J. O'Brien, was one of the select group of business lawyers who argued most of the important litigation heard by the Supreme Court.

[14] *United States v. E. C. Knight Co.,* 156 U.S. 1 (1895).

[15] Benjamin R. Twiss, *Lawyers and the Constitution* (Princeton: Princeton University Press, 1942), p. 209. Among these cases were *Northern Securities Co. v. United States,* 193 U.S. 197 (1904), *Standard Oil Co. v. United States,* 211 U.S. 1 (1911), *United States v. American Tobacco Co.,* 211 U.S. 106 (1911), and *Wilson v. New,* 243, U.S. 332 (1917).

[16] *Southern Textile Bulletin* (June 6, 1918, and September 21, 1916), pp. 14 and 10.

[17] *United States v. American Tobacco Co.,* 211 U.S. 106 (1911).

The great names who created the doctrine of substantive due process and had presided at its heyday were passing from the scene, but the Supreme Court bar still was dominated by a relatively small number of men. In his frequent appearances before the Court, O'Brien's arguments had the same force as Johnson's, but he lacked Johnson's practical inventiveness and consummate ability to shape the results of important constitutional litigation. Johnson had known the Supreme Court bench, the strengths and weaknesses of the justices, as had few other advocates.

O'Brien's business and bar associations were numerous and distinguished. He belonged to the boards of directors of many large financial organizations, including the Metropolitan Life Insurance Company and the Equitable Life Assurance Society, and was chairman of the board of several corporations. He had served for almost twenty years on the New York State Supreme Court, and in 1917 was president of the New York State Bar Association. When consideration is given to the two courts to which test litigation was destined to go, the federal district court in western North Carolina and the United States Supreme Court, the peculiar suitability of the New York firm, with its fortuitous combination of Parker and O'Brien, is easily seen. Its selection undoubtedly resulted from close scrutiny of all available counsel.

Clark's plan for raising the "considerable sums" that constitutional litigation inevitably requires was simplicity itself. The court fight was being undertaken to protect vital interests of the southern textile manufacturers; the mill owners, therefore, should pay for their own protection. The state cotton manufacturers' associations were first approached for funds, after which Clark sent several thousand letters to textile mills throughout the region and to selected individuals, explaining the planned litigation and soliciting contributions.[18] The lack of unanimity within the industry and the opposition to the test were evident in the responses to this and subsequent appeals by Clark. In mid-August, 1917, he wrote that "most of the mills responded promptly and some either gave more than was asked or voluntarily offered to send an additional check if necessary, [but] we are still short of the amount necessary to properly carry the test case to the United States Supreme Court."[19] His editorial, "Tight Wads and Slackers," was largely a violent harangue against those mill owners, apparently a substantial number, who had not contributed as requested. In

18 *Southern Textile Bulletin* (June 6, 1918), p. 15.
19 *Ibid.*, August 23, 1917, p. 10.

his own words, Clark had to "hammer hard" finally to get what he wanted, for he admitted that most of the manufacturers thought the fight was a lost cause.[20]

Several years later, Clark claimed he had succeeded in raising the necessary funds "because of the cotton manufacturers confidence in him," but the difficulties in securing adequate financial assistance lasted until the favorable decision in the *Dagenhart* case was announced. Shortly after the decision, Clark reported that, "it being necessary to raise $4,500 [obviously a substantial portion of the costs of litigation] to complete the payment of the attorneys who won . . . the contest, letters were sent first to the cotton mills of North Carolina and with few exceptions they responded promptly." [21] Following the court victory, the manufacturers generally were more ready to support Clark's self-defined services than earlier. Nevertheless, years later, in a memorial to Patterson, Clark said:

> It happened several times that I found it impossible to proceed without the assurance that funds would be available and invariably the answer of Sam Patterson was, "Go Ahead and if they do not give you the money, I will pay it myself." [22]

Selecting the Most Effective Form of Test Proceeding

Despite his death, John G. Johnson's advice strongly influenced the Executive Committee's action. In late August, 1916, Clark published portions of a letter he had received from a lawyer, who, although not identified, must have been Johnson. This extract comprises a practical guide to the art of creating an effective test case by which to raise an issue of "extraordinary importance." Clark was advised:

> No legal proceeding will lie until the bill is in operation. Some action must be taken under some provision of the bill so that a real and not a moot question is raised. A court, in order to pass upon any phase of it, must have before it an actual case, and if the measure is to be contested, the case should not only be carefully selected in order that the constitutional principle desired to be raised may be clearly presented, but I believe then that when

20 *Ibid.*, June 6, 1918, p. 14.
21 *Ibid.*, June 13, 1918, p. 14.
22 *Proceedings of the Twentieth Annual Conference of the Cotton Manufacturers' Association of North Carolina*, p. 77. Patterson was the owner of the largest cotton damask mill in the world and a man of considerable means.

the issue is raised, if possible, a judicial district should be selected in which the judge is a man of known courage. This is no case to try before a weak character.

It is very difficult to say how long it will take to bring this question to the Supreme Court of the United States. It would depend upon the circumstances of the case. The Facts might present an issue that admitted of an extraordinary remedy that could be taken by the shortest process to the Supreme Court. Thus the issue might be raised by the refusal to permit an inspector of the Department of Labor to enter a factory for the purpose of discharging the duty laid upon him under the bill, or it might be raised by the arrest of a factory manager or corporation officer, or the issue might possibly be raised on behalf of an operative threatened with discharge although this is a delicate and somewhat complex question. If the question went up to the Supreme Court on appeal from a conviction in a lower court, it might take from a year to two years, all depending upon the congestion of the calendar. If raised on an application for a writ to restrain an officer from entering a factory there might be [a] somewhat shorter proceeding. But it is almost impossible to say how long it would take to bring the matter to a final issue, for that is something that is not in the control of litigants or their counsel. The case, however, will be one of such extraordinary importance that the utmost care should be taken in choosing the circumstances and locality of jurisdiction.[23]

Just that much care, in fact, was exercised.

Three months later, Clark told his readers that a test case could not be instituted until the child labor law went into effect.[24] Johnson must have strongly advised against an anticipatory action which a court could declare moot and refuse to pass upon. During the winter, the test case of the Adamson Act was rushed to the Supreme Court. By early March, American entrance into the European war was close at hand; and a critical, nation-wide railway strike also seemed imminent, for the various roads had refused to comply with the statute when it took effect, on January 1. On March 15 the railway brotherhoods announced a general strike order, but two days later they postponed it for forty-eight hours, when the Council of National Defense appealed to both sides to consider the public interest. The following day, March 18, the railroad managers, under pressure from the President, conceded the workers' demands. The Supreme Court, impelled by the emer-

---

23 *Southern Textile Bulletin* (August 24, 1916), p. 10.
24 *Ibid.*, November 30, 1916, p. 10.

gency, delivered its approving decision twenty-four hours later, in *Wilson* v. *New*.[25]

Two weeks later, a conscience-laden Wilson rose before an extraordinary session of Congress "to lead this great peaceful people into war . . . civilization itself seeming to be in the balance." The nation was wrenched from its decade-long preoccupation with progressive reform and became absorbed in prosecuting a war to make the world safe for democracy. Liberal enthusiasm of the kind that characterized Wilson's first term — oriented almost entirely toward domestic reform — would not reappear until the fateful decade of the great depression.

During these months the National Committee concentrated on influencing the administration of the Keating-Owen law; everything, its leaders knew, depended upon how well the statute was enforced. The most important aspect of their endeavor involved close cooperation with the Advisory Board, which had been established under the act to work out operating regulations and procedures. With the nation's entrance into the war, a new phase of activities was undertaken. Efforts were made "to prevent child labor laws and compulsory education laws from being suspended or relaxed and other child welfare activities from being discontinued on the pretext of war necessity."[26] Emergency steps of this kind had been taken in several combatant countries, and various Americans, David Clark prominent among them, advocated similar steps in order to meet the manpower shortage.

From the time the Keating-Owen bill's passage was assured, the National Committee had assumed that test litigation would be instituted, but not until the statute had gone into effect. It awaited the challenge; the initiative lay with the Executive Committee — with David Clark. After the retention of O'Brien, Boardman, Parker, and Fox, the offensive was launched. At this starting point in litigation, as Paul Freund has aptly pointed out, the choice of lawsuit that is to be used is largely in the hands of counsel and their role is often striking. "Should a case be chosen which will present the issues narrowly or broadly? Should an all out contest be risked or should a more limited engagement be fought?"[27] Less cautious than John G. Johnson, the new counsel agreed to Clark's demand that an all-out contest be risked and that it be undertaken as soon as possible.

[25] 243 U.S. 332 (1917).

[26] *Child Labor Bulletin* (August, 1917), p. 86.

[27] Paul A. Freund, *On Understanding the Supreme Court* (Boston: Little, Brown and Co., 1949), p. 92.

In May and early June, Clark and Junius Parker met on several occasions to discuss the kind of case that would be most effective in raising the issues. According to Clark, it was realized that to await the prosecution of a mill for violating the statute "would take a long time and be disadvantageous." In order to obtain a ruling before the statute went into effect, it was decided to employ the form of action that Johnson had characterized as involving "a delicate and somewhat complex question." A scheme was evolved to seek an injunction on behalf of an operative who was employed in compliance with state laws but supposedly was threatened with discharge solely because of the federal statute, to restrain a mill from dismissing him.[28]

This procedure was patterned after the petition used in the Arizona Anti-Alien Law case, *Truax* v. *Raich*,[29] which the Supreme Court had decided two years before. A showing of threatened injury (denial of existing employment) under the requirements of a recently enacted state law had been the basis for requesting an injunction against the employer. Counsel for the employee had successfully argued that the state law was unconstitutional and that only by an equity proceeding could his client's rights be protected. A restraining order had been issued by the state court and upheld on appeal.

The differences between the Arizona case and the case that Clark meant to create were highly significant, however. The challenge to the Keating-Owen law was designed to restrain the enforcement of federal rather than state legislation — legislation, moreover, that was based on an explicit grant of congressional authority. Further, the Arizona statute had required, under the coercion of penalties, that employees be discharged, but the Keating-Owen law merely denied access, for thirty days, to interstate commerce for commodities manufactured in mills or factories that did not conform to the child labor provisions. The managers of industrial establishments could hire and fire whomever they chose, for employment itself was not made a criminal offense.[30]

28 *Southern Textile Bulletin* (June 6, 1918), p. 15.

29 239 U.S. 33 (1915).

30 Under the Arizona statute, 80 per cent of the employees of any concern doing business within the state had to be qualified electors or native-born citizens of the United States. The alien employee in question, Raich, was informed by his employer that, by reason of the law and because of "fear of the penalty," he would be discharged. Counsel filed a complaint against the attorney-general of Arizona and the county attorney upon the allegation that these officers would prosecute the employer unless he discharged Raich. The Supreme Court held that a public official who was about to enforce an un-

Finding a Judge and a Test Vehicle

After deciding to use the equity proceeding, the federal district court in western North Carolina was selected as the most auspicious in which to seek an injunction.[31] More precisely, the judge of this district was selected because he conformed admirably to Johnson's requirement of "a man of known courage." By this characterization Johnson meant a known partisan, a judge who was opposed to the progressive spirit of the times and predisposed to find the Keating-Owen law unconstitutional. As a consequence of the lawsuit decided upon, the choice of a jurist was limited to the four federal districts within the Carolinas. In two of these districts Clark's attorneys had reason to suspect that the justices were "weak characters," perhaps infected by the new jurisprudence of self-restraint. In the third district there was even greater reason for suspicion, because the judge had been appointed by the acknowledged leader of progressive reform, Woodrow Wilson. But there was no need to take chances; not even Johnson could have questioned James Edmund Boyd's "strength of character."

Boyd was that rarity in the post bellum South, a staunch and distinguished Republican. As a youth, he had served in the Confederacy, but soon afterward he was led by his conservative principles to attach himself to the party of the north. The patronage rewards for following his political convictions and renouncing what was becoming the "white man's" party were soon forthcoming. In 1880 he was appointed United States district attorney for the western district of North Carolina by President Hayes. When McKinley took office, in 1897, Boyd became Assistant Attorney General of the United States, and in 1900 he was named to the federal bench in North Carolina.

Boyd was a large, vigorous, handsome man.[32] He bore the stamp of his conservative persuasion proudly in 1917, mirroring an older America, that of Field and Fuller and McKinley. He was then seventy-two years old and had presided over the district court for nearly two decades. By temperament he was disinclined to restrain or moderate his personal views, and they found their way into his opinions. In sum, he was a lawyer of the old, conservative

---

constitutional statute could be enjoined, and ruled that plaintiff's right to this remedy was not affected by the fact that he was employed at will, holding that "the unjustified interference of third parties is actionable though the employment is at will." *Truax* v. *Raich*, 239 U.S. 33, 35–38.

[31] *Southern Textile Bulletin* (June 6, 1918), p. 15.

[32] See Aubrey Lee Brooks, *A Southern Lawyer* (Chapel Hill: University of North Carolina Press, 1950), pp. 37–39.

school, confirmed in his beliefs and the occupant of an entrenched position. Again, David Clark had chosen well.

With the choice of Boyd's jurisdiction as the extremely significant court of first instance, "it was found advisable," Clark later stated, to add further counsel. At the suggestion of W. C. Ruffin, Clark retained the firm of Manly, Hendren, and Womble of Winston-Salem, North Carolina, who were counsel for the R. J. Reynolds Tobacco Company.[33] The senior member of this firm, and one of the most active participants in the litigation, was Clement Manly, another member of the relatively small group of influential leaders of the American Bar Association during its early doctrine-creative years. Still later, it was thought expedient to add William P. Bynum, of Greensboro, North Carolina, to the impressive assemblage of legal talent. Judge Bynum, as he was known locally because of his service on the superior court of North Carolina, had acquired a national reputation and was generally considered one of the ablest southern counsels practicing before the Supreme Court. During his career he served for three years on the executive committee of the American Bar Association and was president of the all-important council for four years.[34]

Clark did not say why additional counsel was retained, but the facts speak for themselves. All were especially prominent lawyers who must have known Boyd for years, both in the courtroom and without. They could expect a friendly reception before his bench and they knew how to appeal to him most effectively. In short, Clark exercised the utmost care to ensure that the responsiveness he anticipated from Boyd would be forthcoming.

Next, Clark toured the western district in search of the "perfect combination of factors." After weeks of intensive effort, he "prepared" four potential test cases, "which were submitted to the attorneys at a conference in New York and that of *Dagenhart* vs. *Fidelity Manufacturing Company* was found to have the best points and was adopted."[35] By preparation, it appears, Clark meant that in each instance he secured the cooperation of the

---

[33] *Southern Textile Bulletin* (March 4, 1926), p. 21. The fact that counsel retained by the two giant tobacco corporations — American and R. J. Reynolds — were among the attorneys for the plaintiff led some southern newspapers to speculate that the tobacco industry was behind the test case or at least aiding the cotton manufacturers, which Clark denied. *Ibid.*, September 6, 1917, p. 10.

[34] See *North Carolina, Rebuilding an Ancient Commonwealth* (6 vols.; New York: American History Society, 1928), III, 3–5.

[35] *Southern Textile Bulletin* (May 18, 1922), p. 18.

child operative, his parents, and the mill in which the child was employed.

This was certainly true in the instance chosen for litigation. The Dagenharts, a father and two minor sons, and the employing concern, the Fidelity Manufacturing Company, were mere figureheads. Clark stressed that it had been necessary to induce the elder Dagenhart to permit his name to be used and that Dagenhart had had no intention of instituting legal proceedings until he had been approached.[36] What form of persuasion proved sufficient is unknown, but apparently neither Dagenhart nor his sons — who later were highly criticial of the constitutional rights of labor that had been secured for them[37] — received financial compensation. The Fidelity Manufacturing Company, Clark made plain, also was merely a facilitating agent.[38] A small cotton mill in Charlotte, it had few employees and its financial position was so insecure that it could hardly have undertaken the costly constitutional litigation.

The circumstances of the Dagenhart children were almost ideal for the test litigation because they illustrated the principal differences between the standards prescribed by the Keating-Owen law and those applied in North Carolina. The older child, Reuben, was fifteen years of age and was employed at piece rates. Under North Carolina law he could work in an industrial establishment for eleven hours a day and up to sixty hours a week, but under the federal statute his daily hours would be restricted to eight, with a corresponding reduction of his income. The young child, John, was thirteen. Under North Carolina law he was permitted to work the same periods as his brother; but under the federal statute he would no longer be permitted to work at all.[39]

In short, David Clark followed John G. Johnson's advice; he carefully chose all the elements of a strong test case: the issue, the judge, the particular circumstances, and even the parties. He left nothing to chance.

[36] *Ibid.*, June 6, 1918, p. 15.
[37] See Lowell Mellett, "Reuben Dagenhart in 1923," *Labor* (November 17, 1923), reprinted in Grace Abbott, *The Child and the State* (Chicago: University of Chicago Press, 1938), pp. 515–16.
[38] *Southern Textile Bulletin* (June 6, 1918), p. 15.
[39] The North Carolina statute of 1907, which prescribed a thirteen-year minimum-age standard, exempted twelve-year-old children who were classified as apprentices. In practice, this exemption tended to mean an effective minimum age of twelve. The standard work shift consisted of eleven hours Monday through Friday and a five-hour half day on Saturday, or a total of sixty hours — the legal maximum for minors and women.

Personal Rights and Associational Virtue

One of the consequences of government-by-lawsuit prior to 1937 was that private litigants often raised constitutional issues of great significance in actions whose form was primarily private.[40] Moreover, then as now, examination of the parties to the record seldom gives a real clue to the actual parties to the proceeding.[41] Both of these matters are illustrated in the complaint that Clark's lawyers prepared. The names of the plaintiffs, the three Dagenharts, gave no indication of the actual identity of those who originated the proceeding. Of greater significance, the constitutional issue was brought forward in a form that was almost wholly private. In short, a direct challenge to the exercise of one of the great general powers vested in Congress was undertaken as a lawsuit to protect personal rights that were vague at best — a lawsuit in which the United States was not even identified as a party.

How did Clark understand and justify this aspect of his activities? Seven years later, in testimony before a congressional committee that was holding hearings on proposed child labor amendments, he admitted creating the *Dagenhart* case to test the constitutionality of the Keating-Owen law (as well as two subsequent cases, to test the second federal child labor law), and he vigorously defended these actions. The following colloquy, which occurred near the end of a lengthy interrogation, furnishes an insight into his thinking. After quoting from Clark's editorial that recounted the necessity for persuading the elder Dagenhart to lend his name to the injunction application, Representative Perlman of New York asked:

> You seemed to have some difficulty at that time to get any employee to test this law, did you not?
>
> MR. CLARK: Yes, sir. Mr. Chairman, it is the right of any citizen of the United States to test any law of the United States, and I do not think I should be held up before this committee as hav-

[40] The seeking of partisan judges to hear litigation challenging federal legislation has been noticeably changed since passage of the Judiciary Act of 1937. A three-judge court is now required to pass upon an application for an injunction to restrain the enforcement of a congressional enactment. Thus litigants are no longer able to "shop" for a promising court of first instance, and they have been deprived of the capacity to raise litigation in essentially private suits.

[41] See Freund, *On Understanding the Supreme Court*, pp. 82–83, and Oliver P. Field, "Judicial Review as an Instrument of Government," Vol. I, *Selected Essays on Constitutional Law*, Association of American Law Schools (4 vols.; Chicago: The Foundation Press, 1938), pp. 734–36. *Selected Essays on Constitutional Law* will be abbreviated *S.E.C.L.*

ing committed an improper act in carrying a law, inflicted upon my State, to the United States Supreme Court, where the Supreme Court held I was entirely correct.

MR. PERLMAN: You did not test it; you got some one to permit his name to be used to test it.

MR. CLARK: I prepared the test case; yes.

MR. PERLMAN: But you did not test it yourself; you got someone who did not want to test it to bring the action.

MR. CLARK: I prepared the best test case I could find, because I wanted to have the thing declared unconstitutional. I had a perfect right to do it; I proceeded along legal lines, and I resent the insinuation I was doing anything improper.[42]

In Clark's view, the fact that the Supreme Court had declared both child labor statutes unconstitutional apparently removed any strain of impropriety attached to the several friendly, and in two instances technically questionable, proceedings. Two decades earlier, Parker had similarly justified the propriety of the friendly procedure that had been employed in another extraordinarily important case, *Pollock* v. *Farmers' Loan and Trust Company*,[43] the great income tax controversy. "Courts try cases on the record," Parker wrote, "and there is not a case which holds that they must go behind the record and determine the motives of each of the controverting parties." [44] Parker seemed to contend that any suit that ostensibly raised a justiciable issue had to be accepted by the courts — certainly an attractive doctrine to a laissez faire advocate who welcomed judicial intervention.

The Proceedings of the Cotton Manufacturers' Association of North Carolina also are instructive.[45] At the seventeenth annual convention, held in 1923 (the first meeting after the Supreme Court declared the child labor tax invalid), Nathan Williams, James Emery's law partner, addressed the delegates. The N.A.M. spokesman-by-proxy complimented his listeners for their support of test litigation and developed a broad interpretation of what their action had accomplished. He quoted Tocqueville's well-

---

[42] Proposed Child Labor Amendments to the Constitution of the United States, Hearings before the Committee on the Judiciary, U.S. House of Representatives, 68th Cong., 2d Sess. (Washington, D.C.: Government Printing Office, 1924), p. 247.

[43] 158 U.S. 601 (1895).

[44] Junius Parker, "The Supreme Court and Its Constitutional Duty and Power," *American Law Review* (May–June, 1896), pp. 362–63.

[45] These proceedings document the close relationship that existed between the Executive Committee and the North Carolina association. To many persons it must have seemed that the committee was no more than the association's instrument, but Clark always maintained his freedom of action.

known statement praising the capacity of free associations to save the common liberties in a democratic society and applied this famous image of associational virtue to the textile manufacturers' support of Clark.

> What would have happened with respect to that unsound and un-constitutional statute . . . that attempted to control the labor of minors in mines and factories if it had not been for the North Carolina Cotton Manufacturers Association? You defended your rights and the rights of the country. A man may say that it will cost him $5,000 to prosecute a suit to declare illegal an unsound enactment or unlawful restriction upon his activities and he pockets his loss and lets Government get its tentacles around his business. Individually, possibly he cannot afford that, but the collective manufacturers of North Carolina can put a halt on that sort of thing and pick one of their number who seems best fitted to shoulder the litigation and go to bat for them and stay until it is finished, and by defending his rights against encroachments of government, save the common liberties of the country.[46]

The question whether Tocqueville would have found this use of voluntary association a praiseworthy one is open to serious debate. Tocqueville, it will be recalled, was particularly apprehensive about the creation of a harsh new aristocracy by the growth of manufacturing. It is doubtful, also, that many of the assembled mill men had previously understood that Clark's attempts to defeat federal child labor legislation was a patriotic service that sought far more than the protection of their economic interests.

The Dagenhart Complaint

On August 1, one month before the Keating-Owen law was to go into effect, the officials of the Fidelity Manufacturing Company posted a copy of the statute on the firm's premises and notified their employees that, after August 31, none of them would be allowed to work in contravention of its provisions. A week later, on August 9, the complaint prepared by Clark's lawyer was filed, under the name of the elder Dagenhart, on his own behalf and on that of his two sons, as next friend.[47] The Fidelity Manufacturing Company and William C. Hammer, the United States district

[46] *Proceedings of the Seventeenth Annual Conference of the Cotton Manufacturers' Association of North Carolina,* pp. 33–34.

[47] *Roland H. Dagenhart, and Reuben Dagenhart and John Dagenhart v. Fidelity Manufacturing Company and William C. Hammer,* North Carolina District Court of the United States, in *Transcript of Record, Hammer v. Dagenhart,* Supreme Court of the United States, October Term, 1918 (Washington, D.C.: Government Printing Office, 1917).

attorney for western North Carolina, were named as defendants. The complaint charged that, although the two minors were employed in strict compliance with the laws of North Carolina, the younger minor had been informed that he would be discharged September 1, and the older minor had been informed that his hours would be curtailed to eight each day. These actions would be taken solely by reason of the federal statute, it was charged, for the officers of the defendant company feared to incur the penalties provided if it was violated. The petition alleged that the threatened actions would deprive the elder Dagenhart of his vested rights, inasmuch as he was entitled to the services of his minor sons and to the enjoyment of any compensation arising from labors he directed them to render. It was further alleged that he was a man of small means and that the receipt of such compensation was essential to the comfortable support, indeed the very subsistence, of his family.[48] (The irony of the petition apparently struck few persons at the time. A prayer to preserve the work opportunities of an obviously poor man's minor sons was presented by a distinguished group of nationally known corporation lawyers, the payment of whose fees would have necessitated the labor, practically in perpetuity, of the two youthful cotton mill operatives supposedly concerned.)

After the assertion of Dagenhart's rights, the complaint charged that the Keating-Owen law was unconstitutional and unenforceable because (1) it was not a regulation of commerce such as Congress was empowered to make; (2) it attempted to regulate conditions of manufacture, an area beyond the powers delegated to Congress; (3) it usurped powers reserved to the states by the Tenth Amendment; and (4) its enforcement would deprive the plaintiffs of their liberty and property without due process of law, in violation of the Fifth Amendment. The petition prayed that the statute be ruled unconstitutional, that the Fidelity Manufacturing Company be permanently enjoined from taking the threatened action against the two minors, and that District Attorney Hammer be permanently enjoined from enforcing the statute against the company or from instituting proceedings against it.

The complaint sought to justify the use of an equity proceeding.

> Plaintiffs are without adequate remedy at law in the premises, and only in a suit of this nature and by the injunctive processes of this Court can they be fully protected in the enjoyment of their property and rights as aforesaid; the granting of the injunc-

[48] *Ibid.*, pp. 2, 3.

tive process as hereinafter prayed will prevent a multiplicity of
suits and prosecutions, and the questions here involved can be
adequately determined only in a suit of this nature.[49]

These remarkable contentions hardly squared with the facts. The
last was wholly fallacious, and those preceding were almost equally
unfounded. The denial of an injunction would not have ex-
hausted the plaintiff's legal protections. The existence of the asserted rights was questionable, and there was no guarantee that
issuance of an injunction would settle the central issues. Nevertheless, Judge Boyd ordered the Fidelity Manufacturing Company and District Attorney Hammer to show cause, within twenty
days (the mandatory waiting period in federal equity proceedings), why a series of injunctions should not be issued pursuant
to the plea, or the bill was to be taken *pro confesso*. The defendants were ordered to appear before Boyd on the twentieth day to
make answer and receive his judgment.[50]

By filing the complaint when they did, Clark's lawyers skillfully exploited the advantages that adhere to those who originate
litigation. The timing ensured that argument of the case would
begin three days before the Keating-Owen law was to take effect.
Clark's compelling desire for a judgment before the statute became operative was virtually assured. In addition, the imminence
of the threatened prejudicial action against the Dagenhart children would tend to obscure the contrived character of the complaint, which was especially important. Boyd's predilections made
it extremely unlikely that he would inquire into the existence of
a genuine controversy; but an attack upon the unusual character
of the petition, then thought probable, would have to be answered.
In that event, a plausible answer was possible, if "the facts" were
accepted on their face.

Commenting on analogous situations, Field pointed out that
the "practice of permitting private parties to take the initiative
in raising questions of constitutional power . . . leaves to the
whim of the individual the determination of the time when such
questions shall be raised and settled";[51] and this fact has considerable importance, because the timing of litigation may decisively
affect the results.[52] Thus Field emphasized that the party initiat-

49 *Ibid.*, p. 5.
50 *Ibid.*, pp. 9–10.
51 Field, *Judicial Review*, p. 737.
52 See Thomas Reed Powell, "The Judiciality of Minimum Wage Legislation," *S.E.C.L.*, I, 554–60. Powell discusses the effect that the composition of

ing litigation as a test of governmental power gains inherent advantages, which must be viewed as defects when seen from another side, that the public, and in light of the fact that the lawsuit is being used as an instrument of political conflict.

The Problem Facing the Justice Department

Judge Boyd's orders were served on District Attorney Hammer on August 10, and he immediately communicated with the Department of Justice in Washington, providing the first information about the test case.[53] At this juncture in the litigation, the initiative shifted to the Attorney General and his assistants. A major problem of strategy confronted them: whether to accept the Dagenhart challenge on its merits, as a means of settling the constitutional issue, or to pursue Fabian tactics until a more auspicious moment for adjudication arrived.[54]

The adoption of the former policy would lead to efforts to secure a prompt hearing before the Supreme Court, as had happened in *Wilson* v. *New*.[55] With war imminent, the public interest had required an authoritative determination rather than uncertainty, and the Justice Department had cooperated with counsel for the railroads in rushing the litigation to the Court. The adoption of the latter policy would lead to efforts to delay a definitive judgment. The public advantage would best be served by waiting for the appearance of a more favorable form of test case with which to defend constitutionality, a change in the temper or composition of the Court, or the withering of resistance as the opponents of the legislation came to live with it.

When the circumstances were analyzed, the Justice Department concluded that the more promising alternative was to accept the complaint and to attempt to expedite an early Supreme Court hearing.[56] Because the only significant opposition to the Keating-Owen law had come from the southern mill owners, it had been assumed that they would initiate constitutional litigation, but, despite Clark's editorial comments, the Dagenhart petition caught the Justice Department unprepared. Officials had anticipated a se-

the Supreme Court and the timing of litigation may have upon the determination of closely controverted constitutional issues.

[53] W. C. Hammer to Attorney General Thomas W. Gregory, August 10, 1917, Justice Department File, *Hammer* v. *Dagenhart*, National Archives, Washington, D.C.

[54] Freund, *On Understanding the Supreme Court*, pp. 109–10.

[55] 243 U.S. 332 (1917).

[56] Memorandum for the Attorney General, August 14, 1917, Justice Department File, *Hammer* v. *Dagenhart*.

ries of lawsuits, based upon prosecutions for violations, once the statute went into effect.[57] But they were denied the opportunity to choose among lawsuits and could not foresee whether or not later litigation would prove more favorable to the defense of the statute. More important, the widespread interest in having the constitutional issue decided as soon as possible, and the expectation that the Court would review the legislation sympathetically, settled the matter. Despite the questionable aspects of the complaint, nothing could be gained by assailing its propriety.

The interested reform groups, pleased with the Justice Department's decision, urged that special government counsel be designated. Because of "the great importance of the action" and "the peculiar character of Judge Boyd's mind," the department needed little encouragement.[58] A. J. McKelway, speaking for the National Committee, suggested to the Attorney General, Thomas W. Gregory, that Thomas I. Parkinson was eminently qualified for the task because of his thorough study of the constitutional questions, his participation in drafting the bill, his presentations before the congressional committees, and his assistance in formulating the administrative regulations. This suggestion was immediately accepted and Parkinson was given a commission as a special Assistant Attorney General.[59] No man in America was more familiar with the constitutional justification for the Keating-Owen law.[60]

Several days later, Secretary of Labor William B. Wilson, at the suggestion of Julia Lathrop, wrote to the Attorney General and requested that Roscoe Pound, Dean of the Harvard Law School, be retained.[61] It was urgent and important, Lathrop argued, that the child labor law be defended by a constitutional authority of national reputation, one who was versed in industrial legislation and skilled in trial work. Parkinson might not be a match for the prominent attorneys on the other side, she implied.[62] Gregory

[57] Thomas I. Parkinson, "The Federal Child Labor Law Decision," *Child Labor Bulletin* (August, 1918), p. 89.

[58] Memorandum for the Attorney General.

[59] "Thirteenth Annual Report, N.C.L.C.," September 30, 1917, p. 3.

[60] In March, 1917, Nathan W. MacChesney, a Chicago lawyer, then president of the Illinois State Bar Association, offered to represent the National Committee's position before the Supreme Court (as Louis D. Brandeis had earlier assisted the National Consumers' League) but the trustees took no action on his offer. "Minutes of the Board of Trustees, N.C.L.C.," March 30, 1917.

[61] W. B. Wilson to T. W. Gregory, August 18, 1917, Justice Department File, *Hammer* v. *Dagenhart*.

[62] Julia Lathrop to W. B. Wilson, August 23, 1917, *ibid.*

had run out of funds, but Pound offered his services without compensation. This offer was quickly accepted, and Pound too was commissioned a special Assistant Attorney General.[63]

A prominent leader in the developing school of sociological jurisprudence, Pound was its chief spokesman within the universities. His writings advanced the thesis that the law was continuously evolving and that the judicial process was creative in nature. There had to be "conscious human effort to shape and so to improve the law," Pound wrote. Philosophical and sociological jurists ought, by interpretation, to adjust "the legal system to the needs of the country." [64] No man in America more clearly represented the current progressive spirit in the field of the law. It was fitting that Pound should help defend one of the satutes that climaxed the progressive movement.

On appeal to the Supreme Court, the Solicitor General, John W. Davis, one of the truly outstanding advocates to hold that office,[65] defended the Keating-Owen law. Before joining Wilson's administration, Davis had twice been elected to the House of Representatives from West Virginia and had practiced law in that state with notable success. He left the post of Solicitor General in September, 1918, to become the United States Ambassador to Great Britain. After his government service, terminated by the Republication triumph of 1920, Davis became a member of a leading New York law firm, Stetson, Jennings, and Russell, and represented the J. P. Morgan financial interests. He was elected president of the American Bar Association, and in 1924 he was the compromise candidate of the Democratic party for President of the United States.

The legal representatives of the nation compared favorably with the formidable array of leading constitutional lawyers Clark had assembled.

Laissez Faire Constitutionalism and Progressive Jurisprudence

On August 27 the Fidelity Manufacturing Company dutifully fulfilled its part in the proceeding by filing an answer to the Dagenhart petition.[66] This reply affirmed that the company would

[63] T. W. Gregory to Roscoe Pound, August 23, 1917, *ibid.*

[64] Roscoe Pound, "Courts and Legislation," *American Political Science Review* (August, 1913), pp. 369, 372.

[65] See John P. Frank, *Marble Palace* (New York: Alfred A. Knopf, 1958), p. 95.

[66] *Transcript of Record, Hammer* v. *Dagenhart*, p. 14.

comply with the provisions of the Keating-Owen law unless enforcement was prevented, presumably by a judicial restraining
order. Fidelity was never heard from again, for its role in the
legal drama had come to an end. From the beginning, however,
its officials had been deeply interested in having the child labor
law declared unconstitutional. Therefore, it was predictable that
the company would neither participate in oral argument nor
appeal from a destructive decision in the district court. Because
the government had been made a party to the action, however,
in the person of District Attorney Hammer, the company's lack
of adversary interest did not impair the defense of the Keating-
Owen law.

On August 29, Hammer filed the expected dismissal motion for
the government; plaintiffs lacked legal standing because the Keating-Owen law was plainly constitutional, he stated.[67] But Boyd
rejected the motion and counsel got down to the business at hand.
At the outset, both sides agreed to narrow argument and decision
in the case to the single issue of constitutionality,[68] which disposed of questions of fact as well as technicalities of procedure.[69]
In effect, counsel and bench abandoned the pretense that the suit
concerned the private rights of the Dagenharts and ignored the
question of whether or not a justiciable controversy existed. Despite the apprehensions of Clark's lawyers, Parkinson, Pound,
and Hammer evidenced no interest in challenging the unusual
character of the proceeding.[70] The agreement reflected the Justice Department's desire to avoid the delays that frequently attend lower court proceedings, and nothing could have served
Clark's purposes better. There no longer was any possibility that
inquiry into the nominal object of the suit might prevent an
immediate judgment on the validity of the statute.

The Executive Committee's counsel fashioned their attack on
the Keating-Owen law out of the same doctrinal underpinnings
of laissez faire that Emery, Kitchin, and the other congressional opponents of the statute had used in their unsuccessful efforts to
prevent its passage.[71] Junius Parker elaborated upon the principal

67 *Ibid.*

68 A. J. McKelway to T. W. Gregory, September 3, 1917, Justice Department File, *Hammer v. Dagenhart.*

69 Parkinson, "The Federal Child Labor Law Decision," pp. 89–90.

70 *Southern Textile Bulletin* (September 6, 1917), p. 10.

71 Although a verbatim transcript of argument does not exist, numerous
sources make possible a fairly full reconstruction of the lengthy legal debate,
which extended over three days. These sources include a fifteen-page account
McKelway sent Attorney General Gregory, Hammer's report to Gregory,

charges set forth in the complaint.[72] His argument was patterned after John G. Johnson's successful contention in the Sugar Trust case, that manufacturing was not part of interstate commerce and that, consequently, congressional authority did not extend to productive activities. In this way the Tenth Amendment was invoked, as it had been so often in the past, to preserve a twilight zone for free enterprise — a region that, despite the explicit holding in the *Hoke* case, neither state nor federal authority could reach. It followed that the child labor law exceeded the powers of Congress and invaded the legitimate sphere of the states.

Bynum's argument centered on the nature of child-made goods. Congress had power to close the channels of interstate commerce to articles that were injurious to public health, morals, or safety, but it possessed no such power over articles that were not inherently injurious.[73] Thus Bynum acknowledged the expansion of congressional regulatory activities of a police power character under the authority of the commerce clause; however, his presentation sought to impose a limitation on this development, distinguishing harmful from non-harmful articles, without regard for prior conditions of manufacture or for subsequent use. Again, the doctrine was not original, having been adapted from the argument made by William D. Guthrie, the losing counsel in the Lottery case.[74] Manly and Hendren, who also appeared for the Executive Committee, merely rephrased familiar contentions against the child labor bill.[75]

Pound led off on the government side, and Hammer, too, argued for constitutionality. Both men followed the general lines of the brief that Parkinson had drafted and submitted to the Justice Department for approval before it had been sent to Judge Boyd.[76] Parkinson, however, presented the most important argument for the government; the decision to give him major responsibility for the defense had been made in a Justice Department

---

Parkinson's brief for the government, correspondence in the Justice Department File, newspaper stories, and additional secondary materials. Indeed, much more information is available about this argument than about oral argument before the Supreme Court in any of the child labor cases.

[72] A. J. McKelway to T. W. Gregory, September 3, Justice Department File, *Hammer* v. *Dagenhart*, and *Greensboro Daily News*, September 1, 1917, p. 1.

[73] *New York Times*, September 1, 1917, p. 16, and A. J. McKelway to T. W. Gregory.

[74] *Champion* v. *Ames*, 188 U.S. 321 (1904); see also Twiss, *Lawyers and the Constitution*, p. 220.

[75] A. J. McKelway to T. W. Gregory.

[76] *Ibid.*

conference on August 25, the day after Pound had received his commission.[77] Parkinson's argument paralleled the testimony he had presented to the Senate and House committees the year before.[78] He admitted the pioneering character of the Keating-Owen law but confidently defended it as being well within the contours of constitutional authority. The arguments advanced against the statute, he insisted, had been repudiated by the most recent decisions of the Supreme Court or had never been countenanced by it. At Boyd's request he discussed the motives that underlay the passage of the statute.[79] He acknowledged that Congress had sought to establish federal child labor regulation but said this had been qualified so that it prohibited only the shipment in interstate commerce of designated products for stipulated periods of time after manufacture. It had not directly attempted to outlaw abusive practices, for this was beyond its authority, nor had it tried to arrogate the police powers of the states.[80]

Pound also had sought to convince the aging jurist that the Keating-Owen law accorded with constitutional principles. Congressional authority over interstate commerce was unlimited, he argued, as long as its exercise met the judicial standard of reasonableness. The method selected by Congress — after careful consideration — to remedy social problems created by changed industrial conditions could hardly be termed arbitrary.[81] Pound, however, purposefully stopped short of a discussion of motives; the only relevant consideration for the court was that enumerated congressional authority had been exercised for an explicitly national purpose.[82] Boyd, who paid close attention to Pound's argument, seemed impressed by having one of the most distinguished legal scholars in the country appear before him. Nevertheless, neither Pound's nor Parkinson's efforts to convert him to the creative need to accommodate law to new circumstances had any effect. Nor was this result unexpected.

The period in the courtroom, former Associate Justice Rob-

---

77 "Thirteenth Annual Report, N.C.L.C.," p. 3.

78 "Minutes of the Board of Trustees, N.C.L.C.," October 4, 1917; A. J. McKelway to T. W. Gregory; and W. C. Hammer to T. W. Gregory, August 31, 1917, Justice Department File, *Hammer v. Dagenhart.*

79 *New York Times,* September 1, 1917, p. 16; A. J. McKelway to T. W. Gregory, and W. C. Hammer to T. W. Gregory.

80 Parkinson, "The Federal Child Labor Law Decision," p. 91, and A. J. McKelway to T. W. Gregory.

81 Paul Sayre, *The Life of Roscoe Pound* (Iowa City: State University of Iowa Press, 1948), pp. 217–18, and A. J. McKelway to T. W. Gregory.

82 A. J. McKelway to T. W. Gregory.

ert H. Jackson once said, "is utterly inadequate to educate an uninformed judge or to overcome old convictions or predilections, or to win a convert to a new position. Success in such an enterprise is apt to be accidental or the result of predetermination."[83] Jackson was commenting on argument before the Supreme Court, where the period allotted to counsel is usually shorter than in the lower federal courts, but his observations apply with equal, perhaps greater, force to the proceedings of the latter. Neither Parkinson nor Pound was able to sway Boyd's mind, for it was closed.

The Judgment of the Court

Judge Boyd's decision, announced on August 31, went against the constitutionality of the Keating-Owen law, but he did not commit his reasons to writing, either then or later. This meant, among other things, that he was not required to cite the applicable precedents and that his contribution to the record consisted solely of his judgment and subsequent orders to the defendants. It was a severe breach of judicial canons for a district judge, sitting alone, to rule so cavalierly upon such important issues, and another of Justice Jackson's generalizations is very much to the point.

> The district courts of the United States are not institutional in their proceedings as much as they are personal. Each such court is an individual, in fact, with a life tenure and independence of every other district court. The district judges . . . include at all times a wide range of abilities, experiences, party affiliations and loyalties, local connections, and economic views and prejudices. A litigant may often exercise a good deal of choice as to the judge or judges who first hear his challenge to an act of Congress. The lower court thus settled upon admits or excludes evidence, expedites or delays proceedings, finds the facts, makes the first decision on the law, and controls provisional and temporary remedies.[84]

The events of the Dagenhart litigation so strikingly illustrate many of these observations that Jackson might have written with this case in mind.

Boyd was gratified by Parkinson's candor, he said when he rendered his decision. The admission that Congress had tried to regulate local conditions within the states narrowed the contro-

---

[83] *The Struggle for Judicial Supremacy* (New York: Alfred A. Knopf, 1941), p. 301.
[84] *Ibid.*, pp. 302–03.

versy to a single issue: "Can Congress do by indirection that which it undoubtedly cannot do directly?" To which he answered: "Congress can regulate trade among the States, but not the internal conditions of labor." Although Boyd emphasized that this judgment rested upon his interpretation of the constitutional limitations upon congressional power,[85] the proposition was mere dictum, as he must have known. Writing in the *New Republic*, Edward S. Corwin dismissed the proposition and found that the decision turned

> either upon the assumption that courts are entitled to pass upon the propriety of the motives of Congress in enacting legislation brought up for review, or that Congress may not exercise its powers when its doing so will affect matters controllable by the states. The latter proposition is absurd — by it Congressional power would be kept in perpetual refrigeration; and the former proposition has been repeatedly rejected by the Court.[86]

Shifting to another supposed ground of unconstitutionality, Boyd spoke for some time about the right of the progenitor to control the behavior of his progeny and warned about social legislation that placed children in the hands of the law or the police.[87] Then he condemned the Keating-Owen law as a deprivation of substantive rights without due process, in violation of the Fifth Amendment, but this discovery eluded even the majority of the Supreme Court, which sustained his decision. And well it might, for Boyd's finding came down to the proposition that Dagenhart's use of his children was an extension of freedom of contract. What is more, that liberty was treated as an isolated human possession, a property largely beyond the domain of social control.

Boyd advanced pure absurdities in further comments. The act, he said, was arbitrary because it would prohibit a thirteen-year-old boy who was stranded in Greensboro from working to secure funds for travel home, and it might sanction another statute that would prohibit a bastard child from traveling on interstate carriers.[88] Although this parade of horrors had no relevance for the litigation at hand, Boyd conjured it up as further justification for his efforts to save the nation from itself. In addition, he hinted at his readiness to administer further relief. He was doubtful, he

---

[85] *New York Times*, September 1, 1917, p. 16.

[86] "Validity of the Child Labor Act," *New Republic* (September 15, 1917), p. 186.

[87] A. J. McKelway to T. W. Gregory, and "Thirteenth Annual Report, N.C.L.C.," p. 3.

[88] *Ibid.*

said, about the wisdom of "too much" child labor legislation.[89] By this reservation, which also had no relevance for the disposition of the case, Boyd suggested that he disapproved of too many or too elaborate regulatory measures. David Clark understood his meaning.

The Response to Boyd's Holding

After the recital of the "plain terms" that condemned the Keating-Owen law, Boyd granted the relief prayed for in the Dagenhart peition.[90] The Fidelity Manufacturing Company was permanently enjoined from discharging either of the Dagenhart children or curtailing their hours of labor. In turn, District Attorney Hammer, his assistants, and his successors, were permanently enjoined from enforcing the provisions of the statute and from instituting any prosecution required under it within the western district of North Carolina. These orders temporarily arrested the enforcement of the child labor statute within Boyd's jurisdiction; however, everyone understood that, like the rulings of other lower courts in such cases, the decision was inconclusive.[91] Both sides henceforth would bend every effort to obtain a conclusive decision from the Supreme Court, and as soon as possible. Before leaving Greensboro, Parkinson and Pound, together with Grace Abbott (chief of the Child Labor Division of the Children's Bureau) and A. J. McKelway, told reporters that special efforts would be made to hasten an appeal.[92] Meanwhile, in Washington, a spokesman for Attorney General Gregory announced that the Justice Department considered Judge Boyd's decision merely a vehicle for getting the legal question before the Court, where officials confidently expected the action of Congress would be sustained.[93]

There was dissension, however, in the party of interested persons who traveled north that night, although it may have been unspoken. Pound soon wrote to Gregory, complaining that

> Through an unhappy misunderstanding, the government did not present a consistent case. At the [Justice Department conference] the District Attorney and I understood that we were to argue that in principle there was nothing about the law which the Supreme Court had not already sanctioned. . . . But Mr. Parkinson did

---

89 *Greensboro Daily News,* September 1, 1917, p. 1.
90 *Transcript of Record, Hammer v. Dagenhart,* pp. 15–16.
91 See Jackson, *The Sruggle for Judicial Supremacy,* p. 303.
92 *New York Tribune,* September 1, 1917, p. 14.
93 *New York Times,* September 1, 1917, p. 16.

not understand it as we did and in his argument conceded the position for which the plaintiffs had been contending . . . and asserted that the case was to be a landmark in constitutional law.[94]

Boyd, Pound reported, stated that it was for a higher court to take such an epoch-making step.[95] In response, Gregory asked Pound for advice on the appeal and assigned William Frierson, an Assistant Attorney General, to investigate the matter.[96] After talking with Parkinson, Frierson concluded that the difference between Pound and Parkinson had been more apparent than real.[97] Whatever the facts, it seems highly unlikely that Parkinson's candor altered the outcome in any way, and Parkinson resented Boyd's putting the "burden" of the holding on him.[98]

The next day, September 1, District Attorney Hammer appeared before Judge Boyd and went through the mechanics of initiating an appeal. He filed an assignment of errors and moved that case be forwarded to the Supreme Court for review. Boyd allowed the motion and entered an order to give it effect. Counsel and bench then agreed upon the content of the record to be certified to the Court.[99] With these actions, Boyd's participation in the Dagenhart case ended, but his role in the political events that centered upon federal child labor legislation had just begun. His convincing demonstration of "strong character" ensured that further constitutional business would flow to his bench.

Boyd's decision exempted a limited geographic area from the operation of the Keating-Owen law but this immunity did not make the lot of the mill owners in the western district an easy one. The constitutional situation was clouded, and the practical question that plagued the manufacturers was what would happen to a company that disregarded the statute if it should be upheld on appeal.

Clark made strenuous efforts to convince the manufacturers that the matter was settled and he encouraged them to continue their operations in conformity with the law of North Carolina. He

94 Roscoe Pound to T. W. Gregory, September 3, 1917, Justice Department File, *Hammer* v. *Dagenhart*. Hammer, too, felt Parkinson had claimed too much (W. C. Hammer to T. W. Gregory).

95 *Ibid.*

96 T. W. Gregory to Roscoe Pound, September 4, 1917, and T. W. Gregory to William L. Frierson, September 4, 1917.

97 W. L. Frierson, "Memorandum for the Solicitor General," September 11, 1917.

98 W. C. Hammer to T. W. Gregory.

99 *Transcript of Record, Hammer* v. *Dagenhart*, pp. 16–18.

promised that no penalties could later be inflicted upon them.[100] However, contrary advice came from other representatives of the industry. Attorney General Gregory sent notice to all district attorneys that the Justice Department considered the Keating-Owen law valid and he instructed them to prosecute all violators within their districts.[101] Hammer was told that, although he was enjoined from acting, manufacturers in the western district would be prosecuted in other states if they shipped goods in violation of the statute.[102] In these circumstances, Clark had little success, for the mill owners chose to obey the measure rather than chance current or future prosecutions.[103]

Like most district court decisions, Boyd's ruling attracted scant attention beyond the immediate locale although it was important news in the southern textile district. In Clark's victory editorial, "Won First Blood," the editor claimed credit for the manufacturers' victory and specifically denied any collaboration with the tobacco companies. He was especially gratified that a decision had been obtained before the law took effect — the mill owners had been spared an army of federal inspectors, and might never have to adjust their operations. Unlikely as it seemed, Clark said, counsel for the government "protested no flaw in the case." [104]

Among newspapers and journals that took notice of the Dagenhart decision, the common expectation followed the lines of an editorial in one of the south's most respected newspapers, Josephus Daniel's *Raleigh News and Observer*:

> There is little doubt, we believe, that the Supreme Court will sustain the law. The trend of decision in that tribunal in recent years has been in line with progressive ideas and [constitutional] doubts . . . have been resolved in favor of . . . what appeared to be the common good.[105]

Most reform groups looked upon the holdings as a temporary setback rather than a lasting defeat. Perhaps no liberal critic better reflected the reaction of progressives to what many considered no

---

100 *Southern Textile Bulletin* (September 6, 1917), p. 10.

101 Circular Letter No. 741. Justice Department File, *Hammer v. Dagenhart.*

102 T. W. Gregory to W. C. Hammer, October 5, 1917.

103 The *Charlotte Daily Observer* reported (June 4, 1918, p. 1) that "all the cotton mills of Mecklenburg County observed the act . . . pending the decision of the Supreme Court. . . ." However, the Children's Bureau pursued a cautious enforcement policy, withholding prosecutions in North Carolina and several other southern states during the appeal period.

104 *Southern Textile Bulletin* (September 6, 1917), p. 10.

105 September 1, 1917, p. 4.

more than judicial fiat, arresting a nonpartisan social advance, than Edward S. Corwin. After caustically analyzing the constitutional arguments that had induced Boyd to come to the rescue of the country and the Constitution, Corwin concluded as follows.

> Judge Boyd's decision cannot stand as law. It is a displaced fossil from a by-gone epoch of constitutionalism and as such merits a place in the cabinet of legal curiosities, but it deserves no weight whatever in the choice of current legislative programs to meet the vital needs of the day. And what makes it the more remarkable is that it should occur at a time when Congress is exercising other of its powers in a way to penetrate the local jurisdictions to their most intimate recesses. At a moment when the government is directing the mines, the factories and the farms of the nation, is saying what price producers shall receive for their products, is conscripting the manhood of the country for the national armies, it is informed that it cannot regulate commerce with the end in view of conserving the health of those of whom its future armies must be composed. It is amazing.[106]

[106] "Validity of the Child Labor Act," p. 188.

5

The Supreme Court Bench: Those Who Would Decide

The Supreme Court during the Progressive Era

But what of the bench that would hear the *Dagenhart* case on appeal? What was its character and tendency? Did the available evidence justify Corwin's confident expectation that the justices would treat Judge Boyd's holding as a fossil from a bygone era of constitutionalism? Did the changed line of judicial interpretation during the progressive era leave little doubt, as reformers frequently asserted, that the Keating-Owen law would be sustained? To treat these questions meaningfully it is necessary to review the main trends of constitutional holdings in the preceding four decades.

As the new industrial society came into being after the Civil War, state legislation was called into play by democratic forces to control capitalistic enterprise and remedy its attendant evils. Fearful of the majority will and finding an invitation to disaster in the injunction of a non-interventionist bench that relief from regulatory injustice must be sought at the polls, business and financial interests turned to the courts and the processes of litigation for protection. Lawyers in their retainer followed the doctrinal lead of dissenters on the bench and drew conceptual substances from a variety of commentaries that proclaimed hitherto unknown limitations upon constitutional powers. They fashioned the prevailing laissez faire ideology and the American philosophy of fundamental rights as a restraint upon government into a chain of formal constitutional limitations. Freedom was erected into a barrier against regulation, individualism translated into a social absolute.[1]

---

[1] For a perceptive discussion of this dramatic chapter in constitutional development, see Benjamin R. Twiss, *Lawyers and the Constitution* (Princeton: Princeton University Press, 1942).

In this remarkable burst of doctrinal creativity, the powerful conceptions of succeeding constitutional law — due process, liberty of contract, and the rule of reasonableness — received their real impetus and elaboration.[2] These doctrines were pressed upon the Supreme Court in case after case by the elite of the American Bar Association, some of them fancying the endeavor a holy war against radical intrusions into American society, and all of them "protecting a philosophy and a way of life which they shared with their clients."[3] What was forcefully proposed at the bar and proselytized by a minority on the bench gradually was read into constitutional decisions as converts were made and justices appointed who mirrored the conservative persuasion of the business community from whence many came.

By the 1890's, the laissez faire doctrines had triumphed. An interventionist bench ushered in the heyday of substantive due process and judicial restrictionism. The Court thrust itself into the interplay between business and government and took upon itself the responsibility of supervising the clash of interests that formed the chief constituent of politics. The dominant group of justices, motivated by distrust for social and economic reform, imposed numerous and ingenious restraints upon popular exercises of authority. During this period in which the Court was overseeing piecemeal state attempts to control business evils, the first national efforts to regulate the economic order (aside from long-standing tariff excises) were undertaken in the Interstate Commerce and Sherman Antitrust acts. The response of conservative counsel and jurists was to develop the constitutional doctrine that Corwin has called "dual federalism." With these developments, judicial review by the Supreme Court for the first time became an important factor in national legislative power.[4]

Such decisions as those in the *Lochner*[5] and Sugar Trust[6] cases, in which state and national legislation was overturned or narrowly interpreted, form the high-water marks of judicial restrictionism. Despite the immense respect that characterized American attitudes toward the judiciary at the end of the nineteenth century,

---

[2] Max Lerner, "The Supreme Court and American Capitalism," *Essays in Constitutional Law*, ed. Robert G. McCloskey (New York: Alfred A. Knopf, 1957), p. 137.

[3] Twiss, *Lawyers and the Constitution*, p. 3.

[4] Edward S. Corwin, *Constitutional Revolution, Ltd.* (Claremont, Calif.: Claremont Colleges, 1941), p. 10.

[5] *Lochner* v. *New York*, 198 U.S. 45 (1905).

[6] *United States* v. *E. C. Knight Co.*, 156 U.S. 1 (1895).

this thwarting of the rising tide of popular efforts to bring business under governmental control and to adjust society to industrial conditions brought bitter criticism down upon the Court, a censure that mounted in intensity as the progressive movement gained greater political momentum. By placing the bench at cross-purposes to the currents of the times, conservative jurists caused a political collision.

The Court's role in government and the validity of its constitutional interpretations were consciously made the battleground by progressive spokesmen. The new teaching bar of the law schools, aided by powerful dissenting voices on the bench, argued for judicial restraint, a return to earlier interpretations of legislative authority, and the need for evolution in the law to accommodate new circumstances. Liberal historians and political scientists sought to destroy the supposed identity between conservative ideology and unchanging constitutional truths, to undermine belief in the pristine character of judicial revelation. And state legislatures continued to pursue various lines of social control, despite judicial holdings that seemed to invalidate them.

This assault on the constitutional imperatives of laissez faire, the permeating influence of changed public opinion, and the liberating effect of new appointees began to free the Court from conservative interpretations — to produce a period of qualified judicial toleration. During the years that followed the landmark *Muller* decision,[7] the Court allowed "legislation to prevail which, in various aspects, regulated enterprise with reference to its social consequences and withdrew phases of industrial relations from the area of illusory individual bargaining."[8] Such decisions as those in the *Hoke*[9] and *Wilson*[10] cases symbolized the disinclination of the bench to stay progressive legislation. As these decisions were announced and sweeping programs of reform were enacted, the restrictive doctrines set forth in numerous earlier holdings seemed to lose much of their vitality, and were thought by many to have been overruled *sub silento*.

Nevertheless, laissez faire philosophy was not stripped from constitutional jurisprudence. The period was no more a period in

[7] *Muller v. Oregon,* 208 U.S. 412 (1908).

[8] Reprinted by permission of the publishers from Felix Frankfurter, *Mr. Justice Holmes and the Supreme Court,* Cambridge, Mass.: The Belknap Press of Harvard University Press, Copyright, 1938, 1961, by the President and Fellows of Harvard College; p. 35.

[9] *Hoke v. United States,* 227 U.S. 308 (1913).

[10] *Wilson v. New,* 243 U.S. 332 (1917).

which legislative judgments about desirable social policies were universally upheld than the preceding period had been one during which they had been universally overthrown. Between the death of Morrison Waite (in 1888) and the decision in the *Muller* case, important constitutional controversies often were decided by narrow majorities, and legislation that involved new forms of social control was sustained as well as struck down. The Lottery and Oleomargarine cases,[11] for example, though decided affirmatively, saw the Court badly split. These decisions had their counterparts in progressive defeats after 1908, and in some near defeats. Notable among the latter were the closely contested holdings in *Bunting* v. *Oregon*[12] and in *Stettler* v. *O'Hara*,[13] which were decided after the passage of the Keating-Owen law. Whether the number of dissenters in these cases heralded a resurgence of judicial restrictionism or merely constituted a recrudescent gasp from a dying era of constitutional construction became crucially important.

Judicial Personality and Motivation

The key to this uncertainty lay in the personality and motivation of the justices. The influence of these factors in judicial decision-making has been commented upon with increasing frequency during this century, and occasionally illuminated by discerning observers, perhaps never more brilliantly than by Benjamin Cardozo. He wrote:

> There is in each of us a stream or tendency . . . which gives coherence and direction to thought and action. Judges cannot escape that current any more than other mortals. All their lives, forces which they do not recognize and cannot name, have been tugging at them — inherited instincts, traditional beliefs, acquired convictions; and the resultant is an outlook on life, a conception of social needs, a sense in James's phrase of "the total push and pressure of the cosmos," which when reasons are nicely balanced, must determine where choice shall fall.[14]

In closely contested cases, typified by plausible, alternative lines of doctrine and the impossibility of achieving consensus, Cardozo

11 *Champion* v. *Ames*, 188 U.S. 321 (1903), and *McCray* v. *United States*, 195 U.S. 27 (1904).

12 243 U.S. 426 (1917).

13 243 U.S. 629 (1917).

14 *The Nature of the Judicial Process* (New Haven: Yale University Press, 1921), p. 12.

suggested, personal philosophy can be expected to influence choice decisively.

After almost a decade on the Supreme Court, Associate Justice Felix Frankfurter commented in similar vein about the influence of personality and motivation upon the jurist's conception of proper social policies.

> Judges like other people have their inborn qualities, deflected and disciplined, enriched or narrowed, by their education, their reading, their experiences, their associations, their depth and drive of creative reflection, their capacity for rigorous, undeceiving self-analysis.[15]

But Frankfurter added a crucial qualification: any "judge worth his salt is held in the grip of his function."

> To assume that a lawyer who becomes a judge takes on the bench merely his own views on social and economic questions leaves out of account his rooted notions regarding the scope and limits of a judge's authority. The outlook of a judge fit to be a justice regarding the role of a judge cuts across his own personal preferences for this or that social arrangements.[16]

Unless he is extraordinarily insensitive and prejudiced, the jurist feels a strong sense of institutional obligation — the responsibility for deciding issues according to established practice, constitutional principles, and public expectations.

Even more important, the judicial function must be recognized for what it is. Walton H. Hamilton has written an extraordinarily preceptive appreciation of the jurist's art:

> In constitutional decision, law encounters the problems of a culture in the making and its path must be broken; judges must find their ways as best they can, through tangles of imperfectly understood situations, past the conflict of values which cannot be resolved, to answers which will do. . . .
>
> The art of judgment is of its own kind. Unlike the poet, the historian, or the essayist, the jurist cannot listen to the promptings in his own heart, choose the subject upon which he would write, say as he would all that is in his mind, and follow his interest to a fresh theme. Instead, as a member of a court, his decisions are a mere step in the process of disposing litigation. He cannot speak until the appropriate cause comes along, he can address himself to the larger issues only so far as a suit of law allows, he must

[15] *Of Law and Men, Papers and Addresses of Felix Frankfurter, 1939–56,* ed. Philip Elman (New York: Harcourt, Brace & World, 1956), pp. 108–9.
[16] *Ibid.,* pp. 40–41.

express a partial opinion and wait for a suitable occasion to continue. Even when his concern is with constitutional issues, and in granting or withholding approval to statutes he is declaring public policy, his manner of speech cannot be that of the statesman. His place is in the institution of the judiciary; he is bound by its usages and procedures; he addresses himself, not directly to a social question but to a matter of policy translated into the language of the law; he cannot escape the values, rules, and intellectual ways of the discipline he professes. On the frontier where a changing social necessity impinges upon the established law, the jurist must possess a double competence; he must employ alike legal rule and social fact, and where they clash, as inevitably they will in a developing culture, he must effect the best reconciliation that may lie between them. The judge must become the statesman without ceasing to be the jurist; the quality of his art lies in the skill, the intelligence, and the sincerity with which he manages to serve two masters.[17]

Mechanical analysis, which represents decision chiefly as the outcome of partisan pulling and hauling, or, worse, portrays the function as one in which judges say what the Constitution is, virtually without restriction, disregards personal integrity, judicial statesmanship, and the uncertainty that frequently disturbs the minds of conscientious and humane justices in resolving choice. Thereby it neglects vital elements in the judicial process.

Severe limitations, therefore, are imposed upon any attempt to explore the influences that shape the outlook of a particular justice or the outcome of a particular case. Yet, despite these limitations, we must attempt to understand what manner of men have sat on the supreme bench if we are to understand why they decided cases as they did. The judicial biographer, no less than others, seeks to reveal the inner forces that direct action, and those who compose collective portraits of judges or judicial behavior, whatever the techniques employed, seek insight into common experiences and uniformities among responses. The results of both approaches have been drawn upon in trying to say something meaningful about the personality and motivation of the men who made up the bench for the Dagenhart case. It has seemed prudent, however, to limit this examination primarily to information about which there is relative certitude; namely, the factors that influenced their selection, and the trends of their alignments after going on the bench.

From the beginning of the nation, Presidents have paid close

[17] "The Jurist's Art," *S.E.C.L.*, I, 591–92.

attention to the outlook of prospective justices toward major policy issues that are likely to come before the Court. They have assumed that the past in which a man was inured would strongly influence his decisions,[18] and they have wished to ensure, as far as possible, that constitutional development would take the direction they approved. This concern was especially stressed during the progressive era. Every President, deeply conscious of the effect his judicial appointments might have, tried to make certain that men who believed as he did were elevated to the supreme bench. In particular, aspirants' economic views were scrutinized as never before.[19]

At the same time, Presidents have always known that no man, once confirmed by the Senate, remains exactly the same as he was before his appointment. The Court's dynamics are its own, and the life tenure that members of the "least dangerous branch" enjoy produces an independence whose results, though usually salutary and broadly consistent with expectations, sometimes surprises, occasionally distresses, the appointing President. "The taking of the robe," Freund observes, "an experience at once emancipating and humbling, is apt to dissolve old ties and to quicken the sense that there is no escape from that judgment of one's successors which is called history." [20]

Even within this limited compass, crystalline clarity, especially about the reasons for appointment, cannot be attained. Sources are limited, frequently ambiguous, and inadequate bases for much that passes as verifiable knowledge. In discussing these problems, Abraham counsels prudence: "All the student of constitutional law or the historian can do with honesty and conviction is to hazard a reasonable inference based on the facts at his disposal." [21]

Generalizations about the patterns of the justices' votes and the justifications for their conclusions as offered in their opinions, although on the surface more reliable than suppositions about the reasons for their appointments, suffer because we can never penetrate the conference to learn why they voted as they did and because of the obscurity of collective pronouncements. Even dissents, despite their seeming singularity, often fail to reveal reliable

18 See Frankfurter, *Mr. Justice Holmes,* p. 13.

19 John P. Frank, "The Appointment of Supreme Court Justices: Prestige, Principles and Politics," *Wisconsin Law Review* (May, 1941), p. 345.

20 Paul A. Freund, *The Supreme Court of the United States* (Cleveland: World Publishing Company, 1961), p. 116.

21 Henry J. Abraham, *The Judicial Process* (New York: Oxford University Press, 1962), p. 58.

insights into particular choices or to illuminate decisional careers. For these reasons, inferences have been hazarded only where what we know about factors influencing selection or explanatory of behavior appear to justify conclusions that transcend speculation.

The Nineteenth-Century Appointees

Except for Chief Justice White and the senior Associate Justice, McKenna, the members of the Court in 1917 had been appointed during the progressive era, and five of them in the period of judicial toleration that followed the *Muller* decision; but not all had been selected by progressive Presidents. Between the administration in which Theodore Roosevelt emerged as a reform leader and the period of liberal reconstruction that was presided over by Woodrow Wilson, William Howard Taft occupied the presidential office, and his single term was all-important. Writing near the end of his life, Associate Justice Robert H. Jackson restated a truism of the Court's history.

> The political branches nominate and confirm the Justices, a control of the Court's composition which results in a somewhat lagging political influence over its trend of decision, and any party that prevails in the Federal Government through several presidential terms will gradually tend to impress its political philosophy on the Court.[22]

Roosevelt and Wilson belonged to different parties but both advocated extensive governmental intervention in economic affairs to achieve equalitarian purposes and to further social amelioration. Taft, on the other hand, represented a more conservative philosophy; his administration interrupted the progressive succession. In itself, this was not necessarily consequential, but Taft had the rare opportunity of reconstituting the Court's majority, and the implications were enormous.

Taft appointed five men to the supreme bench and showed his firm approval of a sixth by advancing him to the Chief Justiceship. The situation was virtually unprecedented; only Washington had been able to impress his philosophy more pervasively upon the Court; but the tribunal of 1910 played an immeasurably larger role in American life than its predecessor of 1789. A more meaningful contrast is that between Taft, and Roosevelt and Wilson.

22 Reprinted by permission of the publishers from Robert H. Jackson, *The Supreme Court in the American System of Government*, Cambridge, Mass.: The Belknap Press of Harvard University Press, Copyright, 1955, by William Eldred Jackson and G. Bowdoin Craighill, Jr., Executors; p. 10.

Although their terms covered almost sixteen years, the two reform leaders were able to nominate only as many justices as bore Taft's commission after four years. Each man had less than the historic average number of appointments per term, but Taft's appointments greatly exceeded the average. If a progressive had been elected President in 1908, constitutional development undoubtedly would have been very different. Under the impact of Roosevelt's leadership of public opinion, the gap between popularly approved policies and judicial holdings was narrowed. If his successor had appointed justices of liberal outlook, and, equally important, continued to champion progressive causes, the gap might have been virtually erased. Whatever chance there had been for permanently impressing the progressive spirit on the bench was lost.

The oldest member of the Court was Chief Justice Edward Douglas White, who became an Associate Justice in 1894 as a result of political warfare between Grover Cleveland and Senator Hill, the leader of the antiadministration Democrats in New York. Cleveland had wanted to replace the deceased Blatchford with an appointee from the New York bar but had turned to White after Hill caused two nominees from his state to be rejected.[23] Why the President did this has never been clear, especially because White vigorously opposed the Wilson-Gorman tariff, one of the principal measures in Cleveland's legislative program. Nevins believes that Cleveland "suddenly realized that a protracted contest with the Senate might result disastrously for the tariff bill" and that he hoped "White's promotion would temporarily weaken the protectionists."[24] White's biographer, on the other hand, feels that other considerations contributed to Cleveland's decision. In her view, White combined impressive legal talent, and — except for his tariff stand — ideological soundness; and he was an acknowledged champion of a graduated federal income tax. In addition, the operation of senatorial courtesy gave Cleveland a way to extricate himself from a grave political stalemate.[25]

White was a Louisiana Bourbon — a wealthy cane planter, president of a sugar refining company, and a man accustomed to playing an influential role in state Democratic politics. More-

---

[23] John P. Frank, *Marble Palace* (New York: Alfred A. Knopf, 1958), p. 57.
[24] Allan Nevins, *Grover Cleveland* (New York: Dodd, Mead and Co., 1933), p. 571.
[25] Sister Marie Carolyn Klinkhamer, *Edward Douglas White* (Washington, D.C.: Catholic University of America Press, 1943), p. 37.

over, he was a former Confederate soldier and a Catholic. After the war he trained as a lawyer by reading the civil law of his native state, and, for a brief period — before he was ousted by judicial reform legislation — he was an elected member of its supreme court. His education in Jesuit schools, perhaps more than his southern background, influenced his philosophy. His opinions frequently invoked conceptions of fundamental principles of liberty and justice, especially in notions of "inherent" powers and "inherent" limitations and in the famous "rule of reason."[26] In addition, White was a fervent champion of dual federalism, as became apparent the year after he went on the bench, when he associated himself with the majority that incorporated this doctrine into constitutional law in the Sugar Trust case. Nevertheless, White voted with the minority in the other great case of that term, *Pollock* v. *Farmers' Loan and Trust Company*,[27] thereby (apparently) deciding exactly as Cleveland had expected.

Associate Justice Joseph McKenna, the single appointee of William McKinley, grew to manhood on the California frontier, his family having forsaken the east after pre-Civil War nativist outbreaks against foreigners. Like White, he was raised a Catholic, read law, and through its practice entered politics; however, he was a life-long Republican. In 1884 he was elected to Congress, where he became one of McKinley's closest personal friends and a confidant of other men in the inner councils of the party of business. His career was that of a faithful party man; he "consistently supported high tariffs, sound money, big business, laissez faire and the railroads,"[28] and never strayed from the conservative path.

His record of Republican orthodoxy and the decisive intervention of the California railroad magnate and political manager, Leland Stanford, led Harrison to appoint McKenna to the Ninth Circuit Court of Appeals. When McKinley became President, these factors, and the ties of friendship, assured him of national office. His nomination to the high bench, after nine months as Attorney General, encountered strong opposition (especially from the Pacific slopes), but the Senate unanimously deferred to McKinley.

McKenna was appalled, when he took his seat, by the magni-

26 Edward S. Corwin, *The Twilight of the Supreme Court* (New Haven: Yale University Press, 1934), p. 24.

27 157 U.S. 429 (1895).

28 Matthew McDevitt, *Joseph McKenna* (Washington, D.C.: Catholic University of America Press, 1946), p. 76.

tude of the responsibility he had assumed. Despite his judicial experience, he was not familiar with constitutional law, and he seems to have been less intellectually able than his brethren. Thus he felt his way cautiously at first, struggling to stay abreast of his work and to satisfy his colleagues' expectations.

His thought, like White's, was grounded in the doctrines of natural law; he frequently justified statutes by reference to their intrinsic reasonableness or accord with the universal sense of mankind. In good conservative fashion, especially during his early years on the bench, he attributed a sacrosanct character to *stare decisis*. Nevertheless, his legal philosophy is not easily definable. Although he was known as a staunch defender of the status quo, he was noticeably more tolerant of economic regulation, and especially of social reform, than the great apostle of laissez faire, Stephen J. Field, whose place he took. With some paradoxical exceptions, he seemed to mold his thought to the dominant trend of opinion.

Progressivism's First Representatives on the Bench: The Roosevelt Appointees

As President, Theodore Roosevelt dominated American life as only a few men have done. The Supreme Court, no less than other institutions of government, came under the force of his personality. His influence was felt directly, through the character of his appointees, and indirectly (but pervasively) through the impact of his militant leadership of public opinion. Roosevelt fervently believed that the Court should protect the conscientious efforts of the President and Congress to serve the interests of the nation. He also believed that personal preferences inevitably influenced judicial holdings. Congress was told, in December, 1908:

> The chief lawmakers in our country may be, and often are, the judges, because they are the final seat of authority. . . . The decisions of the courts on economic and social questions depends upon their economic and social philosophies; and for the peaceful progress of our people during the twentieth century we shall owe most to those judges who hold to a twentieth century economic and social philosophy and not to a long outgrown philosophy, which was itself the product of primitive economic conditions.[29]

Roosevelt attached the utmost importance to the choice of new members of the Supreme Court, especially because the justices

[29] Theodore Roosevelt, Address to Congress, *Congressional Record*, 60th Cong., 2d Sess. (Washington, D.C.: Government Printing Office, 1908), p. 21.

were at that time narrowly divided on many significant constitutional issues. Almost immediately after he took office, Roosevelt was able to act upon his beliefs. In a letter that is often quoted, he discussed the qualifications of the man toward whom he inclined but about whom he had doubts, Chief Justice Holmes of the Massachusetts supreme court.

> The ablest lawyers and the greatest judges are men whose past has naturally brought them into close relationship with the wealthiest and most powerful clients, and I am glad when I can find a judge who has been able to preserve his aloofness of mind so as to keep his broad humanity of feeling and his sympathy for the class from which he has not drawn his clients. . . .
>
> Now a word as to the other side. . . . In the ordinary and low sense which we attach to the words "partisan" and "politician," a judge of the Supreme Court should be neither. But in the higher sense, in the proper sense, he is not in my judgment fitted for the position unless he is a party man, a constructive statesman, constantly keeping in mind his adherence to the principles and policies under which this nation has been built up and in accordance with which it must go. . . .
>
> Now I would like to know that Judge Holmes was in entire sympathy with our views, . . . I should hold myself guilty of an irreparable wrong to the nation if I should put in [Judge Gray's] place any man who was not absolutely sane and sound on the great national policies for which we stand in public life.[30]

The individual views expressed in Holmes's Massachusetts opinion encouraged Roosevelt to believe that Holmes possessed the qualities of a judicial statesman.

Holmes throughout his life was deeply attached to his puritan heritage, his experiences in the Civil War sharply influenced his social philosophy, and the intellectual ferment of his time profoundly affected his mind and spirit. As a judge, he had a remarkable capacity for undeceiving self-analysis and he possessed an outlook on the judicial function that cut across his own preferences for particular social arrangements — the outlook of a thoroughly skeptical man, one whose greatest interest lay in trying to grasp the cosmos by the tail. Unmindful of prestige and political place, he chopped apart outmoded doctrine, gave creative direction to constitutional interpretation, and spoke for the coalescing majority of the progressive era. Within a few years it be-

---

[30] Henry Cabot Lodge (ed.), *Selections from the Correspondence of Theodore Roosevelt and Henry Cabot Lodge, 1884–1918* (2 vols.; New York: Scribner, 1925), I, 517–19.

came apparent that Holmes was the great jurist Roosevelt had sought. Holmes, the proper partisan, powerfully influenced the thinking of his own and later generations. Never, perhaps, has an appointing President's expectation been more richly fulfilled.

Besides Holmes, Roosevelt appointed two other justices to the Supreme Court, and each time he tried to mold the character of the bench by selecting men who were in sympathy with his own convictions on the crucial issues of the day. When Justice Shiras retired in 1902, Roosevelt pressed the appointment on Taft, who twice declined his heart's desire;[31] Roosevelt then appointed William Rufus Day. The "good Day," as Roosevelt once referred to him, was much esteemed by Taft, and Roosevelt greatly valued the judgment of the man who was soon to be his protégé. But the reasons for Day's selection are obscure.[32] With the prosecution of the Northern Securities merger already in progress in the lower federal courts, Roosevelt, it appears, wanted a man who was known to be "absolutely sane and sound" on the industrial question. He also seems to have taken geographic factors into account, considering it advisable to appoint a midwesterner.[33]

Day had grown to manhood in the pre-industrial midwest and was intensely attached to the individualistic tradition that permeated its social philosophy. This influence, together with experience acquired in a common law practice in a small business community (Ravenna, Ohio), greatly affected his mind and character. In 1897, at the bidding of his life-long friend, William McKinley, Day went to Washington to assist the feeble political appointee, former Senator Sherman, who was Secretary of State. With the outbreak of the Spanish-American War, Day became the Secretary, and subsequently headed the peace commission.[34]

McKinley then appointed Day to the Sixth Circuit Court of Appeals, a position that better suited his reflective temperament. As a judge, Day strictly abstained from partisan politics and endeavored "to attain the objectivity that is the essence of judicial temperament."[35] He was never able, however, to escape his preference for particular social arrangements to the extent that Holmes

---

[31] Henry F. Pringle, *The Life and Times of William Howard Taft* (2 vols.; New York: 1939), I, 241–42.

[32] Joseph E. McLean, *William Rufus Day* (Baltimore: The Johns Hopkins Press, 1946), p. 55.

[33] *Ibid.*, pp. 55–56.

[34] *Ibid.*, pp. 17, 35.

[35] *Ibid.*, p. 61.

did. Overall, his constitutional opinions reflect a combination of conservative and (sometimes surprisingly) liberal attitudes.

Soon after Holmes and Day began their careers on the bench, Holmes bitterly disappointed Roosevelt by dissenting in the *Northern Securities* case.[36] Day, on the other hand, won Roosevelt's warm applause by siding with the majority, thereby contributing to the antitrust crusade. The following year, in the *Lochner* case, Holmes again dissented, but this time his words formed one of the great utterances in the Court's history. There is a striking similiarity between Holmes's ringing declaration that the statute of New York did not "infringe fundamental principles as they have been understood by the traditions of our people and our law"[37] and Roosevelt's conviction that a constructive jurist would constantly keep in mind "his adherence to the principles and policies under which this nation has been built up and in accordance with which it must go." Here, as Frankfurter has phrased it, was the great theme of Holmes's judicial life — "the amplitude of the Constitution as against the narrowness of some of its interpreters."[38] Day also dissented, but he concurred in the less fundamental attack upon the argument of the majority, which Justice Harlan wrote. One of the chief articles of his judicial outlook was thereby apparent: the amplitude of state authority for dealing with social and economic problems. However, Day's view of federalism did not permit an equally liberal interpretation of national authority.[39]

In addition to Holmes and Day, Justice White also dissented in the *Lochner* case, and associated himself with the Harlan opinion. McKenna alone, of the sitting justices who would later participate in the *Dagenhart* case, aligned himself with the rigid conservatism of the majority. Thus the newer justices, McKenna aside, formed a readily identifiable liberal bloc in *Lochner*. This bloc, which McKenna usually joined, for the most part maintained its cohesiveness throughout Roosevelt's administration. With few exceptions, the four justices voted to uphold state legislation that regulated labor conditions and national enactments that had police power objectives.

Although the conservative faction, dominated by Fuller and Brewer, usually succeeded in keeping national lawmaking power strait-jacketed, the younger group occasionally won significant

---

36 *Northern Securities Co.* v. *United States,* 193 U.S. 197 (1904).
37 *Lochner* v. *New York,* 198 U.S. 45, 76 (1905).
38 Frankfurter, *Mr. Justice Holmes,* p. 36.
39 McLean, *William Rufus Day,* pp. 68–156.

victories, such as *Champion* v. *Ames*[40] and *McCray* v. *United States*.[41] In the former, a very sharply contested decision, White, McKenna, and Holmes joined Harlan and Brown to form the five-judge majority. The next year, after Day had replaced Shiras, the four newest justices, again in company with Harlan, and this time joined by Brewer, formed the majority in *McCray*. Moreover, White wrote the opinion of the Court, which was less susceptible to differing constructions than the Lottery decision.

However, there were definite limits to the greater liberality of the younger justices, as the *Adair* case [42] (decided in January, 1908) demonstrated. The four men were split, and, when the division in *Lochner* is recalled, the alignment was curious. White and Day sided with the majority; the provisions of the Erdman Act, prohibiting "yellow dog" contracts and employer discrimination against union members, exceeded their conceptions of proper public policy. Holmes and McKenna, on the other hand, dissented, and each wrote an opinion that condemned the supervisory authority over legislative discretion in the field of labor relations exercised by the majority. Thereafter, McKenna rendered liberal opinions more consistently than any other pre-*Muller* justice, with the exception of Holmes.

Less than a month later, *Muller* was announced. Not only were Brewer, Fuller, and Peckham won over — at least for this decision — but Brewer wrote the unanimous opinion. To be sure, he labored to distinguish the *Lochner* holding, but, despite his efforts, it was seriously discredited. The changed temper of public opinion, attributable in significant measure to Roosevelt's dynamic leadership of progressive causes, and the liberal influences of the newer appointees, more responsive than their brethren to the popular will and less attached to *stare decisis*, explain the shift in the Court's emphasis toward judicial restraint. In the years that followed, the doctrines of due process of law and liberty of contract as restrictions upon state regulation of economic affairs fell into partial eclipse. Nevertheless, thanks mainly to White's steadfast efforts, dual federalism did not wane equally.[43]

Reaction to Reform: The First Taft Court

Roosevelt chose Taft as his successor, and his vigorous efforts were sufficient to win the presidency for his trusted subordinate.

[40] 188 U.S. 321 (1903).
[41] 195 U.S. 27 (1904).
[42] *Adair* v. *United States*, 208 U.S. 161 (1908).
[43] See Corwin, *The Twilight of the Supreme Court*, pp. 20–26.

Taft was essentially a conservative, but, under Roosevelt's influence, he shook off some of his former ideas and was looked upon as a reformer. The difficulties he faced as President, however, drove him back toward his deepest convictions. Taft effectively enforced the policies for controlling corporate interests, which he had inherited; nevertheless, popular discontent mounted during his administration. Powerful groups in each of the major parties demanded further revision in the laissez faire character of the economy and greater popular control of political institutions. To make matters worse, a serious cleavage developed between liberals and conservatives within the Republican party, and a disillusioned Roosevelt returned from self-imposed political exile to take command of the insurgents.

Harrassed on many sides, Taft looked to the Supreme Court to protect the essential features of the existing social order. He approved most of the doctrines for the protection of property that the Court's dominant group, under Fuller, had read into law, and he wished to strengthen the bench as a bulwark against progressive reconstruction.[44] Moreover, like many members of the business community, Taft was deeply shaken by the emotional intensity that surrounded reform. It was wholly anathema to one who revered law and legal institutions. Roosevelt might have believed, in 1910, that

> "unless we are prepared to face disaster in the judiciary in the future, there must be a very radical change in the attitude of our judges to public questions,"[45]

but Taft was interested in entrenching men on the bench who would "preserve the fundamental structure of our government as our fathers gave it to us."[46]

Of the five vacancies Taft filled, four occurred within one year. Justice Peckham died in October, 1909; Justice Brewer and Chief Justice Fuller also died (three months apart) in the first half of 1910. Soon thereafter, ill health forced Justice Moody to resign. With the deaths of Brewer, Fuller, and Peckham, the stalwarts of the great interventionist bench were gone, but Taft brought the nucleus of another such bench into being. His first appointment was his long-time friend and former colleague on the circuit court, Horace D. Lurton, nearly sixty-six, and the oldest man

44 Frank, "Appointment of Supreme Court Justices," p. 373.

45 Lodge, *Correspondence of Theodore Roosevelt and Henry Cabot Lodge,* II, 378.

46 Pringle, *William Howard Taft,* p. 536.

ever appointed to the Supreme Court.[47] After this, Taft adhered —
with one notable exception — to a policy of selecting younger
men whose influence could be expected to extend through many
years of service. The first of these, Charles Evans Hughes, was
appointed in May, 1910. Hughes had had a rich political career
and, although he had not had judicial experience, Taft thought
highly enough of him to all but promise his advancement to the
Chief Justiceship when Fuller died.[48]

Six weeks later Fuller was dead, and Taft spent most of the
remainder of the year trying to decide what to do. During this
period Roosevelt became an open adversary — in Taft's view an
enemy of the Supreme Court and the Constitution.[49] On December 12, Taft announced his decisions: Justice White was named
Chief Justice and Willis Van Devanter and Joseph R. Lamar were
named to the vacant places as associate justices. Despite Taft's
indiscreet encouragement of Hughes, the coveted position went
to another man, who was twelve years older than Taft.

Although no one has ever been able to say why Taft finally
decided on White, White's outlook on life and law was similar
in many ways to Taft's, particularly on economic matters. White,
moreover, blended charm and force of person, much as the great
Marshall had, and he was the choice of his colleagues, who took
the unprecedented step of telling this to Taft.[50] Taft could count
on White to lead the Court in the doctrinal direction he desired
and to get its work done. This being so, Taft was not disturbed
about breaking precedent by advancing an Associate Justice, even
one nominally from the opposite party.

The better known of the two new associate justices, Willis Van
Devanter, nevertheless was comparatively unknown. Like many
other able lawyers of the nineteenth century, he had been a
prominent railroad counsel, active in local politics, and then
was named to the bench. He served as chief justice of the Wyoming
Supreme Court, and, after 1903, as a federal circuit court judge.
In Van Devanter's case, the railroad was the Union Pacific and
the politics were those of the Republican party in the mountain
states of the west. He also had served as a member of the Wyoming

---

[47] *Ibid.*, p. 531.

[48] *Ibid.*, pp. 531–33, and Alpheus T. Mason, *William Howard Taft: Chief
Justice* (New York: Simon and Schuster, 1964), pp. 35–36.

[49] Pringle, *William Howard Taft*, II, 557–81.

[50] Corwin, *The Twilight of the Supreme Court*, p. 23; Klinkhamer, *Edward Douglas White*, pp. 45–46; Frankfurter, *Of Law and Men*, pp. 121–22;
and Mason, *William Howard Taft*, pp. 33–40.

territorial legislature and, briefly, as an assistant attorney general attached to the Interior Department. Writing of the reasons for Van Devanter's selection, McHargue observed:

> "[Taft] was probably influenced by the fact that of the Westerners whom he considered geographically available, Van Devanter had fewer enemies who protested his proposed nomination than did his chief competitor." [51]

Both men were staunchly conservative — the proper kind of ideological partisans.

The last Taft appointee, Mahlon Pitney, was selected in the spring of 1912, after the death of Justice Harlan. By this time the final break between Taft and Roosevelt had occurred, and the presidential election loomed ahead. Taft, fighting for his political life, gave no ground to progressives, within his party or without. Pitney was a relatively undistinguished man, despite service in Congress and as chancellor of the New Jersey supreme court. His fellow justices endorsed him, as did members of the state bar, but, more to the point, he was strongly conservative, even reactionary, in his attitudes and was known to have political influence in what appeared to be a doubtful state.[52] On the bench, he proved to be a nonentity, lacking intellectual strength and the capacity to influence his colleagues.

Taft's appointees, without exception were deeply attached to the social arrangements of the capitalist order, especially the protections afforded property, and wished to see these institutions transmitted unimpaired to future generations. Nevertheless, none of them was as rigid and undeviating in his attitudes, nor as interventionist in his "rooted notions regarding the scope and limits of a judge's authority," as such predecessors as Brewer and Fuller had been. "Not a hidebound conservative but a reasonable one," [53] Taft's characterization a decade later of Justice Sutherland, applied to most of his Supreme Court appointees.

The Taft justices generally represented conservative opinion in America, which had shifted significantly as economic conditions and social aspirations changed and as progressivism became a stronger political force. The altered conservative thought largely rejected extreme laissez faire and accommodated moderate pro-

---

[51] Daniel S. McHargue, "President Taft's Appointments to the Supreme Court," *Journal of Politics* (August, 1950), p. 500.

[52] *Ibid.*, p. 56.

[53] W. H. Taft to Horace D. Taft, September 13, 1922, "The Taft Papers," Manuscript Division, Library of Congress, Washington, D.C.

posals for reform, especially if social improvement did not involve interference with vested rights. Because they represented changed opinion, the new majority in the Court did not result in radical reversal of the tendency toward liberal interpretation of governmental powers that had developed in the last years of Roosevelt's administration.

The Court, remade to Taft's specifications, reviewed little truly important constitutional litigation during his administration. Two major antitrust prosecutions, the *Standard Oil* and the *American Tobacco Company* cases,[54] as well as the *Second Employers' Liability* case,[55] were decided without cleavage among the justices. Unanimity also prevailed on two occasions in which the use of the commerce power to accomplish police power purposes was challenged. What had been a badly divided bench in the Lottery case became impressively united in the *Hipolite Egg Company* and *Hoke* cases.[56] These holdings strongly suggested that the tenuous doctrines of the former decision had become settled principles of law. Because of the Court's frequent unanimity and because it seemed to be moving with the times, the consequences of Taft's opportunity to remake the Court's majority were not readily apparent.

Representatives of the New Freedom: McReynolds and Two Thoroughgoing Progressives

As he left office in March, 1913, Taft told reporters that his greatest satisfaction stemmed from the fact that six members of the Supreme Court, the Chief Justice included, bore his commission. " 'And I have said to them,' Taft chuckled, 'Damn you, if any of you die, I'll disown you.' "[57] He had seen to the matter closest to his heart and believed that the Constitution was at least temporarily safe from the progressive attack.

It is a commonplace of constitutional history that Taft's appointees heeded his injunction; two of them, as one commentator put it, "were still saving people from themselves" as late as 1937.[58] But it is usually forgotten that the three Supreme Court vacancies that Woodrow Wilson filled resulted from the death or retirement

---

[54] *Standard Oil Company* v. *United States*, 221 U.S. 1 (1911); and *United States* v. *American Tobacco Company*, 221 U.S. 106 (1911).

[55] 223 U.S. 1 (1912).

[56] *Hipolite Egg Company* v. *United States*, 220 U.S. 45 (1911), and *Hoke* v. *United States*, 227 U.S. 308 (1913).

[57] Pringle, *William Howard Taft*, II, 854.

[58] Frank, "Appointment of Supreme Court Justices," p. 373.

of justices Taft had appointed. Lurton survived only a few years; Lamar died unexpectedly in middle age; and Hughes left the Court to chance larger political fortunes. Had events been different, the first Taft Court — the Court dominated by Taft's appointees — would have merged into the Court over which he presided in the twenties rather than have been partially reconstituted by Wilson.

Wilson's election put a strong progressive in the White House, one who was determined to carry out essential reforms. He looked upon his program as more than a statement of declared purposes; it was a duty incumbent upon the nation. The reform attack upon conservative legalism reached its climax in the first years of Wilson's administration. The controversy swirling about the courts, Swisher writes, "damaged the halo with which the judiciary had been endowed and emphasized the human character of the institution." [59] Wilson had never doubted the wisdom of judicial review but his experiences during the period from which he emerged as a progressive spokesman caused him to stress the creative aspect of the juridical function. As President, he strongly desired to appoint justices who would support the main elements of the progressive program. There had to be an enlightened adjustment of law to new conditions if the forces of humanity were to reconstruct society.

Wilson's first opportunity to put a liberal on the Court occurred in the summer of 1914, but his choice, James Clark McReynolds, is one of the most perplexing in history, for no more illiberal man has ever sat on the bench. Whatever Wilson may have learned of his Attorney General's distinctive characteristics during a year and a half of close personal contact, McReynolds' political career had provided little reason to believe that he was the kind of man Wilson sought. Why was he selected? Frank observes:

> When Justice Lurton died . . . McReynolds was unanimously expected to be his successor. It was rumored that McReynolds did not care to leave the Cabinet with so many important anti-trust actions pending . . . but Wilson was said to regard McReynolds as "the most promising material available." [60]

McReynolds' zeal as a trust-buster was sufficient recommendation. It did not take Wilson long to discover that he had made a grave

59 Carl Brent Swisher, *American Constitutional Development* (Boston: Houghton Mifflin Co., 1943), p. 590.
60 Frank, "Appointment of Supreme Court Justices," p. 463.

miscalculation. Somehow, the psychological and cultural influences that were the source of McReynolds' judicial opinions had escaped him. No justice, not even Field, ever was more conservative, and McReynolds adhered to his convictions with the ardor of a fanatic. It is doubtful that any President has nominated a justice whose views proved so foreign to his own.[61]

[61] An intriguing "twist of fate" occurred at this point. One of the men strongly recommended to replace Justice Lurton was Chief Justice Walter Clark of the North Carolina supreme court. Walter Clark, it will be remembered, was David Clark's father, but a man of radically different political outlook, preeminently the kind of liberal Wilson wished to appoint. Clark had had a memorable judicial career, and, like the deceased Lurton, he came from the south. His supporters had urged his name upon Taft at the time of Taft's first appointment. Now, "the North Carolina delegation in Congress, headed by Congressman Pou from the Raleigh District, called on [Wilson] in a body and urged the appointment of Clark. Pou wrote Clark that the President expressed admiration for his ability and learning and would, he thought, most likely appoint him. . . . Pou again wrote Clark that those close to the White House [presumably Claude Kitchin and Josephus Daniels] and experienced newspaper correspondents in Washington felt certain that the President would name him." Aubrey Lee Brooks, *Walter Clark, Fighting Judge* (Chapel Hill: University of North Carolina Press, 1944), pp. 190–91.

However, Walter Clark was sixty-seven years old, and Wilson did not want to nominate a man of such advanced age. Had Wilson chosen Clark, constitutional development in the ensuing decade would have been very different. Clark's biography, published in 1944, after the Roosevelt Court had come into being, contains this dedication: "To the Supreme Court of the United States which now reflects the views of Walter Clark" (*ibid.*, p. v). With a justice of Clark's liberal outlook sitting in place of the reactionary McReynolds, the Keating-Owen law undoubtedly would have been upheld by a five-to-four vote, rather than overthrown, and David Clark's test litigation brought to naught. Soon after the decision was announced, Clark wrote to Owen, vigorously condemning it. "In passing the Keating Bill, the House and Senate declared the public policy of the people, by whom they were elected, and whose will they represented. The President not only approved but requested the passage of the Act. The odd man on the Court imbued with the ideas of Judicial Supremacy, and the rights of Capital over Labor, handed down from John Marshall and a Court impressed with the necessity of protecting slavery, set the act aside. Where does the governing power reside?" Walter Clark to Robert L. Owen, June 8, 1918, in *The Papers of Walter Clark*, eds. Aubrey Lee Brooks and Hugh Talmage Lefler (2 vols.; Chapel Hill: University of North Carolina Press, 1950), II, pp. 371–73.

The irony of all this was inadvertently expressed in a tribute that William E. Dodd, the University of Chicago historian, wrote to Clark in April, 1919. Dodd stated: "Your opinions are quoted by all the lawyers of liberal views I know, men like Roscoe Pound. I only wish you were endowed with perennial youth. Last September and again in March I had long talks with the President and you will be glad to know, as you undoubtedly already know as well as anyone, that he is entirely of your frame of mind about courts, a change this from the day when he wrote his book on constitutional **govern-**

Wilson did not make the same mistake a second time. When Justice Lamar died, in January, 1916, Wilson climaxed his liberalism by nominating a man whose "vivid public life" left no doubt whatever about the distinctive qualities of his mind and character. Louis D. Brandeis was a thoroughgoing progressive. The violence of the conservative response — the bitterness and vague terror evident in the lengthy confirmation struggle — unmistakably demonstrated that those whose ideas about public policy had been little affected by the progressive period fully understood the implications of Brandeis's social philosophy. It was alien to their own, and the Supreme Court was the crucial battleground. Wilson stuck with his man, marshaled the Democratic membership of the Senate, and quelled the revolt.

Brandeis was a convinced reformer and an equalitarian;[62] Wilson had often consulted him and valued his judgment. He wrote to a friend about the appointment:

> "I need hardly tell you that I named Mr. Brandeis . . . only because I knew him to be singularly qualified by learning, by gifts, and by character for the position."[63]

Brandeis had been "the people's advocate when public interests called for an effective champion,"[64] and Wilson's counselor on antitrust policy. Far more even than Holmes, Brandeis typified the kind of lawyer Roosevelt had described as the greatest judge; his ability had brought him into close relationship with the largest and most powerful clients but he had kept his broad humanity and his feeling and sympathy for all classes. Throughout his judicial career he championed legislative power as an instrument for improving social conditions.[65]

Wilson's last appointment, which was made shortly after Brandeis's confirmation, also was a well-known progressive, John H. Clarke. In sharp contrast, Clarke's selection produced little excitement and none of the dread that Brandeis's nomination

---

ment in 1908. He said he would never appoint another reactionary to the courts, if he could avoid it. But he said: 'It is indeed hard to make appointees continue what they were when appointed.'" Quoted in *ibid.*, pp. 396–97.

[62] See Corwin, *Constitutional Revolution, Ltd.*, pp. 89–90.

[63] 64th Cong. 1st Sess., Senate Documents, XVII (Washington, D.C.: Government Printing Office, 1916), 239–40; quoted in Robert K. Carr, *The Supreme Court and Judicial Review* ("American Government in Action," ed. Phillip Bradley, Vol. VIII [New York: Holt, Rinehart & Winston, 1942]), p. 239.

[64] *Ibid.*, p. 240.

[65] Corwin, *Constitutional Revolution, Ltd.*, pp. 89–90, and Alpheus T. Mason, *Brandeis: A Free Man's Life* (New York: Viking Press, 1946), pp. 514–18.

had inspired. Clarke typified the liberal-patrician dissenter of the late nineteenth century, turned progressive in the first decade of the twentieth. A Democrat and a friend of Tom Johnson, he had been a highly successful railroad attorney, who chose to act as a conscience for the business community he served.[66] In 1914, at the recommendation of Secretary of War Newton D. Baker, Wilson placed Clarke on the lower federal bench as one of several men thought worthy of grooming for subsequent elevation to the Supreme Court. When Hughes resigned, Baker talked with Clarke and drew him out on his views, especially his interpretation of the antitrust laws, that were not already on the record.[67] This interview convinced Wilson that Clarke could be relied upon for a "liberal and enlightened interpretation of the law."[68]

On the bench, Clarke's thought was closer to Brandeis's than to that of any other justice. He believed in broad governmental intervention in the economy to protect the underprivileged and to advance the interests of the "originative" part of America.[69] In this creed, although strongly nationalistic, he was prepared to allow state legislatures wide latitude over internal affairs. If the Court has known a true exemplar of sociological jurisprudence, Clarke, even more than Brandeis, was that justice.

Judicial Outlook of the Supreme Court in 1917

With Clarke's selection, the bench that would hear the *Dagenhart* case came into being. The remaining Taft appointees and their pre-*Muller* brethren had voted unanimously to sustain congressional authority every time they had reviewed exercises of the commerce power for accomplishing police power objectives. During Wilson's first term there was no significant litigation in this area, nor, for that matter, were any extraordinarily important cases decided that conclusively demonstrated the decisional tendencies of his appointees or suggested changes in the alignment of older members of the bench.

This situation changed radically in the winter of 1917. Within a few months, four cases of major importance were decided. The

---

[66] See Hoyt L. Warner, *The Life of Mr. Justice Clarke* (Cleveland: Western Reserve University Press, 1959), pp. iv–v.

[67] *Ibid.*, p. 63.

[68] Ray Stannard Baker, *Woodrow Wilson, Life and Letters* (8 vols.; Garden City, N.Y.: Doubleday, 1927–38), VI 116; quoted in *ibid.*

[69] Warner, *Life of Mr. Justice Clarke*, pp. 67, 74–75, 82–83, 88–89.

first, *Clark Distilling Co.* v. *Western Maryland Railway Co.*,[70] affirmed the validity of the Webb-Kenyon Act, which had been passed over Taft's veto near the end of his administration. The vote was seven to two, Holmes and Van Devanter dissenting. The Court was not unmindful, Chief Justice White said, that opinions adverse to the statute had been expressed in other departments of the government. He held, however, that even though shipments of liquor were part of interstate commerce while in transit, Congress had ample authority to empower state legislatures to prohibit their entrance into the states. Only Van Devanter, of the surviving Taft appointees, voted to sustain Taft's veto.

Two and a half months later, when the Adamson Act — a far more drastic form of regulatory legislation — was reviewed, the lines tightened.[71] Again, White spoke for the Court, accompanied by Holmes, Brandeis, and Clarke, while McKenna concurred, stating his conclusions in a separate opinion. Two Taft appointees, Van Devanter and Pitney, together with Day and McReynolds, found the enactment invalid, in whole or in part. Beyond permanently establishing an eight-hour day for the operating personnel of railroads, the statute provisionally required that their compensation not be reduced below the level previously paid for the then standard ten-hour day. White admitted that the act imposed a mandatory scale of wages; he held, however, that this interference in the essentially private wage relationship, because temporary in character, was fully justified in the circumstances. The "public right of regulation," inherent in the commerce power, clearly obtained and "was subject to be applied to the extent necessary to provide a remedy." [72]

Day and Pitney felt constrained to state the reasons for their dissent. Day granted that congressional action had been necessary to avert calamity; moreover, he was not prepared to deny Congress authority to regulate the hours and fix the wages of railway workers. Governmental control of such an extensive nature, however, had to be lawfully exercised, and Day found conspicuous procedural inadequacies in the act, requirements that clearly violated due process. Pitney's complaint, in which Van Devanter concurred, was more fundamental — a laissez faire stricture that condemned all interference in the wage relationship.[73] Employ-

---

[70] 242 U.S. 311 (decided January 8, 1917).

[71] *Wilson* v. *New*, 243 U.S. 322 (decided March 19, 1917).

[72] *Ibid.*, p. 348.

[73] In a brief dissent, McReynolds characterized the measure as a patent departure from precedent.

ment was a matter of private bargaining between parties, he declared, and the wages paid railway workers had "no real or substantial connection with interstate commerce."[74] For these reasons, the statute was an unwarranted regulation of the internal affairs of the carriers.

Bunting v. *Oregon*[75] and *Stettler* v. *O'Hara*,[76] decided barely three weeks later, involved state legislation that regulated, respectively, maximum hours of employment in industrial establishments and minimum wages for women and minors.[77] Both statutes embodied important elements of the progressive program; both had been enacted as a direct result of the *Muller* decision; and both had been sustained by the Oregon supreme court. Brandeis took no part in either decision because he had participated in the preparation of the briefs. The other justices were divided, five to three, in the *Bunting* case. McKenna, who wrote the opinion, Holmes, Day, Pitney, and Clarke made up the majority, and White, Van Devanter, and McReynolds dissented. Only White, then, of the justices who had participated in the *Muller* decision, resisted the extension of state regulation of hours to men employed in industry. His vote was all the more interesting because he had dissented in the *Lochner* case. McKenna also shifted from the position he had taken twelve years before, toward liberalism.

Because the dissenters declined to state their objections, McKenna was not obligated to distinguish the arguments of the *Lochner* decision, or to correct them outright. The controlling principle, plainly announced, was the doctrine of presumptive constitutionality. If the statute was taken "at its word," McKenna said, there could be no doubt that its purpose was "to fix the maximum hours of service in certain industries." Then he virtually restated the fundamental argument in Harlan's dissent in the *Lochner* case:

> But we need not cast about for reasons for the legislative judgment. We are not required to . . . be convinced of the wisdom of its exercise. . . . It is enough for our decision if the legislation under review was passed in the exercise of an admitted power of government.[78]

[74] 243 U.S. 322, 382.
[75] 243 U.S. 426 (decided April 9, 1917).
[76] 243 U.S. 629 (decided April 9, 1917).
[77] The former statute permitted overtime work but stipulated compensation at time and a half. It raised, therefore, albeit in a secondary way, the question of wage rates for men.
[78] *Bunting* v. *Oregon*, 243 U.S. 426, 435, 437.

In the *Stettler* case, which raised the more important and far-reaching question of the validity of regulating wages, the division was four to four, sustaining the holding of the Oregon supreme court. Because the decision was *per curiam*, the identity of the two sides cannot be definitely ascertained, but it seems certain that none of the *Bunting* dissenters voted affirmatively. The presumption must be that either Day or Pitney felt the statute went too far. And Pitney's explicit declaration when he dissented in *Wilson* v. *New*, that the bargaining relationship was wholly private, leaves little doubt that it was he who shifted.

Several distinct patterns of alignment emerge from these cases. Van Devanter opposed the four enactments[79] and McReynolds opposed the three that involved regulating the conditions of employment. The militant conservatism of the two justices — their antipathy to governmental intervention in the economy — was strikingly illustrated. In contrast, McKenna, Holmes, Brandeis, and Clarke, where they participated, consistently voted to sustain legislative judgment (except for Holmes's dissent in the *Clark Distilling Company* case, the only controversy that did not involve direct regulatory action). White and Pitney, both Taft appointees, and Justice Day fell between these two groups. White voted to uphold the federal but to invalidate the state enactments. Day and Pitney opposed the Adamson Act, by which Congress entered the field of wage regulation, but approved the Webb-Kenyon Act, which used the divesting principle to facilitate state regulatory action. Both men, moreover, voted to affirm the Oregon maximum-hours legislation, although one of them apparently found that the state's minimum wage status was excessive.

Chief Justice White's choices may seem the least consistent among the "center" justices, particularly because of his solicitude for dual federalism, but this apparent inconsistency is deceiving. White's nationalism and his sure grasp of political imperatives seem to explain his votes to uphold the congressional enactments. The paramountcy of public need especially pervades *Wilson* v. *New*. Had the railroad owners not capitulated to the workers' demands, or the Adamson Act been declared invalid, the result might have been industrial war — violence and economic paralysis worse than that of the strike-torn thirties. Further, neither the *Clark Distilling Co.* nor the *Wilson* cases involved demarcating federalism's boundaries or interference in general property rights. The Webb-Kenyon Act bolstered state authority rather than pre-

[79] Here and in the following analysis, the probable votes in *Stettler* v. *O'Hara* are incorporated.

empted it, and the Adamson Act affected workmen who operated instrumentalities of interstate transportation. White was able, therefore, to maintain his restrictive interpretation of national purposes relatively intact and to throw his influence against legislation that decisively interfered with labor conditions.

The Future Realistically Viewed

By the autumn of 1917, Wilson knew the full extent of his miscalculation about McReynolds. Obdurate and reactionary, McReynolds' vote and the vote of the doctrinaire Van Devanter were virtually certain to go against advanced progressive legislation, whatever its nature. Just as clearly, the liberal coalition of McKenna, Holmes, Brandeis, and Clarke seemed almost certain to sustain the Keating-Owen law. It was not likely that McKenna, once a thoroughgoing conservative and no doubt the least predictable justice in the group, would disown his opinions in the Pure Food and Drug and the Mann Act cases or would try to distinguish them. The fact that the child labor act extended the principles of these decisions and benefitted the laboring class virtually ensured that he would support it.

This left White, Day, and Pitney. Because of his highly restrictive interpretation of the commerce power in his dissenting opinion in the *Wilson* case, Pitney's accord was doubtful but not definitely precluded. Thus the outcome seemingly turned on how White and Day would vote. As much as White, Day hewed to a narrow conception of the meaning of commerce and believed that the reserved powers of the states imposed limitations upon the exercise of national authority, but the reasons for his attachment to these doctrines differed, at least in part. White favored industrial consolidation and he facilitated its growth by developing nationalistic doctrines, preeminently the rule of reason, and incorporating them into law. Day, on the other hand, was emotionally tied to the simple, commercial-agrarian order that was symbolized by the small midwestern cities at the end of the nineteenth century. Thus he steadfastly supported antitrust prosecutions because he believed that the discipline of competition should prevail in the marketplace. At the same time, he wished to maintain the states in their accustomed rights, not to avoid regulating business but to prevent centralizations of power, whatever the agency.

On the other hand, powerful forces pushed White and Day toward consensus with the liberal group of justices and a holding of constitutionality. The most significant force was the obligation, personal as well as institutional, to *stare decisis*. Neither man was stubbornly bound to precedent, least of all White, but both were deeply committed by their decisional past to the stream of police power holdings. White's involvement went back, without interruption, to *Champion* v. *Ames.* Both men, moreover, had voted with the majority in the *McCray* case and White had written the forceful, self-denying opinion. The difficulty was especially compounded for White because of his defense (in the *Wilson* case) of "the public right of regulation" for protecting the public interest and because of his deference to the democratic will. Day conceded, in dissenting in *Wilson,* that legislative acts ordinarily bear the presumption of constitutionality and that the Court had no authority to inquire into legislative motives. He asserted, nevertheless, that Congress had itself confessed the arbitrary character of the Adamson Act, to which White had responded:

> The very highest of judicial duties is to give effect to the legislative will and in so doing to scrupulously abstain from permitting subjects which are exclusively within the field of legislative discretion to influence our opinion or to control judgment.[80]

This exchange pointed to the truly elusive factor that shaped the outcome of the *Dagenhart* case: the extent to which deference to legislative judgment and popular conceptions of permissible national purposes had actually penetrated the judicial mind, particularly White's and Day's thought. It was, after all, only seven years since such bitter antagonists of business regulation as Fuller and Brewer had dominated the Court, and not three decades had passed since Congress had begun to use the commerce power to affect the economic order. White had been forty-two years old, Day nearly forty, and much of their outlook on life and law had been shaped when the Interstate Commerce Act was passed. In addition, popular criticism of the judiciary, which had reached a climax early in Wilson's first term, had declined noticeably by 1917. The Court's tolerant attitude toward legislative experimentation had deprived the various political movements that sought to limit judicial authority of much of their vitality and had helped to restore much of the public esteem that previously had been accorded the bench.

The fate of the Keating-Owen law hinged on whether White and Day deferred to their preferences for tightly compartmentalized federal arrangements or whether one or both found enough scope within the Constitution to embrace the measure.

[80] *Wilson* v. *New,* 243 U.S. 332, 359.

6

Reversion to Judicial Restrictionism:
Hammer v. Dagenhart

Preparations for Argument

Immediately after Judge Boyd entered the Dagenhart injunctions, the interested parties, desirous of having the uncertainty of the legislation quickly resolved, laid plans to hasten the constitutional question to the Supreme Court. The Justice Department's motion to appeal Boyd's judgment was enthusiastically supported by the National Committee and the Children's Bureau. On the other side, David Clark made it clear that every means available to appellees would be employed to advance what it was hoped would be a conclusive victory in the final stage of litigation.[1]

When the Supreme Court convened in October, Clark's lawyers contacted the Solicitor General, John W. Davis, to request that the case be set for argument at the earliest date circumstances would permit.[2] Davis was entirely agreeable; he had contemplated such a motion at a later time and would notify counsel beforehand.[3] The problem that preoccupied the reform agencies, however, was ensuring the most effective defense of the Keating-Owen law. The matter had assumed unusual importance because of the friction that had developed over the adequacy of the government's argument in the district court. The Children's Bureau pressed for assurance from Attorney General Gregory that the Solicitor General, rather than an assistant in his office or special counsel, would argue the case. Davis's confirmation that he would personally handle the litigation was warmly received by the Children's Bureau and the Department of Labor.[4]

---

[1] *Southern Textile Bulletin* (September 13, 1917), p. 10.
[2] Clement Manly to J. W. Davis, October 16, 1917, Justice Department File, *Hammer* v. *Dagenhart*, National Archives, Washington, D.C.
[3] J. W. Davis to C. Manly, October 17, 1917, *ibid.*
[4] Louis Post to J. W. Davis, November 12, 1917, *ibid.*

Somewhat earlier, A. J. McKelway had talked with Davis about the plans the Justice Department had under consideration and Davis had asked that the National Committee prepare material bearing on the reasonableness of the Keating-Owen law to assist him in constructing the government's brief. Davis also informed McKelway that the Justice Department might call upon a lawyer of national prominence to assist in arguing the case. One of the men being considered, he said, was Charles Evans Hughes, the former associate justice of the Supreme Court and Republican presidential nominee the year before.[5]

This information convinced the National Committee that there was no reason to worry that the defense of the child labor act might be slighted because of the enormous demands that had been placed upon the Justice Department by the war effort. In mid-November, however, Davis gave the responsibility for the initial draft of the government's brief to William Frierson, the Assistant Attorney General who earlier had mediated the disagreement between Pound and Parkinson.[6] In addition to the material already at hand and that which Wiley Swift had compiled for the National Committee, Frierson had a copy of Pound's argument in the district court.[7]

On January 28, 1918, Davis wrote to Clement Manly and enclosed copies of the motion to advance that he had submitted to the Supreme Court that day.[8] The motion stipulated concurrence by counsel for the appellees and set forth the following grounds for moving the litigation forward.

> The case is of importance to the Department of Labor in the administration of the "child labor law" and to the Department of Justice in the matter of enforcing the criminal provisions of the law. For these reasons and because the case is one of general public interest an early determination by this court is desirable.[9]

A week later Davis informed Manly that the Court had granted the motion and and that argument was set for April 15.[10] The

[5] "Minutes of the Board of Trustees, N.C.L.C.," October 31, 1917.

[6] J. W. Davis to William Frierson, November 15, 1917, Justice Department File, *Hammer* v. *Dagenhart.*

[7] Roscoe Pound to W. Frierson, September 28, 1917, *ibid.*

[8] J. W. Davis to C. Manly, January 28, 1918, *ibid.*

[9] *Motion to Advance,* Supreme Court of the United States, October Term, 1917, No. 704 (Washington, D.C.: Government Printing Office, 1918), January 28, 1918, pp. 1–2.

[10] J. W. Davis to C. Manly, February 5, 1918, Justice Department File, *Hammer* v. *Dagenhart.*

delay of several months in presenting the motion foreshadowed no change in the government's plans. Despite the priority the Justice Department accorded the case, other matters, directly related to the prosecution of the war, were of far greater urgency and claimed the first attention of the Attorney General and his staff.

On March 21, Davis sent copies of the latest version of the government's brief to Parkinson and Pound and requested "such criticism and suggestions as you may care to make."[11] After consultation, they gave Davis the reply he desired. Pound responded immediately, praising the brief, but the Justice Department files do not contain a statement from Parkinson. Pound stated:

> . . . the argument appears to me full, complete and convincing. . . . I shall write to the friends of the Act who have been interested in this litigation saying to them that in my judgment they could not hope to have the case better presented.[12]

Davis acknowledged: "I trust the end will crown the work."[13]

At the same time, Davis had sent copies of the brief to Manly, for Junius Parker and Manly had been pressing Davis, in conversation and correspondence, to see the government's argument as soon as it was completed.[14] Davis's favor, a common courtesy in appellate litigation, was not reciprocated until just before argument.

Clark, who had hoped the case would be argued early in the term, chafed under the delay. His irritation manifested itself in editorial charges that the National Committee and the Children's Bureau were doing everything within their power to delay a Supreme Court decision. In addition, Clark inveighed against what he claimed was a desperate effort by the National Committee to influence the Supreme Court through publicity in the Washington newspapers and speeches in Congress.[15] To counter the alleged campaign and to influence public opinion — especially to affect congressional attitudes about the necessity for further federal legislation if the Keating-Owen law was invalidated — he published a massive, special edition of the *Bulletin* bearing the saccharine title the "Health and Happiness Issue."[16]

[11] J. W. Davis to T. I. Parkinson and R. Pound, March 21, 1918, *ibid.*
[12] R. Pound to J. W. Davis, March 23, 1918, *ibid.*
[13] J. W. Davis to R. Pound, April 1, 1918, *ibid.*
[14] Certified statement, J. W. Davis to C. Manly, March 30, 1918, *ibid.*
[15] *Southern Textile Bulletin* (February 7 and January 31, 1918), p. 10.
[16] *Ibid.*, December 20, 1917.

This largely pictorial propaganda piece was artfully designed to give the lie to critics of the southern textile industry by presenting the "facts" about mill operations and the "truth" about life in the surrounding villages.[17] The highly selective contents, drawn disproportionately from the newer and more progressive mills, contrasts sharply with the memorable photographs Lewis Hine took during the same period to document exploitation in the mills. Neither set of photographs accurately portrayed conditions throughout the industry, but the National Committee had not pretended that Hine's work was representative; it was merely irrefutable proof that shameful practices persisted. Clark's condemnation of the National Committee's publicity efforts similarly distorted reality. The committee worked hard to sustain interest in reform and to counteract the tendency to relax existing regulatory legislation, but it did not try to lobby the bench.

The Strategy of Argument: Written Briefs and Oral Advocacy

The aim of counsel in preparing the briefs that are required in all cases taken to appellate courts and in outlining their oral arguments is to persuade the bench. Neither form of presentation can be neglected, for a well-constructed brief that meets the essential issues that have been raised in litigation can be just as convincing as an outstanding oral argument. Thus the able attorney attempts to integrate the two forms of advocacy: to sustain an organized argument in his brief and to adapt his presentation before the court so that every aspect of the art of persuasion is exploited. Every factor that may give an advantage is taken into account. "Certainly," Carr points out, "any wise present-day lawyer preparing a case for presentation to the Supreme Court gives as much thought to the individual justices, their likes, prejudices, and personal idiosyncracies, as he does to legal arguments or precedents favorable to his side of the case."[18] Ordinarily, experience practicing before the Court and personal force and intellect give an edge in selecting the materials that are likely to be most persuasive in briefs and during the dramatic, and often crucial, moments of argument.

---

[17] Copies were sent to libraries throughout the country and to all members of Congress. Inasmuch as the congressional committees had ignored the cotton manufacturers' invitations to visit southern mills the previous year, Clark, in effect, sought to show them what they had "refused" to see.

[18] Robert K. Carr, *The Supreme Court and Judicial Review* ("American Government in Action," ed. Phillip Bradley, Vol. VIII [New York: Holt, Rinehart & Winston, 1942]), p. 236.

Between John W. Davis and Morgan J. O'Brien, the advantage clearly lay with Davis. Appointed Solicitor General in the summer of 1913, Davis argued an extraordinary number of cases — sixty-seven in all — during five ensuing terms of the Court.[19] None of his predecessors had appeared as often, and few approached his enviable record of success. Davis, moreover, was warmly regarded by the bench and by the Supreme Court bar. Felix Frankfurter, who knew him as a fellow member of Wilson's administration, described Davis as "an enchanting advocate with great grace, charm, and distinction."[20] Handsome and of imposing presence, he was highly cultivated, eloquent in speech, and vastly engaging in personality. The respect that members of the Court had for him is indicated in the following account from a presidential campaign profile.

> When [Davis] appeared in the Supreme Court chamber every in-
> terested observer used to be reminded a lot of doting grandfathers
> enjoying the performance of a precocious and favorite grandson.
> The Court fairly hovered over Mr. Davis in its solicitude, particu-
> larly Chief Justice White. The Court can be most unapproachable
> and aloof in its demeanor toward the bar, as every lawyer who has
> appeared before it knows. But it never heckled its fair-haired boy.[21]

This admiration once prompted the justices to take the highly unusual step of informing President Wilson that they would welcome Davis's appointment to the bench.[22]

On the basis of experience, then, and by reason of his personal qualities and knowledge of the bench, Davis was superbly equipped to defend the constitutionality of the Keating-Owen law. The government's side of the controversy possessed a further, though incalculable, advantage: the history of the progressive movement and the wartime crisis favored a nationalistic decision sustaining congressional authority. In Europe, the crucial weeks of the war were at hand; the great German spring offensive swept relentlessly forward, seeking a decisive advantage before American soldiers could reach the front in sufficient numbers to stem the tide. In America, the necessity of mobilizing the industrial forces

19 Theodore A. Huntley, *The Life of John W. Davis* (New York: Duffield and Co., 1924), pp. 95–96. In a practice extending over half a century, John G. Johnson argued seventy-one cases before the Supreme Court.

20 Felix Frankfurter, *Felix Frankfurter Reminisces*, ed. Harlan B. Phillips (New York: Reynal, 1960), p. 267.

21 Edward G. Lowry, quoted in Clinton W. Gilbert, *You Takes Your Choice* (New York: G. P. Putnam, 1924), p. 63.

22 Huntley, *Life of John W. Davis*, p. 98.

of the nation had led Congress to grant Wilson more extensive powers than any President had ever exercised before. The railroads, as well as other instrumentalities of transportation and communication, had come under federal control; government boards were fixing prices, conscripting labor, regulating hours and wages, and establishing production priorities. In greater measure perhaps than ever before, the doctrine of the paramountcy of public need affected the Supreme Court on decisions that touched many sectors of American life. The justices were manifestly reluctant to cut down national powers.

Nevertheless, as John Frank makes clear, success in constitutional litigation sometimes is precluded.

> The really basic question is: what difference [do written briefs and oral advocacy] make? What is the significance or consequence of the role of the lawyer in Supreme Court litigation?
>
> The answer depends very heavily upon the class of cases involved. If the case is in an area in which the Justices have marked opinions to start with, they may be unpersuadable, and in that situation the arguments are unimportant.[23]

Davis's argument strongly suggests he realized that, because of their special enthusiasms, it was useless to try to persuade Van Devanter and McReynolds to approve progressive social legislation. In turn, the argument presented by Clark's lawyers strongly suggests that they considered the principal exponents of non-interventionist judicial philosophy — Holmes, Brandeis, and Clarke — to be unpersuadable. Both teams of counsel therefore designed their presentations to appeal chiefly to the justices whose positions seemed most in doubt and, consequently, possibly open to persuasion. This meant that argument was directed primarily toward White and Day.

The Government's Brief: National
Powers Affirmed

Davis's defense of the Keating-Owen law differed little in outline from the earlier arguments of William Draper Lewis, Thomas I. Parkinson, and the congressional sponsors of the measure.[24] Nevertheless, Davis handled the elements of the argument in a distinctive way. In previous encounters, those who supported national action had usually dwelt at length on the law; that is, they

23 John P. Frank, *Marble Palace* (New York: Alfred A. Knopf, 1958), p. 97.
24 See *Brief for Appellant, Hammer* v. *Dagenhart* (Washington, D.C.: Government Printing Office, 1918), pp. 3–4.

had sought legal justification for the exercise of the commerce power to promote the public welfare. Davis, however, devoted six pages of terse argument to this phase of the defense. He felt that the Court, in particular the justices who had to be persuaded, needed education in the facts and their proper application, rather than in the relevant legal principles.

This concentration followed Davis's instructions to a later generation of advocates for success in appellate proceedings. The lawyer must first of all provide the judges, who usually "know nothing whatever of the controversy," with what Justice Holmes called "the implements of decision." To do this, he must know the judges' "mental habits" — as far as possible, "change places" with them. The implements consisted of stating the nature of the controversy and its chronology, stating the facts, and stating the applicable rules of law. In an appellate court, the presentation of the facts "is not merely a part of the argument, it is more often than not the argument itself." Then, Davis counseled, "always 'go for the jugular,'" the cardinal point of the case, rather than cast numerous hooks, hoping to sink one.[25]

"Unquestionably," the government brief asserted, after Davis had succinctly cleared away the details of the controversy and the chronology, "the power conferred upon Congress [to regulate commerce] was plenary and embraced all the power which the States had previously enjoyed over the subject."[26] Many judicial decisions had subsequently made clear that commerce involved the transportation of goods, that congressional control attached the instant movement began, and that regulation could take the form of prohibition.

The child labor law, to be specific, applied "only when actual transportation to another State" began, Davis said; it laid no prohibition upon manufacturers as such. This was the cardinal point, and Davis concentrated his argument upon it.

> That [the Keating-Owen law] is a regulation such as it purports to be is clear if the plainest and most unambiguous language can make it so. The contention to the contrary is in effect an attack upon the good faith of Congress and invites the Court to assume that the language used, notwithstanding its explicit character, is a mere pretense adopted in order to cloak a usurpation of State power to make local police regulations. The act, however, must be read as it is written. Its character as a regulation can only be

[25] John W. Davis, "Part II," *Success in Court*, ed. Francis I. Wellman (New York: Macmillan Co., 1941), pp. 221–41.
[26] *Brief for Appellant*, p. 6.

denied by reasserting the now obsolete doctrine that the power to regulate does not include the power to exclude designated articles from the channels of commerce.[27]

The relevant constitutional doctrines were so well established, Davis asserted, that they precluded contradictory interpretation: police power enactments were essentially matters of public policy and were excluded from judicial supervision. The brief said nothing about forging a new epoch in constitutional jurisprudence — precedent amply legitimated the challenged statute.

The remainder of the brief, much the greater part of it, documented the facts — "the implements of decision," which, in Davis's view, more often than not won arguments. Surely and with great economy, Davis described the development of industrial child labor, the rise of the reform movement, the way in which interstate commerce heightened the child labor problem and conditioned state response, and the growth of public consciousness that national action was necessary to remedy the problem. No more incisive analysis of this history has ever been written. Davis's treatment of the practical considerations was brought to its climax in the following summary statement:

> Back of the present law stands the general conviction, clearly evidenced, that child labor is in and of itself immoral in character and injurious to the general welfare; that as such it may be properly abolished by the States within their several borders and by Congress in channels of interstate trade; that the States are deterred from dealing with the matter as they wish for want of harmonious action among them; and that its use by competitors is unjust and immoral.[28]

Everything thereafter was subsidiary — props to support the conclusion that the Keating-Owen law remedied a pressing public problem by permissible means. The attack upon the statute, Davis pointed out, usually took the form of suggested distinctions about congressional authority, said to derive from the Fifth and Tenth Amendments. Although remarkably ingenious, these contentions found sanction neither in law, for the courts had repeatedly rejected them, nor in logic, for their reasoning was not tenable. As for the contention that prohibition extended only to articles that were injurious in themselves, Davis stated:

> Discussion of the inherent badness of things is largely futile. How do we judge of goodness or badness except by their effects?

27 *Ibid.*, pp. 9–10.
28 *Ibid.*, p. 48.

. . . Those things which work ill effects when transported across state lines are for that reason evil. The transportation of the products of child labor, therefore, cannot be classed as innocuous in fact.[29]

As for the contention that the consumer "at the end of the interstate journey" was the only legitimate object of concern, Davis stated:

. . . It is the public, wherever situated, that is entitled to protection. . . .

The truth is that in most cases it is impossible in point of fact to separate the consuming from the producing public. The interstate journey cannot be confined in its effects to the people in the receiving State. Action and reaction pursue each other in the course of human affairs regardless of State lines.[30]

Throughout this part of the argument, Davis repeatedly referred to the precedent police power rulings, especially the *Hoke* case. Other precedents, notably Chief Justice White's opinion in the *McCray* case, were used to answer the secondary attack on the measure, the charge that Congress had not acted in good faith. Again, the contention was neither legally supportable nor logically tenable, Davis argued, for the statute was a legitimate exercise of conceded power. Whatever view individual justices might take of its ultimate purpose, the institutional view of the Court was confined to the objective expressed on its face.

"As every presumption favors validity, the court need not speculate on motives. If any legitimate purpose is discernible on inspection of the act it must be sustained." [31]

The arguments that would induce the Court to go beyond this rule had been specifically condemned in the *McCray* holding, Davis declared. The implication was clear: either White's opinion was controlling or it should be corrected.

Two features of the brief stand out: the skillful portrayal of the practical matters that Holmes termed "the life of the law," and the extent to which argument was directed at White. In particular, the realistic conception of modern industrialism that Davis developed merits attention. Although he consistently referred to transportation as the physical condition of commerce, its substance was conceived as traffic in the sense that Marshall used

29 *Ibid.*, pp. 41–42.
30 *Ibid.*, pp. 64–65.
31 *Ibid.*, p. 67.

the word — but traffic in an economy profoundly altered by technological innovation, a complex, interrelated, and well-understood course of commercial activities that defined separation into artificial compartments.

If one accepted this conception, he thereby substantially approved Davis's argument, and this, no doubt, is exactly what Davis wanted from White, who was noticeably chary about facts that ran counter to his constitutional ideas. Davis knew how to appeal to White (the two men felt almost boundless esteem for each other), and he did so subtly. There was nothing mechanical about his efforts to remove the aging jurist's doubts. Repeatedly, Davis used passages from White's opinions to show that the prohibitions said to limit the commerce power had been rejected decisively in earlier cases. But he must have known that he had to induce White, and perhaps others, to face reality in order to succeed.

The Southern Textile Manufacturers' Brief: Shall There Be Absolutely Nationalized Control of American Life?

Clark's lawyers also used arguments that had been developed by other men, principally the doctrines that John G. Johnson and, especially, William Guthrie had formulated in an effort to narrow the scope of federal authority in the field of interstate commerce. Indeed, the framework of their brief derived almost entirely from Guthrie's losing argument in the Lottery case. Necessarily, O'Brien and his associates took account of the judicial holdings since that time that had sustained federal police power statutes, but they sought to read into them the same limitations that Guthrie had suggested. This meant elaborating supposedly established doctrines, but they contributed nothing of conceptual substance to the fundamental propositions of dual federalism.

The brief began where the southern defense against federal child labor legislation had always begun,[32] with the policy argument that national intervention was unnecessary.

> In every State in the Union, legislation has been enacted with respect to the employment of children. These regulations have

---

[32] Before it reached the constitutional issues, the brief sought to dispose of any apprehension that might have existed about the question of jurisdiction. "The propriety of this suit, as a test of the constitutionality of the statute in question, is not questioned by the defendant-appellant," it was asserted. *Brief for Appellees, Hammer* v. *Dagenhart* (New York: Stillman Appellate Printing Co., 1918), p. 4.

taken into account the conditions of the State affected, having regard to climate, distribution of wealth, social conditions and other
such conditions. . . .

*Of course, these steps have, in a general way, been coincident
with the progress of the States in wealth and prosperity. . . . In
other words, . . . that which might be entirely wise and humane
in a rich community, of cold climate, where weather conditions
make ventilation difficult, inhabited chiefly by Anglo-Saxons, would
be an unwise burden in a community where poverty still stalks,
where weather conditions may make possible constant fresh air
even in a factory, and where the population is, in whole or in part,
of some other and earlier maturing race than the Anglo-Saxon.*[33]

Insinuated in this argument and in several subsequent passages
that questioned the need for federal action was the clear idea that
the south had to exploit the economic advantages that inhered
in the industrial employment of children in order to counterbal-
ance the natural and historical advantages possessed by other regions. Moreover, the thoroughly discredited accusation that the
reform movement generally, and the Keating-Owen law specifically, had been inspired by New England textile interests was
revived. The import of these arguments — that the southern past
and the region's struggle for economic survival justified different
standards of social regulation — might well have appealed to a
member of the bench who had fought in the Confederate ranks,
lived through reconstruction, and vividly remembered the heritage
of poverty, a man who also had represented southern industrial
interests as a member of Congress.[34]

Having wished away the existence of child labor as a national
problem, the brief treated the fundamental issue, as it was characterized in the case — the far-reaching consequences of holding
the Keating-Owen law constitutional.

The question . . . is (and we make this statement with the utmost respect) whether those who earnestly favor an absolutely
nationalized control of every function and activity of life, and
the complete elimination of the States as political entities, have
hit upon a new and yet unused tool to accomplish their purpose.[35]

[33] *Ibid.*, pp. 9–10.
[34] That Chief Justice White recalled the southern past with emotional intensity is demonstrated by remarks he made in a contemporary conversation
with Felix Frankfurter. Frankfurter remembers that White "spent a considerable time descanting on the ruin that the Civil War had wrought in the
South. They were just about emerging from all the devastation and the consequences of such a war." *Felix Frankfurter Reminisces*, p. 98.
[35] *Brief for Appellees*, p. 14.

If Congress could regulate local matters by influencing the movement of persons and things in commerce, it could impose its will upon every aspect of local and personal conduct. This prophecy of impending doom was so familiar that Clark's lawyers found it necessary to assure the Court there was nothing fanciful in their forebodings. The evocation of the "Grand Peur" reached its climax in the crucial passage in the brief.

> There is practically involved in this case the right of Congress to regulate, under the guise of a commerce regulation, every relation of life. . . . If the views of those who assert the constitutionality of this method are sound, there is no practical necessity, nor reason, for State legislatures, and certainly none for constitutional amendments.[36]

The precedents demonstrated, the brief acknowledged, that Congress could regulate commerce with a view to promoting the general welfare, but the evil so reached had to be involved in, or assisted by, commerce to justify regulation or prohibition. Commerce, of course, was defined exclusively as interstate transportation. Although the Lottery and White Slave cases were said to confirm this limitation upon national purposes, the precedent mainly relied upon was White's fervent defense of the federal equilibrium in the *First Employers' Liability* cases.[37] The present Chief Justice's language, counsel for the textile manufacturers said, "seems to us decisive in the case" (the emphasis is theirs):

> It remains only to consider the contention . . . that the act is constitutional, although it embraces subjects not within the power of Congress to regulate commerce, because one who engages in interstate commerce thereby submits all his business concerns to the regulating power of Congress. To state the proposition is to refute it. *It assumes that because one engages in interstate commerce he thereby endows Congress with power not delegated to it by the Constitution, in other words, with the right to legislate concerning matters of purely State concern.*[38]

In addition, the brief stressed *United States* v. *Delaware and Hudson Co.*,[39] which sustained part, but not all, of the Commodities Clause legislation. White had used the occasion to try to restore the ebbing vitality of the distinction between manufacture and commerce that had been announced a decade before. This obscure

---

36 *Ibid.*, p. 16.
37 207 U.S. 463 (1908).
38 *Ibid.*, p. 502; quoted in *Brief for Appellees*, pp. 29–30.
39 213 U.S. 366 (1909).

authority, counsel urged, demonstrated conclusively that, on its face, the Keating-Owen law constituted an exercise of power for a purpose not expressly committed to Congress.[40] Thereby Clark's lawyers tried to undercut the strictures in White's *McCray* opinion that denied the Court authority to examine congressional motives.

In this instance, as in many others, the Executive Committee's brief was aided by the opportunity O'Brien, Parker, Hendren, and the others had had to examine the government's brief. They repeatedly juxtaposed their interpretations of the "facts" to those that Davis had developed. This contrast was perhaps most striking with respect to the implications of the interconnectedness of modern economic life. In their version, the potential for harmful federal interference took precedence over anything else, and this gave meaning to the major thrust of their attack — the emotional warning about the disastrous consequences an affirmative holding would produce. It helped compensate for the sparseness of the legal doctrines that supposedly enunciated limitations upon the commerce power. And it justified the necessity for the Supreme Court to oversee national economic regulation in order to maintain the states in their accustomed power. Both sides, it seems, assumed that practical considerations of public policy rather than abstract legal doctrines would determine the outcome.

Contradictory Doctrines: "The Rightful Scope of Governmental Function"

Late in the day, on April 15, Solicitor General Davis, as counsel for the appellant, opened oral argument in the *Dagenhart* case. He continued his presentation the following day, and Morgan J. O'Brien, accompanied by William Hendren, appeared for the nominal appellees. At both sessions the courtroom was packed with important personages from the various branches of government, many of them legal and business notables who had come to Washington to participate in various phases of the war effort.[41] The significance of the case was widely recognized and the anticipated clash between distinguished advocates stirred excitement.

Davis had hardly begun, following the lines of his brief, before the justices began to raise questions.[42] Throughout the controversy, counsel for both sides were repeatedly interrupted, the members of the bench showing lively interest in the various as-

---

[40] *Brief for Appellees*, p. 51.
[41] *Outlook* (May 29, 1918), p. 187.
[42] *Ibid.*

pects of the pleadings.[43] The interplay of questioning apparently involved occasional harassment, but, for the most part, the justices seemed genuinely to be seeking information from the advocates before them.

Davis must have delighted in this response. Later, he advised lawyers to "rejoice when the courts ask questions" during oral argument because it meant the justices were interested. "A question affords you your only chance to penetrate the mind of the court." It disclosed what the justices were thinking and revealed doubts that might be dispelled, favorable inclinations that might be encouraged.[44] Davis drew a running fire of questions and comments, according to one report, when he contended: "Underlying this statute is the conviction that child labor is always and everywhere inherently an evil thing and all statutes are a reflection of prevailing opinion in the public mind."[45] Davis defended this cardinal point and constantly integrated it with another: that legal doctrine made permissible what dominant opinion justifiably demanded.[46]

Like John G. Johnson, after whose strategy in argument he patterned his own, Davis sought, by keeping always to his main point, to control the pleading and make it "difficult for his adversary to persuade the Court that there was anything else worthy to be considered."[47] O'Brien suffered from this strategy, it appears, but not to the same extent as other counsel on other occasions. The available evidence suggests that his presentation, which never ventured from the Executive Committee's brief, failed to evoke the same heightened interest, although he, too, was asked many questions. In particular, White pursued the query whether, as one correspondent reported it, Congress had not, in passing the Thirteenth Amendment, assumed responsibility for the maintenance of "virile citizenship"; that is, a healthy and informed citizenry, a purpose that might serve as an analogy for the Keating-Owen law.[48]

When counsel's time was up, one fact stood out beyond all others — the freedom the Court had for exercising deliberate choice about the constitutional interpretation it would approve.

43 *Ibid.*; see also *Washington Post* and *Washington Evening Star*, April 16, 17, 1918.

44 Davis, *Success in Court*, p. 234.

45 *Washington Post*, April 17, 1918.

46 *Outlook* (May 29, 1918), p. 187.

47 Davis, *Success in Court*, p. 234.

48 *Outlook* (May 29, 1918), p. 187.

From the briefs and from the oral pleadings, the justices had comprehensive statements of two alternative lines of constitutional doctrine that comprehended the nature and extent of the commerce power. Davis had argued for a uniformly broad interpretation of congressional authority — for the interpretation that had been developed by the Marshall Court, that was extended during the progressive era (mainly in the period of judicial toleration), and that had been repeatedly confirmed in the previous police power rulings. O'Brien (and the counsel associated with him) had argued for a highly restrictive interpretation — the body of doctrine (largely fashioned during the period of judicial intervention) that rested upon the narrow view of the commerce that had been developed in the Sugar Trust case and upon the theory that the reserved powers of the states restricted national purposes.

Both positions had a measure of plausibility, in the sense that various principles and doctrines of constitutional law could be brought to their support, but they diverged sharply from each other, and were, in fact, logically incompatible. Both counsels contended that consistency required a holding in agreement with the position each espoused; to rule otherwise would involve a departure from past decisions. In part, although the magnitudes differed, each was right.

Despite William Draper Lewis's assertion (in 1914) that the contemporary Court had firmly embraced the Marshallian view of the Constitution, a position Davis essentially reiterated, the precedents cited did not include the entire spectrum of relevant holdings. Clark's lawyers could point to the Sugar Trust and *First Employers' Liability* cases, and to other expressions of judicial negativism, as precedents for their position. Some of these decisions, however, had declined in standing; in fact, several were viewed by competent authorities as having been overruled *sub silento*. Nevertheless, a majority of the Court had power, if they chose, to restore their earlier vitality. However one approached it, the decision in the case would involve a judgment about "the rightful scope of governmental function," in Corwin's phrase.[49] One line of judicial rulings would be strengthened, at least for a time, and the other weakened, if not destroyed outright.

Whichever line was approved, Chief Justice White and Justice Day would find themselves in an enviable position. Both had

[49] Edward S. Corwin, *Constitutional Revolution, Ltd.* (Claremont, Calif.: Claremont Colleges, 1941), p. 31.

voted, in cases decided while they were members of the Court, for the holdings that could be said to be controlling, whether they were cited as such or not — be they *United States* v. *E. C. Knight* and the *First Employers' Liability* cases or *Champion* v. *Ames*, *McCray* v. *United States*, and *Hoke* v. *United States*. Such are the vagaries of constitutional adjudication.

Hammer v. *Dagenhart* Decided: "The Far-reaching Result of Upholding the Act"

On June 3, 1918, the Supreme Court, by a five-to-four vote, declared the Keating-Owen law unconstitutional. Crucially, both White and Day rejected the factual "implements of decision" Davis had offered them and resolved their doubts in line with their marked preference for an impotent national authority. Together with Van Devanter, Pitney, and McReynolds — latter-day counterparts of Fuller, Brewer, and Peckham — they formed the bare but decisive majority. McKenna, Holmes, Brandeis, and Clarke, the coalition of justices who were disinclined to stay legislative judgment, dissented, and Holmes wrote a powerful opinion that criticized the majority's position.

Day, the other surviving Rooseveltian appointee, spoke for the Court. The government had insisted, he said, that adjudged cases established the doctrine that the regulatory power granted Congress incidentally included the authority to prohibit the movement of ordinary commodities, but

> the cases demonstrate the contrary. . . . In each . . . the use of the interstate transportation was necessary to the accomplishment of harmful results. In other words, although the power over interstate transportation was to regulate, that could only be accomplished by prohibiting the use of the facilities of interstate commerce to effect the evil intended. This element is wanting in the present case. . . . The act in its effect does not regulate transportation among the States, but aims to standardize the ages at which children may be employed in mining and manufacturing within the States. The goods shipped are of themselves harmless. . . . When offered for shipment, and before transportation begins, the labor of their production is over, and the mere fact that they were intended for interstate transportation does not make their production subject to federal control under the commerce power.[50]

To all intents and purposes, that was it. But the majority chose to drive the decision farther. The government had further con-

50 *Hammer* v. *Dagenhart*, 247 U.S. 251, 270–72.

tended, Day said, that the channels of interstate commerce could be closed as a means of controlling the unfair competition engendered by the differences between state regulatory standards. However, this doctrine was no less erroneous, he declared.

> There is no power vested in Congress to require the States to exercise their police power so as to prevent possible unfair competition. Many causes may cooperate to give one State, by reason of local laws or conditions, an economic advantage over others. The commerce clause was not intended to give to Congress a general authority to equalize such conditions. . . . The grant of authority over a purely federal matter was not intended to destroy the local power always existing and carefully reserved to the States in the Tenth Amendment to the Constitution.[51]

Hence, Day ruled, judged by "its natural and reasonable effect," the Keating-Owen law was in a twofold sense repugnant to the Constitution. "It not only transcends the authority delegated to Congress over commerce, but also exerts a power as to a purely local matter to which the federal authority does not extend."[52] At the same time, Day disclosed the crucial reason behind the decision — the majority's apprehension about what would follow if the act were sustained.

> The far-reaching result of upholding the act cannot be more plainly indicated than by pointing out that if Congress can thus regulate matters entrusted to local authority by prohibition of the movement of commodities in interstate commerce, all freedom of commerce will be at an end, and the power of the States over local matters may be eliminated, and thus our system of government be practically destroyed.[53]

For the majority, in short, the case fundamentally involved the preservation of the rightful character of the federal equilibrium.

With Day's words, laissez faire returned to the Court. The cluster of significant cases decided early in 1917 had indeed heralded a resurgence of judicial restrictionism, but this would not become readily apparent until several years later. The doctrinal triumph unquestionably belonged to William Guthrie, for the principles of the opinion were those of dual federalism and limited national purposes.[54] The ideas that had been rejected as

[51] *Ibid.*, pp. 273–74.
[52] *Ibid.*, p. 276.
[53] *Ibid.*
[54] Benjamin R. Twiss, *Lawyers and the Constitution* (Princeton: Princeton University Press, 1942), pp. 217–20.

a limitation upon the commerce power in the Lottery case were now pronounced to be the law of the land. But the larger triumph belonged to former Chief Justice Fuller, whose foreboding dissent in the Lottery case formed the seminal statement of the "Grand Peur" in the field of federal police power legislation. His opinion had ended with an anguished warning, one whose depth of conviction and emotional intensity has rarely been matched in Supreme Court utterance: "Our form of government may remain notwithstanding legislation or decision, but, as long ago observed, as with religions, the form may survive the substance of the faith." [55]

Fuller had not been sanguine enough. The substance of the faith had survived; and five justices who subscribed to all or a portion of Fuller's strictures now called a halt to federal interference in any phase of the relationships of employment. Congress had gone beyond their rooted notions of permissible regulation, and these preferences for familiar social arrangements determined their judicial choice. Forced to choose between divergent interpretations of the commerce power, they translated their anachronistic convictions into substantive restrictions upon the enumerated powers of Congress. As frequently happened during the height of judicial interventionism, the *feeling* that Congress should not possess certain authority had been transformed into the *belief* that it did not possess that authority.

The greatest triumph in the decision, however, was reserved for William Howard Taft. Three of the justices who helped make up the narrow majority — White, Van Devanter, and Pitney — bore his commission, and a fourth — the opinion writer, Day, his intimate friend and former colleague on the circuit court bench — owed his place primarily to Taft's recommendation to Theodore Roosevelt. Five years before, White and Pitney had disregarded Taft's veto of the Webb-Kenyon Act, but, when a critical decision was reached in a case of extraordinary importance, they responded characteristically. Each of Taft's appointees who was still on the Court voted to invalidate the Keating-Owen law. What is more, Day's opinion essentially restated Taft's frequent denunciations of the idea that federal child labor regulation was constitutional. Defeated for re-election, Taft had accepted appointment, in 1913, to the Law School faculty at Yale University, where he castigated progressivism's radical program for democratizing American life. A movement had arisen, Taft said, "called the New Nationalist

[55] *Champion* v. *Ames* 188 U.S. 321, 375.

School that proposes to put into operation a great many new remedies through the National Government basing the national authority on the failure or unfitness of the States to discharge their proper and exclusive duties under the Constitution."[56]

To arrest this threat, the powers and functions of the states had to be maintained in all their fullness. About child labor reform, one of the new remedies, Taft declared:

> Child labor in the state of shipment has no legitimate or germane relation to the interstate commerce of which the goods thus made are to form a part, to its character, or to its effects. Such an attempt of Congress to use its power of regulating such commerce to suppress the use of child labor in the state of shipment would be a clear usurpation of that state's rights.[57]

Day's syntax was superior but the substance was the same. The Constitution was safe, not for a few more years but for another generation, for kindred conservatives — including Taft himself — would soon join the members of the majority whose tenure was to extend beyond the progressive era.

An Opinion Writer's Dilemma: Distinguishing the Indistinguishable

We know virtually nothing about what occurred when the *Dagenhart* case was discussed in conference and during the period in which opinions were circulated; only the closely contested vote and the antagonistic opinions, testifying to an irreconcilable division, became public knowledge. A number of facts about the alignment, beyond the decisive concurrence of the Taft appointees, are unambiguous, however, and several other aspects of where choice fell are suggestive.

Of the six justices still on the Court who had subscribed to the sweeping terms used to define the scope of federal police power in the *Hoke* case, only McKenna and Holmes were prepared to approve the Keating-Owen law. McKenna's opinion in *Hoke* had reflected the position that Congress had broad authority to use its power over interstate commerce in any manner that would "promote the general welfare, material and moral,"[58] but White, Day, Van Devanter, and Pitney failed to find sufficient latitude within

[56] William Howard Taft, *Popular Government: Its Essence, Its Permanence and Its Perils* (New Haven: Yale University Press, 1913), p. 152.
[57] *Ibid.*, pp. 142–43.
[58] See Robert E. Cushman, "The National Police Power under the Commerce Clause of the Constitution," *S.E.C.L.*, III, 72.

this position to embrace the child labor act. Together with White, McKenna and Holmes were the surviving members of the five-judge majority that had originally sanctioned police power legislation in the Lottery case. Although McKenna and Holmes continued to interpret that decision liberally, White had sided with another five-judge majority to impose hitherto unknown limitations upon the doctrines enumerated in that case — restrictions that had been rejected at the time it was decided. The alignment in *Dagenhart,* furthermore, exactly paralleled the alignment in *Wilson* v. *New,* except that White had shifted to the side of unconstitutionality.

In these circumstances, the canons of judicial propriety and the no less binding imperatives of judicial statesmanship made it virtually incumbent upon White to write the opinion of the Court; the decision, moreover, was extraordinarily important and had been reached by the narrowest possible margin. That White did not assume this burden but assigned it to Day, the other justice likely to have had difficulty resolving his judgment in the case, is surely significant. Day's authorship seems to illustrate the circumstance in which a brother won over, rather than an already deeply committed member of the Court, is priviledged to avow his acquiescence — and thereby is firmly bound to the controlling dispensation. Indeed, this assignment suggests that Day had been less prepared than White to invalidate the Keating-Owen law.

In drafting the opinion, Day encountered an insoluble dilemma: the majority wished to preclude further congressional interference in the realm of industrial labor relations, but it was unwilling to overturn the earlier police power cases. This meant that Day had to try to distinguish the doctrines approved in the earlier holdings from the Keating-Owen law. To find a tenable distinction, Day fell back upon the familiar laissez faire formulations that congressional authority did not extend to inherently non-harmful commodities nor to activities that preceded interstate transportation. But this was unavailing because the earlier decisions simply did not involve constitutional differences in kind. As the Supreme Court unanimously pointed out two decades later, the supposed demonstration was mere assertion, a vain effort to import limitations that had never been enunciated.[59] In the Court's words, the distinction "was novel when made and unsupported by any provision of the Constitution."[60]

---

[59] *United States* v. *Darby Lumber Co.,* 312 U.S. 100 (1941).
[60] *Ibid.,* p. 116.

This failure, despite Day's forceful language, followed inescapably from the inconsistency in what he had set out to do. The enactments sustained in the approved decisions, just as much as those in the Keating-Owen law, affected conditions anterior to transportation and interfered grievously with methods of production.[61] Guthrie left no doubt that the Lottery legislation had been designed to conform the behavior of manufactures to socially acceptable practices, when he argued against its validity in *Champion* v. *Ames*. The regulated subjects were not injurious to interstate commerce but posed a threat to the health, welfare, or morals of the whole country, and the dangers sought to be remedied stemmed from or were augmented by interstate shipment. In short, there was no logical way in which the losing arguments in *Champion* and *Hoke* could be made to co-exist with the doctrines that had been sustained in these and other applicable decisions.

Thomas Reed Powell, who contributed the most telling contemporary commentary upon the majority's holding from outside the bench, summed up the fundamental inadequacy in Day's opinion.

> If we brush aside all the confused and erroneous thinking of the majority, we have left only their fiat that whether prohibition of interstate transportation is a regulation of commerce among the states depends on the locus of the primary benefit of the prohibition. This fiat was essential to the decision, unless earlier cases were to be overruled. The fiat applies, be it noted, only to congressional prohibitions. If a state denied admittance to products of child labor from other states, it would be held to exercise a power which the Constitution, by conferring upon Congress, had denied to the States. But when Congress denies admittance to a state of products of child labor from other states, it exercises a power never conferred. This power over interstate transportation has evaporated by the establishment of the federal Constitution.[62]

Powell might well have added that the inconsistency of this result was dramatically apparent if it was compared with McKenna's emphatic declaration in *Hoke* that such an area of immunity from federal regulation could not exist. An interpretation of the facts that was analogous to that advanced by counsel for the Executive Committee controlled the decision. Still, Davis's cardinal point could not be denied. The majority was forced to

---

[61] See Thomas Reed Powell, "The Child Labor Law, the Tenth Amendment, and the Commerce Clause," *S.E.C.L.*, III, 317–18.

[62] *Ibid.*, pp. 332–33.

resort to a constitutional myth in order not to impugn prior decisions.

Holmes's Dissent: The Logic of the Matter

The extensive collection of legal negativisms that Day had assembled was vigorously condemned in Holmes's dissenting opinion. Holmes's intellectual power and capacity for great utterance, combined with his prestige and tenure, no doubt explain why he spoke for the dissenters. Holmes was deeply disturbed by the character of the decision and by the influences he believed had determined it. To Harold Laski he wrote: "[Thursday] came down an opinion that stirred the innards of Brandeis and me and he spurred me to write a dissent." [63] Having lost the battle in the conference, the minority chose to assail its colleagues in the open.

Holmes conceded that Congress could not legislate directly upon subjects that were under the control of the states, but, he argued, an act within the powers specifically conferred upon Congress could not be voided because of its indirect effects, however obvious it might be that it would have such effects.

> The first step in my argument is to make plain what no one is likely to dispute — that the statute in question is within the powers expressly given to Congress if considered only as to its immediate effects, and that if invalid it is so only upon some collateral ground. The statute confines itself to prohibiting the carriage of certain goods in interstate or foreign commerce. Congress is given power to regulate such commerce in unqualified terms. It would not be argued today that the power to regulate does not include the power to prohibit. Regulation means the prohibition of something, and when interstate commerce is the matter to be regulated I cannot doubt that the regulations may prohibit any part of such commerce that Congress sees fit to forbid.[64]

The question narrowed down, Holmes declared, to whether the Keating-Owen law could be invalidated because of "its possible reaction upon the conduct of the States." He affirmed the con-

[63] Reprinted by permission of the publishers from Mark De Wolfe Howe, *Holmes-Laski Letters: the Correspondence of Mr. Justice Holmes and Harold L. Laski, 1916–1935*, Cambridge Mass.: The Belknap Press of Harvard University Press, Copyright, 1953, by the President and Fellows of Harvard College; May 25, 1918, I, 157.

[64] *Hammer* v. *Dagenhart*, 247 U.S. 251, 277–78. Corwin singled out for special condemnation the narrow conception of commerce employed in the majority's opinion, thereby carrying forward Holmes's argument. See Edward S. Corwin, "The Power of Congress to Prohibit Commerce," *S.E.C.L.*, III, 121–22.

trary, in some of the most trenchant language in the dissenting opinion.

> I should have thought that that matter had been disposed of so fully as to leave no room for doubt. I should have thought that the power to regulate commerce and other constitutional powers could not be cut down or qualified by the fact that it might inter- fere with the carrying out of the domestic policy of any state.[65]

Holmes's purpose was to expose mercilessly the erroneous as- sumptions of dual federalism. Day had ascribed two chief attri- butes to state power: it was by nature "inherent" and it encompassed "matters purely local in character." The former state- ment meant that state authority was exclusive and the latter meant that control over the conditions of manufacture had "never been surrendered to the general government." "If it were otherwise," Day had warned, "all manufacture intended for interstate ship- ment would be brought under federal control to the practical ex- clusion of the authority of the states."[66] But Holmes demonstrated the fallacies in this attempt to separate state and national power into exclusive compartments. The proclaimed constitutional im- peratives were entirely illusory; in addition, the Keating-Owen law neither coerced state action nor practically excluded state power from the field of industrial relations. Holmes's review of the deci- sions that sustained previous regulatory statutes made patent that the precedents lent no support to the majority's insistence that the act violated the commerce clause and the Tenth Amendment.

> The Pure Food and Drug Act which was sustained . . . with the intimation that "no trade can be carried on between the states to which [congressional authority] does not extend," applies not merely to articles that the changing opinions of the time condemn as intrinsically harmful, but to others innocent in themselves. . . . It does not matter whether the supposed evil precedes or follows the transportation. It is enough that, in the opinion of Con- gress, the transportation encourages the evil.
> The notion that prohibition is any less prohibition when ap- plied to things now thought evil I do not understand. But if there is any matter upon which civilized countries have agreed — far more unanimously than they have with regard to intoxicants and some other matters over which this country is now emotionally aroused — it is the evil of premature child labor. I should have thought that if we were to introduce our own moral conceptions

---

[65] *Hammer* v. *Dagenhart*, 247 U.S. 251, 278.
[66] *Ibid.*, pp. 272–73.

where, in my opinion, they do not belong, this was preeminently a case for upholding the exercise of all its powers by the United States.[67]

The last mordant sentences dramatically exposed the central issue in the decision for Holmes — the extraordinary measure of judicial control exercised by the majority. Day had referred ominously to "the thing intended to be accomplished" by the Keating-Owen law, as if the fact that child-made goods were innocuous in themselves had convinced his brethren that Congress aimed at controlling methods of production.[68] Holmes regarded this condemnation of the statute on collateral grounds as an intrusion by the majority of their personal conceptions of public policy into the decision-making process, thereby nullifying the legislative expression of the public will. He denounced the majority's action in scathing terms.

> But I had thought that the propriety of the exercise of a power admitted to exist in some cases was for the consideration of Congress alone and that this Court always had disavowed the right to intrude its judgment upon questions of policy or morals. It is not for this Court to pronounce when prohibition is necessary to regulation if it ever may be necessary — to say that it is permissible as against strong drink but not so against the products of ruined lives.[69]

The Critical Issue: Judicial Supervision or Restraint

Holmes's harshly critical dissent did not express everything that had stirred his "innards." Discretion obviously restrained him from saying publicly all that he might have said about the majority's guardianship of personal values. In his view, the majority had not merely decided the case wrongly but had misconceived the limits of judicial power. To guide its exercise of the delicate function of judicial review, the Court has historically evolved various canons of self-limitation, notably the presumption of constitutionality that attaches to legislative acts and the impropriety of exploring congressional motives. The former provides that statutes not be invalidated unless they are patently contrary to the Constitution, and the latter disavows authority to make judgments about the wisdom or expediency of legislation. To be sure,

67 *Ibid.*, pp. 279–80.
68 Powell, "The Child Labor Law, the Tenth Amendment, and the Commerce Clause," p. 330.
69 *Hammer* v. *Dagenhart*, p. 280.

they are conventions of judicial obligation, which every justice must interpret for himself, and not inexorable commands, but disagreement among the justices usually has been over their application to particular cases rather than with their substance.

Within the conference, it seems certain, the dissenters must have forcibly urged upon their brethren the argument that their decision denied the presumption of constitutionality and consciously involved a supposition about congressional purposes. Congress had passed the Keating-Owen law by decisive margins, after long deliberation, and four of their colleagues found no conflict between the law and the Constitution. How, then, had the majority discovered infirmities so excessive that the statute must be voided?

White and Day, no doubt, were especially hard pressed, for they had repeatedly acknowledged the binding character of these self-denying canons of construction. Both men, for example, had concurred in Justice Harlan's dissenting opinion in the *Lochner* case, in which the controlling character of the doctrine of reasonable doubt was the basis for the charge that, in effect, the five-judge majority had constituted itself perpetual censor over legislative judgment. In the *McCray* case, moreover, White had emphatically denied that the Court might scrutinize the purposes that underlay congressional action. Indeed, his declaration was the most significant statement of this constraint to that time.

> . . . no instance is afforded from the foundation of the government where an act, which was within a power conferred, was declared to be repugnant to the Constitution, because it appeared to the judicial mind that the particular exertion of constitutional power was either unwise or unjust. To announce such a principle would amount to declaring that in our constitutional system the judiciary was not only charged with the duty of upholding the Constitution but also with the responsibility of correcting every possible abuse arising from the exercise by the other departments of their conceded authority.[70]

The remedy, if lawful power was exerted "with the object or motive of reaching an end not justified," lay with the people, "not in the abuse by the judicial authority of its function."[71] All in all, it was an unambiguous rejection of judicial supervisory power based on collateral grounds. Only the year before, in *Wilson* v. *New*, White had firmly restated the Court's responsibility as the conservator of popularly determined policies.

[70] *McCray* v. *United States*, 195 U.S. 27, 54.
[71] *Ibid.*, pp. 54, 55.

In all likelihood, these commitments to disinterested judgment, both personal and institutional, were not the only relevant considerations about the exercise of judicial review that the dissenters urged upon White and Day. Another factor must have been forcefully pointed out: the Supreme Court had invalidated federal statutes by a five-to-four vote on only four previous occasions, and only two of these cases [72] had involved major pieces of legislation. White, in particular, must have been reminded that in the most significant of these decisions, the Income Tax case, he had, in dissenting, eloquently decried judicial supervision that impliedly rested upon "the casting vote of a single judge." White had warned:

> If the permanency of [Supreme Court] conclusions is to depend upon the personal opinions of those who, from time to time, may make up its membership, it will inevitably become a theatre of political strife, and its actions will be without coherence and consistency . . .
> The fundamental conception of a judicial body is that of one hedged about by precedents which are binding on the Court without regard for the personality of its members.[73]

Holmes's public appeal turned White's previous holdings back upon him and upon the other members of the majority. The precedents were said to dispose so fully of the propositions advanced against the Keating-Owen law as "to leave no room for doubt"; White's *McCray* opinion was said to exclude any inquiry into the purpose of the act; and the *Veazie Bank* case [74] was cited as having precluded judicial supervision. "The judicial cannot prescribe to the legislative departments of the government limitations upon the exercise of its acknowledged powers." [75] Writing to Pollock about the opinion, Holmes confided: "I flatter myself that I showed a lot of precedent and also the grounds in reason." [76]

---

[72] *Pollock* v. *Farmers' Loan and Trust Company*, 158 U.S. 601 (1895), and *First Employers' Liability* cases, 207 U.S. 463 (1908).

[73] *Pollock* v. *Farmers' Loan and Trust Company*, 157 U.S. 429, 651. When the Income Tax case was first decided, White wrote a memorable dissent, in which Justice Harlan concurred. After it was re-argued, he contributed a second, much attenuated statement, obviously designed not to distract from the former. The other dissenters wrote separate opinions.

[74] *Veazie Bank* v. *Fenno*, 8 Wallace 533 (1869).

[75] Cited at 247 U.S. 251, 279.

[76] Reprinted by permission of the publishers from Mark De Wolfe Howe, *The Correspondence of Mr. Justice Holmes and Sir Fredrick Pollock*, Cambridge, Mass.: The Belknap Press of Harvard University Press, Copyright, 1941, 1961, by the President and Fellows of Harvard College; I, 267.

Holmes virtually charged the majority with an incapacity to view correctly the question to be decided. They had permitted subjects outside the rightful province of the Court to control their judgment. Day responded to Holmes's attack in his opinion. The terms were reminiscent of his affirmation of judicial sovereignty in *Wilson* v. *New*.

> We have neither authority nor disposition to question the motives of Congress in enacting this legislation. The purposes intended must be attained consistently with constitutional limitations and not by an invasion of the powers of the state.[77]

This weak response, which avoided the critical issue, hardly met Holmes's contention, for the authority renounced in theory had been exercised in fact. The majority's holding obviously rested upon deductions about the motives of Congress in enacting the Keating-Owen law — "to do by indirection what could not be done directly." Nevertheless, this "justification" for intervention had been precluded by White's stipulation in the *McCray* case that resort to the people was the proper remedy when a wrong motive impelled the exercise of a lawful power. The exercise of power itself had to be condemned.

This does not suggest that the majority consciously perverted its process of judgment. To be sure, the justices' laissez faire impulses found a way to invalidate the Keating-Owen law, but this result, we can be certain, was one that each of them believed was required by the Constitution. This was as true for White and Day, the two justices who probably had most difficulty resolving their judgment, as for Van Devanter, Pitney, and McReynolds. Their social philosophies and conceptions of public necessity undoubtedly determined their choice. Neither could have voted in a different manner than he did, we can assume, and have remained consistent with his deepest convictions — especially his conception of the nature of American federalism. This social value took precedence over the other values in the controversy.

On the other hand, it is difficult to believe, in view of their decisional backgrounds and the questions asked counsel during oral argument, that White and Day had become absolutely convinced of the invalidity of the Keating-Owen law; that is, that they found the dissenters' arguments devoid of compelling logic and could announce their conclusions in the case with no anxiety about the result. If nothing else, White's nationalism, during the

---

[77] *Hammer* v. *Dagenhart*, 247 U.S. 251, 276.

height of a great patriotic war, and Day's pronounced humanitarianism — though subjective factors, like many another — must have tugged at mind and conscience. It is this probability that lent force to Holmes's fundamental criticism: the majority had exceeded the limits of judicial discretion.

"It is a pity," Thomas Reed Powell commented,

> that at least one more member of the Supreme Court did not appreciate that the Child-Labor Law regulated a local matter only to the extent that it depended for its existence upon a national matter. It is a pity that the majority was influenced by apprehensions which are entirely visionary. It is unfortunate for the position of the judiciary that the narrow margin by which the decision was reached invites the inference that the judges who composed the majority were influenced by their personal predilections on a question of policy.[78]

The judicial function, however, involves choice not by percentage of certainty about the rightful disposition of each cause but by voting either yes or no and justifying the collective determination with an explanatory compromise that is minimally satisfactory to each justice who makes up the majority.

A Judicial Addendum

The last word belonged to Holmes, whose opinion ended with the assertion that the powers granted to Congress could be exercised to the fullest extent, at its discretion, to serve national purposes as it understood them.

> The act does not meddle with anything belonging to the States. They may regulate their internal affairs and their domestic commerce as they like. But when they seek to send their products across the state line they are no longer within their rights. If there were no Constitution and no Congress their power to cross the line would depend upon their neighbors. Under the Constitution such commerce belongs not to the States, but to Congress to regulate. It may carry out its views of public policy whatever indirect effect they may have upon the activities of the States. Instead of being encountered by a prohibitive tariff at her boundaries, the State encounters the public policy of the United States which it is for Congress to express. The public policy of the United States is shaped with a view to the benefits of the nation as a whole. . . . The national welfare as understood by Congress may require a different attitude within its sphere from that of some self-seeking

[78] "The Child Labor Law, the Tenth Amendment, and the Commerce Clause," p. 335.

State. It seems to me entirely constitutional for Congress to enforce its understanding by all the means at its command.[79]

Seldom had Holmes's eloquence and capacity to strike at the heart of a controversy been employed with more power. Indeed, few dissenting opinions in the Court's history have better illustrated Charles Evans Hughes's observation that a dissent "is an appeal to the brooding spirit of the law, to the intelligence of a future day, when a later decision may possibly correct the error into which the dissenting judge believes the court to have been betrayed." [80]

From the moment it was announced, Holmes's searching argument formed a rallying point for progressives, hopeful that it would some day become law. At first, however, the Justice Department seemed unwilling to delay an attempt to correct the error into which it believed the Court had strayed. On June 10, John W. Davis requested permission to apply for a re-argument of the case. Such applications are rarely granted; nevertheless (after the Court has approved them), the losing side in the original decision occasionally has prevailed, even in great constitutional controversies. Success in such cases usually results from changes in the personnel of the supreme bench — and ordinarily there had been an interval of many months between the first and the second argument. Although such precedents sometimes spur hope that re-argument may prove successful, the narrow margin of votes in an intensely contested case almost always precludes reversal of the original decision, for losing counsel must change the mind of one or more justices and, in effect, induce them to confess that they had handled the case incorrectly. In *Dagenhart*, this possibility was very remote. When the Justice Department abandoned its strategy, on the grounds that it "would be productive of no result," [81] Thomas I. Parkinson acknowledged the well-nigh insurmountable difficulty.

> A reargument in the near future could not reasonably be expected to produce a change in the decision. It may be assumed that Mr. Justice Holmes and those justices who concurred in his vigorous dissent urged their views upon their associates quite as persuasively as counsel for the government could be expected to do on reargu-

[79] *Hammer* v. *Dagenhart*, 247 U.S. 251, 281.

[80] *The Supreme Court of the United States* (New York: Columbia University Press, 1928), p. 68.

[81] J. W. Davis to T. I. Parkinson, June 30, 1918, Justice Department File, *Hammer* v. *Dagenhart*.

ment; and if they were unable to win over one of the majority, it is unlikely that counsel could succeed in doing so.[82]

Why, then, had the Justice Department contemplated action? One possibility is that the request was intended as solace for the reform organizations, aggrieved by the decision; another possibility is that the Justice Department was goaded by the disappointed groups into initiating a motion that conceivably might lead to a different result.[83] Although these possibilities cannot be discounted, another explanation seems equally plausible: the motion was a tactical move, public notice to the Court that the government considered the decision highly political and did not acquiesce in the new limitations imposed upon national power. Indeed, a revival of judicial restrictionism threatened many forms of liberal legislation, and, for this reason, the motion may have been a warning to the Court that the political branches of the government meant to preserve their authority against judicial intrusion.

Whatever the actual reason, David Clark believed that the Justice Department's action threatened the outcome, and he suggested another explanation.

> Should one of the judges who decided the law unconstitutional die before the October term and be replaced by a man who would vote with the other side they might grant the motion to rehear and might eventually reverse the former decision. . . . [Our opponents] are gambling on the death of one of the judges who voted with us.[84]

One week later, Clark reproduced a letter from counsel that assured him his apprehensions were groundless: under the rules of the Supreme Court, one of the justices who concurred in the holding would have to support re-argument for the motion to be granted.[85] "The Dagenhart case is therefore ended," Parkinson wrote, "and its decision until reversed in some future case leaves the act unenforceable."[86]

---

[82] "The Federal Child Labor Law Decision," *Child Labor Bulletin* (August, 1918), p. 90.

[83] The *Survey*, on whose editorial board sat several leaders of the National Committee, reported: "A rehearing is strongly desired by the National Child Labor Committee and other agencies that worked for passage of the law. In more than one instance the court has reversed itself upon such a hearing." June 15, 1918, p. 323.

[84] *Southern Textile Bulletin* (June 13, 1918), p. 14.

[85] *Ibid.*, June 20, 1918, p. 14.

[86] "The Federal Child Labor Law Decision," p. 90.

As we shall see, Parkinson and other liberals nourished the hope that the Keating-Owen law might be preserved on the statute books until a more auspicious time for reconsideration by the Court. But the case was closed and the statute mortified.

The Interested Parties' Response

Among the interested parties, the initial reaction to the *Dagenhart* decision was surprise or astonishment. Invalidation of the Keating-Owen law had not been expected, not even by those who had most strenuously resisted its enactment. Clark's unanticipated triumph was the cause of "intense rejoicing" throughout the southern textile district [87] and an immense personal victory, probably the most gratifying in his career. In turn, the mill men generously acknowledged their debt to him; congratulatory messages and financial contributions poured in, particularly from industry leaders in the Carolinas, and Clark was feted at the annual meeting of the Cotton Manufacturers' Association of North Carolina.

To celebrate his triumph and to claim proper recognition from the industry, Clark brought out a special edition of the *Bulletin*. If anything more than protection of the mill owners' interests had been gained, Clark failed to emphasize this gain in the feature editorial. Reviewing the events of the previous four years, he wrote:

> It seems a long, long time since we began the fight against this Keating law; and we have spent many hours and many days in what seemed an almost hopeless fight. Many of our best friends had long ago considered it a lost cause, and we could count upon the fingers of one hand the men besides ourselves who thought we could win.
>
> We had believed that we would win, and because we realized that it meant so much to the textile industry we kept up the fight.[88]

By "winning," Clark meant

> The Keating law is nothing but a "scrap of paper" and mills of each state will operate in accordance with their State laws.
>
> All of the Federal inspectors and certificate-issuing ladies can pack their trunks and start for home, for there is no longer any Federal child labor law and people of each state can conduct its own affairs.[89]

[87] *Southern Textile Bulletin* (March 18, 1922, and March 4, 1926), p. 18 and p. 21.
[88] *Ibid.*, June 6, 1918, p. 5.
[89] *Ibid.*

The advantages won for the textile manufacturers solidified Clark's position for the remainder of his life. Thereafter, he was statesman as well as servant. Never again did he lack support from rank-and-file mill owners nor from any major segment of the southern industry. Perhaps it was the exhilaration of victory that caused him to neglect the implications for the nation—the "Pandora's box" of federal power was tightly closed and industrial freedom was preserved and protected from the onslaughts of the "agitators" in and out of Congress.

On the other side, the leaders of the National Committee were completely taken aback.[90] They had been so confident the Court would render an affirmative decision that no thought whatever had been given to alternative plans if the culminating achievement of fifteen years of reform should be overturned. Nevertheless, they assured reporters that a campaign would be immediately undertaken to re-establish the standards of the Keating-Owen law. Interviewed in New York, Samuel M. Lindsay, the committee's vice-chairman, stated: "We shall have to study the decision and then frame a bill which will meet the objections which the Court makes."[91] Another trustee, Rabbi Stephen S. Wise, expressed the conviction of most reform leaders that something had to be done and their confidence that something would be done.[92] This attitude involved substantially more than the characteristic optimism of organizational spokesmen. Both men confidently promised renewed efforts to secure national reform legislation because they correctly assumed that a political force as powerful as the child labor reform movement could not be deterred by a single defeat.

For the progressives in Congress who had supported the Keating-Owen law, the implications of the ruling were just as far-reaching, but in a different sense. The Court's action left them "all in a heap," one commented; they interpreted the holding as prohibiting further efforts to achieve objectives of national social and economic welfare through legislation that was based on the commerce power.[93] Many thought the entire progressive program was jeopardized. Senator Kenyon declared: "The decision is hard. I regret it all the more because it closes the door firmly against

90 See *New York Tribune*, June 4, 1918, p. 16; *New York Times*, June 4, 1918, p. 14; *Washington Evening Star*, June 4, 1918, p. 6; and *Washington Post*, June 4, 1918, p. 11.
91 *New York Tribune*, June 4, 1918, p. 16.
92 *Ibid.*
93 *Ibid.*

so many of our plans." [94] Senator Owen and Representative Keating issued formal statements that severely criticized the decision: it dashed the hope for additional social reform.[95] Other progressives pessimistically stated that they could think of no method by which child labor and similar evils could be prevented through federal legislation.

However, before the day was over, Kenyon and Keating announced that a campaign would be launched at once to amend the Constitution or to enact a new child labor law, the latter possibly based on the taxing power.[96] Other interested persons, including spokesmen for the Children's Bureau, also affirmed that efforts to establish national child labor standards would not be abandoned.[97]

In Charlotte, David Clark and his associates prepared for continued constitutional struggle. William Hendren cautioned the cotton manufacturers that a single judicial holding had not drastically altered the progressive temper of the country.

> I would not feel that I had performed my duty with respect to this association if I did not say to you that the fight is going to keep up and that it is backed by the most powerful and ingenious thought of this country. I wouldn't have any man get it into his head that the fight has been won, because it hasn't.
>
> Behind this is the large class who believe that the Congress of the United States should have supreme power to legislate upon all matters that affect the welfare of this nation without regard to the State, and that Washington should be the clearing house of all industrial disputes.
>
> I want to suggest to you that nothing within the power of this association be omitted to deprive your antagonists of the opportunity of success, and so far as it meets with your own good judgment to declare the policy of our own state so that it shall measure up to the conscience and thought of the standard fixed by the United States.[98]

The last comments indicated the real cost of the contest to the North Carolina mill owners.

While the Keating-Owen bill had been before Congress, the

94 *Ibid.*
95 *Washington Post,* June 4, 1918, p. 11.
96 *New York Times,* June 4, 1918, p. 14.
97 *Ibid.* and *New York Tribune,* June 4, pp. 14–16.
98 W. M. Hendren, *Proceedings of the Twelfth Summer Session of the Cotton Manufacturers' Association of North Carolina* (Charlotte: Observer Printing House, 1918), pp. 20–21. Following Hendren's address, Sam Patterson, president of the association, added his own emphasis.

southern manufacturers had generally given ground in the form of improved state legislation. It had become clear that if state laws were made to conform to the bill's standards and adequate provisions for enforcement were provided, there would be minimal interference in state affairs.[99] Nevertheless, the North Carolina mill men continued to resist such legislative change, and they possessed sufficient influence to have their own way in the state's legislature. By the summer of 1918, however, they were ready to make concessions.

As Davidson points out, "The feelings of many people were undergoing a decided change and it was becoming obvious that the state could not much longer cling to old standards regarding child labor which its neighbors were discarding for more progressive forms of regulation."[100] Many manufacturers, moreover, had revised their opinions about the utility of employing child labor in light of their practical experiences while operating under the Keating-Owen law. A leading trade publication, the *Textile World Journal*, explained:

> The decision of the Supreme Court declaring the Keating-Owen child labor law unconstitutional is not nearly as important today as it would have been had it been rendered before the effect of the bill had been given a thorough test. It can be stated without fear of effective contradiction that it has been demonstrated to the satisfaction of most manufacturers that the labor of children under fourteen years of age is not only inefficient in itself, but tends to lower the efficiency of all departments in which they are employed; also children of fourteen to sixteen years, worked on a short time basis, are scarcely less efficient and have a disorganizing effect in the departments where they are utilized. Because of these facts, and entirely apart from humanitarian considerations, large numbers of southern mills will not re-employ children of these ages, and few would do so were it not for the pressure of war work and increasing scarcity of labor in the South.[101]

The labor standards that so often in the past had been condemned as ruinous did not prove so after all; on the contrary, the cotton manufacturers were able to maintain, and even advance, their profit margins, and the unusual wartime demand hardly sufficed as an explanation.

For these reasons Hendren's prudent injunction was heeded, though only partially. The North Carolina association adopted a

---

99 Elizabeth H. Davidson, *Child Labor Legislation in the Southern Textile States* (Chapel Hill: University of North Carolina Press, 1939), p. 170.
100 *Ibid.*, p. 172.
101 June 8, 1918, p. 20.

resolution calling for the enactment of a fourteen-year minimum-age requirement for industrial employment.[102] Because the other southern textile states had already established this standard, Clark explained in an editorial, ammunition would be given the groups who advocated federal legislation if North Carolina failed to conform.[103] Nothing was said, however, about the subject that most immediately involved the mill owners' interests and upon which public attention centered — the hours that children between fourteen and sixteen years of age were permitted to work.

The Popular Response

The initial public reaction to the *Dagenhart* decision, as evidenced in editorial comments, generally involved the same surprise that had been expressed by the interested parties, and disappointment that federal regulation of child labor, at least under the commerce power, had been outlawed. Influential newspapers and periodicals in every region criticized the logic of the Court's holding and questioned the appropriateness of the judicial supervision that had been exercised in the case. More often than not, the journalistic commentators urgently called upon Congress to enact another statute, whose constitutionality would be assured. On the other hand, this predominant response fell short of the virtual unanimity that had been expressed when the Keating-Owen law had been enacted. Indeed, several prominent publications that originally had supported the measure now approved its demise, but such approving editorial voices were a distinct numerical minority.

The *Washington Evening Star*, typical of many newspapers across the country, decried the fact that the Court's decision exposed children to virtual industrial slavery. In some parts of America, its editors asserted, federal legislation was "imperatively needed to protect children from the cruel hardships of industrial occupations that sap their strength and wreck their constitution." [104] The *Springfield* (Massachusetts) *Republican*, still an influential spokesman for the Republican cause, also based its complaint upon practical considerations. The Supreme Court, it charged, had "struck a blow at social reform and economic justice which must be deeply deplored."

> Unrestrained selfish interests are a drag upon reform because in the competition of sections for manufacturing supremacy greed

---

[102] See its *Proceedings of the Twelfth Summer Session,* pp. 74–76.
[103] *Southern Textile Bulletin* (July 11, 1918), p. 10.
[104] June 4, 1918, p. 6.

will seek to maintain a cheap labor market whenever it can . . .
the Court has ignored social and national welfare in order to sustain a narrow view of the privilege of contract and the individual's
right to work.[105]

Similar arguments were repeated, again and again, frequently
in the same heightened emotional form, and invariably culminated in demands for renewed congressional action.

Many editorials, however, discussed the constitutional issues
and condemned the holding as an irresponsible burden upon the
commerce power; it denied Congress full authority to protect
the general welfare. But there was noticeable reluctance to take
the Court to task. Instead, the critics frequently predicted that
future Courts inevitably would restore national power to its proper
place. The *New York Tribune*, for example, expressed marked
optimism about the possibility of enacting further liberal legislation, for its editors believed that national democratic forces irresistibly would shape the country's future.

> It is evident enough that when four of the more progressive type
> judges unite in an opinion against the more old-fashioned law-
> and-precedent jurists, it is only a question of time when the
> present majority will be overruled.
>
> It is extremely interesting to observe how thoroughly what may
> be regarded as public interest always dominates the law, no matter
> how flat and unequivocal the language of the law or statute may
> be.[106]

By its holding, the five-judge majority protected policies that
violated "the national sentiment of humanity." More important,
its constitutional opinions were incongruous when American life
was viewed realistically.

> The exigencies of national life and organization practically de-
> mand a homogeneity of law and custom. It is clear enough that
> if for any reason of local interest any state was to harbor a danger-
> ous contagion, the rest of the nation would not be content to set
> up a mere quarantine against it, if that was clearly inadequate.
> It would invade any right and ruthlessly abrogate any local custom
> to stamp out an epidemic that might threaten the nation's wel-
> fare. In a less radical way such is the purpose of the proposed
> Amendment for the nation-wide suppression of alcohol. That is
> as clear an invasion of state rights and state customs as any law
> could be. But if the nation decides upon it, it will be the law of
> the land; and no court will stand against it.

[105] Quoted in *Literary Digest* (June 15, 1918), p. 16.
[106] June 5, 1918, p. 10.

All of which means that our Constitution is not a rigid coat of mail restraining all chance of freedom of action, as it has long been held and feared by many to be.[107]

The critical editorials of other newspapers usually were more restrained than the *Tribune* in their advocacy of popular government; many, however, were less restrained in their language. The *New York Evening Post* condemned the holding as reactionary, so out of step with conscience and what the law should be that the nation would take whatever steps were necessary to overturn it.

The decision just rendered . . . will not long stay the merciful and protecting arm of national power; the victory of sordidness over our little ones will not long endure. A nation that will give its blood and money on the battlefield for the freedom of mankind throughout the world will surely find a way, despite five to four decisions, to release from slavery the children of its own hearthstone.[108]

For the most part, the editorials that endorsed the holding appeared in conservative publications that were regarded as spokesmen for the business community. Invariably, they contained protestations about the need to remedy the child labor evil, but, with few exceptions, they seemed to be motivated by the same fear of encroaching federal authority that had so greatly influenced the judgment of the Court. The *Chicago Tribune*, retreating from its earlier acclamation of the Keating-Owen law, termed the statute bad policy because it involved the dangerous method of regulation by indirection. Nevertheless, the *Tribune* admitted that the forces that dictated a common national life meant increased federal control of traditionally local affairs. It asked simply for direct intervention.

As federal regulation is extended by necessity it ought to be extended directly and straightforwardly. Many state functions retard nationalization. Others are valuable to it. The process of ruling the states from Washington must be determined — if determined — wisely, not by the evasive use of laws not intended for the purpose to which they are put.[109]

The *Tribune* failed to clarify what it meant by straightforward federal police power legislation but it suggested that some subjects, including child labor, might legitimately be controlled. The *New York Times* was less compromising. Its objection to

107 *Ibid.*
108 Quoted in *Literary Digest* (June 15, 1918), p. 16.
109 June 6, 1918, p. 6.

congressional regulation of child labor, the editors stated — in contrast to their restrained approval of the Keating-Owen law two years earlier — was partly that it was unnecessary and confusing "but chiefly that it is contrary to our political institutions which after all are worth preserving."[110] The plaintive character of this criticism reflected the accumulated frustrations of conservatives who, for many years, had done little more than reluctantly accept progressive restrictions upon business enterprise. The *Times's* argument centered on what, it suggested, was an absence of national consensus on the substantive policy issue.

> When there are forty-eight Varieties, more or less, of temperance laws and child labor laws there is proved to be such a wide Variance of opinion that it would not be right for intolerant opinion on those subjects to impose its will upon others equally entitled to their opinions. There never could have been a United States without local control of local matters, and there is a national danger in forcing Federal regulation upon States in advance of public opinion in each of them.[111]

The editorial gratuitously suggested that those whose motives in opposing child labor were genuine — "based on considerations of humanity, not merely on dislike of competition in the market place" — should direct their efforts to state campaigns. There was great hazard "in seeking crosscuts to reform of any sort in violation of constitutional safeguards of State or national rights."

> When sentiment is unanimous there is no difficulty in getting action. . . . But when sentiment is diverse in such high degree as upon prohibition and child labor and many social reforms the tedious method of securing unity of sentiment in advance of unity of legislation is preferable.[112]

But the *Times* erred. Its curious equation of the popular will with intolerant opinion seriously distorted reality and its complaint that national regulation endangered the federal equilibrium was utterly without foundation. The public interest, as the *Tribune* suggested, dominates the law, even if the time lag occasionally is long.

[110] June 5, 1918, p. 10.
[111] *Ibid.*
[112] *Ibid.*

7

Progressivism's Waning Months: The Second Federal Child Labor Law

The Progressive Temper and American Social Purpose

The Supreme Court's decision against the Keating-Owen law did not end agitation for national regulation of child labor. American humanitarianism and reform consciousness, although partially submerged by the military conflict in Europe, remained vital forces in national life and the masses of people willingly turned to the unfinished tasks in the quest for social justice and economic freedom. These values found expression in the congressional initiation and swift ratification within the states of the Eighteenth and Nineteenth Amendments, the former imposing a national standard of morality and the latter conferring the electoral franchise upon women. No matter that the first was repressive in nature, the crowning symbol of the growing drive for conformity; it sprang from the deep-rooted American impulse to do good. The latter, which extended equality, armed with greatly enhanced power those who, it was thought, would make social betterment the chief concern of their political participation. American idealism and the progressive temper also were reflected in the terms of the peace, the radical program for righting age-old wrongs and meeting legitimate national aspirations, that Wilson announced to the world and that most of the nation enthusiastically endorsed.

Public sentiment also generally supported extensive governmental regulation of economic affairs. In the popular view, this mode of social control was the principal means for achieving the central purposes of progressivism. The wartime crisis had called forth greatly increased federal intervention in the economy. The welding together of distributed sovereignty and the creation of new, centralized power heightened acceptance of strong government. But signs of the approaching conservative reaction were discernible. Many insurgents had returned to Republican ranks in

1916, which made for exceedingly close presidential and congressional contests. States' rights Democrats and business Republicans reasserted their influence in Congress and in public life during Wilson's second term, and political consensus about the desirability of using federal authority to accomplish broad objectives of domestic welfare had begun to wane. Emergency measures, such as government seizure and operation of the nation's railroads, although accepted as temporary expedients, did not foreshadow the attitudes that would predominate once peace had returned. Nevertheless, this reaction had not yet assumed significant proportions; social reconstruction and economic regulation were intimately linked in the public consciousness.

Thus the *Dagenhart* decision provoked an outpouring of popular demands for new federal child labor legislation. The closeness of the holding and the eloquence of Holmes's dissent — its sure implication that a dominant opinion that did not infringe fundamental principles as they have been understood in our traditions and law had been denied its natural outcome — seemed to confirm the inherent justness, as well as the constitutionality, of federal regulation. Armed with this conviction and imbued with a sense of urgency by the plight of child workers deprived of federal protection, the organizations that gave leadership to the reform movement set about exploring alternative means by which national child labor standards could be achieved.[1] They were joined by interested members of Congress (from both sides of the aisle) and sympathetic federal administrative officials. The alternative of turning back exclusively to time-consuming and uncertain state compaigns was rejected out of hand, as virtual abandonment of the child labor cause.

Justice Day had been emphatically correct in two portions of the Court's holding, reform spokesmen concurred — in acknowledging universal agreement that "there should be limitations upon the right to employ children in mines and factories in the interest of their own and the public welfare" and in admitting that uniformity in remedial legislation might be desirable. He had been emphatically wrong, however, when he held that regulation of the hours children might labor in industrial establishments was "a matter purely local in its character," to which federal

---

[1] The Court's action, Samuel Gompers declared, had merely hardened public determination to secure comprehensive federal control: "The Supreme Court could have repealed no other law that would have caused such a degree of popular resentment." "Child Life Must Be Conserved," *American Federationist* (August, 1918), p. 693.

authority in no way extended.[2] On this point, Holmes was seen as the reliable guide: "the power to regulate commerce and other constitutional powers could not be cut down or qualified by the fact that it might interfere with the carrying out of the domestic policy of the state."[3] In keeping with the approach toward the constitutionality of pioneering legislation that Parkinson had recommended during the 1916 congressional hearings, the National Committee respected the *Dagenhart* decision as demarcating the boundaries of the commerce power, at least for the time being. Along with other reform organizations, however, it rejected the conclusion that the substantive objective thereby was made impossible.[4] Only one form of federal control had been annulled; another form might offer a constitutional way to overcome the Court's veto.

However, caution is recommended with respect to understanding the aftermath of the *Dagenhart* decision. First, it is important to differentiate between public response in June and the decisive pressure for new federal legislation that developed during the late summer and autumn. Despite the unexpected result and the widespread critical editorial comment, the Court's holding did not have the same dramatic impact upon the masses of persons as did the invalidation of various New Deal social welfare measures fifteen years later. The reasons for this have little relation to the importance of the decision: the nation was preoccupied with the Great War and the climactic months of the European struggle were at hand. At Chateau Thierry, in early June, 1918, American troops were engaged in their first major battle, and German submarines were destroying shipping close to our Eastern seaboard.[5] In addition, the sense of common purpose imposed by the war and the overriding interest in preserving this nationalistic accord moderated political encounter.

As military victory approached, however, domestic political

[2] *Hammer* v. *Dagenhart*, 247 U.S. 251, 275.

[3] *Ibid.*, p. 278.

[4] At first shock, wrote Julia Lathrop, the Court's holding might seem conclusive, but analysis of the opinions "justifies the conviction that federal regulation to protect children had received not a defeat but only a stimulating setback. . . . It remains only to find a method of national limitation not repugnant to the Constitution." "The Children's Bureau and Child Labor," *American Federationist* (October, 1918), p. 909.

[5] A later generation must read the newspapers and correspondence of the period to comprehend how totally absorbed Americans were with the war in Europe. The progress of the "battle against the Hun" seems to have blotted out virtually everything else.

issues regained their hold on public attention and partisan politics reasserted its traditional influence. No domestic problem attracted greater public attention than child labor in the autumn of 1918, and no other phase of reform was more essentially a nonpartisan social objective. Reformers dramatized the exploitation that followed upon the *Dagenhart* decision, which did not accord with the current moral conceptions of the country, and stimulated an outpouring of outraged public feeling. Congress responded in overwhelming numbers to what its members looked upon as an irresistible demand to frame new federal legislation to end "the servitude of the little children." The Republican victory in November symbolized the dissolution of the wartime nonpartisanship and the return to politics as usual, but the chief representative of immediate postwar Republicanism, Henry Cabot Lodge — as much as any other political figure — lent his prestige and led the drive in Congress to pass the child labor tax.

Respect for the Judiciary

A second caution involves the criticism of the Supreme Court that stemmed from the *Dagenhart* decision. Although many liberals were bitterly disappointed by the holding and vigorously condemned its substance, few of them attacked the institution of judicial review. Most congressmen and many reformers, together with the great body of the people, were far more interested in finding a constitutional alternative to the invalidated statute than in retaliatory action against the Court. In the view of most of these persons, the practical results of the decision were unfortunate, but the immediate, and for many the only, problem was finding some means to ensure that federal protection — stripped overnight from tens of thousands of child toilers — would be swiftly and permanently restored.

Those congressmen who had sponsored the Keating-Owen bill were the first to call the Court to account, and other progressives joined their criticism. Holmes's searching exposure of the logical deficiencies in the majority's reasoning and his condemnation of the justices' lack of judicial temperament were generally applauded. Liberal journals and many newspapers, as we have seen, deplored the holding. Professional commentary in the law reviews sided disproportionately with the minority, and constitutional scholars suggested that the majority had departed from precedent and had clouded doctrine, in a five-to-four decision.

The *Dagenhart* case, Walter F. Dodd wrote, evidenced a narrow interpretation of the commerce clause because clearly granted powers of the national government were "in no way limited through implication, or otherwise, by a general reservation to the states of powers not so granted."[6] Henry Wolfe Bikle suggested that the Court had abandoned previous police power precedents and had reverted to older and unsatisfactory constitutional tests. He characterized the decision as one that "instead of clarifying the scope of the commerce power seems to perpetuate old doubts, if not indeed to create new ones, as to the law on this subject."[7] In the opinion of William Carey Jones, the Court's adjudication rested on "a perverse view of constitutional construction." He hoped that future Courts would exercise enlarged vision when reviewing legitimate acts.[8] Moreover, the few commentators who approved the majority's constitutional position usually acknowledged that the reception generally accorded the decision in the magazines and press was caustic, though not contemptuous. Andrew A. Bruce suggested that the journalistic applause for the minority opinion could be explained only "on the theory that desire often outruns judgment and that when one feels deeply it is difficult to pause and think."[9]

Only to this extent was there the public denunciation of the Court that Senator Brandagee had anticipated if the bench set aside a measure as heavily invested with popular approval as the Keating-Owen bill. The Connecticut lawmaker, it will be recalled, had chided his colleagues in 1916 for shirking responsibility and passing unconstitutional legislation on to the Court, necessarily drawing it into political controversy. Although the bench occasionally suffered vehement censure, most criticism was more temperate than Brandagee had predicted. The journals of the country and the uplifters hurled very few epithets at the Court, and there were few demands "to haul off the bench"— Brandagee's phrase for judicial recall procedures.

This pronounced reluctance to attack the Court appears to be explained chiefly by the role of the bench in the decade since the

6 "Implied Powers and Implied Limitations in Constitutional Law," *S.E.C.L.*, I, 341, 343.
7 "The Commerce Power and Hammer v. Dagenhart," *University of Pennsylvania Law Review* (January, 1919), pp. 21, 29. Bikle argued that if legislation that met new circumstances "should prove contrary to the public interest there is always the opportunity for repeal of the law," rather than reliance upon judicial supervision. *Ibid.*, p. 36.
8 "The Child Labor Decision," *California Law Review* (September, 1918), pp. 412, 417.
9 "Interstate Commerce and Child Labor," *Minnesota Law Review* (January, 1919), p. 92.

Muller case. By 1918 the Court had substantially recovered the public trust that had eroded earlier in the progressive era. Indeed, examination of the congressional debates and relevant editorial commentary suggests that the decline in prestige the Court is frequently said to have suffered early in the century probably has been exaggerated. At the height of the reform assault, when, in Mason's words, "bold measures were proposed to overcome the effects of judicial obtuseness to social and economic change," [10] no other institution of government, not even the presidency, enjoyed the same measure of public esteem. Of course, if the bench had not prudently deferred to legislative discretion, the situation might have been far different, but the progressive movement suffered few major judicial defeats in the ten years after *Muller*. The resentment against judicial supervision and against the Fuller Court's laissez faire doctrines of economic freedom had declined very noticeably.

Although the *Dagenhart* decision represented an interruption in the Court's liberal outlook toward progressive legislation, few contemporaries saw it for what it was: a breach — not a temporary break — in constitutional interpretation that signaled return, for almost a generation, to conservative jurisprudence. Hence progressives were less disposed to lead a crusade against judicial supervision than to express confidence that, in time, and hopefully in the very near future, the dissenters' opinion would become law. Thomas Reed Powell drew an analogy between the overthrow of the offending *Lochner* doctrines and the expected demise of the equally distressing rules announced in *Dagenhart*. The optimism that permeated much liberal commentary is apparent in his words.

> There can be little question that the view of the minority will in time prevail. Decisions which are out of joint with the times, which are not required by any clear mandate of the Constitution, and which meet with strong dissent from some of the ablest judges, are not likely long to remain unmodified. The history of the Supreme Court shows that minorities often persist in their dissent and not infrequently become a majority. The decision denying the power of Congress to make greenbacks legal tender survived but a year. The famous Bakeshop case, which annuled a ten-hour law for bakers, died after a decade. These may ere long be joined, in the limbo of rejected doctrines, by the Child Labor decision.[11]

10 Alpheus T. Mason, *The Supreme Court from Taft to Warren* (Baton Rouge: Louisiana State University Press, 1958), p. 29.
11 "The Child Labor Decision," *The Nation* (June 22, 1918), p. 731.

Because they believed that the minority justices represented the dominant opinion in American society, the critics viewed charitably what most of them considered was only a temporary departure from sound interpretation of constitutional powers. The expectation that national democratic forces would mold the nation's future tempered their response to the fact that progressive legislation had been thwarted by a five-to-four decision.[12] Liberal reaction also was conditioned by confidence that there were acceptable constitutional approaches that offered an end to child labor. Wrote Walter Dodd: "The result sought in vain under the commerce power . . . is likely to be accomplished under a broadly construed taxing power."[13] Powell bespoke the sanguine expectation with greater force.

> The Supreme Court has appreciated the wisdom of not annuling an undoubted exercise of the Federal taxing power because of its necessary collateral effects. While reason and previous authority seem to militate as strongly in favor of disregarding the necessary collateral effects of undoubted exercises of the commerce power, it must be assumed for the present that there is some vital distinction between the two. Until that assumption is no longer necessary, those who believe that the nation should use its power to end the evils which harm the nation must look to the taxing power of Congress.[14]

In addition, progressive leaders recognized, as Professor Jones pointed out, that the existing war conditions had "led to some surprising, even if temporary, upsettings of certain judicial decisions."[15]

---

[12] The severe language employed by some critics struck John A. Ryan as unfortunate. The leader of liberal Catholic social action hoped for omnibus legislation, under the commerce power, providing national control over the conditions of private industry and employment. "While federal action of this sort is for the present impossible," he wrote, "owing to the unfavorable decision of the Supreme Court . . . the analysis that we have made of the majority and minority opinions indicates that a contrary decision is not beyond the range of reasonable hope. . . . This forecast receives powerful support from social thought of our times and the whole logic of events." "The Supreme Court and Child Labor," *Catholic World* (November, 1918), pp. 212, 222–23.

[13] Dodd, "Implied Powers and Implied Limitations in Constitutional Law," p. 343.

[14] Powell, "The Child Labor Decision," p. 431.

[15] Jones, "The Child Labor Decision," p. 415. After the Supreme Court's decision in *Coppage* v. *Kansas* (236 U.S. 1 [1915]), overthrowing a Kansas statute that made it unlawful for employers to require employees not to join unions, the Taft-Walsh board protected the right of workers to join unions. Further, after the Court invalidated, in *Adams* v. *Tanner* (244 U.S. 590 [1917]),

Not surprisingly, then, the bitterest criticism of the Court for the *Dagenhart* decision occurred in 1922, not 1918 — after the *Drexel* case and a series of flagrantly anti-labor rulings clearly disclosed the Court's reversion to judicial restrictionism. That summer, Senator Robert R. La Follette launched his gallant though futile presidential campaign under the Progressive banner. In an impassioned address to the American Federation of Labor he denounced the *Dagenhart* majority, claimed that a judicial oligarchy ruled the United States, and decried judicial sovereignty as incompatible with popular government.[16]

The remarkable self-restraint of Congress also deserves attention. There was little disposition to attack judicial review, and none to criticize individual justices. This acquiescence in the Court's guardianship testified to respect for the judiciary and to the lawmakers' conception of the proper division of governmental powers. As the Senate debates (in 1916) demonstrated, virtually every congressman conceded that the interpretive prerogative inhered in the Court. Progressive spokesmen urged only that Congress not be denied the opportunity to pass on the constitutional question for authoritative construction. Having received that construction, the vast majority of congressmen, whether they approved it or not, and despite the narrow division, accepted the result, which in effect meant acquiescence in the existing exercise of judicial power. Like the constituents they represented, the lawmakers' interest lay in finding some way to harmonize the nation's humanitarian purposes with its organic law.

For some congressional progressives, however, the work of adjusting American life to changed circumstances and the added burdens imposed by the majority's restrictive interpretation of national authority assumed primary importance. Although they were concerned that the results of the Keating-Owen law be realized in another way, their primary interest centered on methods for restraining the Court if it went against congressional enactments that, in their judgment, clearly accorded with the Constitution. The legislature's place in the constitutional system, and that of the popular will, were at stake, not simply an objective of public policy.

a Washington statute that prohibited private agencies from taking fees from those seeking work, President Wilson tried to have the federal employment service pre-empt the field. *Ibid.*, pp. 415–16.

16 "Child Labor and the Federal Courts," *American Federationist* (July, 1922), pp. 269–85.

The Search for Constitutional Alternatives

Several days after the *Dagenhart* decision was announced, the trustees of the National Committee, meeting in emergency session in New York, instructed a special committee "to outline a course of action in connection with Federal legislation." [17] Two trustees, William Draper Lewis and Charles P. Neill, who had taken a leading part in drafting the first child labor bill, were appointed to this group; the other members were Samuel M. Lindsay and V. Everit Macy, another board member of many years' standing. The four men immediately contacted representatives of the Children's Bureau, the National Consumers' League, and the American Federation of Labor — as well as sympathetic members of Congress, notably Senators Kenyon and Pomerene and Representative Keating. Thus the previous child labor reform alliance was quickly refashioned.[18] From the outset, the cooperating organizations agreed completely upon objectives: federal protection had to be restored immediately to children employed in industry, and this program of governmental safeguards had to be established on a permanent basis as rapidly as events would permit.

The strategy initially agreed upon involved finding a temporary expedient, either in administrative action or emergency legislation, that would preserve the benefits that had existed before the invalidation of the Keating-Owen law and that would afford ample time in which to consider a lasting solution to the child labor problem. Having suffered constitutional defeat, the reform organizations' overriding concern was making certain that the alternative now selected would not suffer similar destruction. From the first, it appeared highly likely that congressional legislation based upon the taxing power would be chosen.[19] Nevertheless, several constitutional options were thoroughly studied,

[17] "Minutes of the Board of Trustees, N.C.L.C.," June 7, 1918.

[18] See Lathrop, "The Children's Bureau and Child Labor," p. 909, and Gompers, "Child Life Must Be Conserved," p. 692. The National Committee had dominated the campaign for the first federal child labor law, giving it leadership and direction. Although it remained the greatest single influence in the campaign for the child labor tax, decision-making was more widely shared than before. Effective control was exercised by the committee and the Children's Bureau; the other organizations interested in child welfare essentially followed their lead. The greater part played by the Children's Bureau stemmed from the institutional power the agency had acquired, the strong congressional ties developed, and the enhanced influence possessed in a friendly administration.

[19] *New York Tribune*, June 14, 1918, p. 10.

over a period of several months, in the interest of achieving as much certitude as possible about the final decision. These alternatives included, principally, amending the Constitution, re-enacting the Keating-Owen law in modified form, and enacting new congressional legislation that differed materially from the Keating-Owen law.

Senator Kenyon, in his first comments upon the *Dagenhart* decision, expressed marked skepticism about the possibility of further legislative action: "I do not for the moment see any plan by which a Federal statute could be applied to this problem, in view of the sweeping nature of today's decision." [20] Other members of Congress agreed with this assessment; within ten days, therefore, a number of joint resolutions proposing amendments to the Constitution had been introduced.[21] The obvious merit of this method of establishing the principle of federal control was that it would settle the constitutional question once and for all. This had been recognized when the national reform movement first took shape, but congressional legislation was then looked upon as much easier to attain and almost certain to survive judicial scrutiny. Later, the impressive bipartisan support accorded the Keating-Owen law seemed to ensure that, should it be invalidated, the more fundamental form of popular action could be pursued successfully.

Inevitably, then, the possibility of amending the Constitution received serious consideration after the law had been voided. By this path the notorious *Dred Scott* case had been overcome after the maelstrom of civil war. In this way, also, the graduated federal income tax had been accorded constitutional standing after the five-to-four adverse decision in the *Pollock* case. In the latter, closely precedented situation, success had been foreclosed in the years that immediately followed the Court's action. As progressive sentiment increased, however, irresistible public pressure developed. Understanding the implications of this politically charged opinion and sympathetic with its equalitarian purpose,

20 *Ibid.*, June 4, 1918, p. 16.
21 Child labor amendments had been introduced more than once before. The best-known resolution was drafted by Representative Rogers of Massachusetts after the 1914 legislative hearings before the House Labor Committee. Although he remained convinced that amendment was the preferable way to achieve child labor control, Rogers deferred to the Keating-Owen bill in 1916. After *Dagenhart*, he re-introduced the original resolution, and two other resolutions were offered. All were narrow in scope, providing simply for congressional authority to regulate child labor, and all were introduced by Republican representatives from populous, northern industrial states.

Taft, while President, had taken the lead in passing the Sixteenth Amendment. It was essential, in his judgment, to protect the Court from a second, certainly injurious clash with the democratic will if Congress, as many persons suggested, re-enacted the invalidated statute.[22]

Early in its deliberations the coordinating committee decided against trying to change the Constitution. It was hoped that action could be taken under the "existing powers of Congress and under the rules and precedents already established by the Supreme Court," action that would meet the test of judicial review.[23] The reform groups were not prepared to hazard the difficulties and the delay almost certain to be encountered in an amendment campaign. To have decided otherwise would have entailed an extensive undertaking, reaching into at least three-fourths of the states and bearing correspondingly burdensome expenses. Equally important, even if all went well at each stage in the campaign, it appeared highly probable that at least two years would elapse before an amendment could be ratified; and further delay might ensue before Congress enacted enabling legislation. Furthermore, if matters went bady, other avenues of federal control would in all likelihood be foreclosed, at least for the foreseeable future.

The traditional attachment to the formal constitutional status quo therefore assumed unusual importance. Americans have always been extremely wary of any resort to the amendment procedure, a National Committee official observed, especially when the proposed change would augment national powers.

> The American people are inclined to having their own way, and in this respect, among others, they are progressive; but they are also conservative, and they are not disposed to change their Constitution unless they feel themselves forced to do it. They would much rather get the federal legislation they desire through the Constitution as it stands, if that is possible, than to amend or overturn their Constitution, flying from known to unknown evils.[24]

For these reasons, efforts were bent toward attaining child labor safeguards under the Constitution as it stood, and nothing came of the joint resolutions that had been introduced in Congress.[25] In retrospect, it is clear that an amendment campaign

[22] See Mason, *The Supreme Court*, pp. 18–21.

[23] Raymond G. Fuller, "A Quest for Constitutionality," *Child Labor Bulletin* (November, 1918), p. 207.

[24] *Ibid.*

[25] In an article sympathetic to the Court's holding because it disallowed the method of indirect legislation, a conservative constitutional commentator,

would have been much the wiser course of action. The legislative alternative chosen was struck down by the Court, and when constitutional change was later sought, the campaign went down to defeat. Such a campaign, if undertaken earlier, might well have succeeded.

Political Challenge to the Supreme Court

A second approach comprised several proposals to retain the Keating-Owen law or to re-enact it in such form that it would be immune from, or would survive, judicial inspection. These proposals included: (1) outright assaults upon the institution of judicial review, seeking to circumscribe the Court's jurisdiction or diminish its power, and (2) less dramatic propositions, which, though unmistakable challenges to the bench, did not aim at such fundamental results. The government's request to move for reargument fell within the latter classification. When the Justice Department abandoned the motion, Professor Ernst Freund (among other liberals) proposed that the Keating-Owen law be retained on the statute books, though unenforceable, until such time as change in the personnel of the Supreme Court or in the constitutional outlook of the bench presented a favorable opportunity for reconsideration of its validity. In other words, Congress should not, in future legislation, expressly or impliedly repeal the statute because the decision of subsequent cases might disclose the error in the narrow interpretation of the commerce clause announced by the Court.[26] Of course, as long as the majority was imbued with the negative creed of dual federalism it was unrealistic to hope for reversal of the *Dagenhart* decision. Parkinson recognized this full well; nevertheless, he felt that the holding so severely handicapped progressive efforts to order the life of

Fredrick Green, suggested that the proper way to promote the national welfare was to enlarge the scope of federal police power by a general amendment to the Constitution. "Social Justice and Interstate Commerce," *North American Review* (September, 1918), pp. 387–400.

The possibility of constitutional change was also suggested by a critic of the decision, but for drastically different reasons. If the Court construed the Constitution liberally, William C. Jones maintained, "the instrument will be found flexible and sufficient to satisfy all the developing needs of society. If, on the other hand, the construction be narrow, if acts of Congress are nullified because of incidental conflict with reserved powers of the state, the country will be driven to amendment of the Constitution, or else fail in keeping in line with the progress of enlightened communities in the world." "The Child Labor Decision," pp. 395–417.

26 Thomas I. Parkinson, "The Federal Child Labor Law Decision," *Child Labor Bulletin* (August, 1918), p. 90.

society more equitably that having it contravened was more important than enacting another federal child labor law.[27]

The proposals for re-enacting the Keating-Owen law also stayed within the existing framework of judicial review but they involved challenging the Court more directly and emphatically. One of these schemes, proposed by Roscoe Pound, called for wording the statute exactly as before, except for two additions: an introduction declaring that the states were powerless to forbid the sale within their boundaries of child labor products shipped from other states, and a conclusion declaring that Congress did not intend by the prohibition of interstate commerce to interfere with local conditions.[28] But this mantle of constitutional propriety was transparently thin. The suggested declarations hardly remedied the twin defects Justice Day had proclaimed: that the act overreached congressional authority and invaded purely local affairs. Nothing came of Pound's proposal to reshape the law by congressional disclaimers, nor of other suggestions for its repair.

Parkinson felt that any plan to re-enact the statute would look too much like a collateral attack upon the Court. The view of the interested groups toward all political proposals is evidenced in his counsel.

> It seems likely that the lawyers in the Senate who would resent such an attack, added to those who object to any federal legislation restricting child labor, would defeat such a measure. One of the best friends of the original child labor law in Congress has refused to introduce a bill to re-enact it in substantially its original form on the ground that this is not the time to divert public interest to the consideration of such fundamental constitutional questions as the respective functions of the legislative and judicial departments of the federal government.[29]

All of the congressional friends of the Keating-Owen law did not react in the manner of the representative Parkinson referred to. The Court's action incensed Senator Owen and he immediately countered with a radical proposal to put it in its place. He asked that the invalidated act be passed again — with a new section that denied the Court the right to review its constitutionality.[30] In this way the power vested in Congress to control the Court's appellate jurisdiction would be used to strip the bench of the

[27] *Ibid.*, p. 97.

[28] *Ibid.*, p. 96.

[29] *Ibid.*

[30] *Congressional Record*, 65th Cong., 2d Sess. (Washington, D.C.: Government Printing Office, 1918), pp. 7431–35.

opportunity to condemn the measure a second time. Owen's new section read:

> The constitutionality of this act having been declared by the competent authority of Congress and the President of the United States at the time of its passage shall only be questioned thereafter by the Congress itself and the people of the United States in their sovereign capacity as voters. Any executive or judicial officer who in his official capacity denies the constitutionality of this act shall ipso facto vacate his office. No judge of any inferior Federal court shall permit the question of the constitutionality of this act to be raised in the court over which he presides, and the United States Supreme Court shall have no appellate power to pass upon such questions.[31]

This proposal was far from original. In fact, only the year before, Owen had introduced a far-reaching bill designed to deprive the feral courts of authority to construe the constitutionality of all congressional enactments.[32] In support of the current version, Owen directed an all-out attack upon the exercise of judicial review, but, respecting the prevailing congressional deference toward the judiciary, he showed no contumely to the bench. Its members, though sincere and upright, were only men, no wiser nor more learned than those who served in Congress. Unlike congressmen, however, they were not subject to popular surveillance at regular intervals and therefore could disregard public opinion.[33] The result was more than mere irresponsibility, Owen argued: the justices exercised enormous power, an authority over American life that had never been intended by the founders. Because Congress had the responsibility for determining the policies of the nation, the obvious corrective was to deprive the Court of the authority to consider the constitutionality of congressional enactments.

The language of the attack was timeworn; the substance of Owen's proposal for restraining the Court less so. From the earliest exercise of judicial review, opponents had frequently suggested exempting various matters from the Court's jurisdiction, but, with only one conspicuous exception (during Reconstruction, when the radical Republicans dominated American life and nearly destroyed divided sovereignty),[34] Congress had not used its power

---

31 65th Cong., 2d Sess., S. 4671 (June 7, 1918).

32 64th Cong., 2d Sess., S.J. Res. 193 (January 12, 1917).

33 *Congressional Record*, 65th Cong., 2d Sess., p. 7433.

34 This was the famous case of *Ex parte McCardle* (6 Wallace 318 [1868], 7 Wallace 506 [1869]). A suit had been appealed to the Court, and argued

over the Court's appellate jurisdiction to immunize federal legislation. The notion, on the other hand, that an exemption could
be extended to a bill after the Court had pronounced an identical
statute unconstitutional was not nearly as familiar and had no
precedent in practice. Always, where controversy has developed
over the exercise of judicial discretion, it has been resolved by
indirect means or healed by time.[35] As President Roosevelt discovered in 1937, judicial review is too deeply embedded in the
American political tradition to be extirpated or curtailed. Senator
Owen discovered this earlier. Although he was not a "wild horse"
politically, Owen's drastic curb upon the judiciary was too patently retaliatory to win wide acceptance.

Samuel Gompers, the president of the A. F. of L., demanded
that the nation think further than curative proposals.

> It must deal with this curious political phenomenon unlike any
> other institution of any country. It must regulate the veto power
> of the Supreme Court and eliminate an intolerable situation that
> enables five men to defeat the will of the nation. . . . In a demo-
> cratic country, the vote of one person cannot permanently obstruct
> efforts to protect the making of a stronger, more resourceful
> nation.[36]

Walter Clark, who had influenced Owen's thinking for almost a
decade, warmly congratulated him and spurred him to sustain
the attack.[37] Clark characterized judicial review as "sheer judicial
usurpation."

before it, that seemed to indicate that the Reconstruction Acts would be held
unconstitutional. At this stage in the litigation, Congress hurriedly passed, and
carried over President Johnson's veto, a provision to withdraw the Court's
appellate jurisdiction from cases of the type represented. After re-argument,
the Court unanimously chose to accept the action of Congress to avoid a direct
clash. "We are not at liberty to inquire into the motives of the legislature.
We can only examine into its power under the Constitution; and the power
to make exceptions to the appellate jurisdiction of this court is given by
express words."

[35] "Various political proposals to curb [judicial review] have been directed
mainly, if not always, not against the existence of the power but against the
manner or the finality of its exercise." Thomas Reed Powell, *Vagaries and
Varieties in Constitutional Interpretation* (New York: Columbia University
Press, 1956), p. 19.

[36] "Child Life Must Be Conserved," p. 692.

[37] W. Clark to R. L. Owen, June 8, 1918, in *The Papers of Walter Clark*, eds.
Aubrey Lee Brooks and Hugh Talmage Lefler (2 vols.; Chapel Hill: University
of North Carolina Press, 1950), II, pp. 371–73. After the November election,
Owen reported what he considered vindication at the polls: "I carried my state
by forty-five thousand majority I am told — about fifteen thousand ahead of

If the Judges were infallible, there might be more excuse for this assumption of power. But the effect of the Income Tax decision and many others show why this claim of absolute, irretrievable, and ultimate sovereignty in a majority of the Court is maintained: It's simply because the decision in those cases has inured to the protection of the possessors of aggregated wealth, or self-styled "vested interests." [38]

Most liberals, however, shied away from doing violence to the Court. Thomas Reed Powell condemned as irresponsible any suggestion that the Court's exercise of judicial review be restricted.

We must bow to the decision until it is overruled. If we wish to continue the Federal system, it is idle and foolish to talk of withdrawing the power of the Supreme Court to project the lines of the Constitution which vaguely point to the boundaries between State and National authority.[39]

Criticism that the *Dagenhart* decision was "equivalent to a usurpation of power" was extreme and unjustified, stated John A. Ryan, who singled out Owen's proposal for censure.[40]

Conservatives relished the liberals' ideological discomfiture and angrily branded Owen's suggestion unthinkable if not subversive. In "American Democracy and Russian Democracy," the venerable American Bar Association leader, Everett P. Wheeler, attacked domestic reformers, particularly the Socialist party and its cry for the abolition of judicial review.[41] Another greatly exercised conservative suggested: "Senator Owen's attack against the Supreme Court . . . is aimed toward establishing the supremacy of Congress, and if successful, will result in taking away the equilibrium which marks with regular precision the working and harmony of the three great branches of government." [42] The *New York Times* also heaped scorn on Owen, but the editors seemed fearful of the popular response.

It is probably safe to say that the Senator is alone in [his] view of the purpose and effect of the action of the Supreme Court. It

the ticket, which shows that my views on the Supreme Court have not as yet damaged my prestige." R. L. Owen to W. Clark, November 12, 1918, *ibid.*, p. 383.

[38] "Where Does the Governing Power Reside?" *American Law Review* (September–October, 1918), p. 692.

[39] "The Child Labor Decision," p. 731.

[40] "The Supreme Court and Child Labor," p. 212.

[41] *American Law Review* (September–October, 1918), pp. 657–68.

[42] C. A. Herrshoff Bartlett, "The Co-ordinate Powers of Government," *ibid.*, p. 670.

is not so sure that he is alone in thinking that the short way to child labor reform is to abolish the Supreme Court by Act of Congress. He may have company in thinking, like the Bolsheviki, that anything can be done by a viva voce vote.[43]

Not one member supported Owen's proposal on the Senate floor. A similar fate awaited a broader resolution, entered in the House by Representative Dillon, a South Dakota Republican. Like Owen's earlier proposal, it would have denied the Court the power to review congressional enactments.[44]

New Congressional Legislation

The last approach, and seemingly the most promising, was a new form of federal legislation. There was no dearth of suggestions for the coordinating committee to consider. Within weeks after the *Dagenhart* case was decided, various congressmen had worked several of these proposals into statutory form and had introduced them into Congress. On June 19, Senator Kenyon submitted a bill that would deny use of the mails to persons or concerns who employed child laborers in violation of national standards.[45] Upon certification by inspectors from the Department of Labor that an offense had occurred, postal authorities were to return to the senders all mail addressed to the offending company. This procedure followed closely an existing statute requiring that mail addressed to persons who had violated the Espionage Act be returned.[46]

One week later, Senator Atlee Pomerene, an administration Democrat from Ohio whose career in politics had developed under Tom Johnson's liberal tutelage, introduced two child labor bills, one based on the commerce and the other on the taxing power.[47] The first bill differed from the Keating-Owen bill by incorporating the divesting principle employed in the Webb-Kenyon Act to prevent the shipment of intoxicating liquors into states in which their sale was prohibited. Articles manufactured by children were similarly to be stripped of their interstate character, so that

[43] June 7, 1918, p. 12. See *ibid.*, June 19, 1918, p. 10, for Owen's response and further editorial attacks.

[44] 65th Cong., 2d Sess., H.R. 12416 (June 7, 1918).

[45] 65th Cong., 2d Sess., S. 4732 (June 19, 1918), and a later substitute, S. 4760 (June 27, 1918).

[46] *Survey* (June 15, 1918), p. 323. For a contemporary analysis of the use of the postal power for regulatory purposes, see Robert E. Cushman, "National Police Power under the Postal Power of the Constitution," *S.E.C.L.*, III, 362–96.

[47] 65th Cong., 2d Sess., S. 4762 and S. 4763 (June 27, 1918).

state legislation that made their sale unlawful would not invade the sphere of commercial regulation reserved to Congress. To be effective, the measure had to be completed by prohibitory state statutes, which might, one reform source suggested, necessitate the establishment of a federal licensing system.[48] The taxing bill provided for levying an excise tax upon articles or commodities in whose production child laborers had been employed, ostensibly as a way of raising revenue. In reality, the tax was pegged at a level Pomerene thought would deprive child labor of its profits.

On the floor, Pomerene expressed the hope that one, perhaps both, of these bills would remedy the constitutional defects the Supreme Court had discovered in the Keating-Owen law, and he asked that they be sent to the Committee on Interstate Commerce.[49] Furnifold M. Simmons, the conservative North Carolinian who chaired the Finance Committee, objected: like other revenue measures, the taxing bill should be considered by his committee. Pomerene responded candidly; despite the excise provisions, the bill related more to interstate commerce than to taxation and for this reason should be referred to the committee that previously had considered child labor regulation at great length. Simmons later moved to refer the bill to the Finance Committee, but the motion was narrowly defeated.

Throughout the summer the coordinating committee studied these specific proposals, several other child labor bills based on the taxing power that later were introduced,[50] and various regulatory schemes that were not formulated into bills. It quickly discarded the Kenyon postal bill. Irrespective of questions about the constitutionality of using the postal power to accomplish police power purposes and the difficulties inherent in the regulatory scheme embodied in the bill, the committee thought that the opposition to such a plan of control would prevent its adoption.[51] The Pomerene commerce bill also was rejected, but not out of hand; the *Clark Distilling Company* decision furnished a precedent that deserved more than cursory study; and several variations of the divesting principle were considered. In the end, however, all encountered the same stumbling block. The Court had said

48 *Survey* (June 15, 1918), pp. 323–24.

49 *Congressional Record*, 65th Cong., 2d Sess., p. 8347.

50 Senator Lenroot of Wisconsin (Republican) introduced S. 4823 (July 11, 1918); Representative Green of Iowa (Republican) introduced H.R. 12705 (July 12, 1918); and Representative Gard of Ohio (Democrat) introduced H.R. 13087 (October 17, 1918).

51 Parkinson, "The Federal Child Labor Law Decision," p. 96.

that its holding rested on the exceptional nature of the substance (alcoholic beverages) being regulated. Because of this conscious effort to distinguish the ruling, Parkinson reported, there was "little reason for hoping that the principle of [the *Clark*] case would be extended to the products of child labor by the court which has refused to extend to such products the principles of the Lottery case." [52]

After careful consideration of many legislative proposals, the coordinating committee found itself, at the end of the summer, in firm agreement that use of the taxing power would provide the most efficacious method for establishing permanent federal child labor standards. [53] This agreement was reached by a process of elimination, not default; otherwise, an amendment campaign, despite the numerous difficulties that could be expected, almost certainly would have been pursued. When, in early September, final agreement was reached, the committee deemed unsatisfactory the various taxing bills then before Congress. [54] There was skepticism about their constitutionality and, apparently, doubt that they had been framed in the most effective manner for remedying the problem of industrial child labor. Therefore, a special committee, composed of Parkinson, Pound, and Henry M. Bates, Dean of the University of Michigan Law School, was given the task of drafting an appropriate bill for submission in Congress on behalf of the cooperating reform organizations. [55]

Constitutional Justification for the Child Labor Tax

Although, relatively, the commerce power had been more often used to accomplish broad purposes of national social and economic welfare, the taxing power, as an implement of social control, offered a number of striking precedents, especially Justice White's forceful opinion in the *McCray* case. [56] Beyond this decision, the precedents most often cited by reform agencies in public statements that supported the child labor tax were the prohibitive excises Congress had levied upon state bank notes shortly after the Civil War and upon poisonous white phosphorous matches midway in the progressive era — together with the Supreme Court's

[52] *Ibid.*
[53] *Survey* (September 7, 1918), p. 642.
[54] "Report of the General Secretary on Activities of the Committee since October 1, 1918," unpublished and undated N.C.L.C. memorandum.
[55] *Ibid.*
[56] *McCray* v. *United States*, 195 U.S. 27 (1904).

ruling in *Veazie Bank* v. *Fenno*,[57] in which the former tax had been upheld.[58] To this list was frequently added the scheme of national regulation legislated in the Harrison Narcotic Drugs Act.[59]

The tax laid upon promissory paper that had been issued by state banks was easily distinguishable from the proposed child labor tax because Congress had exercised the taxing power to prevent interference with a subject, the national currency, over which it possessed expressly granted and exclusive authority. Despite the crucial difference, this tax was often cited as an example of a judicially sanctioned excise measure in which the evident purpose of Congress had been regulation to the point of destruction, rather than revenue. However, neither the tax levied on the manufacture of colored oleomargarine nor on "phossy jaw" matches could be distinguished in this way. Both had been imposed for the avowed purpose of suppressing a course of business activity, and in each instance the objective was not one that Congress could achieve by direct legislation.[60]

The constitutional justification for the child labor tax rested primarily upon *McCray* and the doctrine of judicial impotence embraced there. In fact, proponents frequently maintained that the constituent doctrines of this holding foreclosed every question about the validity of such an excise. When *McCray* was argued, counsel for the government had candidly admitted that the statute

[57] 8 Wallace 533 (1869).

[58] Because Congress did not hold committee hearings on the child labor tax, the constitutional justification for a prohibitive excise measure put forward by the child-oriented organizations must be pieced together from journal articles and other public statements. Probably the most significant presentation of the National Committee's position appears in an article written by Raymond G. Fuller, its publicity director: "A Quest for Constitutionality" (pp. 213–14). For other statements, see "Editorial and News Notes," *Child Labor Bulletin* (November, 1918), pp. 150–51, and (February, 1919), pp. 229–35; Irvine L. Lenroot, "Taxing Child Labor Out of Industry," *Child Labor Bulletin* (February, 1919), pp. 254–56; and Raymond G. Fuller, *Child Labor and the Constitution* (New York: Crowell, Collier & Macmillan, 1923), pp. 241–45.

[59] A suit that challenged the validity of the Harrison Act was in the courts at the time but the tax on so-called "phossy jaw" matches was never subjected to judicial test. Avowedly designed to protect laborers in match factories from necrosis and consumers from accidental poisoning, it destroyed, virtually overnight, the manufacture of phosphorous matches, for the industry by mutual consent turned to non-toxic formulas for match heads.

[60] For an analysis of the police power implications of the taxing power, see Robert E. Cushman, "Social and Economic Control through Federal Taxation," *S.E.C.L.*, III, pp. 543–64.

had been enacted to drive colored oleomargarine out of the market
and had no justification as a health measure, colored oleomargarine being no more deleterious than uncolored oleomargarine.
The Court, however, had refused to take cognizance of congressional motives — to see the regulatory purpose that all others could
see — and had sustained the measure as a legitimate exercise of
the taxing power. "Here then," Thomas Reed Powell observed,
"was taxation, not for revenue, but for suppression." [61] Justice
White's famous opinion had set forth the doctrine that, when
determining constitutionality, the Court could not go beyond
the scope and effect of the legislation itself.

> Applying this rule to the acts assailed, it is self evident that on
> their face they levy an excise tax. That being their necessary scope
> and operation, it follows that the acts are within the grant of
> power. The argument to the contrary rests on the proposition
> that, although the tax be within the power, as enforcing it will
> destroy or restrict the manufacture of artificially colored oleo-
> margarine, therefore, the power to levy the tax did not obtain.
> This, however, is but to say that the question of power depends,
> not on the authority conferred by the constitution, but upon what
> may be the consequence arising from the exercise of lawful au-
> thority.[62]

The holding seemed to come to this: a taxing measure had to be
held constitutional if "on its face" it levied a tax,[63] and the Court
was barred from any inquiry into the motives of Congress. If the
Court adhered to this self-denying doctrine, a prohibitory child
labor excise seemingly would stop short, perhaps far short, of the
limits of drastic social and economic control the doctrine permitted.[64] Proponents thought there was no way that this doctrine,
and the *McCray* case, could be preserved if their taxing measure
was invalidated.[65]

Pushed far enough, analysis would reveal differences between

---

[61] "Child Labor, Congress and the Constitution," *S.E.C.L.*, III, 531.

[62] *McCray* v. *United States*, 195 U.S. 27, 59.

[63] Cushman, "Social and Economic Control," p. 557.

[64] Writing on the eve of the *Drexel* decision, Charles Warren concluded:
"While, however, the so-called National police powers may be restricted under
the commerce clause, it is to be noted that there seems to be very little restriction on the extent to which the National Government may regulate, under
the taxing power, the production, manufacture, sale and transportation of
articles within the States." *The Supreme Court in United States History* (3
vols.; Boston: Little, Brown and Co., 1923), III, p. 460.

[65] See Powell, "The Child Labor Decision," p. 731.

the oleomargarine legislation and the proposed child labor statute. The former sought to suppress the manufacture of a specific product but the latter conditioned various business practices upon observance by industrial establishments of stipulated limitations. In other words, every producer of colored oleomargarine faced destructive taxation, but companies that employed children could secure immunity from similar taxation by observing specific restrictions upon their labor policies. In addition, the regulated subjects differed: the oleomargarine tax interfered with an established course of business but the child labor tax interfered with the relationships between capital and labor. Whatever the policy implications of these distinctions, there were no constitutional differences in kind between the two measures. The reformers were right; as long as *McCray* stood, a federal child labor tax was logically permissible.

To Restore Immediately "A Minimum Standard of Protection"

At the beginning of the summer the search for a permanent solution to the child labor problem had been subordinated to finding some means to afford relief to child toilers. Immediately after the *Dagenhart* result became known, manufacturers in many areas of the country rushed to employ children who had been barred from industrial occupations under the Keating-Owen law, and they also restored the longer workdays. Investigations undertaken in a number of states by inspectors from the Children's Bureau disclosed that

> many hundreds of children in [the states involved] had been dependent upon the Federal law for their protection against premature and excessive employment, and that with Federal protection withdrawn the sole effective restriction on the entrance of children into industry was in many cases lost. This situation existed not only in States where the standards fixed by the States' laws were lower than the Federal standards, but also in States in which equal or higher legal standards existed but were not adequately enforced.[66]

The acute shortage of labor, unprecedented high wages, and perverted appeals to patriotism drew vastly more children into

[66] U.S. Congress, Proposed Child Labor Amendments to the Constitution of the United States, Hearings before the Committee on the Judiciary, U.S. House of Representatives, 68th Cong., 2d Sess. (Washington, D.C.: Government Printing Office, 1924), p. 276. See also U.S. Childrens' Bureau, *Seventh Annual Report* (Washington, D.C.: Government Printing Office, 1919), *passim*.

industrial tasks than had been employed only a few months
before. What is more, many of these children apparently were less
than fourteen years of age.[67] Although illegal employment in
disregard of state legislation was especially marked in seasonal
industries, manufacturers in virtually every sector of American
industry also took advantage of the situation.[68]

In these circumstances the cooperating organizations felt great
urgency to provide what the *New Republic* termed a "stay of
execution for the period of the war." That some means of federal
control "be found, and that speedily," Owen Lovejoy wrote, "is
demanded by the exceptional conditions of today and by an
aroused public opinion."[69] The coordinating committee considered several proposals for administrative action, all centered on
the concept of emergency powers. Interested persons urged that
federal officials, who possessed extraordinary authority as a result
of the wartime crisis, exercise discretionary powers to impose
child labor restrictions upon American industry. It was suggested
that the War Labor Policies Board, established to coordinate the
labor practices of numerous government agencies, refuse to award
contracts to companies that employed child laborers; that the
Secretary of State, in his capacity as Director General of Railroads,
deny the facilities of rail transportation to such companies; and
that the federal Fuel Administrator, empowered under the Lever
Act to control the production and distribution of coal and coke,
deny such companies the fuel necessary for carrying on their
operations.[70]

After conferring with relevant officials, the coordinating committee worked out a program that combined administrative action
and legislation, both being justified by the military crisis and
therefore only temporary. On July 12, the War Labor Policies

[67] The literature on this subject is voluminous, in itself an indication of
growing public interest. See Owen Lovejoy, "Children Again Become Prey of
Labor Exploitation," *New York Tribune*, June 16, 1918, sec. 3, p. 6; "Labor
Shortage Forcing Children of School Age to Work," *New York Times*, October 13, 1918, sec. 4, p. 1; "Call Children from War Plants," *ibid.*, November 24,
1918, sec. 3, p. 8; and *Child Labor Bulletin* (August and November, 1918, and
February, 1919), *passim*.

[68] See *Seventh Annual Report*.

[69] "Children Again Become Prey of Labor Exploitation," p. 6.

[70] Parkinson, "The Federal Child Labor Law Decision," p. 96. So perversely
had the illiberal attitudes bred of war influenced American life that it was even
suggested the Attorney General designate uncooperative companies as enemy
aliens, thereby exposing them to public hostility and the possible destruction
of property that such designation might call forth. *Ibid.*

Board, whose chairman, Felix Frankfurter, possessed a well-established reputation as a convinced social reformer, announced that a clause would be inserted in all federal contracts that would make the standards of the Keating-Owen law mandatory for companies engaged in government work.[71] This clause would protect children assigned subsidiary tasks in industrial establishments as well as those directly engaged in manufacturing processes. Although the directive bore the stamp of authority, its effectiveness cannot be fully assessed.

For months the WLPB had inserted clauses in federal contracts that required compliance with state labor legislation, for many companies had claimed immunity from state laws when they produced material for the government.[72] The new child labor clause differed from the earlier requirements, but it seemed to benefit from the established pattern of compliance. "The more conscientious holders of war contracts," the *New York Times* reported in October, "made an effort to toe the line as far as child labor was concerned. Other industries were less open about their objections to the clause. They just simply disobeyed it."[73] Most could do so with relative impunity because a comprehensive inspection system was not worked out until late in September.[74] By October, Frankfurter found it advisable to issue a statement reasserting the WLPB's policy toward the employment of children and encouraging vigorous enforcement of state child labor legislation. This statement was designed to combat recurrent suggestions that the manpower shortage made it necessary to utilize children in war industries.[75]

To extend federal protection to child laborers who were not covered by the WLPB's order and to ensure compliance by all employers, the coordinating committee proposed legislation that was based on the war power and would be effective for the duration of hostilities and six months thereafter. This measure provided for the direct prohibition of child labor, similar to state laws, in the interest of "the national security and defense" and

71 See *Washington Post*, July 13, 1918, p. 5; *Child Labor Bulletin* (August, 1918), pp. 80–81, and *New Republic* (August 3, 1918), pp. 7–8. Earlier, the Board had asked that employers voluntarily respect the standards of the Keating-Owen law in dealings with youthful workers.

72 Carl Brent Swisher, *American Constitutional Development* (Boston: Houghton Mifflin Co., 1943), p. 650.

73 "Call Children from the War Plants," p. 8; see also Parkinson, "The Federal Child Labor Law Decision," p. 94.

74 See "Labor Shortage Forcing Children of School Age to Work," p. 1.

75 *Survey* (October 12, 1918), pp. 49–50.

incorporated the standards of the Keating-Owen law, in identical language.[76] According to Parkinson, the measure rested on the theory that "the war power enables Congress to do directly for the conservation of the manpower and health of the nation what it might not be able to do in times of peace."[77] In other words, an exercise of federal police power was called for and was justified on the belief that crisis enlarged national authority. When opponents charged that an independent war power did not exist, a National Committee spokesman responded (without contributing materially to constitutional theory):

> The war power may be vague, but it is actual and effective, as shown by a long list of legislative and executive acts in the interest of the national morale and efficiency. . . .
> The federal war power is the federal power in wartime. Its exercise is accepted by the people as a matter of course.
> The Child Labor bill is a war measure, designed to take care of a situation which has been greatly aggravated by the war. It is further designed to conserve the man power of the nation.[78]

On August 15, Representative Keating introduced the bill in the House,[79] but immediate congressional action proved impossible, even though President Wilson endorsed the measure.[80] At Wilson's bidding, Congress had remained in session during the sweltering Washington summer, despite the lawmakers' desire for adjournment. After months of strenuous endeavor, energy and enthusiasm failed, even though work on much important legislation was unfinished. From mid-July on, meetings were infrequent.

[76] "Fourteenth Annual Report, N.C.L.C.," *Child Labor Bulletin* (November, 1918), pp. 160–61, and Fuller, "A Quest for Constitutionality," p. 213.

[77] Parkinson, "The Federal Child Labor Law Decision," p. 97; see also Bickle, "The Commerce Power," p. 34, and Jones, "The Child Labor Decision," pp. 415–17.

[78] *Survey* (October 26, 1918), pp. 103–4. Five years later, another National Committee official elaborated the suspension-of-constitutional-provisions theory of the war power: "The war power is a vague and elastic quantity, as was shown on innumerable occasions in 1917–18. It carries nationalism to its highest, or most extreme degree. But in war time, nobody seems to mind very much — except profiteers in goods and human labor. In war time, nobody seems to mind states rights very much — except those same people. Whatever the people at large conceive to be necessary to the national interest can be done at their instance or with their approval under the war power — though it often must be done by stretching pretty far the doctrine of implied powers, or even in defiance of the constitution itself." Fuller, *Child Labor and the Constitution*, p. 279.

[79] 65th Cong., 2d Sess., H.R. 12767 (August 15, 1918).

[80] *Survey* (September 7, 1918), p. 642.

The autumn elections loomed ahead and many congressmen spent long periods in their constituencies campaigning for re-election.

Keating, nonetheless, managed to guide the war power bill through the Committee on Labor in little more than a month. On September 25 it was reported favorably, by a vote of five to three, the dissenters representing southern constituencies.[81] By this time, however, it was becoming increasingly apparent that the war probably would end before winter, although reform leaders discounted the imminent cessation of hostilities. In late October a statement from the National Committee suggested: "Who knows when the war will be over? Congress does not know and does not need to know when the war will end in order to pass war measures."[82] Wilson reaffirmed his support of the Keating bill, reportedly after he had received the initial German request for an armistice.[83] But the attractiveness of legislation based on the war power dimmed perceptibly.

The Pomerene Amendment: The Children's Christmas Present

Late in October, Owen Lovejoy advised the trustees of the National Committee that the apparent approach of peace made it necessary to consider whether it would not be wise to transfer the organization's entire energy to a campaign that would seek enactment of the child labor tax.[84] The question soon became academic — Congress assembled in joint session on November 11 to hear a brief address from President Wilson. Wildly cheering men sprang to their feet as Wilson announced: "the war thus comes to an end . . . its object is attained."[85] The military crisis would no longer furnish a constitutional justification for federal child labor regulation.

The National Committee's leadership summoned the nation to carry reform ahead in the new circumstances. The opening editorial in the November issue of the *Child Labor Bulletin* declared:

> Peace has its need of man power no less than war, and so the end of the war must bring no relaxation of effort to secure a federal child labor law to take the place of the Act of 1916. . . .

81 "Fourteenth Annual Report, N.C.L.C.," p. 161.

82 *Survey* (October 26, 1918), p. 104.

83 *Ibid.*

84 "Report on Activities."

85 Woodrow Wilson, Address to joint session of Congress, *Congressional Record*, 65th Cong., 2d Sess., p. 11538.

Federal legislation on this subject is up to Congress — and the people. Now is the time:
> "Come while the nation feels the lift
> Of a great impulse shouting forward!" [86]

The progressive program of social reconstruction would now be resumed and the temper of the nation, exultant in victory, would make the quest easier.[87] "The President, the Secretary of Labor, and a majority in Congress are believed to be strongly in favor of early action," Julia Lathrop wrote; as soon as the tax measure was presented, its passage would be assured.[88] Evidence of an enormous increase in child labor abuses, all stemming from the war, accumulated daily, according to the National Committee,[89] and the widespread publicity given this evidence generated a decisive consensus that virtually determined congressional action.

By early November the drafting committee had put the tax measure into final form and it was circulated among the cooperating organizations for their approval. In addition, Senator Pomerene had agreed to introduce the proposed legislation as an amendment to the revenue bill,[90] but this plan unexpectedly went amiss. Four days after the armistice Pomerene introduced a modified version of the amendment that he had worked out independently of the committee, with the assistance of two progressive colleagues, Senators Kenyon and Lenroot (the latter a Wisconsin Republican). The amendment, more comprehensive than the Keating-Owen law, applied to every "mine, mill, cannery, workshop, factory or manufacturing establishment" in the nation. It incorporated the employment standards prescribed by the invalidated act and provided for a 10 per cent tax on the net profits for the taxable year for every concern that knowingly violated its provisions.[91] Pomerene, however, failed not only to consult officials of the National Committee and the Children's Bureau, as

86 November, 1918, pp. 150–51.

87 This hopeful view of social welfare's future was advanced by Raymond G. Fuller in "The New Humanitarianism," *American Child* (May, 1919), pp. 29–32, and by Edward T. Devine in "A Nation Wide Drive for Social Reconstruction," *Survey* (March 1, 1919), pp. 784–85.

88 "The Children's Bureau and Child Labor," p. 910.

89 *Ibid.*

90 "Minutes of the Board of Trustees, N.C.L.C.," November 6, 1918.

91 *Congressional Record*, 65th Cong., 2d Sess., November 15, 1918, p. 11560. In other words, the tax remained the same whether the standards were violated on a single occasion or hundreds of times. If a concern had procured a proper certificate of age at the time of hiring a child who later proved to be under age, the tax might not be imposed.

they thought he should, he did not even notify them of his intentions. Moreover, because the rider differed in several important respects from the bill prepared by Parkinson, Pound, and Bates, the reform groups were forced to choose between endorsing Pomerene's rider or trying to substitute their preferred draft.[92]

Of the differences between the two drafts, one greatly troubled the child oriented groups. Their version vested administrative responsibility in the Child Labor Division of the Children's Bureau but the Pomerene version vested this responsibility in the Treasury Department. The reformers felt that the specialized agency created under the Keating-Owen law ensured conscientious enforcement, and they had serious misgivings about a possibly unfriendly or uninterested agency in the Internal Revenue Bureau. However, Pomerene, Kenyon, and Lenroot insisted on this change and on others they had made; each had been introduced solely to strengthen the constitutionality of the amendment, they argued. To place its administration under the auspices of the Department of Labor would be prejudicial, for the Supreme Court might hold it to be a child labor law in the guise of a revenue measure, just as it had held the Keating-Owen act to be a child labor law in the guise of a regulation of interstate commerce. But they assured Lovejoy that, in their judgment, the Treasury Department would utilize the Child Labor Division rather than develop a new enforcement agency.[93]

Lovejoy then tried to elicit policy statements from officials of the Children's Bureau and the American Federation of Labor. When these efforts failed, he advised the National Committee's trustees to endorse the Pomerene amendment and to work for its passage inasmuch as it was the only bill that had any chance of being enacted by Congress.[94] After discussing the situation in full on December 17, the trustees followed his advice,[95] and the other organizations quickly fell in line.

Although the Revenue Bill of 1918 had been introduced the

92 "Minutes of the Board of Trustees, N.C.L.C.," December 17, 1918, and "Report of the General Secretary, N.C.L.C." (unpublished and undated memorandum).

93 "Report of the General Secretary."

94 *Ibid.* Lovejoy talked with Grace Abbott, the chief of the Children's Bureau, on December 14, and concluded that, because of the position taken by Kenyon and Pomerene, it was impossible to gain any modifications in the administrative section of the amendment. "Memorandum re Federal Child Labor Bill" (unpublished and undated memorandum in the files of the N.C.L.C.).

95 "Minutes of the Board of Trustees, N.C.L.C.," December 17, 1918.

previous December, neither house had taken action on it by the end of the summer.[96] The Ways and Means Committee completed its deliberations late in September, and shortly thereafter the House of Representatives approved the measure. The Senate Finance Committee held hearings on the bill during September and October but had not made its report by the time the war ended. Treasury Secretary McAdoo, with Wilson's endorsement, then sent a message to Senator Simmons, asking that the Finance Committee reconsider the bill immediately in the light of the new circumstances. McAdoo urged that an appropriately modified version be enacted as soon as possible,[97] for the new tax year would shortly begin. Congress remained in session a few days more, then adjourned briefly. When the two houses re-assembled on December 2, the members of the Senate realized that passage of the revenue bill had become imperative.[98] On December 6, the Finance Committee reported a revised draft of the bill; its major provisions were debated in the days that followed; and on December 23 a final vote was reached. More than one year after its introduction, the revenue bill finally passed both houses of Congress, though in significantly different versions.

Consideration of the Pomerene amendment paralleled that of the parent measure. On December 4, Senator Henry Cabot Lodge of Massachusetts moved, within the Finance Committee, to attach the amendment as a rider to the revenue bill. Senator Simmons vigorously opposed the motion but was quickly overriden by a large bipartisan majority. Two weeks later, on December 18, the rider was debated for a portion of a day, then enacted by a vote of 50 to 12 — a vote strikingly reminiscent of the approval of the Keating-Owen bill.[99]

Eleven of the twelve negative votes were cast by southerners, and eight of these by senators from the four principal cotton textile manufacturing states — North Carolina, South Carolina, Georgia, and Alabama. The previous token northern support had

---

[96] The Sixty-fifth Congress, elected in November, 1916, was almost evenly balanced between the two parties. The Democrats possessed a majority of twelve in the Senate, 54 to 42, but had organized the House only with the cooperation of a handful of Independents and Progressives, for the Republicans had outnumbered them 217 to 213.

[97] Reported in U.S. Congress, Senate, Committee on Finance, Revenue Bill of 1918, Senate Rep. No. 617, to accompany H.R. 12863, 65th Cong., 3d Sess. (Washington, D.C.: Government Printing Office, 1918), p. 2.

[98] *New York Times*, December 19, 1918, p. 17, and December 24, 1918, p. 1.

[99] *Congressional Record*, 65th Cong., 3d Sess., p. 621.

vanished altogether. Outside the South, only Senator Thomas —
whose extraordinary sensitivity to federal child labor legislation
(reformers suggested) reflected the Colorado sugar beet raisers'
economic stake in thousands of agricultural child workers — voted
against the amendment.[100] The opposition was limited to seven
states, and every dissenting senator came from Democratic ranks.
On the other hand, the fifty affirmative votes were distributed over
the country and between the two parties. Eleven were cast by
senators from southern and border states, twelve by westerners,
sixteen by midwesterners, and eleven by easterners. In all, one or
both senators from forty states voted for the rider. Of the senators
absent from the floor whose intentions were announced, all would
have voted affirmatively. "Just a week before Christmas," the
Survey said, "the Senate hung a gift on the children's tree."[101]

"Loading" the *Congressional Record* for the Supreme Court

The Senate debate on the Pomerene amendment, to no one's
surprise, closely paralleled the debate on the Keating-Owen bill.
Almost all of the time given over from the crowded calendar was
taken up with a clash between the midwestern progressives who
drafted the measure and spokesmen for the southern textile industry who had no chance of defeating it. In addition, the debate
covered much the same ground as before, centering on the constitutionality of the amendment and the implications of enacting
a child labor tax after the Supreme Court had invalidated the
Keating-Owen law.

Again, the southerners' constitutional position relied heavily
upon the proposition that the reserved powers of the states imposed limitations upon congressional authority. Hardwick of
Georgia recalled the destruction of the Keating-Owen law.

> Some time ago . . . the Senate passed a bill, in the identical
> language of this amendment, undertaking to prohibit the trans-
> portation of the products of child labor through the channels of
> interstate commerce. . . . The Supreme Court . . . decided it
> was invalid and unconstitutional. . . .
>
> Mr. President, the question was fairly raised, and it was fairly
> decided. The power of Congress was denied in toto. . . . Now
> we are presented with exactly the same proposition, and in no
> different manner, except that it is proposed that Congress shall
> do what the Supreme Court of the United States had decided we

100 December 28, 1918, p. 405.
101 *Ibid.*

had no right even to touch, by means of a tax levy on the product
of this particular kind of labor. . . .[102]

Hardwick acknowledged that the prohibitory excise tax sustained in the *McCray* case had been enacted in the interest of the
nation's dairymen, for the confessed purpose of suppressing the
manufacture of colored oleomargarine. Further, he acknowledged
the similarity to the Pomerene amendment: "The tax was not
levied in that case, as it is not levied in this case for the purpose of raising revenue."[103] Under questioning, Hardwick
sought to distinguish, once and for all, the *McCray* case,
about whose validity he had not the slightest doubt. The taxing power was plenary in character, not to be questioned on
ordinary grounds or for ordinary purposes, he stated. At the
same time, there were equally valid and potent constitutional
provisions, and Congress was prohibited from exercising the taxing power "in such a way as to utterly destroy and entirely abro-
gate" these fundamental rights and powers. Pre-eminent among
them was the right of the states to regulate their own domestic
and internal affairs, a right that "our people more than any other
cling to."

But the game the southerners had afoot did not call for developing the constitutional argument. Everyone knew the substance
of the *Dagenhart* decision, Hardwick said; that holding controlled
the nation and ought to control the Senate. Unlike the Lottery
case, which the confirmed states' righter had declared wholly repugnant three years before, *Dagenhart* constituted good law and
was binding upon all. Thus the moral proposition, as he termed
it, was introduced.

> We have heard a good deal in the debates on this question, pro-
> tracted a great many years here and throughout the country, about
> the moral side of it, about the moral sentiment that is back of
> it. . . . I want to appeal to Senators on both sides of this Cham-
> ber, because it is no partisan question at all about the morals of
> undertaking to do in this way what the highest court in our coun-
> try has decided we have no power to do at all.[104]

If the decisions of the Supreme Court on questions of constitutionality obligated Congress, how could Senators in good conscience vote for "the exact language of an outlawed proposition
under the guise and pretext of raising revenue for the Govern-

[102] *Congressional Record*, 65th Cong., 3d Sess., p. 609.
[103] *Ibid.*
[104] *Ibid.*, p. 610.

ment?" This was the naked issue, Hardwick declared; and the southerners pounded away at it throughout the debate.

To whom was this argument directed? Certainly not to their senatorial colleagues, for the outcome of the legislative struggle was readily conceded. Instead, they addressed the Supreme Court, as persuasively as they were able. The principle that the federal courts might not inquire into the motives for congressional legislation stood in the way of invalidating the child labor tax. The supreme bench needed assistance if it was to circumvent the theory of judicial impotence enunciated in *McCray* — proof that an apparent revenue measure disguised a design to regulate subjects that were within the exclusive jurisdiction of the states. The congressional intention to do by indirection what had been firmly foreclosed under the commerce power would be made so patent that the justices could not disregard the encroachment upon judicial power nor the conflict with fundamental rights that resulted.

> The power to tax [said Overman] is the power to destroy; and when the Senate of the United States goes out of its way to interfere with another branch of this government, and it appears in the RECORD — and I suppose the Supreme Court will read this RECORD — that it is done for that purpose, that court is not going to uphold this section.[105]

The southerners therefore labored diligently to make certain that even the least perceptive justice would have no difficulty understanding the *Record.* They seized every opportunity to attribute to proponents of the amendment the admission, which none actually made, that Congress sought to nullify the *Dagenhart* decision. This being true, it was implied, the Court was not constrained as it would be in the instance of a legitimate revenue measure and could inquire into congressional motives. Questioned by Pomerene, Overman stated:

> I admit that under the oleomargarine case or the Veazie case, this being a bill to raise revenue, and nothing else, that as the Supreme Court says, we can levy a tax which will destroy; no matter what it does, they can not go behind what Congress has done to ascertain the purpose of it. . . .[106]

If congressmen, however, acknowledged their motives and admittedly inserted a provision in legislation for the express purpose

---

105 *Ibid.,* p. 612.
106 *Ibid.,* p. 613.

of nullifying a Supreme Court ruling, the judicial mind need not remain closed to what all others could see.[107]

A familiar name now reappears. There can be little doubt that David Clark devised the strategy of "loading" the *Congressional Record* for the author of the *McCray* opinion (now the Chief Justice) and his brethren to read. He was already laying plans for test litigation, realistically having abandoned hope of delaying congressional consideration or defeating passage of the amendment.[108] The senators from the southern textile district spoke with assurance when they predicted that the child labor tax would go to the Supreme Court. In addition, having laid the groundwork for the Executive Committee's legal assault, their repeated proclamation of the statute's certain overthrow reflected more than sham confidence.

The Proponents' Justification: Practical Considerations and Constitutional Doctrines

The answer to Hardwick and his colleagues came initially not from the progressive spokesmen for the amendment but from Senator Lodge, who certainly did not belong to the "radical" element in Congress. The leader of the conservative eastern wing of the Republican party spoke directly to the practical situation; in doing so, he seemed to typify the thinking of the vast majority of congressmen.

For a great many years he had been deeply interested in the child labor problem, Lodge stated.

> It is a great evil. The States have had ample and abundant opportunity to deal with it themselves. Most of the States have; some have not. I think it is something that ought to be ended.
>
> Congress passed a bill for that purpose by a large majority. That form of legislation has been held unconstitutional by the Supreme Court, and therefore it would seem to me that our only resort is to the taxing power. I am no fonder of resorting to that power for this purpose than anyone else, but the Government of the United States has resorted to it in more than one case. . . .
>
> It happened that some years ago I carried through a bill which became a law, to exterminate by the use of the taxing power the manufacture of white phosphorous matches, which produced hide-

---

[107] The piedmont senators also contrived to show that the amendment's sponsors adhered to an absolutist interpretation of the taxing power and that the measure neither intended to, nor would, raise revenue — whatever the bearing of either point upon the Court's deliberations.

[108] *Southern Textile Bulletin* (March 4, 1926), p. 21.

ous diseases among the workers. The bill failed in one Congress
and passed in the next. I think the constitutionality of that law
has never been questioned.

The amount of revenue to be raised by this measure may be
little or nothing. The main purpose is to put a stop to what seems
to be a very great evil, and one that ought to be in some way put
a stop to. If we are unable to reach it constitutionally in any
other way, then I am willing to reach it by the taxing power,
which the Courts have held can be used constitutionally for such
a purpose. I see no other way to do it.

It seems to me that we are justified in using the taxing power
for that purpose. It is a constitutional, but extreme method, I
readily admit. I think we are justified in it by the fact that the
police power of the States has failed to regulate it as it should be
regulated.[109]

At this point Hardwick asked if Lodge knew where his interesting doctrine would lead — perhaps to the utter destruction of
the fundamental rights of the locality? There was the crucial
question again. Lodge responded with considerable candor.

I admit that it is a dangerous power to use, but I think cases
have arisen where it is less dangerous to use the power than to
neglect the evil. I think there is very much better and stronger
ground for this legislation than there was for the oleomargarine
legislation. It is the fault of the States themselves. I am as much
opposed as anyone to the absorption of State powers by the Federal Government. The fact that that is proceeding as I think in
very many cases to a very unfortunate degree is owing to the fact
that the States have failed to exercise their powers. There has
been, more than that, a disposition in the States to throw all
sorts of things on the Federal Government instead of attending to
it themselves. I wish the States would be more alive to their rights
and duties under the Constitution than they have proved themselves to be.[110]

Ellison D. Smith suggested that Lodge was not fully informed
about legislative developments in the recent past.

Is it not a fact that in the last few years practically every manufacturing State in the Union where child labor has been more or
less employed has had progressive legislation on its own initiative
on this very question looking toward the very end that this legislation is looking to?[111]

109 *Congressional Record*, 65th Cong., 3d Sess., p. 611.
110 *Ibid.*
111 *Ibid.*

Lodge's answer, like his entire argument, echoed the warning of his intimate friend, Elihu Root, that, if the states failed to provide the controls the people needed, "sooner or later constructions of the Constitution will be found to vest the power where it will be exercised — in the national government." Lodge stated:

> If the State has made adequate laws of course it will be in no wise affected by this legislation; it will interfere in no way with their industries or their economic policies; but if the evil does exist anywhere then this law will, in my judgment, be highly beneficial.[112]

This reply provoked a rhetorical outburst from Smith that involved many of the constitutional shibboleths employed by southern representatives in previous child labor debates. He was amazed, the colorful South Carolinian stated, to hear members of the Senate lend themselves to a social nostrum they knew would be absolutely destructive of the cherished dual system of government. There was the impassioned warning about far-reaching consequences again.

The progressive architects of the amendment chiefly sought to render irrelevant the southerners' harassing questions about the morality of enacting further child labor legislation and their contentions that the *Dagenhart* case precluded such action. For Congress to exercise the taxing power within constitutional limits could hardly be represented as callous disregard of its responsibility, they argued. Such action was neither an encroachment on the Court's sphere of authority nor an attempt to nullify one of its holdings. The *Dagenhart* decision, although not questioned as controlling the commerce power, had no practical relevance for a revenue bill.

Having acknowledged the plenary character of the taxing power and the vitality of the *McCray* case, the southerners were told, their constitutional position was fatally undermined. Limited only by the obiter dictum announced in that case and the restrictions found in the taxing clause, Lenroot stated, the taxing power was "supreme and unlimited." The *McCray* restriction stipulated that the taxing power could "not destroy fundamental inherent rights of an individual, which neither State nor Federal Governments can directly destroy, but it may destroy any rights that a state in the exercise of its police power might destroy." [113] The fundamental constitutional proposition was this: What the states could outlaw the taxing power could destroy. No one, the Wis-

112 *Ibid.*
113 *Ibid.*, p. 615.

consin progressive said, possessed a fundamental right to manufacture and sell colored oleomargarine. Similarly, no one possessed a fundamental right to employ child labor, and the states
possessed unquestioned authority to prohibit such employment.
Congress, therefore, could legitimately impose a destructive tax
upon these practices. Such legislation would neither interfere
with state authority nor annihilate individual rights.

The practical result of the amendment, Lenroot acknowledged,
would be a sharp reduction in industrial child labor, for the
monetary incentive to retain child employees would be removed.
Nevertheless, this prohibitory effect posed no constitutional difficulty, for in a long series of cases the courts had repeatedly
recognized that results quite apart from those directly open to
congressional action might be achieved by otherwise unobjection-
able exercises of the taxing power. Justice White had summarized
these decisions in *McCray*: "If a tax be within the lawful power,
the exertion of that power may not be judicially restrained because of the results to arise from its exercise." [114] White's elaboration of the principle of judicial self-restraint was said to be especially important.

> The judiciary is without authority to void an act of Congress
> exerting the taxing power, even in the case where to the judicial
> mind it seems that Congress had, in putting such power in motion,
> abused its lawful authority by levying a tax which was unwise or
> oppressive, or the result of the enforcement of which might be
> to indirectly affect subjects not within the powers delegated to
> Congress.[115]

This was as plain as language could be, Lenroot said. Under the
taxing power, Congress might indirectly accomplish results that
it could not achieve directly.

To Hardwick's insistence that the taxing power could not be
used to destroy equally valid constitutional provisions, Lenroot
posed a confident challenge: "The Senator can not point to any
decision of the Supreme Court of the United States, from the
beginning to this day, where in a given case the doctrine he now
states has been applied." [116] Scores of decisions, "one long, un-
broken line of consistent doctrine," would have to be overturned

114 Quoted in *ibid.*
115 *Ibid.*, pp. 615–16.
116 Proponents made much of an analogy with the heavy excise taxes
Congress had levied upon munitions manufacturers for the express purpose of
depriving them of excess profits and preventing profiteering. Defending these
objectives, President Wilson had told Congress in May, 1918: "The profiteer

to find the child labor amendment invalid. Lenroot "[had] not gone into any discussion of the question . . . whether or not the Supreme Court would inquire into the motives of Congress in passing a taxing measure because even the opponents of the measure, I understand, admit that the Supreme Court will not so inquire." [117] The justices would accept the amendment for what Congress meant it to be.

The progressives thus narrowed the consideration of congressional responsibility to the boundaries of the 1916 debate. Any senator, Pomerene said, who believed that a vote for the amendment would violate his oath of office should vote against it, but he would vote affirmatively in perfect conscience. "If I thought it even probably unconstitutional I should not vote for it," Pomerene said.[118] For Senator Kenyon, the problem was more complex; long experience had brought him to the conclusion "that there is no constitutional question so clear that it is not without very serious difficulties." Nevertheless, he saw little force in the southerners' contention that those who supported the amendment were trying to nullify the action of the Supreme Court. When the income tax and employers' liability acts were ruled unconstitutional, he recalled, Congress had not hesitated to try other methods to achieve the same objectives; and now, after the "keenly disappointing" decision in the *Dagenhart* case, it was again trying another way, one that inevitably would be passed "on to the Supreme Court for them to state whether or not it is constitutional legislation." [119]

Kenyon stressed his certitude about the constitutionality of the amendment.

> I have no trouble, in my own mind, in reaching the conclusion that, under the circumstances, believing that we are remedying a great wrong, a great evil, and are trying to protect and conserve the children of this country, my duty is to vote for this amendment. . . . It is the only means now presented for curing this evil of child labor.[120]

that can not be got at by the restrictions of conscience and love of country can be got at by taxation."

117 *Ibid.*, p. 616. On one occasion, when Overman charged that the amendment's supporters admitted an unconstitutional purpose, Pomerene interrupted: "No, Mr. President, there is not any Senator who can admit a motive by Congress." To which Overman replied: "Well, everybody knows that what I stated is true, and we might as well be candid with each other." *Ibid.*, p. 613.

118 *Ibid.*, p. 618.

119 *Ibid.*

120 *Ibid.*, p. 619.

In the final analysis, Kenyon said, every senator had to decide the question for himself. To assist any who might not have reached a decision, he recalled a memorable precedent, one associated with his own career. The innovative Webb-Kenyon Act had been passed on to the Supreme Court, over President Taft's veto, and had been sustained, seven to two. The practical issue, thus, had to be met in all forward-looking legislation.

The House Considers the Pomerene Amendment

Once the Senate completed action on the revenue bill, its version and the version passed earlier by the House were given to a conference committee. Even though there were hundreds of differences, some of great importance, between the two versions of the bill, one having been passed while the war was still in progress and the other having been modified after the cessation of hostilities, the conference committee reached agreement with minimum conflict. Late in December the majority leader, Claude Kitchin of North Carolina, publicly assured Keating and several other congressional progressives that the conferees would accept the child labor amendment; the "overwhelming sentiment" of the House would not be disregarded.[121] When the conference committee reported, this commitment was kept.

The only deliberation in the House of Representatives on the Pomerene amendment consisted of an anticlimatic verbal skirmish, lasting less than an hour, on February 8, 1919, when the conference committee's report was taken up. The crucial battle on the amendment had already been lost in the Senate. Although the senators from the southern textile district held powerful positions in the committee structure, their opposition to the rider had been easily overcome by large bipartisan majorities in the Finance Committee and on the floor. Their colleagues in the House also found it impossible to withstand what the *New York Tribune* had called "the national sentiment of humanity." Their hopes became pinned on litigation — the expectation that the battle, lost in Congress, could again be won in the courts. They had no reason, therefore, to pursue delaying tactics. Moreover, the importance of enacting the revenue bill, to which the amendment had been attached, increased with each day.

During the brief debate, Representatives Venable and Humphreys of Mississippi railed against the amendment, restating the familiar charge that it invaded states' rights and threatened the

121 *Ibid.,* pp. 927–30.

destruction of constitutional government. "We all agree that it is an outrageous wrong to abuse the child in a factory," Venable said; however, the rider was "not an exercise of the taxing power in good faith" but "a subterfuge to exercise police powers that were never granted to the Federal Government." Permit the states to be deprived of control over local affairs under the guise of taxation and "you can completely socialize the entire Government in a year." Humphreys' impassioned peroration linked the noxious rider to the rising specter of bolshevism.[122]

Proponents of the amendment, several from southern or border states, repeatedly interrupted the two Mississippians with questions and Representative Gard of Ohio briefly rebutted their arguments. "The public policy of the United States is shaped with a view to the benefit of the nation as a whole," Gard quoted from Holmes's dissent in *Dagenhart*, and he, too, addressed an emotional appeal to the House — to applause.

> We face not a question of unconstitutionality, but we face . . . the question of voting as our conscience demands. As we face the world, we are to vote now not on the question of what the Supreme Court will say, because the Congress has the right to enact this legislation, but we vote as our conscience dictates, and my conscience dictates that I vote for the salvation of American childhood.[123]

What stands out is the casual manner in which the vast majority of congressmen approached the bill, as a routine measure rather than as one endowed with enormous potential for influencing constitutional development.

Venable felt so strongly about the constitutional issue that he moved to re-commit the entire report to the conference committee, with the House managers instructed to disagree on the child labor amendment. Forced to forswear his oath to the Constitution or to vote against the conference report, Venable argued, he chose re-committal, hoping that the unlawful appendage might be stricken from the revenue bill. The motion, however, was defeated by a vote of 171 to 15. Immediately thereafter the decisive vote took place, which resulted in acceptance of the conference report and the Pomerene amendment — by the impressive margin of 312 to 11.[124] Significantly, although every negative vote was

122 *Ibid.*, pp. 3029-33.
123 *Ibid.*, p. 3031.
124 *Ibid.*, p. 3035.

cast by a southern congressman, none of these represented a district in the Carolinas or Georgia.

Several days later the conference committee's report was taken up in the Senate and discussed at length for three days, but the child labor amendment was not even mentioned.[125] With scarcely a quorum present, the report was agreed to by voice vote on February 13. Both parties, declared a *New York Times* editorial, were "responsible for deferring enactment of the Tax bill beyond a date when it can be successfully administered."[126] On February 24, President Wilson returned from the Paris peace conference (bringing with him the Covenant of the League of Nations). One of his first acts was to sign the Revenue Bill of 1918, described in the House as "the greatest revenue bill in the history of nations." Title XII, the "Tax on Employment of Child Labor," was sheduled to take effect two months later, on April 25, 1919.[127]

The Child Labor Tax

Without committee hearings or reports, with little agitation from proponents and only negligible opposition, and after scant deliberation, Congress had enacted the Pomerene amendment in less than three months — a remarkably short and uncomplicated legislative history for a statute that, like the Keating-Owen law, lay on the frontiers of constitutional power. We need not speculate upon all the causes; an unchallengeable, bipartisan coalition complied with the public insistence that child labor be controlled, by whatever constitutional method Congress could find. Neither the masses of persons nor the President had changed their view about federal control of child labor as a consequence of experience acquired under the Keating-Owen law.[128] Rather, this experience

125 *Ibid.*, pp. 3117–39, 3179–94, 3265–71 (February 11–13, 1919).
126 February 14, 1919, p. 12.
127 40 U.S. Statutes 1057 (1919).
128 Wilson's interest in federal child labor legislation did not flag following the invalidation of the Keating-Owen law. Nevertheless, his wartime responsibilities apparently precluded an active role in the efforts to re-establish national regulation while hostilities were in progress, and, soon after the armistice, he sailed for the peace conference, not to return until after Congress had completed action on the Pomerene amendment.

What part, if any, he had in initiating the War Labor Policies Board's contract order remains obscure. He conferred on a number of occasions during the summer with representatives of the interested organizations, and the National Committee announced that he supported both the Keating War Power bill and the principle of permanent legislation based on the taxing power. See Thomas G. Karis, "Congressional Behavior at Constitutional

confirmed the desirability of national standards and the efficacy of national enforcement.

"The scientific and popular opinion is so strong for the prohibition of child labor in this country that it is certain to be obtained sooner or later," a commentator remarked in the *Michigan Law Review*.[129] As for the principle of destructive taxation, the *New York World* — said by Link to have been "the editorial spokesman of the Wilson administration" — declared:

> We can see no [constitutional] objection except that the proposed Federal tax is too small. Ten per centage on the value of the products of enslaved childhood is not enough to emancipate the youth of the South or to curb the greed of its employers or to correct the depraved public sentiment against which the levy is aimed.[130]

The *New Orleans Times-Picayune* reported a strong public demand for federal legislation that would stand the test of constitutionality.[131] Perhaps nothing better illustrates the extent of popular support than the paradoxical circumstance that the organization most interested in child labor reform, instead of being in the forefront, found events passing it by. The Senate vote occurred the day after the National Committee's trustees, under pressure from the membership and the newspapers for a commitment, abandoned their preferred version and endorsed the Pomerene amendment[132] — and there is little reason for believing that this endorsement materially affected the outcome. And nothing more dramatically symbolized the futility of southern opposition than the fact that, although Senator Simmons and Representative Kitchin — two of the most powerful figures in Congress — intensely disliked the amendment, they were unable to prevent its attachment to a statute popularly referred to as the Simmons-Kitchin Act.

That the Senate's vote exaggerated congressional support for the Pomerene amendment or disguised ulterior motives appears

Frontiers" (Unpublished Ph.D. dissertation, Department of Political Science, Columbia University, 1951), pp. 168, 178; Raymond G. Fuller, "Child Labor and the War," *The American Review of Reviews* (November, 1918), pp. 500–2; Lovejoy, quoted in "Call Children from War Plants," p. 8; and Fuller, "A Quest for Constitutionality," p. 210.

[129] "Child Labor Law Case," *Michigan Law Review* (November, 1918), p. 87.
[130] Quoted in *Literary Digest* (January 4, 1919), p. 14.
[131] Quoted in *ibid.*
[132] "Report of the General Secretary."

unlikely. Some senators may have voted for it without enthusiasm, possibly against their better judgment, but the likelihood is that senators who had serious reservations or found open opposition inexpedient were absent from the floor. The vast majority, it appears, agreed with Senator Lodge about the need for national action and concurred in his judgment that the taxing power offered the only remaining path. Many, probably, also agreed that this path involved the exercise of a constitutional though dangerous power, one that might occasionally be used to achieve an important social objective but should not become a common resort for regulatory purposes. For the overwhelming majority of congressmen, as the House vote subsequently confirmed, the Pomerene amendment represented a nonpartisan social advance. Despite Wilson's ill-advised partisan call for a Democratic Congress, the Republicans had triumphed at the polls the month before the Senate vote. Although the Republicans would not organize Congress until later in the year, Lodge, Kenyon, and Lenroot spoke for the majority party, consciously reflecting dominant opinion, when they branded child labor an intolerable evil.

The *Doremus* decision,[133] sustaining the Harrison Narcotic Drugs Act, which was handed down soon after Congress completed action on the revenue bill, stilled lingering doubts about constitutionality and strengthened confidence generally. The importance of the case could not be overlooked, a commentator said in the *American Child*; if the Court followed its principles, an affirmative decision was assured.[134] Speaking for the Court, albeit a majority of five, Justice Day found no obstacle to a taxing measure that had been enacted for the purpose of imposing a national regulatory scheme upon the sale of substances over which the states had not been able to exercise effective control.[135] Although he specified that the decisive question was whether the provisions under challenge had "any relation to the raising of revenue," Day concluded that, considered in themselves, these provisions tended "to keep the [narcotic] traffic above board and subject to inspection by those authorized to collect the revenue" [136] — for all practical purposes an admission that generating revenue was largely incidental. At the same time, Day claimed to shun examination of the patent

133 *United States* v. *Doremus*, 249 U.S. 86 (1919).

134 David Brady, "A Forecast of the Supreme Court Decision on the Child Labor Tax," *American Child* (August, 1919), pp. 115–17.

135 Swisher, *American Constitutional Development*, p. 840.

136 *United States* v. *Doremus*, 249 U.S. 86, 94.

supervisory purpose of the statute. The Court had long held, he declared, that

> The fact that other motives may impel the exercise of the federal taxing power does not authorize the courts to inquire into that subject. If the legislation enacted has some reasonable relation to the exercise of the taxing authority conferred by the Constitution, it cannot be invalidated because of the supposed motives which induced it.[137]

Lest the ruling be misunderstood, Day attempted to incorporate the doctrine that matters purely local in character were beyond congressional control. But the analogy to the Pomerene amendment could not be so easily "distinguished away," especially when Day also tried to preserve the broad character of the power to levy excise taxes. It was not "sufficient to invalidate the taxing authority given to the Congress by the Constitution that the same business may be regulated by the police power of the state," the opinion held. "The act may not be declared unconstitutional because its effects may be to accomplish another purpose as well as the raising of revenue." But no amount of judicial sleight of hand could accommodate *Doremus* under the mantle of *McCray* and simultaneously exclude the child labor tax. The facts simply did not diverge.[138]

---

[137] *Ibid.*, p. 93.

[138] Shortly after the amendment became law, the Secretary of the Treasury established a special enforcement section within the Internal Revenue Bureau to administer it. Although this maximized the statute's appearance as a revenue measure, it produced consternation among the cooperating organizations, especially the National Committee and the Children's Bureau. The assurances that the Child Labor Division of the bureau would be designated the administrative agency proved ill founded. Upon discovery of the Secretary's action, Owen Lovejoy and Julia Lathrop wrote to Wilson, pleading their case, but their efforts to obtain presidential intervention failed. "Report of the General Secretary" (unpublished and undated memorandum, N.C.L.C.).

8

The Curious History of a Judicial
Contrivance:
Atherton v. *Johnston*

The Cotton Manufacturers Plan Another Legal Assault

As the National Committee and the organizations associated
with it sought to re-establish national child labor regulation on a
permanent basis, David Clark worked tirelessly to protect the
economic interests of the southern textile manufacturers. He
carried on an unceasing campaign to win broad public acceptance
for the cotton mill industry. When the Keating-Owen law was
declared unconstitutional, he wrote, the "agitators" in and out
of Congress were amazed and angered, and immediately "began
another campaign of abuse against the cotton mills of the South." [1]
To counteract this supposedly unjustified criticism, Clark published a second "Health and Happiness Issue" of the *Bulletin*.
Like the first, its purpose was to portray "the truth" about southern mill conditions.[2]

Clark's attention, of course, was centered chiefly upon Congress.
When, late in the autumn, it became clear that overwhelming
majorities in both houses supported the Pomerene amendment,
he abandoned his efforts to halt its progress. His afterview of the
passage of the amendment is a counsel in political realism, which,
perhaps unconsciously, acknowledged "a national sentiment of
humanity." From the beginning, he said, the Executive Committee realized that the measure could not be resisted successfully.
Furthermore, because it was attached as a rider to the revenue
bill, "there was little opportunity to delay its passage." Thus a
decision was reached early in the contest not "to waste much time
or any money" on attempts to influence the outcome of the con-

[1] *Southern Textile Bulletin* (May 18, 1922, and March 4, 1926), pp. 18 and 21.
[2] This "beautiful edition of more than 300 pages" — as Clark described the
issue — was published "in December, 1918, and very widely distributed." *Ibid.*,
March 4, 1926, p. 21.

gressional deliberations.[3] Nevertheless, the spokesmen for the mill men had not been altogether frustrated, he boasted: "Just in spite we had an amendment drawn placing the enforcement of the new law under a special bureau in the Treasury Department. We managed to get this adopted."[4] This was an outright deception, but playing free with the truth was nothing new to Clark.[5]

Clark's response to the campaign "to force certain standards upon the States by means of a tax" and thereby to secure "centralization of power indirectly and by subterfuge" was a foregone conclusion. In late December, after the Senate had approved the Pomerene amendment, he announced that the constitutionality of the new federal child labor law would be challenged as quickly as events permitted,[6] a tacit admission that the legislative battle in Congress had been lost. This, however, was of little consequence. With the *Dagenhart* victory still vividly in mind, Clark and his associates welcomed the opportunity to transfer the contest to the courts.

There was none of the uncertainty and hesitation that had surrounded the initiation of the previous litigation. The constitutional position was well prepared and a trusted cadre — the counsel responsible for victory six months before — again stood ready to repulse the progressive attack. Again, they were retained to protect the interests of the southern textile manufacturers — in the name of preserving industrial freedom. To have given any quarter, "aside from its relation to child labor," Clark said, would have meant permitting "the agitators and fanatics to know that they could use the taxing power of Government, to regulate the conduct and affairs of the people of this country."[7] Again, an all-out contest was to be waged. But this time the Executive Committee received significantly greater numerical and financial support from the cotton manufacturers than two years before. The potency of defense-by-lawsuit had been dramatically demonstrated.

[3] *Ibid.*, May 18, 1922, pp. 18, 34.

[4] *Ibid.*, March 4, 1926, p. 21.

[5] Clark was guilty of marked duplicity during the campaign to ratify the child labor amendment. He created a paper organization, the Farmers' States Rights League, that flooded rural areas across the country with vicious anti-amendment propaganda. This was said to originate with southern agriculturalists but it represented only the Executive Committee's interests in disguise.

[6] *Southern Textile Bulletin* (December 26, 1918), p. 10.

[7] *Ibid.*, February 27, 1919, p. 12.

Tried and True: Prochein Ami and
James Edmund Boyd

The initial step in Clark's strategy was implemented in mid-December, when, by loading the *Congressional Record,* the senatorial delegations from the southern textile states virtually invited the five justices of the Supreme Court who had composed the *Dagenhart* majority to inspect the substance as well as the form of the Pomerene amendment when litigation arose. The second step involved selecting the form of litigation to be used. A final decision was not easily reached, however. Clark had several meetings with counsel before he announced, on April 10 — two weeks before the child labor tax was to take effect — that the Executive Committee had perfected its plans for challenging the law's validity.[8]

The main problem that faced counsel, just as in the *Dagenhart* case, was Clark's insistence that an initial decision be obtained at the earliest possible moment, preferably before the legislation took effect. The obstacles, however, were much greater than in 1917 because the constitutionality of a revenue measure could be contested in only a few ways. Indeed, until the *Pollock* decision (1895) it was a "well-established principle that the collection of federal taxes would not be restrained by the courts, and that the rights of persons from whom they were unjustly collected might be protected only by suits to recover the taxes after they had been paid."[9] Despite the Supreme Court's willingness to countenance the procedure used in that case — a stockholder's suit against a corporation to enjoin the illegal payment of taxes — the principle seemed to be only slightly, if at all, impaired.

To have waited until the usual form of suit could be instituted would have meant abandoning Clark's order of priorities. Three years later, again in the flush of victory, he explained the problem: because "no taxes or penalties could be assessed until the end of [the law's] first year of operation, some method other than protesting the payment of taxes had to be devised."[10] The method finally agreed upon was an injunction proceeding directly parallel to the one employed in the *Dagenhart* case. An application for a restraining order would be made in the name of another Roland Dagenhart — to prevent his minor son from being denied employ-

---

8 *Ibid.,* February 20 and 27, April 10, 1919, pp. 14, 12, 14.
9 Carl Brent Swisher, *American Constitutional Development* (Boston: Houghton Mifflin Co., 1943), p. 445.
10 *Southern Textile Bulletin* (May 18, 1922), p. 18.

ment in a cotton mill because of the prohibitions said to be implicit in the Pomerene amendment. This form of action was later acknowledged to be, at best, of very dubious propriety, but it involved negligible risk; Clark hazarded only the expenses involved in bringing the suit. Counsel thus selected the quickest way to raise the constitutional question rather than the method most likely to survive jurisdictional inspection.

After the equity proceeding was agreed upon, Clark returned to Charlotte and, as two years before, set about arranging a series of situations from which Junius Parker and his associates could make a judicious selection. As a result, not only were the actual though undeclared plaintiffs, the counsel they retained, and the form of lawsuit employed the same as in the *Dagenhart* case, but the judicial district in which the petition was to be presented — which is to say the judge before whom the case would be tried — also was the same. James Edmund Boyd's holding on the *Dagenhart* petition and, perhaps more important, the laissez faire strictures he had volunteered about the unwisdom of too extensive or too stringent child labor legislation seemed to ensure that he would not deliberate overly long before invalidating the child labor tax.

In still another particular the circumstances of the second judicial test paralleled those of the first test. Clark again set about raising the necessary funds for the litigation by asking the state cotton manufacturers' associations to make contributions, and he also sent direct appeals to mill owners and managers. Both series of requests met ready responses.[11] (Only once, at an early stage in the litigation, did Clark find it expedient to admonish the manufacturers editorially, and in language that was unusually mild.) By this time Clark undoubtedly knew where to concentrate his solicitation efforts and it no longer was necessary to "hammer hard" at unresponsive mill men.

The Test Case, the Complaint, and Control of the Litigation

The Cotton Manufacturers' Association of North Carolina, it will be recalled, meeting shortly after *Hammer* v. *Dagenhart* was decided, had found it expedient to endorse a fourteen-year

---

[11] Of the various state associations, North Carolina appears to have subscribed the largest amount of money; see *Proceedings of the Thirteenth Annual Convention of the Cotton Manufacturers' Association of North Carolina* (Charlotte: Observer Printing House, 1919), p. 56.

minimum-age standard for industrial employment. A bill incorporating this standard was introduced, with the support of the manufacturers, at the next session of the North Carolina legislature, in late February, 1919, immediately after congressional enactment of the child labor tax. Earlier bills that had sought to establish this exclusionary requirement had always been defeated by the mill owners, but the new measure was enacted, without opposition, in a few weeks.[12]

The last of the southern textile states to hold out against national standards of regulation with respect to excluding grade-school-age children from industrial employment had now come into line. David Clark and other spokesmen for the textile industry thereafter insisted that child labor had been abolished in the south, largely at the behest of the mill owners. However, the acquiescence of the North Carolina legislature strikingly illustrated the truth of Holmes's terse utterance in *Dagenhart*: "The national welfare as understood by Congress may require a different attitude within its sphere from that of some self-seeking State." For the child labor laws of North Carolina and its sister states in the southern textile district still failed to restrict the workday to eight hours for children fourteen to sixteen years of age. It was this difference between the provisions of state and federal legislation that the test case would illustrate.

The first week in April, Clark submitted to counsel for the Executive Committee the details of three prospective cases he had prepared.[13] Their choice as the test vehicle involved a mill operative named Eugene T. Johnston, his son John, age fifteen, and their employer, the Atherton Mills, a cotton manufacturing establishment in Charlotte. In the same way the Dagenhart family and the Fidelity Manufacturing Company had served as figureheads for the Executive Committee, the two Johnstons and Atherton Mills now became the parties to the record. Precisely why the elder Johnston lent his name and that of his son to the proceeding is not known, but it is no doubt significant that Eugene Johnston, like Roland Dagenhart, was employed by the defendant company and that the threat of discharge was available as a means of coercion, other inducements failing. The managers of Atherton

12 See especially Elizabeth H. Davidson, *Child Labor Legislation in the Southern Textile States* (Chapel Hill: University of North Carolina Press, 1939), pp. 173–76. The *Charlotte Observer* endorsed the new act chiefly because it would give future legislatures "immunity from the nagging influence of the New England organization" (*ibid.*, p. 174).

13 *Southern Textile Bulletin* (May 18, 1922), p. 18.

Mills, on the other hand, had immediate and obvious economic motives for cooperating. What other motivation, if any, they may have had is not disclosed by the available evidence.

The sequence of events followed much the same pattern as two years before. On April 12, the officers of Atherton Mills posted notices on the company's premises informing its employees that, solely because of the provisions of the child labor law, all operatives under sixteen years of age would be discharged on April 25, the day the act became effective. Eugene Johnston was specifically notified that his son, John, would be barred from further employment after that date. Three days later the Johnston petition was filed.[14] In form and content it followed the *Dagenart* complaint almost exactly; indeed, the identical language was employed paragraph after paragraph. The only substantive changes, aside from the parties, were modifications in the charges of unconstitutionality due to the fact that a revenue measure was being challenged.

The bill averred that John W. Johnston was employed in compliance with the laws of North Carolina, that his father, Eugene T. Johnston, was entitled to direct his services, and that these rights would be unavoidably lost if Atherton Mills complied with the provisions of the child labor law.[15] It claimed further that the law was unconstitutional because (1) it was not a tax levy such as the Constitution authorized; (2) its sole purpose was to regulate the employment of children engaged in manufacture within the states; (3) it usurped powers reserved to the people and the states by the Tenth Amendment; and (4) its enforcement would deprive plaintiffs of their labor and property without due process of law, in contravention of the Fifth Amendment. For these reasons, the bill concluded, an injunction was prayed.

This remedy was justified, word for word, by the same language that had been used in the *Dagenhart* petition: "Only in a suit of this nature" could plaintiffs' rights be fully protected. The assertion was extraordinary. Any equity proceeding would have been suspect as a means of challenging a federal revenue act, but a

14 *Eugene T. Johnston and John W. Johnston v. The Atherton Mills*, North Carolina District Court of the United States, in *Transcript of Record, Atherton v. Johnston*, Supreme Court of the United States, October Term, 1920 (Washington, D.C.: Judd and Detweiler, Printers, 1910), p. 6.

15 *Ibid.*, pp. 1–3. In order to cover every contingency, the bill averred that, if John W. Johnston was not discharged, his hours of labor would be curtailed below those allowable in North Carolina and his compensation correspondingly reduced (*ibid.*, p. 4).

petition in the same form as the *Dagenhart* petition, particularly
if no effort was made to include a governmental official as third
party, was outrageous.

Again, the timing of the litigation had important implications
for the outcome, even more than previously. This greater significance stemmed from the friendly character of the suit. Inasmuch
as the federal government was not involved, not even in a nominal
way, counsel for the Executive Committee and the legal representatives of the Atherton Mills were for all practical purposes
a single corps of attorneys and exercised virtually complete control over the litigation. This advantage was skillfully exploited.
On April 15, William Hendren and W. P. Bynum appeared before Judge Boyd to request an injunction. In view of the alleged
imminent threat to the Johnstons' rights, they asked that the
mandatory waiting period be dispensed with so that argument
in the case might begin as soon as possible. Boyd granted their
motion. He ordered Atherton Mills to "show cause" on April 25,
or as soon thereafter as counsel could be prepared, why an injunction should not be issued.[16]

Clement Manly immediately sent letters to District Attorney
Hammer, to Alexander C. King, who had succeeded John W.
Davis as Solicitor General, and to Daniel C. Roper, the Commissioner of Internal Revenue, informing them of the injunction
petition and of Judge Boyd's order. The controversy was of such
importance that the Justice Department should be advised, "to
the end, if it was deemed consistent, that the Court might have
the benefit to be derived from an appearance and argument of
Counsel for the United States." [17] Counsel for the Atherton Mills
dispatched similar letters the following day. In effect, the Justice
Department and the Internal Revenue Bureau were invited to
defend the constitutionality of the child labor tax. Several years
later the Solicitor General, James M. Beck, who had little sympathy for the child labor tax, remarked sarcastically that if it had
not been for the "fairness and courtesy" of the Atherton Mills,
the Justice Department might not have heard of the case until
after the holding of the district court had been announced.[18]

Beyond calling the Justice Department's attention to the exist-

16 *Ibid.*, p. 5.
17 C. Manly to A. C. King, April 15, 1919, Justice Department File, *Atherton* v. *Johnston*, National Archives, Washington, D.C.
18 James M. Beck, *Supplemental Brief for the Unilted States as Amicus
Curiae, Atherton* v. *Johnston* (Washington, D.C.: Government Printing Office,
1922), p. 8.

ence of the suit, Atherton Mills did no more to defend the child labor tax than was necessary to serve the interests of the textile manufacturers. To maintain the semblance of an actual controversy, counsel answered the bill of complaint. Not surprisingly, this response followed almost word for word the answer the Fidelity Manufacturing Company had filed to the *Dagenhart* complaint. Its perfunctory part in the jurisdictional masquerade completed, Atherton Mills's participation in the case ceased for the moment. Counsel for the company did not even bother to appear before Judge Boyd for argument. An observation of Paul A. Freund's is pertinent at this point: "Whether or not a stockholder's suit [or any other friendly proceeding] will produce a real contest depends on the attitude of counsel."[19] Here, the attitude was firmly and understandably negative. Again, a "self-selected" defender of the constitutionality of a congressional enactment contrived to destroy it. And again the initiative, though in greatly diminished measure, shifted to the Justice Department, which found the time for decision short indeed. Less than a week remained before argument when information about the suit reached Washington.

Another of Freund's observations is applicable: "Whether or not the government was represented at all in these purely private lawsuits depended upon whether the government had notice that the suit had been brought, and whether participation as a friend of the court was thought advisable."[20] Here the decision was for participation, but the government would enter the case only to raise the question of jurisdiction. The friendly character of the action and "the anxiety of both the plaintiff and the defendant to get the Government into court" were patent to officials in the Justice Department and they sought to eliminate the suit.[21] Apparently it was hoped that even so staunch a partisan of judicial supervisory power as Judge Boyd would be forced to acknowledge the conspicuous defects in the petition; therefore, District Attorney Hammer was instructed to appear as amicus curiae, thereby frustrating the design of the supposedly adversary parties.[22]

[19] *On Understanding the Supreme Court* (Boston: Little, Brown and Co., 1949), pp. 84–85.

[20] *Ibid.*, p. 85.

[21] A. C. King to W. L. Frierson, April 16 and 18, 1919, Justice Department File, *Atherton* v. *Johnston*. In the former memorandum the Solicitor General told Frierson: "I assume that . . . if any real contestation is made it will have to be made by the Government."

[22] A. C. King to W. C. Hammer, April 22, 1919.

Judicial Gamesmanship, Zealous Intervention, and a Curious Appeal

When *Johnston* v. *Atherton* was called, on April 23, District Attorney Hammer, following his instructions, asked permission to appear as friend of the court but did not ask leave for the government to enter the case. Judge Boyd granted the request, and Hammer spoke briefly. He contended that the court lacked jurisdiction over the suit, and for two reasons: there was no allegation in the complaint of a contract for labor that would prevent Atherton Mills from discharging John W. Johnston for any reason the company might see fit, and the case was not properly brought under existing federal statutes so as to empower the court to pass on the validity of the law.[23] In short, the suit was stigmatized as a nonjusticiable contrivance.

David Clark had feared that the Justice Department would make just such an attack and that Judge Boyd might sustain the challenge to the court's jurisdiction.[24] However, his anxiety about the jurist's response proved groundless. Boyd rejected Hammer's argument out of hand and accepted the fiction of a real and justiciable controversy. But rather than decide the cause, he, too, played the judicial game. The court was advised, Boyd said, that the defendant had informed the Solicitor General that the suit was pending; therefore, he announced, he would continue the motion for an injunction until May 2, ostensibly to allow the Solicitor General further time to consider this information. Meanwhile, he entered a temporary injunction against the Atherton Mills, as prayed in the Johnston petition.[25]

Boyd, in fact, had told the Justice Department — in unmistakable language — that further argument on the procedural issue would serve no useful purpose. Having taken jurisdiction, he would decide the case. In effect, the Solicitor General had been invited to take part in the masquerade. His office was asked to shoulder its responsibility to defend the constitutionality of the child labor tax, and so to acquiesce in Boyd's ruling on the procedural question. However, the Justice Department declined Boyd's invitation, as it had the Executive Committee's. District Attorney Hammer again was instructed to try to dispose of the

---

23 *Transcript of Record, Atherton* v. *Johnston*, p. 10.

24 *Southern Textile Bulletin* (April 24, 1919), p. 18.

25 *Transcript of Record, Atherton* v. *Johnston*, pp. 10–11, and W. C. Hammer to Attorney General, April 23, 1919, Justice Department File, *Atherton* v. *Johnston*.

case on technical grounds, when argument was resumed, but under no circumstances to make "the United States in any sense a party to the suit." [26]

It was generally expected, when the court convened on May 2, that argument of the suit, like that in the *Dagenhart* case, would take several days. But this was not to be the case. District Attorney Hammer again called attention to the jurisdictional issue and then deferred to counsel for the Executive Committee. Counsel had barely begun their presentation when Judge Boyd broke in to say that he had already made up his mind and found the statute unconstitutional.[27] For this reason, further argument was unnecessary. Boyd's action is easily accounted for. Hammer's appearance told him all he wanted to know: the Justice Department had not commissioned special counsel, as it had in the *Dagenhart* case, and would not argue the constitutional issue. Plainly, then, it served no purpose to prolong the play-acting in the courtroom.

Boyd's indictment of the child labor tax, in his comments from the bench, repeated the constitutional opinions he had expressed when invalidating the Keating-Owen law: Congress had sought to accomplish by indirection what it could not accomplish by direct prohibition, and the statute invaded the regulatory authority of the states.[28] The statute was pronounced "unconstitutional and without the power of Congress to enact" and the plaintiffs were granted the extraordinary relief requested in the petition.[29]

Counsel for the Executive Committee had hoped that officials of the Justice Department would be sufficiently interested in having the constitutional question raised that they would close their eyes to the form of the suit, despite its vulnerability on technical grounds. In this they were disappointed, but not in their expectation that Judge Boyd would brush aside all questions pertaining to technical issues, if such were raised, in order to condemn the law. There was no showing that a genuine lawsuit existed, which indeed was impossible. Boyd's action can be rationalized only by the adventitious supposition that the invalidity of the statute conferred jurisdiction. Again, his disinclination to stray from the constitutional imperatives of laissez faire proved decisive. And, once more, although having taken the grave step

[26] W. L. Frierson to W. C. Hammer, April 24, 1919.
[27] *Raleigh News and Observer*, May 3, 1919, p. 1.
[28] "The New Child Labor Law," *American Child* (May, 1919), p. 9.
[29] *Transcript of Record, Atherton v. Johnston*, p. 12.

of holding a congressional enactment unconstitutional, he did not deign to write an opinion. It was the most remarkable decision in all of the litigation that challenged federal child labor legislation.

Boyd's restraining order differed markedly in effect from his orders in the *Dagenhart* case, for it reached a single youth. Atherton Mills was forbidden to discharge John W. Johnston, "by reason of the force" of the child labor law, or to reduce his hours of labor below the number allowable under the laws of North Carolina. The company, however, could have discharged the youth or reduced his hours of labor for any other reason, no matter how arbitrary, and thereby deprived the elder Johnston of the fundamental rights Boyd had zealously protected. None of Atherton Mill's other employees was affected. The company stood in the same relationship to those employees under sixteen years of age as every other industrial concern in the nation to which the law applied and had either to comply with its requirements or be assessed the 10 per cent tax on net profits for failure to do so.

Because of the limited effect of Boyd's holding, the Justice Department was content to let the *Johnston* case languish.[30] David Clark, however, was extremely anxious to obtain a conclusive holding from the Supreme Court at the earliest opportunity, and, because of the friendly nature of the suit, he was able to influence events exactly as he wished. When it became obvious that the government would not appeal Boyd's decision, counsel for Atherton Mills re-entered the proceeding. Although the company had shown no interest in defending the constitutionality of the child labor tax during argument, as the supposedly aggrieved party in a case in which a federal act had been declared invalid, it possessed a statutory right to appeal to the Supreme Court, which had to accept the case for review.

Thus, counsel for the company went before Judge Boyd on May 14 and moved to appeal. Boyd, in turn, maintained the fiction of a real controversy and granted the motion.[31] This was an even more flagrant disregard of judicial propriety than hearing the case had been. The friendly counsel later agreed upon the record, and Boyd approved their stipulation. Simultaneously, counsel for Atherton Mills again wrote to the Solicitor General.[32]

30 *Raleigh News and Observer*, May 3, 1919.

31 *Transcript of Record, Atherton v. Johnston*, pp. 13–15.

32 William M. Wilson to A. C. King, May 5, 1919, Justice Department File, *Atherton v. Johnston*. When the case was appealed, a brief for the Executive Committee said the "management and control" of Atherton Mills's action "was

Again, the Justice Department was invited to defend the constitutionality of the child labor tax, this time before the Supreme Court. And the department was asked to do this at a time it had not chosen and in a suit it had tried to have ruled defective because patently collusive and not cognizable under federal law.

Calculated Neglect and a Candid Call for Blindness

During the summer, David Clark was preoccupied by the possibility that the test suit might still be ruled nonjusticiable;[33] he acknowledged that the Supreme Court would have to consider the appropriateness of the proceeding before the constitutional issue could be reached. Although he did not say it directly, he strongly implied that the justices might reach a conclusion different from Judge Boyd's. To guard against such an eventuality, he announced (in September) that another test case — along other lines — was being prepared that would ensure a Supreme Court hearing without further delay.[34]

Early in the autumn, counsel for the Executive Committee asked the Solicitor General to join them in requesting advancement of the case. The limited effect of Boyd's holding was no longer the only powerful stimulus for action; by mid-autumn, John W. Johnston would be sixteen years of age and it could not then be argued that the child labor tax deprived him and his father of fundamental rights. The Justice Department agreed to cooperate, but only to a limited extent. The motion for advancement was made on October 6, in the name of the two Johnstons, with counsel for Atherton Mills and the Solicitor General supposedly associating themselves. Clark's attorneys argued that the case was of general public interest, especially in view of the Court's decision in *Hammer* v. *Dagenhart*, where the former child labor law, "which sought to accomplish the same result . . . was declared unconstitutional."[35] The Solicitor Gen-

placed in the hands of the Solicitor General by the appellant" (*Brief for Appellees on Reargument, Atherton v. Johnston* [Washington, D.C.: Government Printing Office, 1922], p. 3).

[33] The Solicitor General, responding to counsel for Atherton Mills, stated that he very much feared the Supreme Court would decline to consider the constitutional question because the petition did not "show such facts as are proper to raise the case." A. C. King to W. M. Wilson, Justice Department File, *Atherton v. Johnston.*

[34] *Southern Textile Bulletin* (May 8, 1919), p. 34.

[35] *Motion to Advance, Atherton v. Johnston* (Washington, D.C.: Government Printing Office, 1919), p. 3. Following a conference with King, Junius Parker drafted the motion, including the statement of the government's posi-

eral said that the government was not a party to the suit and had
not initiated the motion but had joined in it because of the great
interest various departments had in obtaining a definitive constitutional judgment at the earliest possible moment. For this
reason the government would ask leave to submit a brief as amicus
curiae and to be heard orally.

Clark correctly interpreted the Justice Department's action as
meaning that argument would be restricted almost solely to the
question of constitutionality. Faced with the appeal, and under
pressure from such interested government agencies as the Treasury and Labor Departments and from various reform groups to
endeavor to sustain the constitutionality of the child labor tax,
the Justice Department decided that the public interest lay in
settling the issue once and for all.[36] Also, "an appraisal of the
temper of the Court," to use Freund's phrase,[37] made the chances
for success appear promising. The government had only to hold
the *Dagenhart* dissenters and to win over Chief Justice White, the
author of the *McCray* opinion, or to convince the *Doremus* majority. Thus the jurisdictional issue was virtually discarded.

The government's brief, drafted by the Solicitor General, Alexander C. King,[38] and William L. Frierson, the Assistant Attorney
General who had played a prominent role in the *Dagenhart* litigation, was submitted two months later. An introductory section
expressed "entire willingness" to decide the constitutional question in the *Johnston* case, but fairness to the Court made it incumbent upon counsel to raise the technical issue.[39] There followed
an attenuated account of the proceedings in the lower court that
disclosed the friendly character of the suit and made clear the
need for the government to intervene as amicus curiae.[40]

tion. King accepted this draft verbatim but made clear that he still thought
the Court might find the litigation inappropriate. J. Parker to A. C. King,
September 25, 1919, and A. C. King to J. Parker, September 26, 1919, Justice
Department File, *Atherton* v. *Johnston.*

36 A. C. King to W. B. Wilson, April 18, 1919; Jouett Shouse to A. C. King,
April 19, 1919; W. L. Frierson to J. Shouse, May 27, 1919; J. Parker to A. C.
King, September 25, 1919; W. L. Frierson to Raymond G. Fuller, October 15,
1919, A. C. King to J. Parker, October 15, 1919; and D. C. Roper to W. L. Frierson, October 29, 1919; Justice Department File, *Atherton* v. *Johnston.*

37 Freund, *On Understanding the Supreme Court,* p. 110.

38 King replaced John W. Davis after Davis's appointment as Ambassador
to the Court of Saint James's in September, 1918.

39 *Brief of the United States as Amicus Curiae, Atherton* v. *Johnston* (Washington, D.C.: Government Printing Office, 1919 [filed December 6, 1919]), p. 3.

40 Of the conspicuous absence of the appellant, Atherton Mills, the brief
reported: "The defendant company appealed to the court, but, beyond notify-

On account of its desire for a prompt determination of the question involved, the Government does not press the question of jurisdiction. Having called the attention of the court to that question, it is content to present the case if the court is of the opinion that jurisdiction exists.[41]

The justices were informed, in effect, that they could raise the issue of jurisdiction, if they chose, by addressing questions to counsel during argument.

The brief filed by counsel for the Executive Committee dwelt at great length on the jurisdictional issue and treated the subject with disarming candor.[42] The Solicitor General did not question the propriety of an equity proceeding, it was stated. "This method of testing the validity of the statute is adequate, and if the statute is unconstitutional, the judgment [below] should be affirmed." The implication was clear: because the government acquiesced, the alleged invalidity of the child labor tax should obviate all questions about the adequacy of the suit.

The equity proceedings employed in *Truax* v. *Raich*[43] and, conveniently, *Hammer* v. *Dagenhart* were cited as precedents. The brief admitted the crucial difficulty, however: these supposedly precedent suits challenged criminal rather than revenue statutes. It then sought to dispose of this glaring defect:

> It is true also that the United States statutes . . . provide that there shall be no injunction against the collection of taxes. It has been distinctly held, though, that, while an injunction will not lie against the collecting authorities to prevent the collection of a Federal tax, an injunction will lie at the suit of one who would be injuriously affected, against the tax payer, to prevent the tax payer complying with the statute, if it is void.[44]

A recent case, *Brushaber* v. *Union Pacific Railroad Co.*,[45] in which a stockholder's suit, much like that in the *Pollock* case, had been used to challenge the validity of the Income Tax law of 1913, was said to be controlling.[46] But this contention ignored the

ing the Attorney General of the appeal, has displayed no further interest in the proceeding." *Ibid.*, p. 4.

41 *Ibid.*

42 *Brief for Appellees, Atherton* v. *Johnston* (Washington, D.C.: Government Printing Office, 1919 [filed December 4, 1919]).

43 239 U.S. 33 (1915).

44 *Brief for Appellees, Atherton* v. *Johnston*, p. 6.

45 240 U.S. 1 (1916).

46 The equity bill filed in *Brushaber* sought to enjoin the railroad corporation from complying with the tax statute because it was claimed to be unconstitutional, but the Supreme Court sustained the statute unanimously.

fact that the stockholders who entered the petitions in *Pollock* and in *Brushaber* possessed justiciable rights that could be protected against illegal actions of corporate officers — that is, violations of fiduciary responsibilities — while the Johnstons did not possess similar justiciable rights.

Suggested analogies aside, the crucial argument in the brief was an undisguised request that the bench disregard technical deficiencies.

> We are left only to inquire whether this Court, of its own motion, will be astute to find and declare (in order to dismiss this case, which all parties, and the United States earnestly desire to be decided on its merits . . .) that the complaint states no cause of action cognizable in equity. It might have been argued that there was wanting a basis for equitable relief in the complaints filed in the *Brushaber* Case, and in the *Pollock* Case referred to in it, because no allegation was made of insolvency of directors or officers, nor of impossibility of securing by legal proceedings a refund of taxes improperly paid. The Court did not look upon the bills of complaint filed in those cases with so technical and critical an eye.[47]

The Court had previously tolerated questionable test litigation, it was implied, in order to exercise supervisory power over important constitutional questions, and it should not hesitate to tolerate another contrivance. This contention — "They got away with it, why shouldn't we?" — explained the solicitude counsel for Atherton Mills had shown the Justice Department.

> In the *Brushaber* Case, where the jurisdiction was sustained, this Court averted to the fact that in the argument of the case counsel for the United States Government was present and participated as *Amicus Curiae*, thus implying, as it would seem to us, that with the certainty that full argument in favor of the validity of the law would be made in any event, no practical advantage could come from any technical disposition of the litigation. Precisely the same situation and the same assurance of full argument exist in the case at bar.[48]

Clark's attorneys thus encouraged the Court to close its eyes to the fundamental issue raised by the *Johnston* case inasmuch as full argument of the constitutional issue was assured.

[47] *Brief for Appellees, Atherton* v. *Johnston*, p. 7.
[48] *Ibid.*, p. 9. Additionally, the brief sought to demonstrate that real, not fictitious, interests were involved in the suit. By virtue of the lower court's judgment, plaintiffs were undisturbed in the enjoyment of their rights,

Constitutional Contentions in the *Johnston* Case

In putting together their legal argument, counsel for the Executive Committee relied in large measure, as they had done in the *Dagenhart* case, on constitutional doctrines developed by William Guthrie. His losing argument in the Lottery case had been the basis of their attack on the Keating-Owen law, and now they resurrected, almost intact, the argument he had fashioned as losing counsel in the *McCray* case,[49] which elaborated similar principles of dual federalism and limited national purposes. Although incorporated into what otherwise was a revenue act, the child labor section was not a tax measure, the brief charged. In plain fact it sought to regulate economic activities over which Congress had no legislative authority.[50] The processes of production were purely local in character and subject exclusively to state control. Like the Keating-Owen law, the statute was stigmatized as doubly repugnant to the Constitution: it exceeded congressional authority and encroached upon police powers reserved to the states.

Parker, Hendren, and Bynum augmented Guthrie's argument in only one particular; they dramatized the special relevance of the *Dagenhart* decision and broadly framed its bearing.

> The question before this Court in this case, then, is whether a resort to the Interstate Commerce Clause of the Constitution having failed, Congress may, by a resort to the Tax Clause of the same instrument, control the entire policy of a State, and so open the door to complete nationalization of our Government, so ardently desired by some of the publicists of our day. This is an interesting and an important case, because upon its results depends the question whether the *Dagenhart* Case and its decision was a real, or merely a temporary and *pro forma*, assurance of the continuation unimpaired of State authority over "matters purely local."[51]

The question to be decided, in other words, was whether laissez faire had truly emerged victorious eighteen months before or whether a mere reprieve had been won before the states were reduced to nothing and fundamental rights forever destroyed.

To the careful reader, the Court had already rendered its deci-

---

rights that without such protection would have been unavoidably lost (*ibid.*, p. 8).

[49] Benjamin R. Twiss, *Lawyers and the Constitution* (Princeton: Princeton University Press, 1942), pp. 220–23.

[50] *Brief for Appellees, Atherton v. Johnston*, p. 26.

[51] *Ibid.*, p. 14.

sion, the brief asserted: the *Dagenhart* case demonstrated the patent invalidity of the child labor law. Furthermore, the brief wished away the stumbling block of judicial impotence with the familiar though specious argument that arbitrary legislation, beyond the authority of Congress to enact, empowered the Court to scrutinize congressional motives. The groundwork for this proposition, laid by the senators from the southern textile district who had inserted supposedly damaging material in the *Congressional Record*, was skillfully built upon. All that remained to complete the pattern of earlier assaults was to excite fear of the disastrous consequences, certain to follow, if the Court should sustain such "a departure from our Constitution and from our institutions." The familiar parade of horrors reached its climax.

> If the views of those who assert the constitutionality of this method are sound, there is no practical necessity, nor reason, for State Legislatures, and certainly none for constitutional amendments; therefore, those views are unsound and revolutionary.[52]

There, together again, were the Tenth Amendment as a restriction upon national purposes, the inviolable rights of the locality, which excluded federal interference in labor relations, and the "Grand Peur."

The government's brief was equally emphatic, but the argument rested on the opposite side in the *McCray* case, on White's opinion for the Court. Clark's lawyers had furnished the Solicitor General with an outline of their brief. The source of this laissez faire assault on the child labor tax was correctly identified and its substance was dismissed as timeworn and discredited. To condemn the statute as "a mere police regulation and an encroachment on the reserved rights of the States" was simply to revive the contentions rejected in the *McCray* case, presumably in the hope that the current bench might be disposed to reverse its predecessor's holding. But the opinion of the Court controlled, the brief declared, and not the excrescences upon constitutional law that defeated counsel had advocated. The principles thus set forth foreclosed every question in the *Johnston* case.

> When the exhaustive opinion in *McCray* v. *United States* is called to the attention of the court any further argument in support of the constitutionality of this statute would seem to be superfluous. Indeed, the Government could safely offer that opinion as its brief in this case. Precisely the same questions were presented

52 *Ibid.*, p. 35.

and, in what was said then, is found a complete answer to every contention now made.[53]

Despite the pre-emptive character of White's opinion, the Solicitor General sought the greater safety afforded by a comprehensive defense of the child labor law. Because the statute imposed an excise tax, such as Congress was constitutionally empowered to levy, the brief asserted, its validity could not be questioned, either by inquiry into congressional motives or because its operation might prove onerous. To venture upon such an examination would be "a mere act of judicial usurpation." There was no mistaking the *McCray* doctrine of "on face" constitutionality.

In addition, the brief anticipated and squarely met the legal contentions that in practical terms presented the greatest difficulty for a satisfactory defense of the child labor tax. Congress, it was urged, had unlimited discretion to select, from the subjects within its power, the things to be taxed. The fact that it had imposed an excise tax upon the use of something that was subject to the police power of the states was irrelevant. An answer, likewise, was made to the charge that the statute presaged further legislative invasions of individual rights and local powers. No fear of possible abusive action by Congress could justify the exertion by the courts of a power not conferred by the Constitution. This answer did not represent a challenge to the Supreme Court, it simply reiterated the *McCray* doctrine that, should Congress exercise its acknowledged powers in an improper way, the appropriate recourse was to popular control rather than judicial intervention.

With the exception of its calculated neglect of the jurisdictional issue, the government's brief comprised a technically proficient and persuasive presentation. Apart from the pronounced reliance on White's *McCray* opinion, its most striking feature was the repeated attempts to confine the scope of judicial review. Given the continued vitality of *McCray*, it was the more convincing brief, for Clark's lawyers labored to make tenable the legal contentions explicitly rejected there without in any way incurring White's displeasure by seeming to undercut his opinion.[54] Wilson's

[53] *Brief for the United States as Amicus Curiae, Atherton* v. *Johnston*, p. 7.
[54] Attempts to distinguish the *McCray* holding and, to a lesser extent, the *Doremus* decision were ventured, without success, in the Executive Committee's brief. The prohibitive tax on colored oleomargarine was said to be a bona fide excise tax for revenue purposes; and the Harrison Narcotic Drugs Act, admittedly designed to confine the sale of opium, was said to do so "only as having relation to the real raising of revenue." *Brief for Appellees, Atherton* v. *Johnston*, pp. 20–23.

second Solicitor General used the practical and doctrinal materials available to him as skillfully as had the first, providing the bench with just as useful "implements for decision" of the constitutional question.

Further Refusal to Treat the Fundamental Issue

When the *Johnston* case was argued, on December 10, 1919 — more than seven months after Judge Boyd's original ruling — Solicitor General King and Assistant General Frierson appeared for the government as amicus curiae and William Hendren represented the Executive Committee. Had the Justice Department been concerned with technical requirements and had officials bothered to ascertain the facts, King could have foreclosed argument, without even reaching the jurisdictional issue, by showing that the Johnston youth had already celebrated his sixteenth birthday. The statute no longer had application to him and could not affect his rights of employment detrimentally, whatever may have been the legal reality of these rights in relation to it. King, in fact, knew this. On November 26, the Solicitor of Internal Revenue wrote to Frierson, presumably after a field check by agents, and informed him that John W. Johnston was "now past the age of sixteen."[55] The purported controversy had become inescapably moot.

During King's presentation, Justice Brandeis responded to the apparent suggestion in the government's brief that, should they be interested, members of the bench might raise the issue of jurisdiction by means of questions addressed to counsel. Brandeis repeatedly encouraged King to plead that the case was not properly brought but these efforts to rescue the fundamental question were resisted by the Solicitor General. King did not want to discuss the issue, and could not be induced to do so at the urging of a single justice. David Clark, who attended this session of the Court, regretted that the liberal jurist would not let sleeping dogs lie.[56]

Brandeis's colleagues showed no interest in the issue, despite the highly unusual character of the proceeding. Whether because of personal desire to hear and decide the case, as seems likely, or from deference to the express desire of the government to obtain a determinative judgment on the constitutionality of the

55 Robert N. Miller to W. K. Frierson, November 26, 1919, Justice Department File, *Atherton v. Johnston.*
56 *Southern Textile Bulletin* (December 11, 1919), p. 18.

child labor tax, they gave no indication that they looked upon the bill with "technical and critical eyes." None besides Brandeis called attention to its obvious defects. Moreover, the conspicuous absence of counsel for Atherton Mills, which had appealed the case, was passed over without comment, although it should have been sufficient in itself to condemn the supposed controversy as clearly fictional.

Undeterred by Brandeis's interruptions, King spoke to the constitutionality of the statute and his argument followed the lines of the government's brief.[57] Brandeis did not bother to question Hendren, whose remarks hewed closely to the familiar contentions in the Executive Committee's legal position.[58] Presumably, Brandeis decided it was better to pursue the problem of want of jurisdiction in the conference rather than try to compensate for the deficiencies in the government's presentation from the bench.

Almost three decades earlier the Supreme Court had summarized previous opinions that enunciated long-standing principles that defined the extent of its jurisdiction, and this statement was highly relevant.

> Whenever in pursuance of an honest and actual antagonistic assertion of rights by one individual against another, there is presented a question involving the validity of an act of any legislature, State or Federal, and the decision necessarily rests on the competency of the legislature so to enact, the court must, in the exercise of its solemn duties, determine whether the act be constitutional or not; but such an exercise of power is the ultimate and supreme function of courts. It is legitimate only in the last resort, and as a necessity in the determination of real, earnest and vital controversy between individuals. It never was thought that, by means of a friendly suit, a party beaten in the legislature could transfer to the courts an inquiry as to the constitutionality of the legislative act.[59]

But the latter is exactly what had occurred — with the full knowledge and consent of the Justice Department. When King brusquely dismissed Brandeis's questions about whether *Johnston* met jurisdictional requirements, he knew it was technically faulty — that it was not an actual controversy between adversary parties and that it did not involve cognizable legal rights. More important, however, he failed to point out, as propriety even more insistently

57 *Ibid.*
58 *Washington Evening Star*, December 11, 1919, p. 12.
59 *Chicago & Grand Trunk Railway Co.* v. *Wellman*, 143 U.S. 339, 345 (1892).

dictated, the mootness of the proceeding. King's action, in short, involved a serious disservice to the bench, and perhaps actual dereliction in office.

The Failure to Decide the *Johnston* Case

Charles Evans Hughes, in the interval between his two periods of service on the supreme bench, provided a revealing description of the inner working of the Court. He looked back upon his experiences between 1910 and 1916 and generalized about a bench whose composition remained substantially the same through the next three years. In discussing oral argument, Hughes offered the following judgment about the time at which justices tend to reach a conclusion on the issues that have been raised in a case.

> I suppose that, aside from cases of exceptional difficulty, the impression that a judge has at the close of a full oral argument accords with the conviction which controls his final vote. . . . This is so because the judges are conversant with their special material, that is, the prior judgments of the court, and when they apprehend the precise questions to be decided they are generally not slow in reaching a conclusion.[60]

A later appraisal was provided by Associate Justice Robert H. Jackson.

> I think that the Justices would answer unanimously that now, as traditionally, they rely heavily on oral presentations. Most of them form at least a tentative conclusion from it in a large percentage of the cases. This is not to say that decisions are wholly at the peril of first impressions. Indeed, deliberation never ceases and there is no final commitment until decision actually is announced. It is a common experience that a Justice is assigned to write an opinion for the Court in accordance with a view he expressed in conference, only to find from more intensive study that it was mistaken. In such circumstances, an inadequate argument would have lost the case, except that the writing Justice rescued it.[61]

Of course, neither statement is, nor was intended to be, an exhaustive analysis of the process by which opinion takes final form. The possibilities are numerous, and all must be kept in mind, in considering the Court's disposition of the *Johnston* case.

---

[60] *The Supreme Court of the United States* (New York: Columbia University Press, 1928), pp. 61–62.

[61] "Advocacy before the United States Supreme Court," *Cornell Law Quarterly* (Fall, 1951), p. 2.

Although the controversy was argued in December, 1919, it was not decided — at least the Court's holding was not announced — during the ensuing year and a half; that is, while Chief Justice White lived. After his death the case was consolidated with two other suits that challenged the constitutionality of the child labor tax, re-argued, and declared moot, in May, 1922.

The Court's docket was extremely crowded during the last years of White's Chief Justiceship. The justices were heavily burdened by the workload thrust upon them, and advanced age had noticeably impaired the faculties of several. Cases often were heard many months, even years, after their appeal. Nevertheless, once a case was argued the Court's holding ordinarily was forthcoming in a few months. Because of this — and because of the importance of the constitutional question and the government's request for an early ruling — the inescapable conclusion is that disposition of the *Johnston* case was inordinately delayed. What makes the matter deeply perplexing is the probability that most members of the Court soon were ready to decide the case. The importance of the child labor tax, the publicity that surrounded its passage, the certainty that the Court's holding would have far-reaching consequences, and especially the virtually unanimous alignment of the bench in the *Drexel* case refute the contention that most of the justices were unable to resolve their personal judgments in the months that immediately followed the hearing.

Speculation upon the cause for the delay must center upon Chief Justice White and Justice Brandeis. The child labor case placed White in a very embarrassing position, from which he may have found it impossible to extricate himself. The circumstances seemed to require that he either repudiate his *McCray* opinion in favor of his preference for limited national purposes or deny the latter in order to preserve doctrinal consistency. Brandeis, on the other hand, was deeply distressed by the patently contrived character of the case. He was certain it had no standing in a federal court and believed that the jurisdictional issue vastly transcended the constitutional one.[62] The two justices' peculiar interests suggest several plausible explanations for the delay: (1) White was unable to resolve his personal dilemma and used his

[62] Reprinted by permission of the publishers from Alexander M. Bickel, *The Unpublished Opinions of Mr. Justice Brandeis*, Cambridge, Mass.: The Belknap Press of Harvard University Press, Copyright, 1957, by the President and Fellows of Harvard College; pp. 1–20.

position as Chief Justice to postpone decision in the case; (2) Brandeis convinced a majority of the Court that the case violated jurisdictional requirements but his colleagues preferred to wait until they could inconspicuously declare the case moot; (3) the Court was so badly split on how the case should be decided, whether on constitutional or jurisdictional grounds, that it was unable to reach a satisfactory conclusion.

Chief Justice White's Dilemma

By reason of his office and usually by reason of the personal qualities that gained him his office, the Chief Justice exerts great influence over what the Court does or does not do. He controls the conference and thereby the disposition of cases, and he is responsible for managing the work of his colleagues. The practice of the Court in 1919 (little different from today) was to discuss at the Saturday conference the cases heard during the preceding week. Most cases were voted upon at the same conference and, if satisfactory conclusions were reached, responsibility for writing the opinions was assigned. Once drafted, an opinion was circulated among the justices, perhaps re-written on the basis of individual returns, and then announced.[63]

When the *Johnston* case was reached in conference, much undoubtedly depended upon how White handled the situation. He was caught in the grip of an agonizing problem, perhaps so distressing that it provoked his well-known propensity to procrastinate. Thomas Reed Powell suggested the dimensions of this dilemma.

> It could hardly be doubted that [White] would be naturally disposed to follow the substance of [the *Dagenhart*] decision and find similar flaws in the child labor tax. Yet his opinion in the oleomargarine case had been so sweeping that even his unrivalled intellectual ingenuity must have paused before the task of writing an opinion annulling the child labor tax which would have squared with his opinion sustaining the oleomargarine tax.[64]

If anything, Powell understated the repugnance White felt toward the child labor tax. Although he had voted to sustain the oleomargarine excise, he considered it unwise legislation and dangerous in the highest degree. Moreover, his dissent in the *Doremus* case dispelled, once and for all, any doubt about his attitude

---

63 John H. Clarke, "How the United States Supreme Court Works," *American Bar Association Journal* (February, 1923), pp. 80–82.

64 "Child Labor, Congress, and the Constitution," *S.E.C.L.*, III, 532.

toward the use of the taxing power for regulating local economic activities. The Harrison Narcotics Drugs Act should have been declared unconstitutional, he said, as "a mere attempt by Congress to exert a power not delegated, that is, the reserved police powers of the States."[65]

On the other hand, White's prestige and some of his personal convictions were heavily invested in *McCray*. In particular, he firmly adhered to the need for judicial consistency. "The fundamental conception of a judicial body," he proclaimed in pained outcry when dissenting in the *Pollock* case, "is that of one hedged about by precedents which are binding on the Court without regard for the personality of its members."[66] The principle of *stare decisis* bound not only successors but sharply restricted the discretion of men who had originally enunciated decisions. At the same time, distinguishing the *McCray* case so as to preserve its vitality while permitting the overthrow of the offending statute would have required no mean feat of doctrinal juggling. Indeed, White's "undoubtedly doctrine" simply couldn't have been gotten around on logical premises.

> Undoubtedly, in determining whether a particular act is within a granted power, its scope and effect are to be considered. Applying this rule to the acts assailed, it is self-evident that on their face they levy an excise tax. That being their necessary scope and operation, it follows that the acts are within the grant of power. The argument to the contrary rests on the proposition that, although the tax be within the power, as enforcing it will destroy or restrict the manufacture of artificially colored oleomargarine, therefore the power to levy the tax did not obtain. This, however, is but to say that the question of power depends, not upon the authority conferred by the Constitution, but upon what may be the consequence arising from the exercise of the lawful authority.[67]

White had another alternative, however; to avoid the dilemma by preventing the conference from coming to a final commitment, and this was the practical way out. White might have reasoned that in a few months the Johnston youth would be sixteen years of age and it would be possible to declare the case moot. But this would not have eliminated the dilemma permanently; further, complementary explanation is possible. The effects of White's physical deterioration were readily apparent by the time the

65 *United States* v. *Doremus*, 249 U.S. 86, 95.
66 *Pollock* v. *Farmers' Loan and Trust Company*, 157 U.S. 429, 652.
67 *McCray* v. *United States*, 195 U.S. 27, 59.

Johnston case was argued. His hearing was failing badly and he no longer possessed the stamina to keep up with his work. His tenure as Chief Justice would soon end, either through resignation or death; but he clung to the office, for personal and for political reasons. On the day White died, Justice Holmes, writing to Harold Laski, commented on his stubborn resistance to retirement.

> With us the main event has been the death of the Chief Justice (White — May 19, 1921). Poor man, he suffered long and bore up against it heroically — but life could not have been satisfactory longer, even if his pain had ceased. . . . I cannot judge whether his delaying any operation was due to determination not to give the appointment to Wilson or to love of the office or to mistaken sense of duty — possibly all combined. For I think he loved the office as an end in itself.[68]

White was determined not to surrender the Chief Justiceship while the dangerous progressive, Wilson, could name his successor. He may, however, have planned to retire after the new administration was settled, and he must have realized that death was not far off. He died only a few weeks after Harding took office. His love of the place he occupied, as well as his sense of obligation to his brethren, would explain why he stayed on through the last weeks of the term. For these reasons he may have pursued delaying tactics in the conference, hoping that the painful dilemma need never be faced. It is not difficult to envision most of his colleagues sympathetically refraining from being troublesome about the case, knowing that soon it would be resolved to their satisfaction.

"The Most Important Thing We Do Is Not Doing"

After hearing argument in *Johnston,* Justice Brandeis set about writing an opinion that condemned the textile manufacturers' suit and castigated the lower court for tolerating such a plainly contrived and nonjusticiable petition. Within six weeks he had com-

---

[68] Reprinted by permission of the publishers from Mark De Wolfe Howe, *Holmes-Laski Letters,* Cambridge, Mass.: The Belknap Press of Harvard University Press, Copyright, 1953, by the President and Fellows of Harvard College; I, 339.

The day before, Holmes had mentioned White's illness in writing to Frederick Pollock. "The poor old boy is the object of nothing but sympathy just now. He has stuck to his work (I think unwisely) in the face of illness. . . . His infirmities have made the work harder for others, and I imagine that he has suffered much more than he has told" (Reprinted by permission of the publishers from Mark De Wolfe Howe, *Holmes-Pollock Letters,* Cambridge, Mass.: The Belknap Press of Harvard University Press, Copyright, 1941, 1961, by the President and Fellows of Harvard College [II, 68]).

pleted a relatively finished draft that he titled "Memorandum to the Court." Alexander M. Bickel, who published this opinion and accompanying commentary in *The Unpublished Opinions of Mr. Justice Brandeis*,[69] wrote that the *Johnston* case "was identified in Brandeis's mind with the problem of collusive suits arranged to obtain quick and convenient adjudication of constitutional issues." His draft opinion is a devastating commentary upon the defects in the *Johnston* proceeding and contains a strong statement of one of the principal themes in his outlook upon the judicial function: the absolute necessity for self-restraint in constitutional litigation.[70] As he once told Felix Frankfurter, "The most important thing we do is not doing." [71]

Because of the craftsmanship of Brandeis's opinion and its biting specificity, it would be folly to paraphrase any portion of it. He declared that the lower court's action in entertaining the bill in equity "was a clear usurpation of power; and the jurisdiction of this court is limited to reversing the decree below and directing that the bill be dismissed . . . for want of jurisdiction." [72] He was severely critical of the increasing tendency by federal courts to invalidate congressional enactments, and especially by district judges who sat alone.

> For nearly a century after the adoption of the Constitution federal courts approached with great reluctance the exercise of their high prerogative of declaring invalid an act of Congress. This reluctance was finally overcome; and then there was manifested a disposition, encouraged by the acquiescence or active cooperation of the Department of Justice, to facilitate the efforts of litigants to secure decisions on the validity of statutes of wide public interest, when their constitutionality was questioned. Lately single judges sitting alone in trial courts have declared acts of Congress invalid without even stating the reasons for their decisions.[73]

Turning to the specific issues, Brandeis stated: "No federal court has jurisdiction of a proceeding brought specifically to have

---

69 Pp. 2–20.

70 Brandeis cited the *Johnston* Memorandum in the notable compilation (part of his concurring opinion in *Ashwander* v. *T.V.A.* [297 U.S. 288, 345–48]) of self-denying rules the Court has imposed on the exercise of judicial review.

71 "Brandeis-Frankfurter Conversations," Manuscripts in the Library of Harvard Law School, Cambridge, quoted in Bickel, *The Unpublished Opinions of Mr. Justice Brandeis*, p. 17.

72 "Memorandum to the Court," quoted in *ibid.*, p. 5.

73 *Ibid.*, pp. 5–6.

an act of Congress declared unconstitutional, because such a
proceeding is not a 'case' within the meaning of the Constitution. . . ."[74] In *Johnston,* he continued,

> it is clear that the alleged controversy between the parties to the
> suit is not actual: that this proceeding . . . is a device to secure
> an adjudication of an important question of constitutional law, —
> in short, the fruit of collusion, to which this court should not,
> and under ordinary circumstances would not shut its eyes; and
> that the infirmity of the proceeding is not overcome by the acqui-
> escence of the Department of Justice. Surely this is not a "real,
> earnest and vital controversy between individuals."[75]

But the suit suffered from an even more fundamental defect.

> The proceeding below was not a "case" within the meaning of
> the Constitution. . . . For it is clear . . . the bill set up no right
> of the plaintiffs as against the defendant and . . . the act threat-
> ened is not a wrong against the plaintiffs or as against anyone else
> in the present case. . . .
>
> No principle is more firmly established in English and American
> law than the right of the employer to discharge the employee forth-
> with, if there is no agreement express or implied for a definite
> period of service or for notification before the termination.[76]

Brandeis's indictment went further. "The bill in the present
case not only fails to set forth a cause of action, but it is fatally
defective also, specifically for want of equity." Mere assertion,
clothed in legal form, did not create justiciable rights: "The
well established rule that a plaintiff must show that he would
personally suffer an injury by application of a law before he can
institute a bill for relief to test its constitutionality demands that
the bill be dismissed."[77]

Brandeis concluded with a ringing warning, derived from
historical and political considerations, that stressed the impropriety and unwisdom of exercising judicial supervisory power
unless this was absolutely necessary to dispose of a valid case at law.

> For nearly a century and a half Federal courts, as an incident
> to deciding cases rightfully before them, have necessarily exercised
> at times the solemn duty of declaring acts of Congress void. But the
> long continued, uninterrupted exercise of this power has not
> sufficed to silence the doubt originally expressed whether the
> framers of the Constitution intended to confer it. On the con-

[74] *Ibid.,* p. 6.
[75] *Ibid.,* p. 7.
[76] *Ibid.,* pp. 7–8.
[77] *Ibid.,* pp. 11, 12.

trary, the popular protest against its exercise has never been so vehement, nor has it ever secured the support of so many political thinkers and writers, as in the last decade.[78]

In Bickel's apt summary, Brandeis's memorandum was "urgent with a sense of the truly fundamental issue of the division of powers between those organs of the government which are responsible to the electorate, and the judiciary, which is not." [79]

It is more than likely, Bickel feels, that the memorandum was circulated to the Court. An initial return from Holmes indicated vigorous support: "I don't see the answer to this. Count me with you unless the discussion discloses some reason I have not thought of." Another return from Holmes, entered on a second draft, "This is a powerful discourse and I agree with it," may have been written on the occasion of a general circulation.[80] In the conference, certainly — and through the draft if it was circulated — Brandeis's "reproach to their jurisdictional conscience" undoubtedly forced his brethren to come up hard against the technical question.

Had Brandeis convinced a majority that the case ought to be dismissed it seems certain that a holding reversing Judge Boyd's decision and directing return of the proceeding to the district court would have been forthcoming. Indeed, the majority's concern for preserving jurisdictional proprieties, it can be assumed, would have strongly argued for an immediate and explicit ruling along the lines of the memorandum. But such a holding was not announced. Nevertheless, when in 1922 the *Johnston* case was declared moot, Chief Justice Taft suggested that it might earlier have involved serious jurisdictional issues. This recognition, certainly not required to dispose of the case and perhaps not directly related to prior deliberation within the conference, is the chief evidence to support the inference that a majority of the Court concluded the proceeding should be dismissed on technical grounds but chose, for reasons of judicial statesmanship, to let it languish.

The Possibility of an Unsatisfactory Division

The last, seemingly plausible explanation is that *Johnston* was an exceptionally difficult case, one that the Court could find no satisfactory way of resolving. Such a result might have occurred, it can be argued, because of human failings and institutional

[78] *Ibid.*, p. 13.
[79] *The Unpublished Opinions of Mr. Justice Brandeis*, p. 20.
[80] *Ibid.*, p. 14.

pressures. White's infirmities and his inability or unwillingness to dominate the Court during his last years as Chief Justice, the advanced age of other justices and their inability to work as they once had, the crowded calendar, the disorganized character of deliberations, and the serious divisions within the conference are factors that may have made a resolution impossible.

Such a thesis may go too far but none of the practical considerations can be dismissed, especially White's role as the Court's administrative head. White never managed its business as expeditiously as certain other chief justices, and by 1920 his intellectual hold on his colleagues had greatly loosened. Still, he was a formidable jurist, usually the master of others in personal relationships, and surrounded by colleagues who were ideologically akin. Had he wished to, he could have expedited the *Johnston* case (litigation of such importance cannot be deferred unduly except by deliberate choice) unless the court had become so badly fragmented it was unable to agree on the precise question to be decided.

Again, Brandeis's "Memorandum to the Court" is suggestive. Bickel reached a most surprising conclusion after he had examined the original, heavily corrected copy.

> An early, incomplete draft of his opinion in *Atherton Mills* v. *Johnston* makes it plain that Brandeis, no matter how reconciled he may eventually have become to the opposite result, would in that case have upheld the Child Labor Tax Act, had he been prepared to reach the merits. In fact, this draft carries the startling suggestion that when *Atherton Mills* was first argued, there was a majority so inclined.[81]

The sentence that is said to sustain this truly remarkable inference was eliminated from the second draft as a tactical move, Bickel feels, so as not to antagonize those members of the Court who felt differently about the merits. It reads:

> If I believed that this Court had jurisdiction to pass in this proceeding upon the constitutionality of Section 1200 of the Revenue Act of 1918 . . . I should have no difficulty in holding the act valid, on the authority of *Veazie Bank* v. *Fenno*, 8 Wall. 533, and *McCray* v. *United States*, 195 U.S. 27, and for the reasons expressed in the dissent by Mr. Holmes in *Hammer* v. *Dagenhart*, 247 U.S. 251, 277, in which I joined.[82]

81 *Ibid.*, p. 16.
82 "Memorandum to the Court," quoted in Bickel, *Unpublished Opinions of Mr. Justice Brandeis*, pp. 16–17.

This sentence was preceded by two others that Brandeis had crossed out.

> I agree that the decree entered below by the District Court must be reversed with directions to dismiss the bill. But in my opinion the dismissal should be for want of jurisdiction.[83]

According to Bickel,

> there is no blinking the fact that these passages — and especially the two sentences last quoted — sound as if it had been decided at conference to ignore the jurisdictional difficulties in *Atherton Mills* v. *Johnston* and to hold the Child Labor Tax Act constitutional. No doubt one can force the language — though it takes quite a little forcing — and surmise that Brandeis was addressing himself not to what he expected to emerge as the majority opinion, but to what he thought would be a colleague's — perhaps Clarke's — dissent on the merits. That could account as well for his eventually dropping these sentences as inappropriate to a memorandum directed at the entire Court and meant to convince all, regardless of their views on the merits. But the other possibility cannot be ignored.[84]

It is one thing to ignore such a possibility; it is another thing to shut one's eyes to the great weight of evidence that makes Bickel's inference appear not simply improbable but unlikely in the highest degree. To create a seemingly plausible five-judge bloc desirous of affirming the constitutionality of the child labor tax, Bickel had to group Brandeis, Clarke, Holmes, McKenna (who dissented in the *Doremus* case), and Chief Justice White — the last too unlikely to credit. Moreover, Bickel leaves unanswered, for he had no evidence to draw upon, the question whether the *Johnston* case was reached in conference before Brandeis had worked out his original draft. Was the memorandum written, at White's assignment, as the opinion of the Court, or was it drafted in an effort to compensate for the inadequacies in the Solicitor General's argument? The latter seems much more likely. Had White voted with a majority to sustain the child labor tax (what conceivable majority could have existed without his concurrence?), it would have been practically incumbent upon him to write the opinion of the Court rather than pass this responsibility on to Brandeis or another justice. Equally likely, an affirmative holding on the merits, had one been reached, would

[83] *Ibid.*
[84] *Ibid.*

surely have been announced.[85] In addition, the substance of Holmes's two returns strongly suggests that they were recorded before the case was reached in conference.

The greatest difficulty in Bickel's supposition, however, is that he fails to provide a satisfactory explanation for the dramatic reversal of conviction that would have been necessary to produce the virtually unanimous alignment in *Bailey* v. *Drexel*. Can we believe that three members of the Court, and possibly a fourth, changed their minds within a period of two years about such fundamental questions as those involved in the child labor tax, or that they were induced by tactical considerations to shift their votes? To ask the question is to answer it — emphatically in the negative.

Is it conceivable, then, that a majority position did not coalesce? Holmes and Brandeis, it appears, preferred to dismiss the case on technical grounds. Day, too, who forcefully restated (in the *Muskrat* case [86]) the Court's concern that jurisdictional requirements be respected, might have been sensitive to the flagrant defects in *Johnston*. Van Devanter, Pitney, and McReynolds, on the other hand, almost certainly felt that the child labor tax threatened the federal equilibrium as grievously as had the Keating-Owen law, and no doubt preferred to void the statute. Clarke, it stands to reason, strongly preferred to uphold the act, because he alone voted to do so two years later. McKenna, because of his *Doremus* vote, was scarcely likely to look upon the law sympathetically. And White probably hoped that the case need never be decided.[87] The "numbers game," therefore, can be indulged in numerous combinations, all characterized by the absence

---

[85] Because Bickel argues, on the basis of Brandeis's citation of *McCray*, that White might have voted affirmatively on the merits, it is certainly pertinent to observe that Brandeis also cited Holmes's dissenting opinion in *Dagenhart* in the same sentence. A justice speaking for the Court, or concurring, or trying to shift a tentative majority (one that necessarily would have included one or more justices who voted to invalidate the Keating-Owen law) to a different ground hardly could be expected to cite a dissenting opinion unless the precedent was being overthrown; and reversal of the *Dagenhart* case is too farfetched to credit.

[86] *Muskrat* v. *United States*, 219 U.S. 346 (1911).

[87] It is perhaps relevant that White objected strenuously to the proceeding employed in the *Pollock* case: "The decisions of this court hold that the collection of a tax levied by the government of the United States, will not be restrained by its courts." The complainant was seeking to do exactly what statute and precedent made impossible, White protested. *Pollock* v. *Farmers' Loan and Trust Company*, 157 U.S. 429, 609 (1895).

of a majority of justices in agreement. But such suppositions are essentially sterile — too highly speculative.

Of the plausible conclusions about the curious history of the *Johnston* case, only one judgment is relatively certain: Brandeis's reproach to his colleagues' "jurisdictional conscience" was unavailing. The fact that the Court did not dispose of the litigation while White lived must be laid primarily to an irreconcilable split or to White's resistance. For the former, it is enough to say that, if a stalemate occurred, White's probable reluctance to reach a conclusion might well have been the crucial factor. As for the latter, other justices might have gone along with White for various reasons, not the least being tactical, for in all human affairs it usually is preferable that a result that cannot be reached in accord with one's convictions at least not go against them.

A Period of Anxious Waiting

When spring approached in 1920, David Clark expressed his growing anxiety about the Supreme Court's failure to render a decision in *Johnston*. The first year of operation under the child labor tax was drawing to an end and "every cotton mill" would soon be "obliged to file returns admitting or denying liability for the 10 per cent tax." Because the justices undoubtedly realized the importance of rendering a decision before tax returns had to be made, it could only be assumed, Clark wrote, that "a serious division" existed among them.[88] Clark had good reason for his alarm, especially when the Court adjourned without disposing of the case. As the weeks stretched into months, the Johnston youth grew older and it became more and more difficult to maintain the textile manufacturers' resistance.[89]

Many mill men began to look upon the law as permanent and to make long-term adjustments in their operations. Experience demonstrated conclusively that the prosperity of the southern mills did not depend upon the employment of child labor.[90] Of even greater significance, however, economic conditions in the south were changing, and with these altered circumstances came perceptible changes in attitudes. The increasing industrialization

[88] *Southern Textile Bulletin* (March 4 and 25, 1920), p. 22.

[89] See Davidson, *Child Labor Legislation in the Southern Textile States*, p. 267.

[90] See "The Passing of an Old Excuse," *American Child* (November, 1919), pp. 157–58. Not only improved standards of legislation and higher adult wages but the substitution of machinery in place of poorly paid children and the increased demand for skilled workmen helped diminish child labor.

of the region pushed the problems of labor acutely to the fore[91] and the first large-scale attempts at unionization forced the owners' hands. Prosperity brought irresistible demands for social welfare advances, improved working conditions, and greater compensation — as well as more southern spindles.

Practical economic considerations, in addition to the heightened social consciousness, contributed to the attainment of reform objectives. The old-time mill owners, like Daniel Tompkins, were fading from the scene. They had lived in a predominantly rural society, and many had viewed competition with northern interests in a heightened emotional perspective, bred of the Civil War. Others, frequently allied with northern financial interests, were imbued with laissez faire economic notions. These men were being replaced by a new generation of mill owners and managers, less paternalistic but more conscious of the social problems produced by industrialism. Southern manufacturers, however grudgingly — and despite or because of the virtual labor wars of the early twenties — were moving slowly into the twentieth century.

Clark nevertheless had busied himself with publicity campaigns to influence opinion in Washington and the nation. A third "Health and Happiness Issue" of the *Bulletin* was published on Christmas Day, 1919.[92] During the summer of 1920 the Executive Committee ran a series of illustrated advertisements, labeled "Life in Southern Mill Towns," in the *Washington Post*. These advertisements purported to lay "before the American public the true story of the remarkable strides" made by the southern textile industry.[93] No doubt Clark hoped to influence the judicial mind as well as congressional attitudes. Then he revived the demonstrably false but shrewdly calculated southern indictment of reform. "It is well known," the mill men were told, "that the movement for the Federal Child Labor Law was financed to a considerable extent by New England cotton manufacturers in order to reduce competition."[94] It was a crude attempt to sustain the will to resist.

[91] For discussion of these changes, see Davidson, *Child Labor Legislation in the Southern Textile States*, pp. 267–68, and Broadus Mitchell, "The End of Child Labor: How Labor Is Finishing What Social Work Began," *Survey* (August 23, 1919), pp. 747–50.

[92] *See Southern Textile Bulletin* (March 4, 1926), p. 21.

[93] For an account of the series, see "Life in Southern Mill Towns," *American Child* (August, 1920), pp. 108–10.

[94] *Southern Textile Bulletin* (May 19, 1921), p. 30. Clark was sharply criticized for this statement in a number of southern newspapers because he adduced no proof. But he refused to retract the charge.

By autumn, as the anniversary of argument in *Johnston* neared, the Supreme Court's continued silence caused apprehension among the leaders of the National Committee as well. Their concern centered upon the quality of enforcement, and, more immediately, upon the disquieting fact that the cost of administering the child labor tax greatly exceeded the revenue it derived. Owen Lovejoy was informed by the Bureau of Internal Revenue that approximately $90,000 had been allocated for enforcing the act during its first year of operation but only slightly more than $2,000 had been collected in fines.[95] Lovejoy conveyed this information to the trustees early in November. The figures were interpreted as a sign that the child labor law was regarded only as a regulatory measure, and it was thought that this impression might prejudice the Court's holding. Lovejoy asked for a decision on future action if the law was invalidated and the trustees appointed a steering committee to formulate a policy.[96] Earlier in the year the members of the National Committee had been told that "an adverse decision would bring to the fore the question of a constitutional amendment that would permit adequate national action against the evil of child labor, at least so far as concerns child labor in the mining and manufacturing industries." [97]

Because of the form of the child labor tax, it was difficult to determine its impact. The Internal Revenue Bureau reported in November that, although no statistical estimate was available, a marked reduction in child labor had been observed in various sections.[98] Later in the winter, Lovejoy received confidential information that seemed to throw new light on the administration of the law. Informants in the Bureau of Internal Revenue reported that a series of inspections had disclosed widespread violations.

[95] Letter from Owen Lovejoy to members of the National Committee, October 30, 1920. Under the law's provisions, penalties could not be levied until the end of the fiscal year, and an additional sixty days was allowed for filing returns. In fiscal 1919, when the measure had operated for barely two months and before an inspection system became effective, not a cent in revenue was derived; and the following year the return was insignificant.

[96] "Minutes of the Board of Trustees, N.C.L.C.," November 8, 1920.

[97] "Federal Action and Child Labor," *American Child* (February, 1920), pp. 276–77. Speaking to the American Child Hygiene Association in October, 1920, shortly before the presidential election, Herbert Hoover, soon to proselytize the virtues of "rugged individualism," advocated a child labor amendment to make possible comprehensive federal control, for the existing tax was said not to reach "the great mass of children employed in street trades and various blind-alley occupations." Quoted in *American Child* (November, 1920), pp. 203–4.

[98] *American Child* (November, 1920), p. 203.

Infractions supposedly had been found in two-thirds of the plants visited, but taxes had been collected in only two cases. The sources estimated that several hundred thousand dollars would have been obtained had vigorous efforts been made to enforce the statute. This information made it appear that the Child Labor Tax Division, created in the Bureau of Internal Revenue, was not performing its work effectively. Again Lovejoy sought the guidance of the trustees about verifying the information and approaching authorities in the bureau to find out exactly "what they are doing."[99] These reports, it was later found, had been greatly exaggerated, but the winter of 1920–21 was a distressing period for the National Committee.[100]

The Supreme Court maintained its silence into spring, nearly a year and a half after *Johnston* had been argued, and a strong suspicion developed that the justices had shunted the case aside. Through the winter and the first months of spring, Chief Justice White's health and spirit declined rapidly. A serious blow had been dealt those who wished to see the child labor tax voided, Clark commented on White's death, for White's "decisions had stamped him as being against the Federal usurpation of States Rights."[101] His replacement, Clark suggested, would hold the balance on the Court.

Before adjourning, on June 6, the Court restored the *Johnston* case, now one of the oldest controversies on its docket, to the calendar for re-argument when the new session would open, in October. However, it must have been clear to everyone that the test vehicle was indisputably moot.

99 Memorandum, Executive Committee of the Board of Trustees, N.C.L.C., January 27, 1921. Apparently, sympathetic employees of the bureau passed this information on without the knowledge of their superiors.

100 The annual reports of the Child Labor Tax Division show that the section (under Nila F. Allen) conscientiously sought to enforce the child labor tax in all sections of the country, including the western district of North Carolina, and that its inspectors were largely concentrated in the south, where state standards fell below the national minimum.

101 *Southern Textile Bulletin* (May 26, 1921), p. 18.

9

Preserving the Ark of the Covenant:
Bailey v. *Drexel*

The Reaction to Progressivism

The new administration that took office in the spring of 1921 symbolized far more than the transference of political power from one party to another. It represented a momentous shift in public opinion. The nation, as it were, did not pause for a breathing period to consolidate the comprehensive reform program that had been enacted by Congress during Woodrow Wilson's first term; rather, the masses of people rejected some of these gains, as well as further reforms. Conservative ideology, which had declined greatly in popular appeal during a period of pronounced social innovation, reasserted its former influence after the war as the weary populace yearned for and desperately sought to recapture more satisfying social conditions, which had supposedly existed before the progressive era.

Within a year after the armistice, the wartime unity and wartime prosperity had ended.[1] The country was not prepared for the resultant economic dislocation and the difficulties in readjusting life to the conditions of peace. Americans had expected far more from victory than they saw about them, and many rapidly became disillusioned. The nation's attention turned inward — redirected toward its traditional isolationism — and the Senate rejected American participation in the League of Nations. In addition, many persons were frightened by the Red Scare and feared or imagined widespread subversive movements, said to have been spawned by the Russian revolution. Fear of the bolsheviki would henceforth stigmatize all reform efforts.

The country sought security, and prosperity above all else. Re-

1 William Miller, *A History of the United States* (New York: Dell Publishing Co., 1958), p. 389.

pressive measures, carried over from wartime, were used by nativists, by super patriots, and by persons who ordinarily respected freedom of expression in an almost hysterical drive for conformity and for rooting out foreign influence and stemming labor agitation.[2] The widespread interest in restoring ordered social conditions and the illiberal influences bred by the war affected many aspects of American life. The progressive movement rapidly lost its popular appeal as the wellsprings of humanitarianism began to dry up. Americans became preoccupied with their own concerns; they had little time or taste for social innovations. But, more important than any other development in the immediate postwar years, the business community began to reassert its former dominance in economic and political affairs, to reconquer the American mind for conservatism.

The results of the election of 1920 clearly demonstrated that the country no longer was progressive in temper. Harding and Coolidge emerged almost over night as the kind of new leadership the nation preferred — well-meaning nonentities, interested in renouncing governmental powers and returning the control of national affairs to the monopolistic and privileged interests that had managed industrialism during the last decades of the nineteenth century.

Harding had been nurtured in the Social Darwinian economic philosophy that underlay orthodox business Republicanism. He announced the ascendancy of business influence with a wonderfully simple and simplistic slogan: "We want less government in business and more business in government." Coolidge typified the drive for security and conformity. He had been brought to national attention and his place on the Republican ticket by the singular distinction of having used coercion to suppress the Boston police strike. The two men, conservative in outlook and "countrified" in background — the apotheosis of middle-class virtues — presided over a country that was hurrying toward the political right while Woodrow Wilson, the former progressive hero, bitter and broken in spirit, awaited death. Wilson's vision of a better

---

[2] A dramatic symbol of the change in the national mood is furnished by the transformation of A. Mitchell Palmer. This ardent liberal representative, who first introduced in Congress the bill destined to become the Keating-Owen law, became the vengeful "fighting Quaker" Attorney General who instituted the notorious "Palmer Raids" to combat the Red Menace. Woodrow Wilson, diminished in stature and no longer representative of the country's will, was unable to control the illiberal excesses of the former progressive.

world seemingly was dashed to pieces. A thoroughgoing reaction to progressivism had set in.

It was not surprising, then, that the man Harding chose to head the Supreme Court — even more than his election as President — represented the changed mood in the nation. For although Harding was a politician of minor stature (and even though he was enormously popular during his presidency), William Howard Taft was the acknowledged statesman of American conservatism. "To an amazing extent," Frank observed two decades later, "Taft in 1921 was the choice of all America." [3] The Republican president, repudiated by the country in the triumph of progressivism in 1912, was returned to a major position in American politics.

Taft's Chief Justiceship

All his life Taft had hungered for a place on the supreme bench. In his eyes, every other political office, even the presidency, paled before the Chief Justiceship.[4] When, in 1913, he retired to the tranquil setting of Yale University, technically as a professor of public law, his appointment to the Court seemed a remote possibility, although not definitely precluded. Taft had elevated a justice twelve years his senior to head the Court, which made it virtually certain that the Chief Justiceship would become vacant once more while he lived.[5] What followed is explained less by

[3] John P. Frank, "The Appointment of Supreme Court Justices," *Wisconsin Law Review* (July, 1941), p. 469.

[4] When Justice Clarke retired, a year after Taft's appointment to the Supreme Court, Taft wrote to him: "You are 65 and leaving the Bench — I am 65 and have just begun. Perhaps it would have been better for me never to have come to the Court but I could not resist an itching for the only public service I love." W. H. Taft to J. H. Clarke, September 5, 1922, quoted in Hoyt L. Warner, *The Life of Mr. Justice Clarke* (Cleveland: Western Reserve University Press, 1959), p. 114.

[5] Taft, we know, wished to appoint to the Court younger men, whose influence could be expected to extend over several decades, and he departed from this conviction only twice — to honor the aged Lurton and to elevate the trusted White. What is usually lost sight of in discussing White's appointment is that Taft believed strongly in the desirability of mandatory retirement for federal judges at the age of seventy. The legislation that made it possible for them to leave the bench with full salary at that age (if they had served for ten years or more) was enacted before Taft became president. Once in office, Taft chafed because Chief Justice Fuller and Justices Harlan, Brewer, and Peckham did not choose to retire. More important, White was sixty-five when he was elevated to the Chief Justiceship and had served on the bench for sixteen years. In five years he would be eligible to retire. See William Howard Taft, *Popular Government: Its Essence, Its Permanence and Its Perils* (New Haven: Yale University Press, 1913), p. 159.

calculation than by the vagaries of events; nevertheless, as Taft well knew, there was much to recommend him for a place on the supreme bench. He had served on the federal circuit court of appeals for eight years and had been Solicitor General and Secretary of War, as well as President of the United States. These were imposing qualifications — too imposing for any office but the Chief Justiceship. Furthermore, Taft's eager re-entry into the struggle over political ideology and national purposes soon after the 1912 election signified his availability. Quite as important, Taft was a formidable antagonist when striving for objectives that mattered to him, and never more than when he promoted his candidacy for appointment to the Court.

During the years of his exile from national office, Taft's gaze never left the "sacred shrine." On each occasion that Wilson had the opportunity to nominate a justice to the Court, Taft had encouraged the campaigns that were undertaken to win the appointment for him. When Harding was elected President, Taft happily received assurance that his fellow Ohioan would name him to the supreme bench, hopefully as its head.[6] When White died, Taft expected to be selected; he felt that the place was his just due, as if White had deeded a feudal office and Harding was the bounden executor. He had the unqualified backing of the business community, anxious that one whose constitutional opinions thoroughly accorded with its own should succeed White. And had not White, as Taft repeatedly asserted, promised to hold the place for him?[7] Not anticipating conflict, Harding had promised his first Court appointment to a close congressional associate, Senator Sutherland, and Taft worried that the treasured place might pass to another. In the end, after weeks of delay, Harding

6 Henry F. Pringle, *The Life and Times of William Howard Taft* (2 vols.; New York: Holt, Rinehart & Winston, 1939), II, 954–56; see also Alpheus T. Mason, *William Howard Taft: Chief Justice* (New York: Simon and Schuster, 1964), pp. 77–79.

7 Pringle, *William Howard Taft*, II, 955. The nature of this so-called promise can easily be misinterpreted. Taft and White entered into no bargain concerning advancement to and surrender of the office of Chief Justice; instead, over a period of years, something approaching a personal concordance seemed to develop between them. They were tied to each other by strong bonds: mutual respect, similar beliefs, intimate knowledge of large political events, and realistic political practice. Both saw the possibility that Taft might succeed White and increasingly felt that such a succession was indispensable to preserve the constitutional values they believed in. It was natural that they should come to feel that Taft ought to become Chief Justice, that White should "transfer" the office to him upon retirement or death.

sent the nomination forward and the Senate, in a burst of good feeling, confirmed Taft (though not unanimously) the same day.[8]

Taft knew exactly how he wished to use the long-cherished office — to preserve stability in society and to achieve stability in judicial decisions.[9] Taft was more enlightened than many conservatives of the period but he had retreated substantially from the liberal views he had expressed thirteen years before, when he was reputed to be a reformer. As he looked back on the previous two decades, especially the disastrous 1912 campaign, he felt vindicated by events, certain that they had demonstrated the correctness of his views about the permissible limits of governmental functions. He hoped to repair the inroads progressivism had made in the Constitution during his eight years' exile from national power.

For Taft, judicial review was the fundamental institution of American government, distinguishing it from other democratic societies. Its purpose was to ensure considered public action, to restrain popular passions, and to impose strict prohibitions upon political interference in social and economic affairs in order to protect personal liberty and the fundamental rights of property. These freedoms, he deeply believed, were indispensable to the existence and progress of society.[10] Taft felt, moreover, when he assumed the Chief Justiceship, that he spoke for dominant opinion in the country, and this became increasingly true.

The Court, as we have seen, functioned badly during White's last years. Serious divisions existed within the conference and the Court fell far behind in its work. Taft could do little about the over-age members of the bench, except encourage them to retire and compensate for their incapacity by taking on a disproportionately large burden of opinion writing, but he tried hard to moderate conflict, to mass opinion, and to expedite the Court's work. Beyond all else, he sought to recreate the conception of a tribunal that spoke decisively upon the constitutional questions that came before it. His purpose was to strengthen judicial review and to put the Court beyond popular control and above criticism.[11] When the October term began in 1921, the mood of the nation was vastly different from the spirit immediately after the

[8] *Ibid.*, pp. 955–59, and Mason, *William Howard Taft, Chief Justice*, pp. 76–85.

[9] Alpheus T. Mason, *The Supreme Court from Taft to Warren* (Baton Rouge: Louisiana State University Press, 1958), pp. 48–49.

[10] *Ibid.*, pp. 45–49, and Pringle, *William Howard Taft*, II, 965–68.

[11] Mason, *The Supreme Court from Taft to Warren*, p. 47.

armistice, when the second federal child labor law had been enacted. This change permeated the judicial chamber and the
Court's decision-making.

The Creation of a New Test Vehicle

When the *Johnston* case was restored to the Court's docket for
re-argument, the order contained an assignment directing the
attention of counsel to the question of jurisdiction. Clark's lawyers
plainly understood the implications: the test vehicle had become
doubly vulnerable, for lack of vitality and for jurisdictional deficiencies, and almost certainly would be condemned on one or
both counts.[12] For these reasons it was deemed imperative to
institute another lawsuit to challenge the validity of the child
labor act and this time to employ the established legal procedure
for contesting allegedly unconstitutional federal taxation — a suit
to recover tax monies which had been paid under protest. Clark,
however, was unable to locate a cotton mill in the western district
of North Carolina that, having been assessed the 10 per cent tax
upon net profits, had resisted paying the penalty. Without exception, the textile concerns had conformed to the child labor provisions of the revenue act or, if apprehended for having violated
these provisions, had paid the tax.[13]

This unanticipated difficulty complicated the Executive Committee's plans, for Clark was not prepared to go outside the western district, that is, beyond Judge Boyd's benign jurisdiction. It
was necessary, therefore, to find another figurehead firm, one engaged in another form of industrial enterprise. From the district
collector of internal revenue in Raleigh, North Carolina, counsel
secured a list of the manufacturing establishments in the western
district that had recently been assessed the 10 per cent penalty
under the child labor tax. Clark then approached officials of
these corporations to determine whether any were disposed to
cooperate with the Executive Committee, and he "investigated the
conditions surrounding each case."[14] The officials of the Drexel
Furniture Company, representative of another southern industry
that generally resisted progressive economic reforms, proved
amenable to Clark's proposals, and their attorneys worked closely
with counsel for the Executive Committee in arranging the details
of the test litigation.

12 *Southern Textile Bulletin* (March 9 and May 18, 1922), p. 18.
13 *Ibid.*, March 4, 1926, p. 21.
14 *Ibid.*, May 18, 1922, p. 18.

During this period, Manly and Hendren suggested to the new Solicitor General, James M. Beck, that re-argument in *Johnston* be delayed because of "the probability of a case being docketed during the early months of the term which will be free from any question of jurisdiction."[15] Beck had put them on guard by writing that he felt obligated, because of the Court's direction, to discuss the technical issue. Hendren's intelligence pleased Beck, for he wanted to settle the constitutional question promptly but thought it would "be difficult, if not impossible" for counsel "to overcome the jurisdictional objection." He therefore agreed to consider delaying *Johnston* until "the unnamed case" to which Hendren referred was docketed,[16] but he needed immediate information about this case. Subsequently, Parker and Hendren talked with Beck in Washington and explained their "purpose to have one or more prospective tax payers pay the tax under protest and then bring suit to recover it."[17]

On October 1, Beck wrote to Hendren and asked that he telegraph the name of the new litigation, implying that little time remained for formulating strategy before the Court assembled for the autumn term.[18] Beck, who found Hendren's response inadequate, was unable to determine whether the proceeding "has actually been commenced, or is only prospective litigation." He intended to instruct the United States Attorney in the western district to expedite a decision, but, if the case did not come up soon, he would be forced to proceed with *Johnston* and another case (also patently defective), "which are now before the Supreme Court."[19] Counsel worked quickly in order not to miss their opportunity. Hendren wrote, on October 7, that the suit had "not actually been commenced for the reason that it was only within the last few days that client had received a notice of assessment."[20] However, J. W. Bailey, the collector of internal revenue for North Carolina, had sent a notice on September 20 that $6,312.79 was assessed because Drexel during the preceding tax year had em-

[15] W. Hendren to J. M. Beck, September 15, 1921, and C. Manly to J. M. Beck, September 15, 1921, Justice Department File, *Atherton* v. *Johnston*, National Archives, Washington, D.C.

[16] J. M. Beck to W. Hendren, September 13, 22, 1921.

[17] W. Hendren to J. M. Beck, October 4, 1921.

[18] J. M. Beck to W. Hendren, October 1, 1921, Justice Department File, *Bailey* v. *Drexel*, National Archives, Washington, D.C.

[19] J. M. Beck to W. Hendren, October 4, 1921, *ibid.*

[20] W. Hendren to J. M. Beck, October 7, 1921, *ibid.*

ployed two youths who allegedly were under fourteen years of age.[21]

Hendren, who assured Beck that payment would be made within a few days, tried to impress upon Bailey "our desire" to expedite the matter and he asked David Blair, the Commissioner of Internal Revenue, for preferred treatment so that conditions would soon be mature for entering the suit.[22] Hendren indicated his trust that Beck's representative would file a motion to dismiss and thus bring on the case for immediate hearing. Beck, who had informed the Internal Revenue Bureau that he wanted to expedite the new, non-vulnerable suit, received prompt assurance that the agency would cooperate fully, for it wanted the constitutionality of the law determined.[23] Because the Commissioner had discretion to withhold action on claims for six months, it was imperative that he acquiesce; otherwise, the new lawsuit could not be adjudged, appealed, and consolidated before *Johnston* was reached. The cooperation continued, and Beck wrote Blair a second time to be absolutely certain he understood it was "necessary to get some case before the Supreme Court that is free from jurisdictional defects." [24]

On October 20, officials of the Drexel company transmitted the amount of the assessment to Bailey, giving notice that the corporation would institute proceedings to recover this payment. The test suit then was drafted, challenging the validity of the child labor tax and requesting return of the tax monies alleged to have been improperly collected; Bailey was named as defendant. Extreme care was taken to ensure that the complaint conformed exactly to technical requirement [25] — *Johnston* was so gravely threatened that counsel could not afford mistakes that might leave the substitute litigation vulnerable on procedural grounds.

The child labor tax had now been in effect for two and a half years — far too long for Clark and his associates. Moreover, the enforcement agency in the Bureau of Internal Revenue was administering an effective and comprehensive inspection system, which cost $130,000 in 1921 (but the Treasury Department re-

21 *Transcript of Record, Bailey* v. *Drexel* (Washington, D.C.: Government Printing Office, 1921), p. 2.

22 W. Hendren to J. M. Beck, October 7, 1921, Justice Department File, *Bailey* v. *Drexel.*

23 Mabel W. Willebrant to David H. Blair, October 7, 1921, and D. H. Blair to M. W. Willebrant, October 14, 1921, *ibid.*

24 J. M. Beck to D. H. Blair, October 10, 1921. Justice Department File, *Atherton* v. *Johnston.*

25 *Southern Textile Bulletin* (May 18, 1922), p. 18.

ceived only $24,233 in tax penalties).[26] Satisfied that criticisms of the Child Labor Tax Division had little basis in fact, the main concern of the National Committee was whether the Court, under Taft's leadership, would uphold the tax — for Taft was not bound by previous judicial pronouncements, as White had been, to the principle of taxation for regulatory purposes. "The fight for federal protection of children against child labor has not been lost, perhaps it has only just begun," an editorial in the *American Child*[27] stated while commenting upon Judge Boyd's reaffirmation of the unconstitutionality of the child labor tax in an independent proceeding (the Vivian Cotton Mills case).

During the summer the National Committee passed two milestones, one in personnel, the other in policy, that had important implications for the future. Felix Adler, who with Edgar Gardner Murphy had founded the committee in 1904, retired as chairman (having served for seventeen years) and was replaced by David F. Houston, Wilson's Secretary of Agriculture between 1913 and 1920 and Secretary of the Treasury in 1920 and 1921.[28] Houston's appointment suggested the committee's greatest concern during the twenties, the problem of agricultural child labor, which — perhaps more than any other factor — contributed to the defeat of the child labor amendment. However, none of those who heard Houston's inaugural remarks realized that their determination to expand reforms to the largest uncontrolled sector of production would prejudice the entire reform program. "There is more to be done than has yet been done to end child labor in factories and cities, but [Houston said] . . . the next great task of the Committee, no longer to be neglected, should be to give our assiduous attention to child labor in agriculture."[29]

The affairs of the southern cotton manufacturers also reached a significant turning point in 1921. The manufacturers faced a new threat to the autonomy of their operations, which greatly disturbed Clark, when the American Federation of Labor launched a coordinated drive to organize the textile industry in the south. The mill owners bitterly resisted this first large-scale attempt to

[26] Untitled and undated N.C.L.C. files. In 1922, when the law was in effect for less than five months, its administrative cost ran to $88,000 and somewhat more than $15,000 in penalties was collected.

[27] November, 1921, p. 206.

[28] See *American Child* (August, 1921), pp. 100–103, for tributes to Adler and policy statements for the future.

[29] *Ibid.*, p. 101. Besides being an able administrator, Houston was a classical economist, conservative in outlook, and far removed by personality and persuasion from such militant reform leaders as Florence Kelley.

equalize bargaining relationships by establishing labor self-help institutions. Clark placed himself in the vanguard of the defense; his editorials lashed out at misguided strikers and poured unrestrained invective upon the intruding labor organizers. He purchased hostile advertisements in newspapers throughout the piedmont and sought every opportunity to present the textile manufacturers' story. In the end, the industry destroyed the organizing drive but the mill men could not re-establish the virtual immunity from labor agitation that had hitherto existed.

The *Drexel* and *George* Complaints

Immediately after it paid the tax assessment — under protest — the Drexel company submitted a petition to the Commissioner of Internal Revenue requesting a refund, another step in meeting technical requirements (Blair had previously instructed Bailey to expedite the claim[30]). On October 28, Hendren wrote to Beck and reported progress on "speedily instituting" the new litigation, and he suggested that Beck prod Blair to act on the claim.[31] Blair had already done this, rejecting the claim in the familiar language of such proceedings. Blair complimented Beck on his management of the various cases and indicated that the viable suit could be instituted without delay.[32] One week later the *Drexel* complaint was filed in Greensboro. The allegations set forth as proof of the invalidity of the "pretended act" conformed exactly to those contained in the *Johnston* petition.[33]

Upon receiving the complaint, Judge Boyd ordered Bailey to appear on November 21 to answer its charges; however, the complaint was later amended and the case was not argued until December 10. At that time, F. A. Linney, the newly appointed district attorney for western North Carolina, filed a demurrer contending that the child labor tax was constitutional.[34] Beck had instructed Linney to take such action as would avoid all procedural and jurisdictional questions and obtain a decision upon the merits of the constitutional question.[35] After hearing Linney and Bynum,

30 D. H. Blair to J. M. Beck, October 19, 1921, Justice Department File, *Atherton* v. *Johnston.*

31 W. Hendren to J. M. Beck, October 28, 1921, *ibid.*

32 D. H. Blair to J. M. Beck, October 28, 1921, *ibid.,* and D. Blair to Drexel Furniture Company, October 29, 1921, Justice Department File, *Bailey* v. *Drexel.*

33 *Transcript of Record, Bailey* v. *Drexel,* p. 3.

34 *Ibid.,* p. 8.

35 J. M. Beck to F. A. Linney, December 9, 1921 (telegram), Justice Department File, *Bailey* v. *Drexel.*

Boyd summarily dismissed the demurrer and again held the act unconstitutional. The questions had previously been considered by the court, he stated, "and it is deemed sufficient now to refer to the opinion in the case of *George* v. *Bailey*," which relied chiefly upon *Hammer* v. *Dagenhart*.

> The great principle emphasized in [*Dagenhart*] . . . is that the preservation of the States and the maintenance of all the rights remaining in them after the adoption of the Constitution and the Tenth Amendment thereto are: "As much within the design and care of the Constitution as the preservation of the Union and maintenance of the National Government." [36]

The threat to the sovereign rights of the locality loomed so large that Boyd rejected the *McCray* doctrine of "on face" constitutionality. "This court feels it to be its duty to disregard the form of the Act and to look at its substance." He found the congressional purpose to be the standardization of labor conditions across the country — avoidance of *Dagenhart* by the duplicity of a supposed taxing measure.[37]

After receiving Judge Boyd's ruling, District Attorney Linney filed an assignment of errors; then he requested and was granted a writ for appeal.[38] The entire performance was well-nigh perfunctory, as if the legal drama had been repeatedly rehearsed, as in fact it had. Everyone concerned with the litigation anticipated a negative holding, for Boyd had twice before declared the child labor tax unconstitutional — in the *Johnston* case and during the preceding summer in an independent suit (one not sponsored by the Executive Committee).

The latter case, *George* v. *Bailey*,[39] involved a request by the Vivian Spinning Mills of Cherrydale, North Carolina, for an injunction restraining the collector of internal revenue from enforcing the child labor act against it. During 1919 the plaintiff had manufactured cotton yarn under the name of the Vivian Cotton Mills. On November 9, 1920, George was assessed $2,098 for having employed children in violation of the statute's provisions.[40] In the interval, title to the business had been transferred

---

[36] *Transcript of Record, Bailey v. Drexel*, p. 10.

[37] *Ibid.*, p. 11.

[38] *Ibid.*, pp. 12–13.

[39] 274 Fed. 639 (1921).

[40] *Transcript of Record, Bailey v. George, Trading and Doing Business as Vivian Cotton Mills, et al.*, 259 U.S. 16 (Washington, D.C.: Government Printing Office, 1921), p. 2.

to the Vivian Spinning Mills, which sought to escape liability for the tax against the former owner. Bailey was ordered to collect the overdue assessment, together with a stipulated penalty and accrued interest, or if unable to do this, to seize the property and dispose of it by sale to satisfy the assessment. To prevent seizure and forced sale, a complaint was filed on July 7, 1921; it asked that Bailey be restrained and it claimed that the company had not knowingly employed children in violation of the child labor act and would suffer great loss, the market value of textile properties having recently fallen, should Bailey proceed as ordered. In addition, the bill asserted that the tax was unconstitutional, being contrary to the Fifth and Tenth Amendments.[41]

The complaint was widely recognized as defective because it went directly counter to the statutory provision that no suit for restraining the collection of federal taxes could be maintained by any court. Judge Boyd nevertheless responded exactly as counsel for the company had hoped. He waved aside a government motion to dismiss the complaint because of its glaring technical inadequacy, for the second time held the child labor tax invalid, and entered the requested injunction.[42] It was an audacious, because flagrantly improper, act, but Boyd apparently had no compunction about disregarding unambiguous statutory limitations in his determination to impose his constitutional opinions upon litigants.

Perhaps to offset his shocking disregard of propriety, Boyd rendered an opinion, put together from timeworn constitutional stuff and cotton mill propaganda. He labored to show that the child labor legislation of North Carolina afforded "as much protection to the health and physical condition of children" as the federal statute; indeed, better protection, because it promoted mental training and provided criminal sanctions against violators.[43] Although irrelevant, Boyd's reason for incorporating these propositions appears obvious: he wanted to educate the Supreme Court about the supposed "facts." Congress had engaged in a laudable undertaking, prompted by the highest motives of humanity, but Boyd suggested that its purposes had already been accomplished, although unknown to Congress, by existing state legislation. Not surprisingly, however, this defense neglected the crucial fact: the North Carolina legislation did not restrict the workday to eight hours for children fourteen through sixteen years of age.

41 *Ibid.*, pp. 2–4.   43 *Ibid.*, p. 26.
42 *Ibid.*, pp. 1–30.

Boyd also tried to justify having taken jurisdiction in the case.

> It is insisted that the statute [prohibiting injunctions] renders the courts powerless to intervene where the Government is proceeding under assessments to collect taxes, no matter whether the tax is legal or illegal, well founded or erroneous, constitutional or unconstitutional. If this position be maintained, then Congress, under the guise of raising revenue by taxation, can overcome all constitutional barriers.[44]

In effect, Boyd contended that the courts could prevent the collection of unconstitutional taxes despite statutory limitations upon jurisdiction; otherwise, invalid measures would become permanent because they would be invulnerable to attack. The flaw in Boyd's reasoning, however, requires little comment. The fact that injunctive relief was disallowed in no way barred subsequent legal remedies if the taxing power was improperly exercised.

With his decision in *Drexel*, Boyd achieved a distinction of sorts. It is highly unlikely that any other federal district judge ever declared a single congressional enactment unconstitutional on three different occasions. This distinction, however, was an exceedingly dubious one, even though the Supreme Court ultimately sustained the holding of invalidity, because two of the suits were disposed of on technical grounds. In other words, although Boyd undoubtedly felt he had been vindicated by the supreme bench, he had treated two patently defective suits as justiciable. Any conscientious jurist who was seriously interested in preserving jurisdictional proprieties would have rejected both suits outright, but Boyd cared only to preserve the federal system from "overreaching" national authority.

"Remove Not the Ancient Landmark, Which Thy Fathers Have Set"[45]

Early in October, when the Court met for the new term under Chief Justice Taft, the Justice Department (as we have seen) agreed with counsel for the Executive Committee to delay consideration of the *Johnston* case until it could be consolidated with new litigation that did not suffer from technical defects. Various officials of the new administration, in turn, cooperated with Clark's lawyers to advance the *Drexel* case because they believed the pub-

---

44 *Ibid.*, p. 27.
45 Prov. 22:28, quoted in frontpiece of James M. Beck, *The Vanishing Rights of the States* (New York: George H. Doran Co., 1926).

lic interest required expeditious determination of the constitutionality of the child labor tax. On December 15, less than a week after Judge Boyd decided *Drexel,* Beck informed Hendren — and a day later Parker — that he was considering a motion to advance argument in the two cases for the first week in January, if they could be ready by that time.[46] He did not want to "crowd" opposing counsel, he told an associate.[47] After considering the matter, both sides opted for delay, first until late January, and then, at Beck's suggestion, which Parker readily approved, until March 6.[48]

The underlying premise of the adversary system is that counsel for the opposing parties will disclose in open contention all the facts and points of law necessary to dispose equitably of litigation; in other words, judges read briefs and hear oral advocacy to assist them in deciding cases. For this reason, Justice Jackson once wrote, to do justice to their task in constitutional litigation, counsel must believe that "both sides in every controversy should be worthily presented with vigor — even with partisan zeal — so that all material for judgment will be before the Court and its judgment will suffer no distortion."[49] This premise was severely strained in the *Drexel* case, however, because Beck was thoroughly convinced of the unconstitutionality of the child labor tax.

Propriety dictated that Beck choose one of two alternatives: submerge his personal convictions and present a wholehearted defense of the legislation entrusted to his care or acknowledge its irremedial defects despite the political hazards. "Candor," Freund writes, "has impelled counsel for the government to confess error in a substantial number of cases reaching the Supreme Court on the opponent's petition."[50] But Beck was unequal to either choice. To resolve his dilemma, he tried to give his brief and oral advocacy the appearance of an energetic defense while, in fact, he contrived a self-defeating argument, one deliberately calculated to

---

46 J. M. Beck to W. Hendren, December 15, 1921, Justice Department File, *Atherton* v. *Johnston,* and J. M. Beck to Junius Parker, December 16, 1921, Justice Department File, *Bailey* v. *Drexel.*

47 J. M. Beck to F. A. Linney, December 17, 1921, Justice Department File, *Bailey* v. *Drexel.*

48 J. M. Beck to J. Parker, January 10, 1922, and J. Parker to J. M. Beck, January 13, 1922, Justice Department File, *Atherton* v. *Johnston.*

49 Robert H. Jackson, "Advocacy before the United States Supreme Court," *Cornell Law Quarterly* (Fall, 1951), p. 15.

50 Paul A. Freund, *The Supreme Court of the United States* (Cleveland: World Publishing Co., 1961), p. 114.

destroy rather than preserve the statute.[51] He could not escape from his past and his conservative convictions.

As an Assistant Attorney General in Theodore Roosevelt's first administration, Beck had defended the federal lottery act (besting William Guthrie) in *Champion* v. *Ames*. However, he clearly recognized the threat to laissez faire enterprise created by that decision and by the *McCray* holding. When, several years later, after he had returned to private practice, this danger materialized in the Beveridge bill, Beck discussed it in a journal article, "Nullification by Indirection."[52] In Twiss's words, this article "was a strong protest against acquiescence by the Supreme Court in the nullification of what was, in effect, the doctrine of 'limited purposes' through the use by Congress of granted powers for ends properly within the jurisdiction of the states."[53] The regulation of child labor, Beck argued, was "a subject beyond question exclusively within the police power of the state."[54] His answer to the theory of judicial impotence, which in his view was the constitutional prop for federal police power legislation, was to impose a saving qualification — the familiar contention used throughout the history of child labor reform — that the Court was duty bound to examine the substance as well as the form of legislation so as "to determine whether a federal power had been exercised for a federal end or for some ulterior purpose."[55] Not surprisingly, Beck had heartily approved the *Dagenhart* decision; and he told the St. Louis Bar Association, three weeks before *Drexel* was argued, that if the courts continued to sustain congressional taxation without inquiry into motive, "little will be left of the rights of the State."[56]

His argument in the *Drexel* case was meant to assist the Court to retreat further than it had retreated in *Dagenhart* from the highly destructive, perhaps fatal, position announced in the *McCray* decision. In form, his brief was a strong argument for legislative supremacy and against judicial supervision.[57] It drew heavily upon the presentation made by Solicitor General King

---

51 See Morton Keller, *In Defense of Yesterday: James M. Beck and the Politics of Conservatism* (New York: Coward-McCann, 1958), pp. 171–73.

52 *S.E.C.L.*, III, 90–103.

53 Benjamin R. Twiss, *Lawyers and the Constitution* (Princeton: Princeton University Press, 1942), p. 232.

54 "Nullification by Indirection," p. 97.

55 *Ibid.*

56 Keller, *In Defense of Yesterday*, pp. 171–72.

57 Twiss, *Lawyers and the Constitution*, p. 233.

when the *Johnston* case was first argued. But Beck drastically overstated the argument and presented a sweeping conception of congressional power, one almost certain to antagonize the judicial mind. Indeed, he virtually challenged the Court to override the principle of judicial impotence. At the same time, he repeatedly undercut the child labor tax with numerous candid admissions that it carried far — clearly beyond political limitations, and in effect beyond constitutional ones.

Early in the brief, Beck said that the child labor law was a tax, whether valid or not — hardly the customary way of launching a constitutional defense. Should the courts assume the burden of declaring legislation unconstitutional, "not because of that which it directly provides, but because of some inferable unconstitutional motive," the function of judicial review would become more delicate than ever. This being true, Beck stated,

> candor requires me to add that it may also be true that if, in our complex civilization, where steam and electricity have intricately unified the relations of life, the powers of the National Government can be utilized to secure objectives which are beyond the scope of Federal power, then our constitutional form of Government may prove to be a less effective distribution of power than is generally believed.[58]

There followed exaggerated statements, interspersed with damaging admissions that supposedly were introduced in "the spirit of candor," and the weaknesses in the constitutional position often were magnified rather than forthrightly answered. At one point, Beck argued

> This excise tax may be unreasonable, arbitrary or oppressive, but as the cases herein before cited show, such considerations are within the discretion of Congress, and that body, representing in a peculiar way the popular will, has the exclusive right of determining the reasonableness of selecting one class for taxation or exempting another, with all the attendant consequence of such discrimination. If it uses its power tyrannically, the remedy can only be with the people who elect the members of Congress.[59]

As for judicial review, Beck reached an extreme conclusion — at least for America in 1922.

---

[58] *Brief on Behalf of Appellants and Plaintiffs in Error, Bailey* v. *George* and *Bailey* v. *Drexel* (Washington, D.C.: Government Printing Office, 1922), p. 15.

[59] *Ibid.*, p. 39.

Our constitution provides that the judiciary has no power of revision whatever, except where a concrete case is presented between
litigants, and if, in such a case, an *invincible, irreconcilable, and
indubitable repugnancy* develops between a statute and the Constitution, the Court applies the Constitution, and thus virtually
nullifies the statute.[60]

If the field of operation of any statute came within the delegated
powers of Congress, it lay beyond judicial censorship. "Undoubtedly Congress can pass many laws which are hostile to the spirit,
even to the letter, of the Constitution and which are, therefore,
politically anti-constitutional," and the Court is not empowered
to intervene.[61] The challenge to the bench was carried still further,
beyond every prudent limit.

> Congress may pass many laws within the scope of its powers,
> and yet the real motive or objective of the laws may be the accom-
> plishment of a design which is equally in excess of its true func-
> tions and plainly an attempt, by indirection, to accomplish an
> unconstitutional end.
>
> That is deplorable. It is anti-constitutional. It may be subversive
> of our form of Government; but, here again, the only remedy is
> with the people.[62]

Beck concluded: "However plausible the conjecture, this Court
is powerless to say judicially that the motive of Congress in levying the tax under consideration was not to impose a tax, but to
regulate child labor." [63]

The Executive Committee's brief, in contrast, was characterized
by vigorous but restrained advocacy. It virtually recapitulated the
statement submitted when *Johnston* was originally argued and
it incorporated long passages from the *Dagenhart* brief. The controversy was still pictured in vivid emotional terms: Had the
Dagenhart case halted or only retarded the unconstitutional centralization of power that threatened to destroy the states and to
subject every vestige of local affairs to national control? [64] Guthrie's rejected brief in *McCray*, which justified judicial intervention
in support of dual federalism, again was the principal constituent
of the committee's position. When federal powers were used

60 *Ibid.*, p. 46.
61 *Ibid.*, p. 49.
62 *Ibid.*, p. 51.
63 *Ibid.*, p. 53.
64 *Brief for the Defendant in Error*, Bailey v. Drexel (Washington, D.C.:
Stillman Appellate Printing Co., 1922), p. 49.

for ulterior purposes, the brief asserted, the Supreme Court was obligated to look beyond the form of legislation to its nature and effect. The congressional purpose necessarily appeared from a consideration of the child labor act, and, should any doubt remain, the argument continued (exploiting the southern legislators' efforts to load the *Congressional Record*), reference to the Senate debates would show the clearest expression of the congressional will and purpose.[65] Congress, in short, possessed no power to regulate child labor within the states and any attempt to accomplish this purpose, whatever implement of national control it sought to employ, violated fundamental constitutional principles.

The attack was mounted from the supposedly determinative grounds of the *Dagenhart* decision. To compensate for the difficulties presented by other precedents, especially *McCray*, counsel talked around the authorities, further articulated the theory of limited purposes, and appealed for a saving exercise of judicial censorship. The child labor tax, the brief contended, "certainly goes beyond anything yet attempted, and as far as anything that can be imagined." [66] The Court therefore was implored, in the name of values that transcended the Constitution, to interpose, proclaiming "thus far but no farther."

> Cases such as this that involve great constitutional questions are not to be solved by an attempt to write out a legal formula that reconciles all preceding cases that have been decided. There inevitably is involved in the decision of such cases the quality of statesmanship as well as the qualities of a lawyer. Throughout the history of this country . . . there have appeared . . . trends or tendencies of statutes and of decision, one serving as a precedent for a next further step in the same direction — and then there has come before the Court a case which, if decided in accordance with the theretofore existing trend or tendency, would constitute, to quote a memorable phrase recently uttered by a member of this Court, the "step from the deck to the sea." [67]

The argument against permitting that step resembled less a legal brief than a plea to kindred souls to preserve the laissez faire philosophy.

Questions from the Bench: Prelude to Destruction

The oral presentations, like those in *Dagenhart*, provoked many questions from the bench. Bynum, who shouldered the major

65 *Ibid.*, p. 7.   67 *Ibid.*, pp. 42–43.
66 *Ibid.*, p. 12.

burden for the Executive Committee, was treated gently, but Taft and the other conservative justices, seeking information to buttress the conclusions they appeared already to have reached, subjected Beck to repeated harassments. Bynum, for example — who left posterity a sixty-five page abstract [68] he could hardly have read in the alloted time — relished discussing, in reply to questions from Taft, the great difference between the cost of administering the child labor tax and the revenue it produced.[69] Beck had been furnished with a statement from the Secretary of the Treasury, Andrew Mellon, that placed the proper interpretation on these differences, but this information seemingly did not register on closed minds. ("An explanation . . . lies principally in the fact that after the passage of the Act employers found it inadvisable to employ child labor, with the result that few businesses fell within the purview of the statute." Mellon pointed out, moreover, that because costs were incurred during the year and penalties were assessed subsequently, substantial amounts were outstanding, monies that greatly narrowed the differential.[70])

Beck, constantly forced on the defensive, frequently displayed a negative attitude. In response to questions from McReynolds, he argued that Congress could impose heavy taxes on wheat sales in order to restrict production, and Van Devanter was told that Congress could impose taxes on products manufactured by organized laborers for shipment in interstate commerce, presumably as a deterrent to unionization.[71] Taft thereupon said he was unable to understand where Beck would have the Court draw the line between construing the meaning of legislation, as the Constitution required it to, and scrutinizing the motives of Congress. Beck's reply is not recorded, but earlier he had insisted that Congress could enact such excise taxes as those imposed in the child labor law and that the only question at issue was whether the Court would follow precedent and decline to inquire into congressional motives or would choose to sit as a censor over motives. To the various questions, in short, Beck either responded in language that pushed his challenge to judicial power to extreme lengths or candidly admitted that sustaining the tax would carry federal regulatory authority far into the states' domain.

[68] *Abstract of Oral Argument for the Defendant in Error, Bailey v. Drexel,* pp. 1–65.
[69] *Washington Post,* March 9, 1922, p. 5
[70] Andrew W. Mellon to Harry M. Daugherty, March 4, 1922, Justice Department File, *Atherton v. Johnston.*
[71] *Washington Post,* March 9, 1922, p. 5.

In *Dagenhart*, Davis had aimed for the jugular, but Beck's "unwilling defense" only spelled out the vulnerable aspects of the government's case, which eased the task of Bynum and Hendren. Little more was demanded of them than the amenities of stating their case, even though it was studded with wholly illusory apprehensions about "teeming nationalism" destroying not only the states but the nation.[72]

At the conclusion, the opinion of observers was almost unanimous that the child labor tax was lost. Beck, the author of *The Passing of the New Freedom*,[73] had helped put the axe to one of the last legislative expressions of the progressive era. Little wonder, then, that Beck wrote to Taft after *Drexel* was announced:

> You may be surprised to know that, although I presented the Government's contention in the Child Labor Case as strongly as I was able, yet none who heard you deliver the opinion may have welcomed the decision more than I. Had the Court adhered tenaciously to the views of the late Chief Justice White in *McCray* v. *United States*, our form of government would have sustained a serious injury.[74]

Thus Beck agreed fully with Bynum and Hendren, and his cooperation with them throughout the litigation is more easily understandable. Taft had slight regard for his fellow conservative but made a courteous though hardly candid acknowledgment: "I had the impression that your soul was not wrapped up in the Child Labor Cases, although you certainly made as strong a case as could be made out of the previous authorities."[75]

The Disposition of the *Johnston* and *George* Cases

The *Drexel* case, it was generally recognized during argument, was the battleground on which the constitutionality of the child labor tax would be settled; nevertheless, counsel for the Executive Committee played the game of litigation to its conclusion in *Johnston*. Instead of abandoning the moribund vehicle, a perfunctory effort was made to show that the suit involved a justiciable cause, and its mootness was disregarded.[76] As for the lack of

[72] *Ibid.*, March 8 and 9, 1922, p. 6 and p. 5.

[73] New York: George H. Doran Co., 1920.

[74] J. M. Beck to William H. Taft, May 16, 1922, "The Taft Papers," Manuscript Division, Library of Congress, Washington, D.C.

[75] W. H. Taft to J. M. Beck, May 17, 1922, *ibid.*

[76] *Brief for Appellees on Reargument, Atherton* v. *Johnston* (Washington, D.C.: Stillman Appellate Printing Co., 1921), pp. 1–14.

precedent for the injunctive relief Judge Boyd had granted, the brief declared:

> If, in order to restrain a wrong or afford means of protecting a right, it is necessary to take a forward step, it should be taken unless there is likely to come out of that step more harm than good or some doctrine of existing law stands as an insuperable obstacle.[77]

Again, counsel tacitly admitted that the district court lacked jurisdiction over the proceeding, but they argued that, where rights of great dignity and importance were impaired and genuine adversary contention had been arranged ("the appellant has, it seems, surrendered to the Solicitor General the control of the defense"), no heed should be taken of unimportant technicalities.[78] Clark and his associates were not greatly concerned about the outcome but must have thought it advisable to continue the pretense of an actual controversy, possibly for fear that another course of action might have reflected adversely upon the *Drexel* case. The fact that counsel in both test proceedings and in the *Dagenhart* case were the same could not have been lost on the Court.

The government's brief as amicus curiae, on the other hand, vigorously attacked the suit, as if the Solicitor General was compensating for his failure to defend the child labor tax wholeheartedly. To his credit, Beck was concerned that the Court's jurisdictional rules should not be arbitrarily disregarded. After demonstrating that the suit had become moot,[79] he criticized its technical defects. The proceeding was so obviously friendly and so patently nonjusticiable that he seemed scarcely to refrain from open criticism of his predecessor and, less obviously, of the justices who made themselves party to the masquerade. Beck declared:

> This method of challenging a statute is not to be commended. It is quite obvious that the suit is a friendly one. Both plaintiff and defendant desire the same result. While their good faith is not questioned, yet the United States is thus brought into a litigation in which it has technically no status and in which its counsel must appear as *amicus curiae*. In purpose and effect this is a suit against the United States to challenge one of its laws, and yet

77 *Ibid.*, pp. 11–12.
78 *Ibid.*, pp. 3–12.
79 *Supplemental Brief for the United States as Amicus Curiae, Atherton* v. *Johnston* (Washington, D.C.: Government Printing Office, 1922), p. 4.

the United States is not a party to the record. Such a proceeding is questionable. If the statute in question is to be assailed in the courts, it should be assailed in a more direct manner.[80]

Collusive suits were never an acceptable means for deciding constitutional issues, no matter how important such issues might be. Otherwise, "the invalidity of statutes, instead of being decided in a direct proceeding, where a plaintiff has a direct and necessary legal interest in the question involved, could be raised collaterally by the mere averment, which could take various forms, that if a statute had not been passed some individual, with whom the plaintiff had some kind of relation, might have acted differently than he otherwise would." [81] Further examples, such as the *Johnston* case, the brief suggested, in which eagerness to resolve large issues led the government and the bench to close their eyes to the fictional character of the suits, might endanger the function of judicial review.

Brandeis must have read the government's brief with pleasure, and the disposition of the *Johnston* case must have given him great satisfaction — the Court held the proceeding moot.[82] In addition, Taft, who delivered the terse opinion, made it plain that it might once have involved serious jurisdictional questions.[83] The interment of the case, for it rapidly passed into oblivion save for Brandeis's citation in his special concurrence in *Ashwander*, marked a significant victory for Brandeis's conviction that the most important thing the Court did was "not doing." From the beginning the suit was a friendly and far-fetched contrivance, but most of the bench had been willing, initially at least, to shut their eyes to its manifest defects. Although the case was soon forgotten, it can hardly be viewed as anything other than a self-inflicted wound, an occasion on which judicial canons were imprudently disregarded. To our knowledge, only Brandeis and Holmes could

80 *Ibid.,* p. 6.
81 *Ibid.*
82 *Atherton* v. *Johnston,* 259 U.S. 13 (1922).
83 *Ibid.,* p. 15. Taft's language suggests that he had read Brandeis's "Memorandum to the Court" concerning *Johnston* before he framed his opinion. "The record further raises the doubt whether on its face this is a real case within the meaning of the Constitution upon which the judgment of this court upon the validity of an act of Congress under the Constitution can be invoked, and whether it does not violate the principle and ignore the caution of the words of Mr. Justice Brewer in *Chicago & Grand Trunk Ry. Co.* v. *Wellman.* . . . These are serious questions requiring full consideration. We only state them in order that it may not be thought by our conclusion that we here decide them."

reflect upon their part in the *Johnston* litigation with the conviction that they had done full justice to their constitutional
obligations.

The government's brief in the *Vivian* case scored the proceeding as patently irregular. Even though a revenue measure was unconstitutional, Beck declared, the judiciary lacked authority to
restrain the collection of federal taxes.[84] The rights of appellee,
if justiciable, were afforded protection by the procedure of a suit
to recover monies illegally paid. The Court disposed of the case
on the technical ground and remanded it to the district court
with directions to dismiss.[85] "The averment that a taxing statute
is unconstitutional does not take this case out of [the section
which barred injunctive relief]," Taft stated. "There must be
some extraordinary and exceptional circumstance not here
averred or shown to make the provisions of the section inapplica-
ble." [86] The case was a mere incident in the sequence of litigation
that challenged the child labor tax.

The Ark of Our Covenant: Highwater Mark
of Judicial Negativism

Although the consolidated child labor cases were argued late
in the term, the Court, under Taft, needed little time — barely
two months — to dispose of them. On May 15, 1922, three years
after the child labor tax had become effective, it was declared
unconstitutional, in the *Drexel* case. Although the decision was
not unanimous, the alignment involved none of the precarious-
ness of the *Dagenhart* division. Only Justice Clarke differed from
his brethrens' consensus, but personal circumstances prevented
him from writing a dissenting opinion. The other eight justices,
with Taft speaking for the Court, held that on its face the child
labor tax constituted an invasion of exclusively state functions

---

84 *Brief on Behalf of Appellants and Plaintiffs in Error, Bailey v. George*
and *Bailey v. Drexel,* pp. 1–2.

85 *Bailey v. George,* 259 U.S. 16 (1922).

86 *Ibid.,* p. 20. On the question of constitutionality, counsel for George
adopted the brief submitted by Clark's lawyers in *Drexel,* and subsequently
virtually abandoned their cause. Inasmuch as *Drexel* treated the constitutional
issue, their brief stated: "The question of jurisdiction in this case becomes
purely academic. . . ." *Brief on Behalf of Appellees, Bailey v. George,* p. 6.
The available evidence suggests that the Vivian company, although not disposed to challenge the factory inspector's report of the facts, tried to avoid
paying the assessment in the hope that the statute would be voided in *Johnston* before collection was enforced; having miscalculated, it had concocted
a device for staying enforcement as long as possible.

and an unconstitutional enlargement of federal authority. The identical saving qualification upon the theory of judicial impotence that led to the invalidation of the Keating-Owen law — namely, that the validity of legislation be determined by its natural and reasonable effects — resulted in the nullification of its successor. By its action the Court again gave constitutional standing to previously rejected doctrines. Together with a host of rulings that denied self-help weapons to labor organizations,[87] and the notorious *Adkins* case,[88] which even Taft couldn't stomach, the decision symbolized judicial reaction to liberalism during the 1920's.

From the outset, Taft tried to establish that the Court had not gone behind the child labor tax to inquire into the motives of Congress.

> We must construe the law and interpret the intent and meaning of Congress from the language of the act. The words are to be given their ordinary meaning unless the context shows that they are differently used. Does this law impose a tax with only that incidental restraint and regulation which a tax must inevitably involve? Or does it regulate by the use of the so-called tax as a penalty? If a tax, it is clearly an excise. If it were an excise on a commodity or other thing of value we might not be permitted under previous decisions of this Court to infer solely from its heavy burden that the act intends a prohibition instead of a tax. But the act is more. It provides a heavy exaction for a departure from a detailed and specified course of conduct in business.[89]

Taft thus drew two distinctions, apparently crucial to the decision, between incidental restraint and a prohibitory penalty of the kind associated with criminal statutes, and between a commodity as a subject of taxation and a course of conduct in business. After describing the operation of the act — namely, that profits were taxed without regard to the extent of departures from the measure's provisions, and only where an employer knowingly departed — he reached the fundamental conclusion in the case.

> In the light of these features of the act, a court must be blind not to see that the so-called tax is imposed to stop the employment of children within the age limits prescribed. Its prohibitory and regu-

---

[87] See *Duplex Printing Co.* v. *Deering*, 254 U.S. 443 (1921); *American Steel Foundries* v. *Tri-City Central Trades Council et al.*, 257 U.S. 184 (1921); and *Truax* v. *Corrigan*, 257 U.S. 312 (1921); all sustaining injunctions entered to restrain trade-union activities.

[88] *Adkins* v. *Children's Hospital*, 261 U.S. 525 (1923).

[89] *Bailey* v. *Drexel*, 259 U.S. 20, 36.

latory effect are palpable. All others can see and understand this. How can we properly shut our minds to it?[90]

All that followed was made inevitable by this conclusion, obviously designed to harmonize the Court's judgment with the *McCray* doctrine of "on face" constitutionality. The child labor act was condemned because of its nature and inevitable effects, Taft said, and not because of unsupportable suppositions about congressional intentions. It became the Court's high duty and function to invalidate the statute, for — the proposition went without saying — the remedy of popular control specified in *McCray* applied only when valid constitutional powers were wrongly employed.

> We cannot avoid the duty even though it requires us to refuse to give effect to legislation designed to promote the highest good. The good sought in legislation is an insidious feature because it leads citizens and legislators of good purpose to promote it without thought of the serious breach it will make in the ark of our covenant or the harm which will come from breaking down recognized standards. In the maintenance of local self-government, on the one hand, and the national power, on the other, our country has been able to endure and prosper for nearly a century and a half.[91]

We can seriously doubt that Taft or any other members of the majority, with the exception of Holmes and Brandeis, found this act of judicial supervision in defense of dual federalism in any way painful. The result accorded too closely with their constitutional preferences.

Taft had only to sketch the far-reaching effects of upholding the child labor act to make the opinion a classic statement of laissez faire constitutionalism.

> Grant the validity of this law, and all that Congress would need to do hereafter, in seeking to take over to its control any one of the great number of subjects of public interest, jurisdiction of which the States have never parted with, and which are reserved to them by the Tenth Amendment, would be to enact a detailed measure of complete regulation of the subject and enforce it by a so-called tax upon departures from it. To give such magic to the word "tax" would be to break down all constitutional limitations of the powers of Congress and completely wipe out the sovereignty of the States.[92]

90 *Ibid.*, p. 37.
91 *Ibid.*
92 *Ibid.*, pp. 37–38.

Counsel for the Executive Committee had their answer: The *Dagenhart* decision was held the controlling precedent, plainly applicable to the facts, and the *McCray* rules were overriden, although Taft labored hard to demonstrate that they retained vitality. The opinion declared:

> . . . The congressional power over interstate commerce is, within its proper scope, just as complete and unlimited as the congressional power to tax; and the legislative motive in its exercise is just as free from judicial suspicion and inquiry. Yet when Congress threatened to stop interstate commerce in ordinary and necessary commodities, unobjectionable as subjects of transportation, and to deny the same to the people of a state, in order to coerce them into compliance with Congress's regulation of state concerns, the Court said this was not in fact regulation of interstate commerce, but rather that of state concerns, and was invalid. So here the so-called tax is a penalty to coerce people of a State to act as Congress wishes them to act in respect of a matter completely the business of the state government under the Federal Constitution.[93]

But neither the commerce nor the taxing power, in this constitutional position, was complete or unlimited; both were narrowly confined through the instrumentality of the Tenth Amendment. The doctrine of limited purposes, determinative in *Dagenhart*, had not merely stemmed the tide of disastrous centralization momentarily, it was erected into a well-nigh impenetrable barrier against the exercise of major federal powers for influencing the course of economic development.

The substance of the decision and its antecedents were altogether familiar. Once again, to quote Twiss, "Guthrie's prophetic ability in blazing a doctrinal trail for the Court's laissez faire impulse was ultimately vindicated." [94] The *Drexel* case reads page and paragraph straight from Guthrie's brief condemning the destructive tax that had been laid upon colored oleomargarine. White's doctrine of democratic control was rejected out of hand, and was not even discussed; judicial willingness to inquire into motives and to transform personal preferences into substantive restrictions upon constitutional power aborted the *McCray* theory of judicial restraint. And once more Taft's convictions about American federalism triumphed; but this time, as chief magistrate of the supreme bench, he unified the Court and drafted the

93 *Ibid.*, p. 39.
94 Twiss, *Lawyers and the Constitution*, p. 223.

opinion, rather than stand on the sidelines. Guthrie's doctrinal creativity and Beck's self-defeating defense, Taft's leadership and the temper of the times, and perhaps, most of all, the justices' predilections for halting use of the taxing power to achieve social welfare purposes contributed to the decision. The Court was unwilling to acquiesce in the results of popular sovereignty, particularly after Beck had branded them as politically anticonstitutional.[95]

From Judicial Impotence to Judicial Supervision, without Prejudice to the Past

The most interesting feature of Taft's opinion was his attempt to clarify the substance of the holding. Why he venured upon this task is not clear, for the decision did not make such an undertaking mandatory; indeed, the result was to moderate its extreme character. On the other hand, the recognized standards Taft referred to certainly were not widely understood before the decision. The distinction between a commodity and a course of conduct in business as subjects of taxation, no less than the doctrine that the Constitution prohibited taxation primarily for regulatory purposes, found little authority in the precedent holdings. Every revenue measure, as Taft indirectly acknowledged, incorporates a scheme of regulation; the burden of taxation induces changes in conduct in line with preferred objectives of public policy. What Taft announced was not a universal rule, readily applicable in every instance, but a calculus that vested the Court with supervisory power to render decisions that were based upon

[95] *Hill* v. *Wallace*, 259 U.S. 44 (1922), was decided the same day as *Drexel*. Taft's opinion, which relied heavily upon the conclusion in the child labor case, branded as impermissible a tax supposedly burdensome to the extent of causing discontinuance of a particular business. He stated: "The [Grain Futures Trading] act is in essence and on its face a complete regulation of boards of trade, with a penalty of 20 cents a bushel on all 'futures' to coerce boards of trade and their members into compliance. When this purpose is declared in the title of the bill, and is so clear from the effect of the provisions of the bill itself, it leaves no ground upon which the provisions we have been considering can be sustained as a valid exercise of the taxing power" (*ibid.*, pp. 66–67).

Corwin argues that the two cases hardly occupied a common footing: "In the one [*Drexel*] an act of Congress, otherwise valid, was banned for a supposed purpose, in the other [*Hill*] for its actual content." Edward S. Corwin, "Constitutional Law in 1921–1922," *American Political Science Review* (November, 1922), p. 617.

subjective considerations, for the difference between tax and penalty admittedly was sometimes difficult to define.

> Where the sovereign enacting the law has power to impose both tax and penalty, the difference between revenue production and mere regulation may be immaterial; but not so when one sovereign can impose a tax only, and the power of regulation rests in another. Taxes are occasionally imposed in the discretion of the legislature on proper subjects with the primary motive of obtaining revenue from them, and with the incidental motive of discouraging them by making their continuance onerous. They do not lose their character as taxes because of the incidental motive. But there comes a time in the extension of the penalizing feature of the so-called tax when it loses its character as such and becomes a mere penalty, with the characteristics of regulation and punishment. Such is the case in the law before us. Although Congress does not invalidate the contract of employment, or expressly declare that employment within the mentioned ages is illegal, it does exhibit its intent practically to achieve the latter result by adopting the criteria of wrongdoing, and imposing its principal consequences on those who transgress its standards.[96]

If this rule means anything, it means that the Court will decide when a tax, imposed upon a legitimate subject, inflicts a burden that can be said to be more penalty than excise. But the criteria for making such delicate judgments are somewhat obscure because various principles are not spelled out. As long as Congress selects proper subjects, it may levy taxes and incidentally regulate. At some point, however, where regulation loses its incidental character, Congress exceeds its powers and the Court is duty bound to intervene. Here the calculus becomes virtually unmanageable for want of precision, because Taft, by his silence, acquiesced in the principle that whether or not a tax measure actually returns revenue is not decisive.

Perhaps it would be more accurate to say that Taft had to approve this damaging ambiguity because the Court did not wish to reverse earlier holdings that sustained regulatory taxes. Just as Day had done in *Dagenhart*, Taft tried to distinguish the precedents; if anything, however, even more remarkable ingenuity was required to square *Drexel* with *McCray* than *Dagenhart* with *Hoke*. Day had failed, and so did Taft. Of *Veazie* he said: "The sole objection to the tax was its excessive character. Nothing else appears on the face of the act." [97] And the object fell within con-

[96] *Bailey* v. *Drexel*, 269 U.S. 20, 38.
[97] *Ibid.*, p. 41.

gressional authority. Again, in *McCray*, Taft admitted the regulatory purpose that was obvious to all: "This Court held that the discretion of Congress in the exercise of its constitutional powers to levy excise taxes could not be controlled or limited by the Courts because the latter might deem the incidence of the tax oppressive or even destructive." [98] In both cases, in other words, subjects properly taxable were regulated. Taft therefore summed up: "In neither . . . did the law objected to show on its face as does the law before us the detailed specifications of a regulation of state concern and business with a heavy exaction to promote the efficiency of such regulations." [99]

Of Taft's efforts to distinguish *McCray* and similar cases, Edward S. Corwin, perhaps the most severe critic among the professional commentators, said "he is unable to do so convincingly, since he is unable to deny that the regulatory purpose of Congress was not fully as palpable in those cases as in his." [100] Felix Frankfurter, although he approved the holding, was even more emphatic.

> To my taste the distinction thus made between the Oleomargarine and the Child Labor Taxes is not only a fine one — it's too fine. Certainly some of the language used in, and the lead of the earlier cases have been repudiated, and respect for law would not have suffered if the repudiation had been made explicitly. It is not healthy that the broad issues involved in delimiting the proper scope of Federal and State powers should rest on grounds so subtle that intelligent lawyers, no less than laymen, cannot readily grasp them.[101]

Thomas Reed Powell, who similarly endorsed Taft's result, also concluded that *McCray* had been deprived of procreative power. "The oleomargarine tax was in all substance as much a perversion of the taxing power as was the tax on child labor." [102] And no one

98 *Ibid.*, p. 42.
99 *Ibid.* In *Doremus*, Taft declared, the validity of the special tax was unquestioned. "The provisions for subjecting the sale and distribution of the drugs to official supervision and inspection were held to have a reasonable relation to the enforcement of the tax and were therefore valid" (*ibid.*, p. 43). But Taft said nothing about White's charge in dissent that the Harrison Narcotic Drugs Act grievously invaded exclusive state concerns.
100 "Constitutional Law in 1921–1922," p. 613.
101 "Child Labor and the Court," *New Republic* (July 26, 1922), p. 249.
102 "Child Labor, Congress and the Constitution," *S.E.C.L.*, III, 541. "The difference," Powell argued, "lay rather in the amount of objective evidence needed to convince the court that it had clearly caught Congress in unconstitutionality."

since, except by sophistry, has separated *McCray* and *Drexel*, for there is no difference in kind.[103]

Drexel remains the authority, and forty years later is still the law of the land, conditioning congressional action and judicial decision-making. The judicial revolution that overtook the commerce power in the late thirties did not bring reversal. However, the evidence suggests that, should a suitable occasion arise, the dominant opinion that produced the revolution — that freed national power from the doctrine of limited purposes, that revitalized state exercises of the police powers for social welfare purposes, and that made possible federal and state taxation programs that radically adjusted the distribution of national income and hastened social equality — would sanction taxation purely for regulatory purposes, almost without regard for the subject; and the contemporary Supreme Court likely would acquiesce. The fact that regulation by indirection need no longer be resorted to virtually assures this result.

Chief Justice Taft and the *Dagenhart* Dissenters

The result of the Court's deliberations in the *Drexel* case now seems so decisive we have difficulty realizing that an almost unanimous holding was not generally taken for granted. Most of those who heard the case argued apparently believed that the child labor tax would be invalidated, but the masses of people had no such definite expectation. Only one point was generally agreed upon: Taft's influence would be decisive.

For us, the truly interesting matter is Taft's success in massing the bench and incorporating his personal convictions in the opinion. On the one hand, the consensus achieved (given the frequent fragmentation of the Court in the immediately preceding terms) suggests the likelihood of an institutional decision in which preferred constructions necessarily would be modified to gain maximum adherence. On the other hand, the opinion was so

---

[103] Robert E. Cushman, in the Thirties, concluded: "*Bailey* v. *Drexel Furniture Co.* and *Hill* v. *Wallace* do not overrule the *McCray Case*, and yet the two groups of cases are logically irreconcilable. Chief Justice Taft's reasoning in the child labor tax case and the grain futures trading case lead inevitably to the conclusion that the oleomargarine tax imposed a 'penalty' rather than levied a tax and was therefore void. . . . No amount of analysis will disclose any inherent difference between these various taxes which can provide a logical basis for classifying them into different categories as to their validity." "Social and Economic Control through Federal Taxation," *S.E.C.L.,* III, 563.

revelatory of Taft's constitutional creed that, in Corwin's judg-ment, it deserved special attention.[104] For that very reason, how-ever, certain portions must have offended Holmes and Brandeis. Holmes's dissent in *Dagenhart*, Bickel points out, "speaks at least implicitly to the issue of the *Child Labor Tax Case.*"[105] Still, the two liberal justices acquiesced, and therein lies the problem.

That Taft voted as he did should not have occasioned surprise; the doctrine that federal power could be employed to regulate business enterprise, especially labor relations, was foreign to his conception of American constitutionalism. Taft consistently ex-pressed the conviction, in the years after the Beveridge bill was proposed, that control over child labor was vested exclusively in the states and that their power was protected from federal inter-ference by the Tenth Amendment.[106] Even more important for Taft, we can assume, was the threat to judicial review if Congress's attempt to circumvent the practical effect of the *Dagenhart* deci-sion was not permanently thwarted. The child labor tax sought "to do the same thing" as the Keating-Owen law, "and the effort must be equally futile," he declared in his opinion. "In other words" — as Alpheus T. Mason points out about the priority of Taft's values — "the modern need for national power . . . had to yield before the even greater need of preserving the sanctity and inviolability of judicial decisions."[107]

[104] Corwin, "Constitutional Law in 1921–1922," p. 612.

[105] Reprinted by permission of the publisher from Alexander M. Bickel, *The Unpublished Opinions of Mr. Justice Brandeis*, Cambridge, Mass.: The Belknap Press of Harvard University Press, Copyright, 1957, by the President and Fellows of Harvard College; p. 18.

[106] Taft was impressed by the contention in the Executive Committee's presentation that the child labor tax was a weapon of northern textile inter-ests that sought to equalize conditions with the south. The legislation (he wrote to his brother Horace) was "a mere effort of good people, who wish children protected throughout the country, to compel certain States to con-duct their police powers in accord with the views of the good people, as well as an effort by the manufacturers of Connecticut and Massachusetts to in-crease the cost of production of commodities in which they compete with the Southern States, by depriving them of child labor. Unfortunately we cannot strain the Constitution of the United States to meet the wishes of good people." W. H. Taft to Horace Taft, May 15, 1922, "The Taft Papers." Plainly, Taft's conviction about the role of the New England textile manufacturers resulted from his willingness to believe those who opposed the act rather than from investigation of the facts. Moreover, the "good people" Taft referred to in-cluded numerous spokesmen for the business community and conservative interests, men such as Henry Cabot Lodge, who generally were opposed to governmental interference in the economy.

[107] *The Supreme Court from Taft to Warren*, p. 57.

Justice McKenna's choice presents no greater difficulty than Taft's. After his *Doremus* vote there was every reason to believe that he would oppose a revenue measure whose regulatory purpose was equally apparent and more far-reaching. With advancing age and approaching senility, his commitments often took an erratic turn, but his propensity to conform his judgments to shifts in popular opinion largely explains his judicial career.

The question that defies easy explanation concerns Holmes and Brandeis. Why did Holmes, and especially Brandeis, who we know once believed the child labor act was constitutional, concur in the retrogressive course of their conservative brethren? The answer to this question is unusually important because their acquiescence greatly enhanced the authority of the precedent and apparently resulted in subsequent deference that otherwise might not have occurred.[108] It is doubtful that Beck's self-defeating argument was of much consequence; Holmes's and Brandeis's intellectual powers were such that they surely went beyond counsel's presentations to their own conclusions. Other and more significant factors must have determined their final commitment. Among these, no doubt, was Taft's "unusual capacity for keeping the brethren in line." Mason writes:

> The Chief Justice pressed hard for unanimity. Deep rifts were screened by his colleagues' natural desire to assist his effort. Sometimes as many as three Justices would relucantly go along with the majority because no one of them felt strongly enough about the issue to raise his voice in protest. During the early years of Taft's Chief Justiceship, it was not unusual for Justices to write on the back of circulated slip opinions: "I shall acquiesce in silence unless someone else dissents"; or, "I do not agree, but shall submit." For the sake of harmony staunch individualists such as Holmes, Brandeis, and Stone, though disagreeing, would sometimes go along with the majority. It seems probable that such considerations help in accounting for the unanimity achieved in the reactionary Child Labor Tax decision.[109]

There is little basis for speculation about Holmes's vote except that the views about taxation that he subscribed to throughout his career conflict, at least in part, with the *Drexel* holding. His commitment may not have been reached until after it became clear that only Clarke would join in dissent — an insufficient basis for an effective opposing opinion. On the other hand, Bickel

---

108 See Bickel, *The Unpublished Opinions of Mr. Justice Brandeis*, p. 19.
109 Mason, *The Supreme Court from Taft to Warren*, pp. 57, 58.

points out that Holmes was reluctant to dissent after he had once had his say on any subject,[110] and he may have decided to accommodate his brethren, despite disagreement on the merits, in the belief that nothing consequential could be added to the *Dagenhart* dissent. The trouble with this supposition is that Holmes and Brandeis, when deeply stirred, often dissented more than once on the same issue. For example, having had their say early in 1921, in the *Duplex Printing Co.* case [111] (about injunctive processes applied against labor organizations) did not prevent them from dissenting later in the year — with great vigor — in *Truax* v. *Corrigan.* [112] This is a substantial difficulty and is not easily gotten around.

It seems probable that Holmes concluded the child labor law went too far and he preferred to hit the other side hard. Two weeks after *Drexel* was decided he chided Laski good naturedly about his attempts to convert him to the cause of social reform. "If you think that I am going to bother myself again before I die about social improvements or read any of those stinking upward and onwarders — you err." [113] Holmes did not vote in *Dagenhart* out of passion for social reform but from his settled convictions about constitutional power and popular government. In this connection, Taft's careful attempt to clarify the holding is suggestive. His calculus of discretionary power for establishing different lines of social policy, depending upon their effects, may have been a concession to the jurist who several years later criticized Marshall's celebrated dictum that the power to tax is the power to destroy. Holmes, again the dissenter, maintained:

> In those days it was not recognized as it is today that most of the distinctions of the law are distinctions of degree. If states had any power it was assumed that they had all power, and that the necessary alternative was to deny it altogether. But this Court, which has so often defeated the attempt to tax in certain ways, can defeat attempts to discriminate or otherwise go too far without wholly abolishing the power to tax. The power to tax is not the power to destroy while this Court sits.[114]

[110] Bickel, *The Unpublished Opinions of Mr. Justice Brandeis*, p. 18.
[111] *Duplex Printing Co.* v. *Deering*, 254 U.S. 443 (decided January 3, 1921).
[112] 257 U.S. 312 (decided December 19, 1921).
[113] Reprinted by permission of the publisher from Mark De Wolfe Howe, *Holmes-Laski Letters*, Cambridge, Mass.: The Belknap Press of Harvard University Press, Copyright, 1953, by the President and Fellows of Harvard College; Holmes to Laski, June 1, 1922, I, 430.
[114] *Panhandle Oil Co.* v. *Mississippi Ex rel. Knox*, 277 U.S. 218, 223 (1928).

The previous December, Holmes had remarked on Taft's "happy success in uniting the Court" on a difficult boycott case;[115] and on May 1, two weeks before *Drexel* was announced, he confided to Laski: "Taft continues to give me great satisfaction as Chief Justice."[116] He was impressed by Taft's capacity to understand big movements and to portray issues effectively, and he found him amiable and comfortable. The personal situation, then, was propitious for accommodation, if not concession, and Taft's formula for determining social gradients through the agency of judicial supervision could have appealed to Holmes. Taft nevertheless rested the opinion on the doctrine of limited purposes and the clear analogy he proclaimed to the *Dagenhart* case cannot be blinked, for it meant invalidation on collateral grounds. Why would Holmes have acquiesced in doctrines that sharply challenged the constitutional position he had brilliantly defended when he dissented in *Dagenhart* if he had not found unbridgeable constitutional differences in kind?

Brandeis and Clarke: The Sociological Jurists Disagree

Brandeis's concurrence, in silence, in the invalidation of the child labor tax is even more puzzling. Why did a thoroughgoing progressive, a jurist who two years before believed the statute was constitutional, compromise his convictions or change his mind? Why did he endorse a position "not easily reconciled with views to which he subscribed before and after?"[117] Bickel, who offers several plausible suggestions, inclines to the view that Brandeis became reconciled to the majority position for practical reasons, having found it impossible to reverse the conference's conclusion on the merits.

> Brandeis once remarked that the "great difficulty of all group action, of course, is when and what concession to make." There is no doubt that Brandeis sometimes suppressed dissents for tactical reasons. "Can't always dissent," he said. And: "I sometimes endorse an opinion with which I do not agree. I acquiesce."[118]

---

115 Holmes to Laski, December 22, 1921, I, 389. The "success," probably *American Steel Foundries* v. *Tri-City Central Trades Council et al.* (257 U.S. 184), decided December 5, 1921, was followed two weeks later by *Truax* v. *Corrigan* (257 U.S. 312), decided December 19, 1921, which greatly disappointed Holmes.

116 Holmes to Laski, May 1, 1922, I, 423. Holmes referred to *Stafford* v. *Wallace* (258 U.S. 495 [1922]).

117 Bickel, *The Unpublished Opinions of Mr. Justice Brandeis*, p. 15.

118 *Ibid.*, p. 18.

The decision in *Johnston*, Bickel says, "was a victory on the issue which for Brandeis was of overriding importance," a victory achieved against considerable odds. And another long battle, stretching over two years, the *Coronado* case,[119] also culminated in success two weeks later. "Victory brings let-down, and a desire for pacification. It might have seemed to Brandeis churlish, and a disservice in the long run to his effectiveness in the cause of jurisdictional observance and to his future relations with the new Chief Justice, Taft, to turn around at this juncture and register a dissent."[120]

In this supposition Taft offered Brandeis the concession, which was not required to dispose of the cause, that *Johnston* did not decide previously existing jurisdictional questions, and Brandeis in turn suppressed his views on the merits in *Drexel*, though obviously not as a negotiated quid pro quo. This rests heavily upon the proposition that Brandeis, for tactical advantage and to foster amicable relations, would deliberately misinform the country and succeeding Courts about his convictions in perhaps the most important case that was decided that term. Brandeis, it is true, was apprehensive about working with Taft, and for good reason; his nomination had been "a fearful shock" to Taft, who fiercely battled to prevent his confirmation and in the following years repeatedly condemned "the new school of constitutional construction" that Brandeis and Clarke represented.

The fault in Bickel's surmise, however, is that neither Taft nor Brandeis was inclined to make a constitutional compromise for expediency, even when concession would not affect the outcome of litigation.[121] Every justice owes his contemporaries and his successors the forthrightness of his commitments.

> While I recognize the annoyance to the bar of dissenting and con-
> curring opinions [Justice Jackson wrote], I think they are the
> lesser of evils. A court opinion which puts out a misleading im-
> pression of unanimity by avoiding, or confusing, an underlying
> difference is a false beacon to the profession. Far better that the
> division be forthrightly exposed so that the profession will know
> on what narrow grounds the case rests and can form some estimate

119 *United Mine Workers* v. *Coronodo Co.*, 259 U.S. 344 (1922).
120 Bickel, *The Unpublished Opinions of Mr. Justice Brandeis*, p. 19.
121 About the possibility of strained relations between Taft and Brandeis, Mason concludes: "There was little likelihood that either man, least of all Brandeis, would have allowed personal differences to interfere with the effectiveness of the Court's work." *Brandeis*, p. 537.

of how changed facts may effect the alignment in a subsequent case.[122]

Brandeis was obligated to dissent if he differed from the Court, or to submit a concurrence if he possessed reservations about or disagreed on the principles of the holding. Because he did not, we must be skeptical. Moreover, Taft's supposed concession in *Johnston* cost nothing; it was a non-binding appendage, not the basis for the holding. In addition, Brandeis's concern about jurisdictional observance was part and parcel of a larger commitment, to limiting judicial control over the popular will. This commitment chiefly prompted the *Ashwander* concurrence, just as it had the *Johnston* Memorandum, but *Drexel* involved, for many liberals, a notorious exercise of judicial control.

Mason, in contrast to Bickel, and writing before the *Johnston* Memorandum became available, represents Brandeis's vote as his genuine conviction. His analysis therefore suggests that Brandeis changed his mind on the merits rather than acquiesced because he had reconciled himself to an irreparable result. Taft's suggestion that "to give such magic to the word 'tax' would . . . break down all constitutional limitations of the powers of Congress and completely wipe out the sovereignty of the states," in Mason's view "struck responsive chords for the apostle of localism."

> "Perhaps it will be recognized someday as the beginning of an epoch, an epoch of States Duties," Brandeis commented in passing Taft's opinion along to Norman Hapgood. "States Rights succumbed to the Rights of Nations. States Duties were ignored and State functions atrophied. The extremes of concentration are proving its failure to the common man. . . . The new progressivism requires local development—quality not quantity." Here Brandeis foreshadowed sharp differences of later years with the New Dealers whose headlong drive for national power threatened, he believed, to destroy one of the great bulwarks of liberty—federalism.[123]

For Bickel, Brandeis's letter merely put the best possible face on the decision—"consoling himself and his friends with its potential for the achievement of broader purposes."[124] But Brandeis had company in liberals who had changed their minds about the

---

122 Jackson, "Advocacy before the United States Supreme Court," pp. 13–14.
123 Mason, *Brandeis*, p. 558. Bickel refers at length to these passages from Mason but he excised Brandeis's striking sentence that characterized large-scale concentration as a failure.
124 Bickel, *The Unpublished Opinions of Mr. Justice Brandeis*, p. 15.

permissible extent of federal authority and feared the onrush of centralization. Felix Frankfurter, the former chairman of the WLPB, applauded Taft's opinion because the child labor act involved "the dishonest use of the taxing power" and violated the bond of union. Also, Frankfurter put virtually the identical interpretation upon the holding as did Brandeis: "We must pay a price for Federalism." [125] Looking to the future, Frankfurter suggested the wisdom of "a renewed energetic movement to rouse the States to action."

> Nothing less seems to be involved than the refashioning of responsible citizenship. It is too easy to look to Washington and a centralized administration for the correction of all our national shortcomings. I do not speak from any regard for traditional states' rights . . . but as one with some knowledge of the functioning of the Federal machinery and its power further to absorb and discharge effectively nationwide duties, especially duties of intimate local concern, affected by local conditions of great variety throughout the country.[126]

Thomas Reed Powell furnishes another example of altered opinion. After the destruction of the Keating-Owen law, Powell urged reform forces to utilize the taxing power to achieve their aims, but four years later, in commenting upon *Drexel,* he said: "The decision . . . was essential to safe-guarding the federal system from being warped beyond recognition." [127] Like Frankfurter, Powell expressed apprehension about the survival of traditional political arrangements.

These conclusions, although not representative of liberal commentaries, cannot be wished away nor denied. They teach a memorable lesson: never to underestimate the tremendous psychological and philosophical shock Americans (especially those attached to the Jeffersonian democratic persuasion) suffered as a result of the unprecedented centralization that was necessary to put the nation on a war footing in World War I. The immense bureaucracy, the coercive power of gathered sovereignty, and the restrictions imposed publicly and privately upon mind and expression indelibly influenced men who were sensitive — as Bran-

[125] Child Labor and the Court," *New Republic* (July 26, 1922), p. 248. The price consisted in "at one time the impotence of the Federal Government to correct glaring evils unheeded by some of the States, at other times the impotence of States to correct glaring evils unheeded by the Federal Government."

[126] *Ibid.,* pp. 249–50.

[127] Powell, "Child Labor, Congress, and the Constitution," p. 543.

deis and Frankfurter were — to the libertarian credo that power corrupted and paralyzed local responsibility but that a wide dispersion of political and economic authority fostered democratic virtues and militated against arbitrary assaults upon individuals. There had never before been such far-reaching national control, and many persons hoped it would never again be necessary.

It is not implausible, then, to conclude that Brandeis changed his mind. His vote in *Drexel* would be that of the early New Freedom economic adviser, reasserting the values inherent in the traditional, decentralized regime as adapted to industrial conditions — competitive enterprise, economic freedom, and local control — rather than to the national dominance implied in Croly's New Nationalism. Although seemingly a vote against social welfare, it may have represented — in compromised form — the deepest values of Brandeis's constitutional creed. The judicial process was a conscious social process for Brandeis; practical matters rather than "revealed truths" informed his choices. And the "faithful maintenance of the federal balance," for these reasons, Freund lucidly demonstrates, pervaded his philosophy.[128]

Clarke's dissent without opinion, although notable in itself, is doubly so if — as Bickel suggests — his position represented Brandeis's conviction on the merits, and perhaps Holmes's as well. Certainly, there must have been pressure from Taft and other justices for unanimity in such an important holding. What fortified Clarke in his decision, if his vote can be viewed as a reasoned choice?

We know that Clarke's tenure on the bench was soon to end and that he was tired in body and deeply depressed in spirit when he resigned several months later, on September 1, 1922. The death in the preceding year of his two sisters seemed to blot out all earthly interests, his biographer reports.[129] In addition, the rejection of American participation in the League of Nations, which Clarke felt undermined peace in the world, and Woodrow Wilson's paralysis and impending death (he had become an intimate friend) greatly saddened Clarke. Life must have seemed profoundly tragic, virtually devoid of purpose, for this idealistic jurist after so many severe shocks. Moreover, Clarke suffered hypochondriacal dread that his own health would soon be impaired.

---

128 Freund, *The Supreme Court of the United States*, pp. 116–44.
129 Hoyt L. Warner, *The Life of Mr. Justice Clarke* (Cleveland: Western Reserve University Press, 1959), p. 112.

"This black mood," Warner believes, "was decisive in his decision to resign, for it darkened his attitude toward the Court and
made unsupportable his continuation in that 'cave.'" His depression "made even more galling 'the trifling and technical character' of much of the Court work he was obligated to do and led
him to exaggerate the inevitable differences between himself and
his colleagues." [130]

Was Clarke's dissent, then, a judicial testament to his passion
for social welfare, chiefly the result of his humanitarianism and
instinctive sympathy for the underprivileged? He was, we know,
deeply skeptical about judicial objectivity, and believed that
"each [justice] should become in a measure the advocate of his
own conclusions rather than the coldly, neutral, impartial
searcher after a wise and just conclusion which the ideal judge
is supposed to be." [131] Or was his dissent a more reasoned determination, representing his view of constitutional powers and the
legitimate objectives of public policy? Because he must already
have decided to retire, there would have been no reason for him
to accommodate his colleagues and suppress his convictions. He
was free to speak his mind and had no need to compromise over
differences. During the spring of 1922 he dissented from his
brethren or entered concurring opinions more often than at any
other period in his career on the bench. He objected to the increasingly reactionary trend of decisions, a trend that indirectly
reflected the mood of the country, and he found occasion to say so.

The facts of which we are certain must be treated cautiously.
Clarke did not even attend the Supreme Court sessions when the
child labor cases were argued [132] and he seems to have been absent from the conference when they were voted upon — in both
instances presumably because his second sister was dying. In other
words, he formed his decision from the briefs, if he read them, or
more likely on the basis of his personal outlook and commitments.
The same event that prevented his participation in deciding the
Drexel case also immobilized him, he later made known, to the extent that he was unable to construct an opinion — although he
thought a strong rejoinder to Taft was possible, one that would

---

[130] *Ibid.*, p. 113.

[131] See John H. Clarke, "Reminiscences of the Courts and the Law," *Proceedings*, California State Bar Association, Fifth Annual Meeting (1932), p. 22.

[132] Supreme Court of the United States, *Minutes, 1921.* Clarke was absent
the entire week of March 6–10, 1922.

have tarnished *McCray* or forced the majority to modify its justification.[133]

Clarke's state of mind is especially regrettable because a dissent from him might have induced Brandeis or Holmes to construct a concurring opinion. In that event society would have been provided a more accurate beacon than is available in *Drexel*. This also would have been the case had *McCray* been overruled or clearly distinguished. The best we can say about *Drexel* is that it is a collective judgment, one that peculiarly fails to inform us about judicial behavior.

The Impact of the Child Labor Case

The *Drexel* decision cast a pall of gloom over progressivism, although liberals were less of one mind than they had been about the *Dagenhart* case. To many, the destruction of the child labor tax unmistakably signaled the death knell of contemporary reform; this loss, following upon the invalidation of the Keating-Owen law, deprived the reform movement — permanently, as far as anyone then knew — of the two most important national powers as implements for achieving social welfare objectives. At the federal level, nothing consequential seemed any longer attainable, with the possible exception of a child labor amendment. The quest for social justice was thrown back into the cockpit of the separate states, so often a futile battleground.

Some prominent liberals genuinely applauded the decision. Despite the compelling character of its claims, one said, humanity conveyed no warrant to distort the Constitution. Like Powell, some of these men had changed their minds and reversed their earlier positions in reaction to centralization or after re-analysis of competing constitutional principles.[134] Other liberals had never

[133] John H. Clarke to Woodrow Wilson, September 9, 1922, quoted in Mason, *William Howard Taft: Chief Justice*, pp. 165–67. In recent years professional commentators have placed great stress on Clarke's disenchantment with Brandeis and the deterioration in his relationships with other justices as the main reasons for his resignation. However, this conclusion neglects the man and the terrible trauma he suffered in 1921 and 1922. He had endured judicial service for almost a decade, on the lower and supreme benches, and clearly recognized the value of liberal votes in the latter, but the devastating personal experiences, as he explained to Wilson, so changed his outlook that "continuing the work became simply unsupportable."

[134] In June, 1918, Powell stated: "Those who believe that the nation should use its power to end the evils which harm the nation must look to the taxing power of Congress. And when in the future the taxing power is thus employed, it is hoped that an undivided Court will accept and apply the closing sentences of Mr. Justice Holmes's dissenting opinion . . . : 'The national

been enthusiastic about using the taxing power for distinctly regulatory purposes.

Although no single statement can generalize the critical reaction, Corwin's judgment about the implications of the Court's action conveys a sense of the disaster many progressives saw in the *Drexel* case.

> The logic of the decision of this case, overriding previous decisions, makes the Court the supervisor of the purposes for which Congress may exercise its Constitutional powers. It thus cancels out the third dimension, so to speak, of the sovereignty of the national government within the field of its granted powers. At one stroke a new canon of constitutional interpretation is created and an out-of-date one revived; legislative motive becomes a test of legislative action; and any effort on the part of Congress to bring within its control matters heretofore falling to the states alone, raises the question of valid motives. The notion of the cooperation of the National Government and the states in the furtherance of the general welfare, which was voiced a few years ago in *Hoke* v. *United States* . . . has apparently dropped out of view.[135]

For the *New York Tribune*, the decision was profoundly disappointing; it meant that America could pay little heed to the bitter cry of children caught mercilessly in the wheels of industry,

> for it is obvious that forty-eight states cannot be brought to enact parallel legislation and that factories will tend to be located where regulations are the most lax. Inexorable economic law will exert its steady pressure to make all states standardize at the lowest level.
>
> Scarcely less discouraging is the evidence given that the Supreme Court, after a period of liberalism with respect to social legislation, is seemingly on the backtrack — is retreating to the caverns of states' rights, with their frigid and dogmatic legalism.[136]

welfare as understood by Congress may require a different attitude within its sphere from that of some self-seeking State. It seems to me entirely constitutional for Congress to enforce its understanding by all means at its command.' " "The Child Labor Decision," *The Nation* (June 22, 1918), p. 731.

Four and a half years later, however, Powell asserted: "One must have an exalted sense of judicial gullibility to disagree with the Chief Justice when he concludes: 'In the light of these features of the act, a court must be blind not to see that the so-called tax is imposed to stop the employment of children within the age limit prescribed. Its prohibitory and regulatory effect are palpable.' " "Child Labor, Congress, and the Constitution," pp. 539–40.

[135] Edward S. Corwin, "The Child Labor Decision," *New Republic* (July 12, 1922), p. 179.

[136] "Reversing Justice Chase," May 17, 1922, p. 10.

This catalogue of liberal complaints was a far cry from the *Tribune's* optimistic editorial on *Dagenhart* that confidently predicted the destruction of the ancient fortress of states' rights. America had not achieved the measure of centralization that would enable the federal government to emulate other civilized nations.

And worse was to follow, despite La Follette's bitter attack that summer upon judicial sovereignty and other criticisms of the Court's growing intrusion upon popular processes. As many liberals had feared, Corwin's dire forecasts proved correct. Under Taft's stewardship, during normalcy, the Supreme Court functioned as supervisor of the purposes for which Congress might exercise its constitutional powers.

"For progressives," in Goldman's characterization of the growing frustration and discouragement of the early Twenties, "here was certainly a post-Civil War all over again, only worse. Reform in the Seventies and Eighties had the buoyancy of a movement that was just taking the offensive. Progressivism of the Twenties was a beaten army, muscles aching, its ranks seriously depleted." [137] *Drexel* helped make painfully clear what many liberals preferred to ignore: conservatism dominated the country and business was ascendant.

Ironically, on May 16, the day *Drexel* was reported, the *New York Times* editorially celebrated the developing pattern of associated industries.

> The modern pressure towards organization and co-operation in business is salutary and indispensable, even irresistible. . . . A full generation of the administration of anti-trust laws has demonstrated the futility of attempting to destroy co-operation, even combination. . . .
>
> To all appearances, we are at the beginning of a new era of self-government. A decade ago Elihu Root sounded a warning that, if the States hoped to withstand the increasing encroachment of national regulation, they must exercise their "rights." This warning has not availed: the States are steadily diminishing as a factor in government. Meantime, a new set of "States" . . . has arisen — industries integrated on a national scale.[138]

The next day, taking care neither for the diminishing states nor its applause when an industry as inherently local as building construction organized nationally, the editors enthusiastically en-

[137] Eric F. Goldman, *Rendezvous with Destiny* (New York: Alfred A. Knopf, 1952), p. 289.
[138] "Self-Government in Industry," May 16, 1922, p. 18.

dorsed the Supreme Court's referral of "the subject of child labor to the States, where it properly belongs."[139]

Unlike the *Dagenhart* decision, the *Drexel* decision came as no great surprise to the National Committee's leaders. With few exceptions, they had become convinced that the child labor tax probably would be invalidated. None, however, was fully reconciled to this result. After the decision the committee announced, with characteristic optimism, "cheerful determination to go on and finish the tasks of child labor reform." There were "no signs of pessimism" at the annual conference, the membership was informed. And several speakers cautioned that there was no justification for curbing judicial power as a way out of constitutional difficulties.[140] Once more a special subcommittee was created and charged with formulating a course of action in the new circumstances.[141] When the trustees met, on June 9, they concluded that there was "no opportunity to secure legislation regulating child labor by federal authorities under the present constitution" and they endorsed a resolution favoring an amendment campaign.[142] But others had already taken the lead; Samuel Gompers had formed the Permanent Committee for the Abolition of Child Labor, an association of representatives from many national reform and social welfare organizations that was dedicated to enacting a child labor amendment.

Later, the National Committee marshaled its forces to influence the formulation of the proposed amendment and launched an extensive campaign to win ratification within the states for whatever version was forthcoming from Congress. These efforts were undertaken with enthusiasm, in general with the expectation that a conclusive victory for child labor reform was in sight.[143] Fifteen years earlier the plight of exploited children had excited a passionate humanitarian crusade; by the mid-twenties, however, improving child labor regulations had become a nagging, unfinished business — a workaday social objective that was routinely ap-

[139] *Ibid.*, May 17, p. 18.

[140] *American Child* (August, 1922), p. 70.

[141] *New York Tribune*, May 17, 1922, p. 4.

[142] "Minutes of the Board of Trustees, N.C.L.C.," June 9, 1922.

[143] Although the majority of the trustees voted for the amendment, the leadership was split; a sizable minority felt that, as a matter of policy, such a campaign should not be undertaken, or they perceived that the prospects for success were less than promising. "Results of Inquiry as to the Attitude of Trustees and Advisory Committee re: Constitutional Amendment," unpublished and undated N.C.L.C. memorandum. See also "Minutes of the Board of Trustees, N.C.L.C.," May 16, May 31, and June 9, 1922.

plauded by public figures but rarely supported energetically. The conservative social forces that in a prosperous and unconcerned America would destroy the amendment campaign had taken shape and needed only to be energized to inflict that unsuspected but devastating result.

The *Drexel* decision was a sweet victory indeed for David Clark. The southern textile industry again was deeply in his debt, and generous acknowledgments were plentiful.[144] William Hendren initiated the industry's celebration (a month earlier) by addressing the Cotton Manufacturers' Association of North Carolina. With the end of a six-year contest at hand and victory on every point in sight, Hendren's mood was exultant: "You gentlemen have been instrumental in presenting for consideration one of the most important and far-reaching constitutional questions with respect to the form and substance of our Government that has been considered in more than a quarter of a century."[145] There followed a recital of horrors, of grave evils certain to have befallen the industry had the child labor tax not been successfully challenged. The address foreshadowed the violent laissez faire attack upon New Deal legislation that Hendren, as a member of the National Lawyers' Committee of the Liberty League, would help direct in the mid-thirties. Writing at the same time, Clark was more candid about the textile manufacturers' interests. "If the Federal Child Labor Law is held constitutional almost every phase of our cotton manufacturing industry will be regulated by National legislation so as to remove any advantage that we now have over New England."[146]

A year later, when the North Carolina association again assembled Clark was still being publicly feted as the two-time victor over unconstitutional federal legislation that had been aimed directly at the southern industry. "The fundamental conception of the formation of our Government," a representative of the N.A.M. told the mill owners, "was that the National Government should never undertake anything which the States could do and that the States should never attempt to do anything which the individual could do."[147] Clark did not rest on his laurels when this

144 See *Southern Textile Bulletin* (May 25 and June 1, 1922), p. 18 and p. 22.

145 *Proceedings of the Sixteenth Annual Convention of the Cotton Manufacturers' Association of North Carolina* (Charlotte: Observer Printing House, 1922), p. 60.

146 *Southern Textile Bulletin* (April 6, 1922), p. 18.

147 *Proceedings of the Seventeenth Annual Convention of the Cotton Manufacturers' Association of North Carolina* (Charlotte: Observer Printing House, 1923), p. 33.

philosophy of extreme individualism was again threatened. Early in 1923 he consented ("reluctantly," his editorial declared) to lead the southern textile manufacturers' fight against the child labor amendment that was certain to issue from Congress.[148] That autumn, in the thick of the struggle, he summed up the personal benefits that redounded from his unflagging efforts to serve the mill men's vital interests. "The *Southern Textile Bulletin* comes to the end of 1923 with the largest amount of advertising and the largest subscription list in its history and it is certainly more firmly fixed in the hearts of the cotton manufacturers of the South than ever before." [149]

[148] *Southern Textile Bulletin* (January 18, 1923), p. 18.
[149] *Ibid.*, December 27, 1923, p. 20.

Epilogue

In his only book, and his last constitutional commentary, Thomas Reed Powell offered the following conclusion about the Supreme Court's power of invalidity.

> Unwelcome common law and statutory interpretations admit of but slightly delayed prospective change of legislation. The correction of judicial infelicities in assuming constitutional negatives is much more difficult, whether by judicial recantation or by constitutional amendment.[1]

After the overthrow of the Keating-Owen law, many progressives hoped for judicial recantation within a few years, but correction of the *Dagenhart* decision proved difficult indeed. When the child labor tax suffered from similar judicial infelicity, child labor reformers undertook to amend the Constitution, but the campaign floundered badly during the mid-twenties, when public opinion was inhospitable to the extension of federal control over the economy.[2]

All this changed with the depression. The electoral revolution of 1932 symbolized just as drastic a transformation of popular sentiment as had the Republican triumph of 1920. The economic emergency brought about the enactment of the National Industrial Recovery and Fair Labor Standards Acts, both of which included provisions restricting child labor, and carried governmental intervention in social and economic life well beyond the provisions

---

[1] *Vargaries and Varieties in Constitutional Interpretation* (New York: Columbia University Press, 1965), p. 14.

[2] Although judicial misconstruction theoretically can be cured by changing the organic law, "the period of gestation of a constitutional amendment," Robert H. Jackson pointed out, "or of any law reform, is reckoned in decades usually; in years, at least. And, after all . . . it may not be the Constitution that was at fault." *The Struggle for Judicial Supremacy* (New York: Alfred A. Knopf, 1941), p. 297.

of the Keating-Owen law. The child labor history culminated in the *Darby Lumber Company* case,[3] in which, to apply Felix Frankfurter's phrase, "that impalpable but controlling thing, the general drift of public opinion" penetrated the judicial mind and conformed the decision.[4] The Supreme Court, its majority reconstituted and its philosophy re-oriented since the judicial revolution four years earlier, unanimously recanted its predecessor's judicial infelicity of 1918. The *Dagenhart* case had fallen into desuetude; the majority's holding was scored as a departure from the principles that had "prevailed in the interpretation of the Commerce Clause both before and since the decision"; and Holmes's "powerful and now classic dissent" was pronounced the law of the land.[5] In the language of Holmes's *Lochner* dissent, the Court's legitimizing action permitted a dominant opinion that did not "infringe fundamental principles as they have been understood by the traditions of our people and our law" to have its natural outcome.[6]

Although the child labor history has not been brought full circle, the events narrated contribute to our understanding of the way in which constitutional powers are adapted to meet changed patterns of social and economic life. In particular, the study seeks to portray the antagonism between popular sovereignty and judicial supremacy in an earlier period of constitutional development. Our judicial world is far different from that of the progressive era. As Pritchett makes clear, "the economic questions with which Holmes mainly dealt — basic constitutional authority to regulate or protect — have, in fact, simply ceased to be issues."[7] Because these conflicts are far off — not in point of time but in our conception and experience of American political history — we may misinterpret the way in which contemporaries viewed them and their significance for democratic society.

Congress in the first decades of the twentieth century had great difficulty comprehending the implications of the highly complicated civilization that was taking shape; older practices failed to provide ready answers to the problems that arose in an industrial

3 *United States* v. *Darby Lumber Co.*, 312 U.S. 100 (1941).
4 *Law and Politics: Occasional Papers of Felix Frankfurter, 1913-38*, eds. Archibald MacLeish and E. F. Prithard, Jr. (New York: Harcourt, Brace & World, 1939), p. 197.
5 *United States* v. *Darby Lumber Co.*, 312 U.S. 100, 115-16.
6 *Lochner* v. *New York*, 198 U.S. 45, 76 (1905).
7 C. Herman Pritchett, *The Roosevelt Court: A Study in Judicial Politics and Values, 1937-1947* (New York: Macmillan Co., 1948), p. 271.

society. The altered character of the public questions was percep-
tively delineated by Justice Stone.

> Public problems are no longer exclusively questions of individual
> right. They involve an understanding of the new and complex
> economic forces we have created, their relationship to the lives
> of individuals in widely separated communities engaged in widely
> differing activities, and the adaptation to those forces of old con-
> ceptions of law developed in a different environment to meet
> different needs.[8]

Finding effective legislative remedies for the new problems was
exceedingly difficult at best, but, in the instance of child labor,
Congress's discretionary power to mold public policy according
to its conception of public needs was further handicapped by
subsequently discredited judicial supervision. The five-judge majority's apprehensions about the abuses of national power that
surely would follow if the Keating-Owen law was permitted to
stand mirrored the conviction that the popular branches of government could not be trusted to respect constitutional limitations.
Reliance, therefore, had to be placed upon judicial control.

Four decades later, however, after judicial approval of vastly
more far-reaching federal powers, those fears have been demonstrated to be fully as fanciful as they appeared in 1918. National
minimum-wage legislation exists, to be sure; but Congress has yet
to outlaw red-headed passengers from interstate transit. More important, the political significance of state government has not
been impaired nor has the Constitution been abrogated — as was
dramatically predicted by the opponents of federal regulation.
The "Grand Peur" was entirely visionary, given the American
genius for concentrating political power but distributing its effects
through various levels of government and given the great variety
of interests that influence policy formation in our highly plural-
istic society. The federal system has survived, with remarkable
vitality. No one can plausibly contend that, had the Court decided *Dagenhart* differently, horrendous results would inevitably
have been our lot, for Congress has exercised national powers with
uncommon restraint. On the other hand, it is beyond contest that
the nation's capacity to confront pressing social and economic
problems was greatly burdened for two decades, and especially
during the depth of the depression, because of the way the case
was decided.

---

[8] Harlan F. Stone, "The Public Influence of the Bar," *Courts, Judges, and
Politics*, eds. Walter F. Murphy and C. Herman Pritchett (New York: Ran-
dom House, 1961), p. 136.

As we look back it is useful to recall that judicial review had become a factor in determining the extent of national legislative power little more than a generation before the *Dagenhart* case was decided. Today, almost all constitutional commentators believe that the American political tradition requires the Supreme Court to follow the precedent that was established in *Marbury* v. *Madison*.[9] "The debate over the legitimacy of judicial review, long lived as it has proved to be," Rostow writes, "is settled by history."[10] Brandeis nevertheless asserted in his *Johnston* Memorandum, and for more than hortatory purposes, that

> the long continued, uninterrupted exercise of this power has not sufficed to silence the doubt originally expressed whether the framers of the Constitution intended to confer it. On the contrary, the popular protest against its exercise has never been so vehement, nor has it ever secured the support of so many political thinkers and writers, as in the last decade.[11]

Brandeis's statement must be read in light of the infrequent destruction of federal statutes prior to *Dagenhart* as well as the virtually unanimous acquiescence within Congress to the exercise of the sovereign prerogative by the supreme bench. No one can reasonably contend that the progressive era held the possibility of fundamentally altering the institution of judicial review. On the other hand, it is conceivable that the sphere in which the Court functions might have been restricted significantly and judicial power made more democratic in character if closely contested decisions such as *Dagenhart* and *Adkins* had gone the other way.

It is a commonplace of constitutional commentary to assert the controlling place of popularly determined policies in American democracy. However, the child labor history instructs — if nothing else — the vulnerability of this principle when conflict exists, as it almost always does, over "the extent of powers actually granted" Congress and over the purposes that government can legitimately pursue, whether the achievement of social welfare or the effectuation of equality.

[9] 1 Cr. 137 (1803).

[10] Eugene V. Rostow, *The Sovereign Prerogative* (New Haven: Yale University Press, 1962), p. xxxiii.

[11] Reprinted by permission of the publishers from Alexander M. Bickel, *The Unpublished Opinions of Mr. Justice Brandeis*, Cambridge, Mass.: The Belknap Press of Harvard University Press, Copyright, 1957, by the President and Fellows of Harvard College; p. 13.

Bibliographic Notes

The progressive era presents unusual problems for the scholar. In the first place, social change occurred with a rapidity hitherto unknown in American life and men found it difficult to comprehend what was happening. In the second place, their efforts to cope with the new conditions encouraged them to explore afresh American experience and the origins of the Republic. The founders' intentions and the course of national development became a source of controversy as never before or since. In consequence, the period is peculiarly subject to interpretation, and the researcher, examining any aspect of it, seems inevitably to encounter disquieting paradoxes and inexplicable problems.

In writing this book, I have sought to achieve understanding by treating what men said as the most reliable guide to what they thought and by treating what they did as the most reliable guide to what they wanted. This approach affords no guarantee that discrepancies, where they existed, would be detected. The hazard, nevertheless, appeared preferable to the probably greater pitfalls involved in trying to appraise whether or not public statements and actions and private records and correspondence should be accepted at face value.

Without exception, the persons who figure prominently in the narrative of events — leading politicians, Supreme Court justices, government officials, and spokesmen for the contending interest groups — are now dead. It was not possible to question them. Even if this had been possible, vagaries of personality and institutional constraints would have foreclosed many crucial lines of inquiry. The dependence ultimately had to be upon the characteristic decency and openness of American politics.

The sources chiefly relied upon were government documents, contemporary legal and journalistic commentaries, organizational records and publications, personal correspondence and reminiscences, biographical works, and historical accounts of the progressive era. The first category includes congressional committee hearings and reports, the *Congressional Record, the United States Reports* and the "records" of decided cases, Justice Department case files, and various departmental and agency orders, reports, and publications.

A conspicuous gap in this essential documentation is the absence of verbatim transcripts of oral arguments before the Supreme Court. Like many another student, I deeply regret that the bench has not, until very recently, permitted such records to be made and has never permitted them to be distributed. We are thereby deprived of invaluable information — insight into the strategy of advocacy and the interplay between the justices and counsel. The practice of tape-recording arguments, inaugurated under Chief Justice Warren's leadership, has not changed this situation because the recordings are reserved exclusively for the use of the Court.

My journey into the past was enriched by many perceptive commentaries on the legal doctrines of constitutional law and by the greater willingness of influential publications in an earlier era of American journalism to take clearly defined editorial positions. The articles and books of Edward S. Corwin and Thomas Reed Powell, in particular, have been heavily, and respectfully, drawn upon. These works rigorously scrutinize the relevant judicial holdings, point out consistency of development, mercilessly expose logical shortcomings, and speculate — frequently in brilliant fashion — on the implications of these decisions for law and public policy.

In this connection, the usefulness of the four volumes of *Selected Essays on Constitutional Law* (Chicago: The Foundation Press, Inc., 1938) can hardly be exaggerated. Contemporary students are deeply indebted to the editors of this invaluable collection (issued under the auspices of the Association of American Law Schools), who, during an unsettled period of legal development, hewed to the highest standards of selection. Their choices have been amply vindicated in the years that have followed.

The newspapers and journals cited were selected because they represented the opinions of substantial portions of the citizenry in the nation or in their regions. Such publications as the *New York Times,* the *New York Tribune,* the *New York World,* the *New Republic,* the *Independent,* and the *Survey* were recognized spokesmen for political parties and factions or for major social

and economic interests. Their editorials greatly facilitated the
task of relating public opinion to policy formation.

The important role organizational records and publications
played in making possible a comprehensive narrative of events
is so clear that comment becomes superfluous, especially because
the crucial contribution of David Clark's disclosures in the *Southern Textile Bulletin* has previously been acknowledged.

With one exception, the contribution of personal correspondence and reminiscences has been much less marked — an occasional illumination of significant decisions and actions. This exception involves a series of lengthy conversations, extending over
several weeks, with Gertrude Folks Zimand, then General Secretary of the National Child Labor Committee. Mrs. Zimand,
daughter of Homer Folks, a committee founder and long-time
trustee, devoted forty years of her life to the organization. With
rare objectivity and unfailing graciousness, she drew upon her
rich store of information, recalling the National Committee's history, the personalities of its leaders, allies, and opponents, and
the record of success and failure. These conversations were an
inestimable assistance to understanding the past.

To account for the results of the Supreme Court's deliberations
in the child labor cases, I found it necessary to explore judicial
biography for insight into personality and motivation. There is
one or more book-length study of each of the justices, except
Mahlon Pitney, but only a few of these works can be considered
definitive in character — such as Mark De Wolfe Howe's unfinished biography of Justice Holmes, *Justice Oliver Wendell
Holmes*, Vol. 1, *The Shaping Years, 1841–1870*, and Vol. 2, *The
Proving Years, 1870–1882* (Cambridge, Mass.: Belknap Press of
Harvard University Press, 1957–), and Alpheus T. Mason's several volumes about Justice Brandeis, *Brandeis: Lawyer and Judge
in the Modern State* (Princeton: Princeton University Press, 1933)
and *Brandeis: A Free Man's Life* (New York: The Viking Press,
1946).

We badly need more such penetrating analyses of the justices'
shaping years and their public careers before they ascended to
the bench. In particular, a definitive biography of Chief Justice
White (comparable to Mason's remarkable study, *Harlan Fiske
Stone: Pillar of the Law* [New York: The Viking Press, 1956])
would contribute greatly to understanding constitutional development and judicial processes.

Of the various historical studies of the progressive era, Harold
U. Faulkner, *The Quest for Social Justice, 1898–1914* (New York:

Macmillan Co., 1931), is still the most informative portrayal of the development of the various movements for social reform; and Arthur S. Link, *Woodrow Wilson and the Progressive Era, 1910–1917* (New York: Harper & Row, 1954), provides unusual insight into political dynamics during the period in which reform consciousness reached its peak.

Works that deal with the various aspects of the child labor reform movement are few in number and frequently are marred by partisan bias; the latter is especially true of material that appeared in the 1930's. The nineteen volumes of the *Report on the Condition of Women and Child Wage Earners*, U.S. Department of Labor (Washington, D.C.: Government Printing Office, 1910–13) are important for two reasons: the preceding investigation was a pioneer empirical survey of a mass social phenomena, and several of these volumes, especially *The Beginnings of Child Labor Legislation in Certain States* and *Cotton Textile Industry* (Vols. VI and I), significantly influenced public opinion and governmental action. Elizabeth H. Davidson, *Child Labor Legislation in the Southern Textile States* (Chapel Hill: University of North Carolina Press, 1939), unfortunately limited in circulation, contains the best scholarly treatment of any aspect of the modern reform movement. Students will also find great value in another study that makes unusual sense of the subject, Thomas G. Karis, "Congressional Behavior at Constitutional Frontiers: From 1906, the Beveridge Child Labor Bill, to 1938, the Fair Labor Standards Act" (unpublished Ph.D. dissertation, Columbia University, 1951).

The following individuals and publishers have kindly granted permission to quote from copyrighted works. Paul A. Freund, *On Understanding the Supreme Court* (Boston: Little, Brown and Co., 1949); Association of American Law Schools, *Selected Essays on Constitutional Law* (4 vols.; Chicago: The Foundation Press, Inc., 1938); Alexander M. Bickel, *The Unpublished Opinions of Mr. Justice Brandeis* (Cambridge: The Belknap Press of Harvard University Press, 1957); Robert K. Carr, *The Supreme Court and Judicial Review*, Vol. VIII of "American Government in Action," ed. Phillip Bradley (11 vols.; New York: Holt, Rinehart & Winston, 1942); Edward S. Corwin, *Constitutional Revolution, Ltd.* (Claremont, Calif.: Claremont Colleges, 1941); John P. Frank, *Marble Palace* (New York: Alfred A. Knopf, 1958); Felix Frankfurter, *Felix Frankfurter Reminisces*, ed. Harlan B. Phillips (New York: Reynals and Co., 1960); Felix Frankfurter, *Mr. Justice Holmes and the Supreme Court* (Cambridge, Mass.: The Belknap Press of Harvard University Press, 1938, 1961); Felix Frankfurter, *Of*

Law and Men: Papers and Addresses of Felix Frankfurter, 1939–1956, ed. Philip Elman (New York: Harcourt, Brace & World, 1956); Paul A. Freund, *The Supreme Court of the United States* (Cleveland: The World Publishing Co., 1961); Eric F. Goldman, *Rendezvous with Destiny* (New York: Alfred A. Knopf, 1952); *Holmes–Laski Letters: The Correspondence of Mr. Justice Holmes and Harold L. Laski, 1916–1935*, ed. Mark De Wolfe Howe (2 vols.; Cambridge, Mass.: The Belknap Press of Harvard University Press, 1953); *Holmes–Pollock Letters: The Correspondence of Mr. Justice Holmes and Sir Fredrick Pollock*, ed. Mark De Wolfe Howe (Cambridge, Mass.: The Belknap Press of Harvard University Press, 1941); Robert H. Jackson, "Advocacy before the United States Supreme Court," *Cornell Law Quarterly*, 37 (Fall, 1951), I, 1–16; Robert H. Jackson, *The Struggle for Judicial Supremacy* (New York: Alfred A. Knopf, 1941); Robert H. Jackson, *The Supreme Court in the American System of Government* (Cambridge, Mass.: Harvard University Press, 1955); Arthur S. Link, *Woodrow Wilson and the Progressive Era, 1910–1917*, Vol. I of "The New American Nation Series," eds. Henry Steele Commager and Richard B. Morris (New York: Harper & Row, 1954); Alpheus T. Mason, *Brandeis: A Free Man's Life* (New York: The Viking Press, 1946); Roscoe Pound, "The Courts and Legislation," *American Political Science Review*, 7 (August, 1913), 361–83; Henry F. Pringle, *The Life and Times of William Howard Taft* (2 vols.; New York: Holt, Rinehart & Winston, 1939); *Selections from the Correspondence of Theodore Roosevelt and Henry Cabot Lodge, 1884–1918*, ed. Henry Cabot Lodge (2 vols.; New York: Charles Scribner's Sons, 1925); Francis Butler Simkins, *The South Old and New* (New York: Alfred A. Knopf, 1949); Carl Brent Swisher, *American Constitutional Development* (Boston: Houghton Mifflin Co., 1943); and Benjamin F. Wright, Jr., *The Growth of American Constitutional Law* (Boston: Houghton Mifflin Co., 1942).

Index

passim; pursues legal challenge (district court), 81–93, 96–103 *passim*; brief and oral argument in *Dagenhart* case, 148–51, 152; plans to continue constitutional struggle, 171–73; brief in *Johnston* on reargu-child labor tax, 220–31 *passim*; brief and argument in *Johnston* case, 233–37, 238, 239; creates second test vehicle, 260–63, 267–68; brief and oral argument in *Drexel* case, 271–73; brief in *Johnston* on reargument, 252, 274–75; 280, 285n

Fair Labor Standards Act, xiv, 300
Farmers' States Rights League, 221n
Federal Fuel Administrator, 199
Federal Reserve Act, 28, 31, 80
Fidelity Manufacturing Company; facilitates litigation challenging Keating-Owen law, 93, 96, 97, 98, 101, 102; 107, 224, 227
Field, Oliver P., 98–99
Field, Justice Stephen J., 91, 121, 131
Fifth Amendment, as limitation on commerce and taxing powers, 35, 36, 52, 63, 106, 146, 225, 266
First Employers' Liability cases, 207 U.S. 463 (1908), 150, 153, 154
Folks, Homer, 68n
Frank, John P. 129, 130, 144, 257
Frankfurter, Felix, 113, 115, 124, 143, 149n; as chairman of W.L.P.B., 200; 245, 283, 291–92, 301
Freund, Ernest, 188
Freund, Paul A., x, 89, 117, 227, 232, 268, 292
Frierson, William, 108, 140, 227n, 232, 238
Fuller, Raymond G., 187, 201n
Fuller, Chief Justice Melville W.: dissents in *Lottery* case, 15–16; mentioned, 124, 125, 126, 127, 128, 138, 154, 156, 182, 257n

Gallinger, Jacob H., 71
Gard, Warren, 194n, 215
Gibbons v. *Ogden*, 9 Wheaton 1 (1824), xi, xiv
Goldman, Eric F., 23, 296
Gompers, Samuel, 42, 75, 178n, 191, 297

Graham, William A., 42
Grain Futures Trading Act, 281n
"Grand Peur," 53, 150, 156, 236, 302
Gray, Justice Horace, 122
Green, Fredrick, 187–88n
Green, William R., 194n
Gregory, Thomas W., 100–101, 107–8, 109, 139
Guthrie, William D.: argument in *Lottery* case, 103, 148, 155–56, 159; argument in *Oleomargarine* case, 235, 269, 271, 280, 281

Hamilton, Walton H., 115–16
Hammer v. *Dagenhart*, 247 U.S. 251 (1918), xiii, 87, 94; argued in district court, 101–5; Judge Boyd decides, 105–8; public response, 107–10; 124, 133, 138; briefs on appeal to Supreme Court, 144–51; oral argument, 151–52; Day's opinion for the court, 154–59; Holmes's dissent, 160–67; motion to reargue, 167–69; interested parties response, 169–73; popular response, 173–76; professional commentary on, 180–83; cited in Senate debate on Pomerene Amendment, 207–13; cited in briefs and argument in *Drexel* case, 271–77; cited in Taft's opinion, 280–82; mentioned, 173, 178–79, 184, 185, 186, 188, 192, 193, 198, 215, 221, 222, 223, 224, 229, 230, 231, 233, 235, 236, 242, 248, 250n, 265, 269, 285, 287, 288, 294, 296, 297, 300; significance, 302–3.
Hammer, William C., government counsel in *Dagenhart* case (district court), 96, 97, 98, 99, 102, 103, 107, 108, 109; 226, 227, 228, 229
Harding, Warren G., 244, 256, 257; names Taft Chief Justice, 258–59
Hardwick, Thomas W.: opposes Keating-Owen bill (Senate), 69–73, 76; opposes Pomerene Amendment (Senate), 206–8, 209, 210, 212
Harlan, Justice John Marshall: opinion for Court in *Lottery* case, 14, 15, 16; mentioned, 124, 125, 128, 135, 163, 164n, 257n
Harrison, Benjamin, 120